LACAN AND LANGUAGE

A Reader's Guide to *Écrits*

LACAN AND LANGUAGE

A Reader's Guide to *Écrits*

John P. Muller

and

William J. Richardson

INTERNATIONAL UNIVERSITIES PRESS, INC.
New York

Library of Congress Cataloging in Publication Data

Muller, John P., 1940
    Lacan and language.

    Bibliography: p.
    Includes index.
    1. Psychoanalysis—Addresses, essays, lectures.
2. Lacan, Jacques, 1901–   , Ecrits. I. Richard-
son, William J. II. Lacan, Jacques, 1901–
Écrits. III. Title.
BF173.M822   150.19'5'0924   81-23681
ISBN 0-8236-2945-7   AACR2

Second Printing – 1985

Manufactured in the United States of America

To

Otto A. Will, Jr., M.D.,
who made this book possible,
the authors dedicate it
with respect, admiration, and gratitude.

Contents

Acknowledgments

Grateful acknowledgment is made to the following publishers for permission to use material from:

Point du Jour, by André Breton, ©1970 Éditions Gallimard, Publishers, Paris.

Schizophrenia, by A. De Waelhens, Duquesne University Press, Publishers, Pittsburgh.

The Standard Edition of the Complete Psychological Works of Sigmund Freud, revised and edited by James Strachey, Sigmund Freud Copyrights Ltd., The Institute of Psycho-Analysis and The Hogarth Press.

Beyond the Pleasure Principle, by Sigmund Freud, W. W. Norton & Company, Inc., Publishers, New York.

The Ego and the Id, by Sigmund Freud, W. W. Norton & Company, Inc., Publishers, New York.

The Interpretation of Dreams, by Sigmund Freud, translated from the German and edited by James Strachey, published in the United States by Basic Books, Inc., by arrangement with George Allen & Unwin Ltd. and The Hogarth Press Ltd., London.

An Outline of Psycho-Analysis, by Sigmund Freud, W. W. Norton & Company, Inc., Publishers, New York.

Truth and Method, by Hans-Georg Gadamer, copyright ©1975 by Sheed and Ward Ltd. Used by permission of The Seabury Press, Inc.

Hermes: Guide of Souls, by K. Kerényi, Springer Publications, Inc., Publishers, Dallas.

Introduction to the Reading of Hegel, by A. Kojève, translated by J. Nichols, Jr., Basic Books, Inc., Publishers, New York.

Écrits, by Jacques Lacan, Éditions du Seuil, Publishers, Paris.

Écrits: A Selection, by Jacques Lacan, translated from the French
    by Alan Sheridan. Copyright © 1977 by Tavistock Publi-
    cations Ltd. Used by permission of W. W. Norton &
    Company, Inc.
*De la psychose paranoïaque dans ses rapports avec la personnalité suivi
    de premiers écrits sur la paranoïa,* by Jacques Lacan, Éditions
    du Seuil, Publishers, Paris.
Le Séminaire: Livre I. Les Écrits techniques de Freud, 1953–1954, by
    Jacques Lacan, Éditions du Seuil, Publishers, Paris.
"Some Reflections on the Ego," by Jacques Lacan. Published
    in *International Journal of Psycho-Analysis,* Vol. 34, 1953, pp.
    11–17.
Memoirs of My Nervous Illness, by Daniel Paul Schreber, trans-
    lated and edited by I. Macalpine and R. A. Hunter,
    Dawson & Sons, Ltd., Publishers, London.
The Language of the Self, by Jacques Lacan, translated and
    edited by A. Wilden, The Johns Hopkins University
    Press, Publishers, Baltimore.

We would also like to acknowledge that the following chapters
were originally published, in a slightly different version, in *Psychoanalysis and Contemporary Thought:* Introduction and Chapter 1
in Vol. 1, No. 3, pp. 323–372 (1978); Chapter 2 in Vol. 1, No. 4,
pp. 503–529 (1978); Chapter 3 in Vol. 2, No. 2, pp. 199–252
(1979); and Chapters 5 and 6 in Vol. 2, No. 3, pp. 345–435
(1979).

Introduction

Few interpreters of Freud fail to acknowledge the epoch-making significance of *The Interpretation of Dreams* (1900a), and for Jacques Lacan, in particular, the most radical of Freud's contemporary interpreters, this work contains the "essential expression of [Freud's] message" (1977, p. 159/509).[1] Nowhere, perhaps, is that message expressed more succinctly than at the beginning of Chapter VI ("The Dream-Work"), where Freud describes the dream as a rebus:

> Suppose I have a picture-puzzle, a rebus, in front of me. It depicts a house with a boat on its roof, a single letter of the alphabet, the figure of a running man whose head has been conjured away, and so on. Now I might be misled into raising objections and declaring that the picture as a whole and its component parts are nonsensical. A boat has no business to be on the roof of a house, and the headless man cannot run [etc.]. . . . But obviously we can only form a proper judgement of the rebus if we put aside criticisms

[1] In citations of Lacan, the first pagination refers to the English translation of *Écrits* (1977), the second to the French original (1966).

1

such as these of the whole composition and its parts and if, instead, we try to replace each separate element by a syllable or word that can be represented by that element in some way or other. The words which are put together in this way are no longer nonsensical but may form a poetical phrase of the greatest beauty and significance. A dream is a picture-puzzle of this sort [1900a, pp. 277–278].

Lacan's own great design is to "return to Freud" in order to articulate the full import of Freud's "essential message" that was expressed in this landmark work. This means taking Freud's designation of the dream as a rebus "quite literally." But what does that mean? Lacan's own response to such a question is, at first blush, puzzling: "This derives from the agency [*l'instance*] in the dream of that same literal (or phonematic) structure in which the signifier is articulated and analysed in discourse" (1977, p. 159/510). Puzzling or not, this response nonetheless contains "the essential expression" of Lacan's own message about how to interpret Freud's fundamental insight, namely, that "the unconscious is structured in the most radical way like a language" (1977, p. 234/594). But Lacan's own message is locked up in an expression so obscure and enigmatic that for the uninitiated it constitutes a kind of rebus in itself.

The essential elements of that rebus have recently (1977) appeared in English translation: nine essays, selected by Lacan himself from his more extensive major work, *Écrits* (1966). English-speaking readers now have the opportunity to decipher for themselves the same rebus that has puzzled or provoked or scandalized or inspired students of psychoanalysis in the French-speaking world for over 40 years. But if an English translation makes these essays available, it does not thereby make them intelligible. For the normal reader of English, a rebus they remain.

It does not seem unfair to characterize Lacan's writings in this way, whether one refers to their substance or to their style. For their substance deals with the nature of the unconscious as Freud understood it, hence with that dimension of human experience that lies beyond the ken of conscious, rational discourse and emerges into awareness only through a kind of diffraction that may assume many forms—in the case of the dream, for example, the form of a rebus. By saying, then, that Lacan's work, in terms of its substance, is a rebus, we mean to suggest that it is dealing with a theme that of its very nature escapes the constrictions of rational exposition.

But we call Lacan's writings a rebus with even better reason because of their style. For the style mimics the subject matter. Lacan not only explicates the unconscious but strives to imitate it. Whatever is to be said about the native cast of Lacan's mind that finds this sort of thing congenial, there is no doubt that the elusive-allusive-illusive manner, the encrustation with rhetorical tropes, the kaleidoscopic erudition, the deliberate ambiguity, the auditory echoes, the oblique irony, the disdain of logical sequence, the prankish playfulness and sardonic (sometimes scathing) humor—all of these forms of preciousness that Lacan affects are essentially a concrete demonstration in verbal locution of the perverse ways of the unconscious as he experiences it. And he makes no apology for the consequent difficulty for the reader. On the contrary, he relishes a "kind of tightening up . . . in order to leave the reader no way out than the way in, which I prefer to be difficult" (1977, p. 146/493).

The result is a hermetic obscurity in Lacan's writings that is all the more infuriating for being so deliberate. That is why they seem so much like a rebus: the reader feels that something significant is being said if only he could find out what it is. It is the modest purpose of these pages to follow the sequence of these essays—to work with the puzzle and try to comprehend this use of language—in order to gain some sense of what that something might be.

But first, who is Jacques Lacan? Although he is usually catalogued among the French structuralists, the fact is that, born in 1901 of an upper-middle-class Parisian family, he was already an established psychiatrist and psychoanalyst in France by the time the early essays of Claude Lévi-Strauss began to appear in the late '30s and '40s and structuralism in the contemporary sense was born.[2]

Lacan's clinical training in psychiatry began in 1927 and culminated in a doctoral thesis entitled *On Paranoia and Its Relationship to Personality* (1932). This work already marked a certain evolution in his thought inasmuch as his very first essays, no doubt heavily influenced by his teachers, had focused on the *organic* determinants of psychopathology. These initial researches left him convinced that no physiological phenomenon could be considered adequately, independent of its relationship to the entire personality that engages in interaction with a social milieu (1932, p. 400). It was to ground this conviction in an exhaustive case study that the doctoral work was undertaken.

The nub of the matter is the word "personality." Lacan speaks of it in the loosest terms as a kind of "psychic synthesis" (1932, p. 14) that adapts man to the milieu of society. As Lacan's own thought began to take shape after the doctoral thesis, two themes in particular intrigued him: the role of the image and the role of milieu in personality formation. The first, the role of the image, found articulation in an unpublished paper given at the Fourteenth International Psycho-Analytical Congress, Marienbad, 1936 (with Ernest Jones presiding), and entitled simply "The Mirror Phase." Mannoni (1971, p. 99) suggests that this was a first indirect answer to the question that arose out of the doctoral thesis as to why the paranoid attacks his own ideal in the image of someone else. The second theme, the role of milieu, found articulation in an article on "The Family" (1938) in de Monzie's edition of the *Encyclopédie française*.

But it was the doctoral thesis itself that brought Lacan his first renown—and, indeed, in unconventional circles. For at that time in France the scientific credentials of psychoanalysis were still highly suspect—particularly by the medical profession. If Freudian theory was accepted with enthusiasm by any-

---

[2] For a general introduction to structuralism, the reader may find the following helpful: De George and De George (1962), Ehrmann (1970), Gardner (1973), and Piaget (1968).

one, it was not by psychiatrists but by the literati and artists, principally the surrealists, who saw in it a confirmation, somehow, of their claim that dream and reality are ultimately reconciled in some sort of absolute synthesis that they called "surreality." Lacan's thesis appealed to the surrealists. What he said about the nature of symptoms was relevant to the problem of automatic writing and poetry. Beyond that, Salvador Dali, working on his own theory of the "paranoiac style" as it related to art, was intrigued by Lacan's theory and they became friends. Soon Lacan was a full-fledged member of the artistic set, rubbing elbows with Bataille, Malraux, Jean-Louis Barrault, etc. (Turkle, 1975, p. 335; 1978). Let these strange bedfellows — strange, at least, for the staid world of Parisian psychiatry — suggest something of the versatility of Lacan's thought and of the flamboyant theatricality of his personal — at least public — style.

Style notwithstanding, Lacan was well known on the Parisian psychoanalytic scene by 1949 when, at the Sixteenth International Psycho-Analytical Congress in Zurich, he delivered a second, much revised paper on the nature of the ego, entitled "The Mirror Stage as Formative of the Function of the 'I' as Revealed in Psychoanalytic Experience (1977, pp. 1–7/93–100). Here his thought develops the notion of "image," which he takes to be a principle of in-*form*-ation, i.e., of giving form to the organism in the sense of guiding its development. Lacan starts from what he takes to be a basic ambiguity in Freud's conception of the ego. On the one hand, "the ego takes sides against the object in the theory of narcissism: the concept of libidinal economy. . . . On the other hand, the ego takes sides with the object in the topographic theory of the functioning of the perception-consciousness system and resists the id" (1951, p. 11). We take him to mean that in the period when Freud's theory of narcissism was developing the ego was conceived as a love object and in that sense was in competition with ("takes sides against") other objects and was not identified with the subject's internal world as a whole (1914a, pp. 78–79). But after 1920, and particularly in 1923, Freud speaks of the ego as seeking "to bring the influence of the external world to bear upon the id and its tendencies, and endeavour[ing] to substitute the reality principle for the pleasure principle which reigns unrestrictedly in the id" (1923, p. 25), thus giving rise to the common conception of the ego as an agency of adaptation.

Lacan, for his part, explores the implication of the earlier conception and argues about the origin of the ego in this way: the newborn is marked by a prematurity specific to humans, an anatomical incompleteness evidenced in motor turbulence and lack of coordination. This state of fragmentation becomes camouflaged through the infant's jubilant identification with its reflection, experienced as a powerful gestalt promising mastery, unity, and substantive stature. Since this reflection (whose prototypical image is as seen in a mirror) is an external form, to identify with it as ego means to install a radical alienation and distortion in the very foundation of one's identity. The consequences of all this, of course, are enormous.

The nature of these consequences, e.g., the infant's experiencing of himself as a totality, of that totality as the idealization of all that it can be, and of that idealized totality as the rigid and armorlike structure that grounds the mechanisms of defense — all of that we must leave for the moment, for it will be thematized in the chapters that follow. Let us be content for now with observing that this was the level of Lacan's reflection (at least from what we can infer from his published work) when Lévi-Strauss' seminal essays began to appear. We can hypothesize that one reason why their impact on Lacan was so profound was that they suggested a radically and creatively new way to come to grips with his old preoccupation with the social component of personality.

Which essays of Lévi-Strauss were particularly meaningful to Lacan? His direct reference to two of them (1977, pp. 3, 73/ 95, 285) suggests that they had a special impact on him at this time: "The Effectiveness of Symbols" (Lévi-Strauss, 1949a) and "Language and the Analysis of Social Laws" (1951). In "The Effectiveness of Symbols," Lévi-Strauss interprets an 18-page South American shamanistic text, a long incantation whose purpose is to facilitate difficult childbirth. How is the cure effected? Lévi-Strauss sees it as a matter of making an emotional situation explicit in words and thereby making acceptable to the mind pains that the body refuses to tolerate. The transition to this linguistic expression that the medicine man provides induces the release of the physiological process—not unlike the work of psychoanalysis. In both cases, unconscious resistances are made conscious, and conflicts materialize in an orderly way that permits their free development and leads to their resolution. In the one case, a social myth provided by the healer specifies the patient's actions; in the other, the patient constructs an individual myth with elements drawn from her past. In both cases, homologous structures of organic processes, unconscious mind, and rational thought are related to one another through the "inductive property" in which the effectiveness of symbols consists (1949a, p. 201), as in poetic metaphor, which, according to Rimbaud, can change the world.

What is the nature of this unconscious mind for Lévi-Strauss? First, it is not the reservoir of personal recollections, images, and experiences, for these merely form an aspect of memory and are more properly called "preconscious." The properly unconscious consists of the aggregate of structural laws by which individual experiences are transformed into "living myth":

> The unconscious ceases to be the ultimate haven of individual peculiarities—the repository of a unique history which makes each of us an irreplaceable being. It is reducible to a function—the symbolic function, which no doubt is specifically human, and which is carried out according to the same laws among all men, and actually corresponds to the aggregate of these laws [1949a, pp. 202–203].

Lévi-Strauss draws on language itself in offering an illustrative analogy. The preconscious is the "individual lexicon" containing the vocabulary of personal history that becomes meaningful to the extent that the unconscious structures the vocabulary according to its laws like grammar, "and thus transforms it into language" (1949a, p. 203). These laws are the same for all people and number only a few. Thus there are many languages, but few structural laws valid for all.

The fundamental, unconscious, and all-pervasive effect of linguistic structures constitutes the key theme of "Language and the Analysis of Social Laws" (1951). Here Lévi-Strauss begins by examining the view that the social sciences cannot lend themselves to mathematical prediction because of the biasing effects of the observer as well as the absence of statistical runs commensurate with the life span of the individuals and societies studied. In opposition to this view, he offers structural linguistics, especially phonemics, as a social science in which the requirements for mathematical study are rigorously met. The influence of the observer is negligible, since he cannot modify language merely by becoming conscious of it — indeed, much of linguistic behavior occurs on the unconscious level, including syntactic and morphological laws and the phonological oppositions that give each phoneme distinctive features. Furthermore, the variety and abundance of written texts in some traditions provide linguistic runs of four to five thousand years and hence the scope required for reliable statistical analysis. Following Jakobson (Lévi-Strauss, 1976), he goes on to suggest just such statistical studies of phonological structures, eventually leading to "a sort of periodic table of linguistic structures" comparable to the table of elements in chemistry. The ultimate purpose of such scientific analysis is "to attain fundamental and objective realities consisting of systems of relations which are the products of the unconscious thought processes" (1951, p. 58), thus leading to the following questions:

Is it possible to effect a similar reduction in the analysis of other forms of social phenomena? If so, would this analysis lead to the same results? If the answer to this last question is in the affirmative, can we conclude that all forms of social life are substantially of the same nature—that is, do they consist of systems of behavior that represent the projection, on the level of conscious and socialized thought, of universal laws which regulate the unconscious activities of the mind? [1951, pp. 58–59].

How all of this affected Lacan at the time begins to be discernible in the famous "Discourse at Rome" (September 1953), later published under the title "The Function and Field of Speech and Language in Psychoanalysis" (1977, pp. 30–113/237–322), which was the first comprehensive statement of his program. There he alludes to Freud's famous passage in "Beyond the Pleasure Principle" (1920, pp. 14–15), where Freud describes how his grandson dealt with separation from his mother by throwing a spool tied to a string over the edge of his curtained crib; while doing this, he would vocalize "o-o-o-o" and *"Da"* (*"Fort!"* and *"Da!"*; "Gone!" and "Here!").

For Freud, the meaning of the game is obvious. "It was related to the child's great cultural achievement—the instinctual renunciation (that is, the renunciation of instinctual satisfaction) which he had made in allowing his mother to go away without protesting" (p. 15). For Lacan, the "cultural achievement" here does not consist simply in the child's "renunciation of instinctual satisfaction" but rather in his experience of desire for the mother precisely in separating from her and in dealing with his frustrated desire through the little game of which inchoatively verbal sounds were an essential part. In Lacan's words, the moment "in which desire becomes human is also that in which the child is born into language" (1977, p. 103/319). The statement is portentous, and careful consideration of it offers a convenient opportunity to gain some sense of what Lacan is about.

Let us begin with the latter part. What does it mean to say that at this point the child is "born into language"? Lacan's own enigmatic answer is as follows:

> [The child's action,] immediately embodied in the symbolic dyad of two elementary exclamations, announces in

the subject the. . . integration of the dichotomy of the phonemes, whose. . . structure existing language offers to his
assimilation; moreover, the child begins to become engaged in the system of the concrete discourse of the environment, by reproducing more or less approximately in his
Fort! and in his *Da!* the vocables that he receives from it
[1977, p. 103/319].

There is much here to be unpacked.

For Lacan, Freud's greatest insight was into the nature of
the "talking cure," and a close reading of Freud's early work,
principally *The Interpretation of Dreams* (1900a), *The Psychopathology of Everyday Life* (1901), and *Jokes and Their Relation to the Unconscious* (1905b), convinced Lacan of the importance for Freud of
language and speech in psychoanalysis. Scientifically trained,
however, Freud wanted to make his insights scientifically respectable, but the dominant scientific model available to him at
the time was that of nineteenth-century physics. In our own
day—and this is something that Lévi-Strauss helped Lacan
appreciate—we have available another scientific model (a more
characteristically human one) for understanding the psyche: the
science of linguistics—a science that explores the structures discernible in the one phenomenon that is coextensive with man
himself, i.e., human language. Lévi-Strauss had suggested the
possibility of using linguistics as the paradigm of analysis in all
of the social sciences, and Lacan follows this suggestion with
regard to psychoanalysis. His task becomes, then, to explore the
"universal laws which regulate the unconscious activities of the
mind" (Lévi-Strauss, 1951, p. 59), where these "universal laws"
are the laws of language and the "unconscious activities" are the
processes that Freud discovered and that he designated simply
as "the unconscious."

Any discussion of the universal laws of language must begin with reference to the work of Ferdinand de Saussure (1857–
1913), whose *Course in General Linguistics,* first published posthu-
mously in 1916, must be considered the principal inspiration of
linguistics in the contemporary sense. For the present, it will

suffice to recall that it was Saussure who emphasized the importance of distinguishing between language *(la langue)* and speech *(la parole)*. For him, language is a "system of signs," essentially "social" in nature, existing "perfectly only within a collectivity," whereas speech is the "executive side" of language, i.e., the actual execution of it—"willful and intellectual"—in the individual subject (1916, pp. 13–16). That is why the issue here is the laws of language, not of speech. This distinction will prove central for Lacan.

Again, it was Saussure who in modern times stressed the fact that if language is a system of signs, then these signs are composed of a relationship between a signifying component (sound image) and a signified component (concept), the relationship itself being arbitrary, i.e., not necessary (e.g., there is no necessary connection between the word "horse" and our idea of horse—*cheval, Pferd, equus,* etc., will do as well).

Now in one of his essays Lacan speaks of these signifiers as composed of "ultimate distinctive features," which are the phonemes, i.e., the smallest distinctive group of speech sounds in any language. These signifiers in turn are combined according to the "laws of a closed order," e.g., laws of vocabulary and of grammar according to which phonemes are grouped into units of meaning of increasing complexity (words, phrases, clauses, sentences, etc.) (1977, p. 153/502).

The elementary particles of language, therefore, are the phonemes. In a classic study, Jakobson and Halle (1956) reported that all possible linguistic sounds may be divided according to a system of bipolar opposition into 12 sets of complementary couples, i.e., binary pairs. It was this method of reducing masses of data to basic elements that can be grouped in sets of binary pairs that Lévi-Strauss made his own (e.g., in classifying myths), constructing from the results an algebra of possibilities that for him designates underlying structures.

Given this analysis, then, when Lacan sees in the *Fort! Da!* experience an articulation "embodied in the symbolic dyad of two elementary exclamations [that] announces in the subject

the. . .integration. . .of the dichotomy of the phonemes, whose
. . .structure existing language offers to his assimilation" (1977,
p. 103/319), he seems to be saying that in this primitive fashion
the child first experiences the bipolar nature of the ultimate ru-
diments of language, the phonemes.

Now the units of meaning composed out of phonemes
(words, phrases, clauses, etc.) relate to one another along one or
the other of two fundamental axes of language: an axis of combination and an axis of selection. Here again Lacan is indebted
to the work of Jakobson (1956, pp. 53–87). Along the axis of
combination, linguistic units are related to one another insofar
as they are copresent with each other. Thus the words that form
this sentence, even though stretched out in a linear sequence
that suspends their full meaning to the end, are related to each
other by a type of copresence, i.e., they are connected to each
other by a certain temporal contiguity. Saussure speaks of such
a relation as unifying terms *in praesentia,* and calls it "syntagmat-
ic" (1916, p. 123). The second axis along which linguistic units
relate to each other, however, is an axis of selection. This means
that they do not relate to each other by reason of a copresence
but rather by some kind of mutually complementary nonpres-
ence, i.e., mutual exclusion, whether this is because one word is
chosen over another as being more appropriate (e.g., we speak
of Lacan as a "psychoanalyst" rather than simply as a "physi-
cian") or because one word implies the rejection of its antonym
(e.g., by calling him a "structuralist," we imply that he is not an
"existentialist"). Saussure speaks of such a relation as unifying
terms *in absentia,* and calls it "associative" (1916, p. 123). Thus,
to select one unit is to exclude the other, but at the same time
the excluded other is still available to be substituted for the first
if circumstances warrant. The axis of selection, then, is also an
axis of possible substitution.

These two principles of combination and selection permeate the entire structure of language. Thus Jakobson (1956, pp.
63–75) was able to analyze the nature of aphasia according to
whether the patient's speech is deficient along the axis of combi-

nation or the axis of selection. Now, when these two axes of combination and selection function in terms of the relationship between signifiers, we find either that signifiers may be related to each other by a principle of combination, i.e., in terms of some kind of contiguity with each other (e.g., a relationship of cause/effect, part/whole, sign/thing signified) — in other words, by reason of what the old rhetoric of Quintilian called "metonymy"; or that they may be related by reason of similarity/dissimilarity, hence by a principle of selection in virtue of the fact that one is substituted for the other — in other words, by "metaphor." For example, on the morning following the first Nixon-Frost interview in 1977, CBS radio news announced: "Nixon discusses Watergate; Australia has its own Watergate." Here, "Watergate" is twice used as a signifier, and the signified is both times the same, i.e., a political scandal. But the relationship between signifier and signified is different in the two instances. In the first case ("Nixon discusses Watergate"), the signifier ("Watergate") signifies "political scandal" by designating the place where it first began to be uncovered, hence by contiguity along the axis of combination, i.e., by metonymy. In the second case ("Australia has its own Watergate"), the signifier "Watergate," already clothed in metonymic associations, is used to substitute for the term "political scandal," hence is plotted along the axis of selection and functions as a metaphor. If we say, then, that signifiers are related to each other in the guise of either metonymy or metaphor, this is simply to transpose the laws of combination and selection into another key. Let this suffice, then, to indicate the sort of thing that is meant when Lacan speaks of the "laws of language."

But how do these relate to the nature of the unconscious as Freud experienced it? It is Lacan's thesis that Freud's insight into the nature of the talking cure was an insight into the way the laws of language work in a relationship between signifiers that may be described as either metonymy or metaphor. Let us be content with mentioning two ways in particular by which this may be understood so as to gain some appreciation of the flavor

of his thought. The first concerns the principle of free association as the "fundamental law" of psychoanalysis; the second concerns the function of the dream-work in shaping the manifest
dream.

To be concrete, let us recall the analysis that Freud makes
of one of his own dreams, the "Dream of the Botanical Monograph."

CONTENT OF THE DREAM. — *I had written a monograph on
an (unspecified) genus of plants. The book lay before me and I was
at the moment turning over a folded coloured plate. Bound up in the
copy there was a dried specimen of the plant.*

The element in this dream which stood out most was
the *botanical monograph*. This arose from the impressions of
the dream-day: I had in fact seen a monograph on the genus Cyclamen in the window of a bookshop. There was no
mention of this genus in the content of the dream; all that
was left in it was the monograph and its relation to botany.
The 'botanical monograph' immediately revealed its connection with the *work upon cocaine* which I had once written.
From 'cocaine' the chains of thought led on the one hand to
the *Festschrift* and to certain events in a University laboratory, and on the other hand to my friend Dr. Königstein,
the eye surgeon, who had had a share in the introduction
of cocaine. The figure of Dr. Königstein further reminded
me of the interrupted conversation which I had had with
him the evening before and of my various reflections upon
the payment for medical services among colleagues. This
conversation was the actual currently active instigator of the
dream; the monograph on the cyclamen was also a currently active impression, but one of an indifferent nature. . . .

Not only the compound idea, 'botanical monograph',
however, but each of its components, 'botanical' and 'monograph' separately, led by numerous connecting paths deeper
and deeper into the tangle of dream-thoughts. 'Botanical'
was related to the figure of Professor *Gärtner* [Gardener], the
blooming looks of his wife, to my patient *Flora* and to the lady

[Frau L.] of whom I had told the story of the forgotten *flowers*. Gärtner led in turn to the laboratory and to my conversation with Königstein. My two patients [Flora and Frau L.] had been mentioned in the course of this conversation. A train of thought joined the lady with the flowers to my wife's *favourite flowers* and thence to the title of the monograph which I had seen for a moment during the day. In addition to these, 'botanical' recalled an episode at my secondary school and an examination while I was at the University. A fresh topic touched upon in my conversation with Dr. Königstein—my *favourite* hobbies—was joined, through the intermediate link of what I jokingly called my *favourite flower,* the artichoke, with the train of thought proceeding from the forgotten flowers. Behind 'artichokes' lay, on the one hand, my thoughts about Italy and, on the other hand, a scene from my childhood which was the opening of what have since become my intimate relations with books. Thus 'botanical' was a regular nodal point in the dream. . . . So, too, 'monograph' in the dream touches upon two subjects: the one-sidedness of my studies and the costliness of my favourite hobbies [1900a, pp. 282–283].

Here we see Freud associating to one of his dreams in order to decipher the rebus. Now for Lacan, the flow of associations is a flow of signifiers. Each signifier has what Saussure would call a corresponding conceptual content (signified), but for Lacan the signifier does not refer to its individual signified but rather to another signifier/association, and this in turn to another in a chain of signifiers. Lacan describes this "signifying chain" as "rings of a necklace that is a ring in another necklace made of rings" (1977, p. 153/502). Surely the complex concatenation of Freud's thoughts here may be described in the same terms: "rings of a necklace that is a ring in another necklace made of rings." And it is important to note that the meaning (signified) of this series of associations resides not in any association in particular but in the whole sequence. As Lacan puts it, "it is in the chain of the signifier that the meaning 'insists' but. . .

none of its elements 'consists' in the signification of which it is at the moment capable. We are forced, then, to accept the notion of an incessant sliding of the signified under the signifier" (1977, pp. 153–154/502). In any case, the signifiers in this stream of associations relate to one another along the two great axes of combination and selection.

Perhaps this will become clearer if we look at the second way in which Lacan sees the "laws of language" structuring the operation of the unconscious, namely, in that operation by which the raw materials of the dream, such as the dream-thoughts or day residues, are transformed (usually with distortions) into the manifest content of the dream, i.e., by the "dream-work." The distorting process, according to Freud's economic theory, has two basic modes: "condensation," where a single idea represents several associative chains insofar as it is located at the point where they intersect (Laplanche and Pontalis, 1967, p. 82), and "displacement," where the intensity of an idea is "detached" from it and passed on to another idea(s) of less intensity but related to the first by a chain of associations (Laplanche and Pontalis, 1967, p. 121). Now Lacan, following the suggestion of Jakobson but developing it in his own way, claims that condensation is a form of substitution, grounded in the principle of similarity/dissimilarity, hence to be located linguistically along the axis of selection: in other words, it is basically metaphor. Displacement, however, functions by reason of contiguity, hence is to be located linguistically along the axis of combination: in other words, it is metonymy.

The dream of the botanical monograph Freud himself presents is an example of both condensation and displacement. First, of condensation:

> This first investigation leads us to conclude that the elements 'botanical' and 'monograph' found their way into the content of the dream because they possessed copious contacts with the majority of the dream-thoughts, because, that is to say, they constituted 'nodal points' upon which a great number of the dream-thoughts converged, and be-

cause they had several meanings in connection with the interpretation of the dream. The explanation of this fundamental fact can also be put in another way: each of the elements of the dream's content turns out to have been 'overdetermined'—to have been represented in the dream-thoughts
many times over [1900a, p. 283].

What Lacan adds to—or makes explicit for—Freud is that these
"nodal points" function as such because the laws of language, in
this case the axis of selection/substitution, first make their metaphoric structure possible.

Again, according to Freud, the same dream from a different point of view is an example of displacement:

. . . in the dream of the botanical monograph, for instance,
the central point of the dream-content was obviously the element 'botanical'; whereas the dream-thoughts were concerned with the complications and conflicts arising between
colleagues from their professional obligations, and further
with the charge that I was in the habit of sacrificing too
much for the sake of my hobbies. The element 'botanical'
had no place whatever in this core of the dream-thoughts,
unless it was loosely connected with it by an antithesis—
the fact that botany never had a place among my favourite
studies [1900a, p. 305].

What Lacan makes explicit for Freud here is that the loose connection between "botanical" and the "dream-thoughts," i.e., an
ironic antithesis, is grounded in the axis of combination/conti-
guity that makes all such metonymy possible.

If Lacan says that the unconscious is structured "like a language" (1977, pp. 81–82, 159–164, 234/293–294, 509–515,
594), then the sense is that its processes follow the axes of combination and selection as all language does. In the "Discourse at
Rome" we are told: "The unconscious is that part of [our] concrete discourse, in so far as it is transindividual, that is not at the
disposal of the subject in re-establishing the continuity of his
conscious discourse" (1977, p. 49/258). Transindividual, it is

"other" than individual consciousness, "the other scene," or simply the Other. Other, it is yet discernible in bodily symptoms; childhood memories; one's particular vocabulary, life style, and character; traditions; legends; and distortions.

Let us return now to the child's game of *Fort! Da!*, the moment when he is "born into language," the fundamental sense of which we have tried to outline. That the child has the capacity to simulate the *Fort! Da!* with his "o-o-o-o" and "da" is a matter of native equipment. That at this point he begins to exercise it is a matter of maturation. Let us note, then: given a matrix of possible phonemes, it is the environment of the natural language that determines which ones the child assimilates; the pair that is assimilated expresses the experience of presence through absence; and what characterizes this moment for Lacan is the fact that although the natural language has surrounded the child from the beginning of life, it is only now that he actively begins to make it his own.

But how the child passes from this moment of incipient speech into the domain of language as a social institution is for Lacan much more than what it is, say, for a Piaget — simply a matter of "self-regulating equilibration." Lacan sees here a profound evolution from a dyadic relationship with the mother into a pluralized relationship to society as a whole. The father, then, is more than the third member of the oedipal triangle — he is the symbol and representative of the social order as such, into which the child, by the acquisition of speech, now enters. The social order is governed by a set of relationships that governs all forms of human interchange (e.g., the forming of pacts, gift-giving, marriage ties, kinship relations). This mapping of human relationships with their symbolic arrangements Lacan speaks of as "law," presumably to suggest the patterning, compelling quality of it. In any case, this law is characteristically human, for, Lacan writes, "in regulating marriage ties [it] superimposes the kingdom of culture on that of a nature abandoned to the law of mating. The prohibition of incest is merely its subjective pivot" (1977, p. 66/277). This law is what Lévi-Strauss

(1949a, p. 203) has called the "symbolic function" structuring the primordial arrangement of society. Lacan, following Lévi-Strauss here (1977, pp. 61–62/272), finds that this primordial law that sets the pattern for human relationships is the same law that sets the pattern of human language. "[T]he law of man has been the law of language," he writes, "since the first words of recognition presided over the first gifts" (1977, p. 61/272; cf. p. 66/277).

In any case, the symbolic order represented by the father is the field, or domain, in which the child becomes an active citizen when he acquires the power of speech. The essence of Freud's discovery, Lacan claims, was to see the relationship between the individual and the symbolic order in terms of man's unconscious dimension. "Isn't it striking," he writes, "that Lévi-Strauss, in suggesting the implication of the structures of language with that part of the social laws which regulate marriage ties and kinship, is already conquering the very terrain in which Freud situates the unconscious?" (1977, p. 73/285).

Let this suffice, then, to suggest what Lacan has in mind when he speaks of the child being "born into language." But the full statement goes further. He tells us that the moment "in which the child is born into language" is also the moment "in which desire becomes human." Let us conclude this brief orientation, then, by trying to get some feel for what he means by that.

For Lacan, the fundamental driving force of the human subject, the dynamic power that propels him, is not libido or Eros, as for Freud, but desire. It is here, perhaps, that another great influence on him, namely Hegel, is most profound.

The Hegel with whom Lacan became familiar was Hegel as interpreted by Alexandre Kojève, a Marxist, whose brilliant lectures on the *Phenomenology of the Mind* (Hegel, 1807a) at the École des Hautes Études (Paris) from 1933 to 1939, were of seminal importance for Parisian intellectuals of pre-World War II France, among whom Lacan obviously found himself. There the role of desire in the Hegelian dialectic emerged in bold relief.

Kojève carefully elucidates the Hegelian argument: Man is basically self-consciousness, and he becomes conscious of himself when for the "first" time he says "I." But this occurs not in an act of knowing, in which he is absorbed by the object he knows, but by an act of desire, whereby he can experience himself in his desire by acknowledging his desire as *his*, and as distinct from its object. Now desire moves to action that will satisfy this desire. This action takes the form of negation, i.e., the destruction, or at least the transformation, of the desired object (e.g., to satisfy hunger, food must be destroyed, or at least transformed). Generally speaking, then, the "I" that desires, inasmuch as it desires, is experienced as an emptiness with regard to the object of desire and receives its positive content by a negating action of this kind, i.e., by destroying, transforming, or "assimilating" the object of desire.

Thus the "I" receives its positive content from the negated object of desire. "And the positive content of the I, constituted by negation, is a function of the positive content of the negated non-I" (Kojève, 1939, p. 4). If this desired "non-I" is thinglike (or "natural"), then the "I," through its negation of it, experiences itself as thinglike (or "natural") and achieves not self-consciousness but at best the mere sentiment of self that characterizes an animal. Hence, for the "I" to experience itself as self-consciousness, the non-I toward which its desire is directed must be another self-consciousness, i.e., another desire. Thus in the relationship between a man and a woman, for example, desire is human only if the one desires not the body of the other but the other's desire (1939, p. 6).

Now to desire a desire is to want to substitute oneself for the value desired by this desire. Therefore for me to desire the desire of another is in the final analysis to desire that the value that I am or that I "represent" be the value desired by this other. I want the other to *recognize* my value, i.e., my autonomy, as his value. Moreover, for the full human status of such a desire to come to light, man's specifically human desire (i.e., for recognition) must actually win out over his specifically animal desire (e.g., for the preservation of life), so that the quest for recognition must be engaged in even at the risk of life, i.e., in a struggle unto death. To be sure, there must not be a real death in this struggle for recognition, lest the victory be a Pyrrhic one insofar as it destroys, through the death of the other, the very possibility of recognition by him. At best, the struggle can end only in the submission of one desire to another, as occurs in the eventual surrender of slave to master.

How this proceeds further in Hegel need not concern us now — the struggle between domination and submission (i.e., between master and slave) as it is reflected in the analytic relationship is a theme that recurs again and again in Lacan, and will be treated in its own time below. It suffices to say that Lacan's conception of desire presupposes the Hegelian model. For the moment it is more important for us to see in what way desire for Lacan "becomes human" coincidentally with the child's "birth" into language.

What Lacan means by the expression "desire becomes human" is hard to say with certainty. It may mean in strictly Hegelian terms that up to the moment of the *Fort! Da!* experience, when absence becomes present through language, the infant's so-called "desire" is not different from the appetition of an animal seeking the satisfaction of its bodily needs. Such gratification yields at best what Hegel calls a "sentiment" of self, but not consciousness of self as an "I" that is enunciated in speech. For his part, Lacan would describe this strictly biological appetition not as "desire," but only as "need." Desire, as he uses the term, could be said to "become human" at the birth of speech in the sense that for him desire in its specifically human sense emerges then for the first time in the initial experience of "want."

It is clear that for Lacan this is a crucial moment in human development. Up to that time the infant has been engaged with the mother in an essentially *dual* relationship — a quasi-symbiotic tie that psychologically prolongs the physical symbiosis in the womb, in terms of which the mother is the infant's All. But with the *Fort! Da!* experience that tie is ruptured. Ruptured, too, is the infant's illusion of totality, its presumption of infinity. It experiences for the first time the catastrophe of negation (it is *not* the mother), the trauma of limitation, the tragedy of its finitude — in other words, its own ineluctable *manque à être* (to use Lacan's expression).

Now this use of the word *manque* is suggestively ambiguous. In itself, *manque* in French may mean "lack," "deficiency," or "want." Hence, *manque à être* would mean "lack of being," or "deficiency in regard to being," or "the state of being in 'want of' being." But this "being in want of" being may be understood also as "wanting" being, so that the most recent English translator renders *manque à être* — indeed, at Lacan's own suggestion (Sheridan, 1977, p. xi) — as "want-to-be." It is precisely this "want-to-be" that we take to be the key to Lacan's understanding of desire: the radical and humanly unsatisfiable yearning of the infant for the lost paradise of complete fusion with its All — a wanting born of want.

The moment is portentous. Desire erupts in the rupture of the primitive union with the mother. Now for Lacan, the signifier par excellence of desire is the phallus. He is not referring simply to the sexual organ of the male (penis), but uses the term in a way that it has been used many times before, i.e., symbolically — here as a symbol of perfect union between every infant (male or female) and its All. In the words of Serge Leclaire, it is a "copula." "It is even, one might say, the hyphen [*trait d'union*] in the evanescence of its erection; the phallus is the signifier of the impossible identity" (cited in Lemaire, 1970, p. 145). Cut off from its "copula" simply by reason of its finitude, the subject thereby suffers a primordial castration. This is also a moment of death, for if we can accept Heidegger's notion of death as the ultimate limit that de-fines a human being (i.e., sets him within definitive limits) — and Lacan alludes to Heidegger precisely in this context (1977, p. 105/321), suggesting that Heidegger is as significant a part of his philosophical background as Hegel — then the moment when "desire becomes human" is not only a primordial castration but also the first experience of the child as Being-unto-death.

Wrenched away from a dyadic relationship with its mother in the world of inarticulate images, the infant must now relate to her through a dialectic of desire, in which the subject's ultimate quest is for recognition by the desired. Traumatized by its want, the child wants, i.e., desires, to recapture its lost plenitude by being the desired of its mother, her fullness — in Lacanian language, by being the phallus for its mother. Alas, that is impossible. For the father (who *has* the phallus) is there: the real father, the imaginary father, and most of all the symbolic father, i.e., the "law of the father" — the symbolic order, structuring all human relationships and making it possible that absence become present through language.

How the oedipal struggle, transposed into these terms, finds its resolution, i.e., how the child comes to forgo its desire to "be" the mother's phallus and settle for the condition of merely "having" a phallus or "not having" it, or, to put the matter differently, how the child learns to accept its indigenous want *(manque)*, i.e, finitude, with the consequence that the same law (of the father) that prohibits indulging the child's want to be the mother's phallus is the law that henceforth mediates this want through the linguistic structures by which desire will express itself (i.e., the symbolic order) — all this is too far-reaching a problem for appropriate discussion here. We shall return to it below. Let it suffice to say that from this point forward the child's desire, its endless quest for a lost paradise, must be channeled like an underground river through the subterranean passageways of the symbolic order, which makes it possible that things be present in their absence in some way through words — passageways whose labyrinthine involution resembles in its complexity the "rings of a necklace that is a ring in another necklace made of rings."

All of this does not add up to an "introduction" to the work of Jacques Lacan so much as an introduction to the studies to follow that takes the form of a mapping out of the most general

contours of the terrain they cover.[3] If the reader is to understand their nature, a word of explanation is in order.

We are convinced that Lacan has something to say that is
worth hearing, and are interested in the larger import of it:
theoretically (i.e., in terms of psychoanalysis), clinically, and
philosophically. However, we have found (as has many a reader
of the French text before us) that in order to gain access to whatever hidden wealth is here, an extraordinarily painful ascesis is
necessary. These pages are a partial record of our own effort to
submit to such an ascesis, and are shared with a larger public
that others may be spared some of its rigors. What is offered
here, then, is a kind of workbook for the reading of Lacan's
Écrits: A Selection (1977). At best, it is only a beginning, i.e., a
set of tools (to change the metaphor) to help the reader get started
in his own reading of the text. In any case, it should be clear
that nothing more is intended here than this set of tools—the
real labor of reading Lacan's text is left to the reader (a reading,
by the way, that we have found, as teachers, to benefit from
reading aloud).

How are these tools designed? Each essay is considered as
a separate unit and examined from three different points of
view: (1) an overview of the argument that strives to articulate
as succinctly as possible the substance of the essay—a look at the
forest, so to speak, without becoming lost among the trees; (2) a
mapping of the text that strives to follow, step by step, Lacan's
own tortuous path through the underbrush; (3) notes that explicate the text where practicality suggests that this might be
useful. In all of it, we are aware of how tentative our own
judgments must remain, and have made certain choices in the
face of Lacan's obscurity that subsequent understanding may
well prove wrong. But a beginning must be made somewhere—
and readers are invited to clarify and supplement our efforts

---

[3] For a more comprehensive introduction to Lacan's thought, the following
may prove helpful: Bär (1971, 1974), Lemaire (1970), Mannoni (1971), *Times Literary Supplement* [London] (1968), and Wilden (1968). Perhaps the best general overview in English is Bowie's (1979) chapter.

In trying to ferret out the meaning of some of Lacan's allusions, we found *The
New Columbia Encyclopedia* (Harris and Levey, 1975) very useful.

with suggestions of their own. At any rate, these tools are not intended to stand on their own. They will make sense only to the extent that they are used as instruments to help break the code of Lacan's text itself.

But when all is said and done, it would be unfair to expect too much from a set of tools. After all, the fundamental rule of psychoanalysis is itself only a tool — the enigma of any given rebus remains to be deciphered. But if this quest for the understanding of one rebus in particular seems caught in a chain of signifiers that "is the ring of a necklace that is a ring in another necklace made of rings," let us take what cold comfort we can from the fact that "it is in the chain of the signifier that the meaning 'insists' [though] none of its elements 'consists' in the signification of which it is at the moment capable. We are forced, then, to accept the notion of an incessant sliding of the signified under the signifier" (1977, pp. 153–154/502), even when that happens in the text of Lacan himself.

Chapter 1

The Mirror Stage as Formative of the Function of the I as Revealed in Psychoanalytic Experience

Overview

Lacan first presented his views on the nature of the ego to the Fourteenth International Psycho-Analytical Congress at Marienbad, July 31, 1936, but failed to submit a written text to be included in the proceedings of the Congress (1966, p. 67, fn. 1). Hence the present text, dating from 13 years later, is the first full articulation of this important theme that we have. But even in 1936, Lacan's formulation did not fall completely out of the blue. To gain a better sense of the import of this essay, then, it may be useful to review briefly the course of Lacan's intellectual career up to that time.

We have seen already that Lacan's clinical training culminated in a doctoral thesis *On Paranoia and Its Relationship to Personality* (1932), in which he examined in a detailed case study the interaction between personality and social milieu. In that monograph, "personality" was understood loosely as "the ensemble of specialized functional relations that establishes the originality of man-the-animal, adapting him to the enormous influence exercised by the milieu of mankind, or society, on the milieu of his life" (1932, p. 400; our translation).

More precisely, the personality is polarized around three different foci: an individual one that relates to a particular life story; a structural one that relates to typical elements that affect every human development; and a social one that relates to one's social interaction with others (1932, pp. 42, 313–315). Of these three, Lacan in his doctoral thesis underlined particularly the last, the *social* component of personality. It is worth noting, too, that in this early work, he recognized clearly the ambiguities involved in Freud's theory of narcissism (1932, pp. 321–322) as well as of the *moi* (pp. 323–326), promising to return to the subject in his later researches (p. 326). The unpublished (1936) essay on the "Mirror Phase" was clearly an effort to fulfill this promise.

Between the doctoral thesis of 1932 and the "Mirror Stage" essay of 1949, there are one essay and one article that are interesting because of their transitional nature. A third piece, "Aggressivity in Psychoanalysis," dates from 1948, one year before the "Mirror Stage" essay, but since the two are cut from the same cloth and the former appears immediately after the latter in the *Selection*, we shall examine them in the order in which they appear in the English edition.

The first transitional essay dates from 1936, the same summer as the first (unpublished) presentation of the "mirror phase" theme, and may be presumed to reflect a comparable level of development. It bears the title "Beyond the 'Reality Principle' " (1966, pp. 73–92), in obvious allusion to Freud's essay "Beyond the Pleasure Principle" (1920), and it takes that "fundamental principle" of Freud's doctrine as a reference point with regard to which the second generation of Freud's disciples can define both their debt to Freud and their task for the future.

In the first part (to have been followed by two others that never appeared), the essay focuses on the import of Freud's

epochal discovery: the method of "free association." This involves a critique of nineteenth-century associationism in psychology (against which Freud was reacting), followed by a
phenomenological description of the new psychoanalytic experience. Here Lacan sees Freud's recognition of "*psychological* reality" as of major importance (1966, p. 88). Of interest to us is his
insistence on two elements that help structure this "psychological reality": (1) the image and (2) the complex.

According to Lacan, the essential function of an image is
"in-form-ation," which we take literally to mean "giving *form* to"
something—whether this be the intuitive form of an object as in
knowledge, or the plastic form of an imprint as in memory, or
the form that guides the development of an organism (1966, pp.
77, 88). In any case, the image is a form that in-forms the subject and makes possible the process of identification with it.
Identification with a constellation of images leads to a behavioral pattern that reflects the social structures within which those
images first emerged. It is this constellation that is called a
"complex," a notion that is far richer for Lacan that that of "instinct." "It is through the *complex* that images are established in
the psychic organization that influence the broadest unities of
behavior: images with which the subject identifies completely in
order to play out, as the sole actor, the drama of conflicts between them" (1966, p. 90; our translation).

The second interim work is the article on "The Family"
(1938). Clearly Lacan sees the family as more significant as a
social milieu than as a biological fabric out of which the subject
is cut, hence his insistence on the importance of the complex
rather than instinct in the development of psychic mechanisms
within it. Here he is more detailed in his description of the complex. The complex, he tells us, is dominated by social factors. In
its content, it is representative of an object; in its form, it represents this object insofar as the object influenced the subject at a
given state of psychic development; in its manifestation of what
is objectively absent at a given point of time, the complex is understood by reference to an object. With regard to the individual

integration of different forms of objectivization, it is the work of a dialectical process that makes each new form arise out of conflicts between the preceding form and the "real." In any case, the complex, at least as understood by Freud, is essentially part of the unconscious dimension of the subject. The image, on the other hand, is seen as one element in the composition of the complex. Thus Lacan speaks, for example, of the weaning process as constituting a complex in the newly born, of which the image of the maternal breast is one element (1938, p. 6). The most important of the complexes is the so-called "Oedipus complex," which includes as a constituent element an image of the father (pp. 11–15). The Oedipus complex is, of course, rich with implications for the social dimension of man, and receives lengthy treatment in the article.

When we come, then, to the landmark essay of 1949, "The Mirror Stage as Formative of the Function of the I as Revealed in Psychoanalytic Experience," two themes have clearly preoccupied Lacan up to this point: the role of the image in the development of the subject and the manner in which social experience evolves. In a certain general way, these two themes polarize the content of the essay, and in any case may serve to structure our remarks about it.

Lacan's principal thesis is that the newly born human infant, initially sunk in motor incapacity, turbulent movements, and fragmentation, first experiences itself as a unity through experiencing some kind of reflection of itself, the paradigm for which would be self-reflection in a mirror. This normally occurs between the ages of six and 18 months. This mirrorlike reflection, then, serves as the form that in-forms the subject and guides its development. So it happens that there is an "identification" between infant and its reflection "in the full sense that analysis gives to the term: namely, the transformation that takes place in the subject when he assumes an image" (1977, p. 2/94). It is this reflected image of itself with which the infant identifies that Lacan understands by the "I." The consequences of this conception are manifold.

What is meant by the initial experience of the "fragmented body" is understandable enough, given the *specific prematurity of birth in man* (1977, p. 4/96), his anatomical incompleteness, which few would wish to challenge. But are we to take literally the suggestion that every infant must perceive himself in a physical mirror in order to discover his own ego? It would seem not:

> . . . the recognition by the subject of his [own] image in the mirror is a phenomenon that for the analysis of this stage [of development] is significant for two reasons: the phenomenon appears after six months, and the study of it at that moment reveals in demonstrative fashion the tendencies that then constitute the reality of the subject; the mirror stage, by reason of these affinities, offers a convenient symbol of this reality: of its affective valence (illusory like the image) and its structure as a reflection from a human form [1938, p. 10; our translation].

The essential here apparently is that a human form be the external image in which the infant discovers both himself and the "reality" around him, but presumably that human form could also be — and in the concrete is more likely to be — the mothering figure.

What, more precisely, does the infant discover in experiencing his form reflected in the mirror? First of all, a total unity that replaces his prior experience of fragmentation. This totality becomes idealized into a model for all eventual integration and, as such, is the infant's primary identification — the basis for all subsequent "secondary" identifications (1977, p. 2/94). This model, however, although it "fixes" the subject in a certain *permanence* that contrasts with the "turbulent movements that the subject feels are animating him" (1977, p. 2/95), does so through a form that initially (i.e., before the subject's assumption of it through identification) is "other" than the subject, exterior to it, hence an "alienation" of it. The stability of this form, contrasting as it does with the instability of the initial fragmentation, assumes a tensile strength that eventually becomes rigid and armorlike—the basis of "the inertia characteristic of the formations of the *I*" (1977, p. 7/99), i.e., its defense mechanisms. That is why Lacan can speak of the process as "the assumption of the armour of an alienating identity, which will mark with its rigid structure the subject's entire mental development" (1977, p. 4/ 97).

There is another aspect of this primitive alienation that must be underlined—its "fictional" quality (1977, p. 2/94). This may be understood in the sense that the ideal of total unity, projected onto this alienating identity, is an unattainable one, wherein "the subject anticipates in a mirage the maturation of his power" (1977, p. 2/94). It can be approached by the developing subject only asymptotically.

But "fictional" may be understood in another sense as well, for the reflection in the mirror is an inversion of what stands before the mirror. Thus the child experiences "the relation between the movements assumed in the image and the reflected environment, and between this virtual complex and the reality it reduplicates—the child's own body, and the persons and things, around him" (1977, p. 1/93). Initially, then, the external world with all its spatial relationships is experienced in an inverted way and, to that extent, awry. Thus, "the mirror-image would seem to be the threshold of the visible world" (1977, p. 3/ 95), in the sense that it establishes "a relation between the organism and its reality—or, as they say, between the *Innenwelt* and the *Umwelt*" (1977, p. 4/96). But since this relationship is filtered through a prism of inversion, there is a primitive distortion in the ego's experience of reality that accounts for the miscognitions (*méconnaissances*) that for Lacan characterize the ego in all its structures (1977, p. 6/99).

Given the fact that the infant subject first discovers himself in an external image, it is easy to understand how he confuses this external image of himself with the images of other subjects among whom he finds himself. It is in such fashion that the "social dialectic" begins. This confusion leads to a misidentification of himself with the other and has far-reaching effects, not only on relationships with others but on knowledge of external things as well. This new development, called "transitivism" by Lacan, is the result of "a veritable captation by the image of the other" (1966, p. 180). Lacan points out how the child's use of language reflects this, speaking in the third person before using the first person. In his 1948 essay, "Aggressivity in Psychoanalysis" (which we will take up next), he writes of the period from six to 30 months:

> During the whole of this period, one will record the emotional reactions and the articulated evidences of a normal transitivism. The child who strikes another says that he has been struck; the child who sees another fall, cries. Similarly, it is by means of an identification with the other that he sees the whole gamut of reactions of bearing and display, whose structural ambivalence is clearly revealed in his behaviour, the slave being identified with the despot, the actor with the spectator, the seduced with the seducer [1977, p. 19/113].

In discussing transitivism, Lacan refers to a well-known study by Charlotte Bühler (1927); Wallon (1934), in a detailed description of this study, describes (in the case of pairs of infants separated in age by no more than two and one-half months) the children's reciprocal attitudes in terms of a reciprocal stimulation formed by a dyadic situation: "The roles are distributed according to age, but the two partners are equally captivated by the situation born of their reciprocal nearness. By it they are confused between themselves: the one who is showing off being as excited by the expectation of the other whose eyes are fixed on him" (p. 194). As a result of Bühler's research, Lacan (1951) tells us, "we can assess the role of the body image in the various ways children identify with the Socius," with the result that the child's "ego is actually alienated from itself in the other person" (p. 16). How this gives rise to jealousy, aggressivity, and the Hegelian dialectic will be the main focus of the next chapter. For now, let it suffice to say that the mirror stage comes to an end in this "paranoiac alienation, which dates from the deflection of the specular *I* into the social *I*" (1977, p. 5/98).

By "paranoiac alienation" in this context, then, Lacan seems to mean both the alienation, i.e., misidentification of the subject himself with his own reflection, and the misidentification of this reflected image with the image of the other in the process of transitivism. But this double alienation has its effect on the infant's experience of external things, too. Just as it leads to a distorted grasp of the subject's reality and to interpersonal confusion, it leads to a fundamental miscognition of external things, to which Lacan gives the term "paranoiac knowledge" (1977, p. 2/94).

More precisely, how is this to be understood? There seem to be two steps to Lacan's argument. The first has to do with the role of desire, an essentially Hegelian term that has to do with prestige and recognition. Once the ego is identified with the other, "the object of man's desire . . . is essentially an object desired by someone else" (1951, p. 12). Desire now mediates human knowledge and "constitutes its objects in an abstract equivalence" (1977, p. 5/98). What becomes salient in the object is its desirability, not any "intrinsic" quality: "One object can become equivalent to another, owing to the effect produced by this intermediary, in making it possible for objects to be exchanged and compared. This process tends to diminish the special significance of any one particular object, but at the same time it brings into view the existence of objects without number" (1951, p. 12). This "instrumental polyvalence" of objects and their "symbolic polyphony" (in part through their role as gifts) introduces "a certain rupture of level, a certain discord" between man and nature, and at the same time "extends indefinitely his world and his power" (1977, p. 17/111).

This extension of man's world appears to involve, in addition to the movement of desire, a second step in the process, whereby "we are led to see our objects as identifiable egos, having unity, permanence, and substantiality; this implies an element of inertia, so that the recognition of objects and of the ego itself must be subjected to constant revision in an endless dialectical process" (1951, p. 12). But once the square of identification is complete (subject-ego-others-things) and things are treated narcissistically as reflections of the ego, they take on the role of "defensive armour" (1977, p. 17/111), and a certain rigidity grips human knowledge: "Now, this formal stagnation is akin to the most general structure of human knowledge: that which constitutes the ego and its objects with attributes of permanence, identity, and substantiality, in short, with entities or 'things' that are very different from the *Gestalten* that experience enables us to isolate in the shifting field" (1977, p. 17/111). Lacan seems to say, then, that human knowledge is paranoiac because imaginary ego-properties are projected onto things; things become conceived as distorted, fixed, rigid entities; and things have salience for man insofar as they are desirable to others. Whether and how knowledge can be other than paranoiac are questions for later discussion.

In the end, then, the image dominates this period of Lacan's thought: the subject is in-formed by his own image, is captivated by the other's image, and objects themselves take on the rigid features of the ego: "What I have called paranoiac knowledge is shown, therefore, to correspond in its more or less archaic forms to certain critical moments that mark the history of man's mental genesis, each representing a stage in objectifying identification" (1977, p. 17/111). The impact of "objectifying identification" on social relationships will serve as the main theme of the next chapter.

Map of the Text

I. Introduction.
    A. Our goal in calling attention to the mirror stage is to shed light on the formation of the I
       1. as experienced in psychoanalysis
       2. and as opposed to Cartesian philosophy.
II. This conception is rooted in an aspect of human behavior

highlighted by a finding of comparative psychology.
A. The chimpanzee can recognize his image in a mirror
   1. but this soon loses its interest.
B. The child jubilantly recognizes his own image in the mirror from the age of six months
   1. with far-reaching *effects* on his development.
      a. The mirror image stage is an identification in which the subject is transformed.
      b. This assumption of his image by the child precipitates the I in a primordial form.
      c. This form is the Ideal I, "the source of secondary identifications"
         i. prior to the form's social determination.
            (a) This form orients the agency of the ego in a "fictional direction"
            (b) and will remain irreducibly discordant with the subject's own reality.
   2. The *process* involves the anticipation of bodily maturation in a gestalt
      a. which is exterior,
      b. of different size,
      c. and whose symmetry is reversed, leading to:
         i. a rigid structure of the I;
         ii. alienation;
         iii. and its resemblance to statues.
   3. The *evidence* for formative effects of a gestalt is:
      a. gonad maturation in the female pigeon;
      b. social maturation of the migratory locust;
      c. significance of space in mimicry.
   4. The *preconditions* for this spatial captation are:
      a. man's organic insufficiency,
         i. requiring that his relation to nature be mediated by an image;
      b. man's prematurity at birth.
III. Some of the intrapsychic implications of this stage are:
A. the image of the fragmented body

      1. as present in dreams, painting, and hysteria;
- B. the fortification of the I,
      1. as suggested in dreams and obsessional symptoms;
- C. a means of symbolic reduction
      1. based on linguistic techniques rather than pure subjectivism;
- D. and a genetic order of ego defenses, whose sequence is:
      1. hysterical repression;
      2. obsessional inversion;
      3. paranoiac alienation
         a. when the mirror stage gives way to jealousy and the social dialectic begins.
- IV. Some philosophical implications follow:
- A. Knowledge becomes mediated through the desire of the other.
- B. The I becomes defensive regarding natural maturation
      1. so that normalization requires cultural mediation.
- C. In relating to others, the narcissistic, alienating I becomes aggressive.
- D. Existential negativity cannot be based on a self-sufficiency of consciousness.
- E. The ego is not centered on the perception-consciousness system or the reality principle
      1. but is characterized by the function of miscognition (*méconnaissance*)
      2. and marked by denial and defensive inertia.

Notes to the Text

1*b*/93[1]   The experience of insight is described in Köhler (1925).

1*c*/93   Recent research (Gallup, 1977) points to the chimpanzee and orangutang as the only primates, other than man, capable of recognizing their mirror images as their own. While the chimpanzee's "jubilant activity"

---

[1] This form of reference includes the page in the English text (1), the paragraph in the same text (*b*—the second), and the page in the French text (93).

may perhaps be exhausted, Gallup reports that the animal settles down to a pragmatic use of the mirror for grooming. Köhler (1925, pp. 317–319) also describes how his chimpanzees persisted in mirroring themselves in polished tin, pools of water, etc.

1*d*/93   In this teasing allusion to Baldwin, Lacan may be pointing us to the American tradition of philosophical social psychology of Baldwin, Cooley, and Mead, whose notions of genetic epistemology, the looking-glass self, and the generalized other are congenial to Lacan's concerns, if not at all to be confused with his own notions of paranoiac knowledge, the mirror stage, and the Other.

Baldwin, many of whose works were translated into French (and other languages), wrote the following dedication to his first volume of *Thoughts and Things* (1906): "To his friends who wrote in French — Janet, Flournoy, Binet, and to the lamented Tarde and Marillier — This book is inscribed by the author in testimony to the just criticism and adequate appreciation his other books have had in France."

According to Baldwin (1902, p. 206), imitation first appears in the infant after six months of age. Freud refers to Baldwin in Letter 74 to Fliess (1887–1902, p. 228) and in his *Three Essays on the Theory of Sexuality* (1905c, p. 174n). For a recent review of Baldwin's work, see Cairns (1980).

Wallon is credited by Laplanche and Pontalis (1967, p. 251) with providing data for the mirror experience in 1931. In a chapter titled "Le corps propre et son image exteroceptive," Wallon (1934) reports examples of infants responding to their reflections between their eighth and ninth months. M. Lewis (1977) reports that infants were aware of seeing their own images in the mirrors of his laboratory at nine months of age. Lacan places the onset of the experience at over eight months in a later paper (1951, p. 14).

2c/94   *Imago* is defined literally as "an imitation, copy of a thing, an image, likeness (i.e., a picture, statue, mask, an apparition, ghost, phantom)..." (C.T. Lewis and Short, 1955, p. 888). For further discussion in Lacan, see *Écrits* (1966, pp. 188–193).

2d/94   The child, incapable of speech (*infans*), assumes the image in the mirror as his idealized identity, establishing the foundational reference for his "I" which he cannot yet speak. This referent is not yet given as an object to the barely inchoative subject, since self-consciousness has not yet emerged through the dialectic of desire and the struggle to be recognized by the other, as will be explained later.

2e/94   Lacan's point seems to be that there are two irreducible aspects of the "I," one fictional and experientially prior, the other social and structurally prior. Laplanche and Pontalis summarize:

> As far as the structure of the subject is concerned, the mirror phase is said to represent a genetic moment: the setting up of the first roughcast of the ego. What happens is that the infant perceives in the image of its counterpart—or in its own mirror image—a form *(Gestalt)* in which it anticipates a bodily unity which it still objectively lacks (whence its "jubilation"): in other words, it identifies with this image. This primordial experience is basic to the imaginary nature of the ego, which is constituted right from the start as an "ideal ego" and as the "root of the secondary identifications." ... It is obvious that from this point of view the subject cannot be equated with the ego, since the latter is an imaginary agency in which the subject tends to become alienated [1967, p. 251].

2f/95   The gestalt law of *Prägnanz* states: "Wholes tend to be as complete, symmetrical, simple, and good as possible under prevailing conditions" (Avant and Helson, 1973, p. 422). The formal properties of the specular image, not the concrete behavior reflected, fix the ego in a rigid, externalized manner analogous to the statue, the phantom, the automaton.

3b/95   The *double*, as discussed by Freud (1919), is linked originally with primary narcissism and ego preservation, but has now become a death omen. Both Freud and Lacan (1951) refer to Otto Rank, who discussed the double's relation to reflections in mirrors (e.g., 1925, pp. 8ff.).

3c/95   In his later paper (1951) Lacan provides references for this research. See also *Écrits* (1966, pp. 189–190) for additional details. Lacan ends the paragraph typically, with a broad reference to the thought of Plato.

3d/96   Roger Caillois is mentioned by Lacan (1964) for his work on mimicry in animals.

4c/96   In presenting additional evidence for man's premature birth, Gould (1976) reasons that the human embryonic brain, only one-fourth of its final size, has to leave the pelvic cavity before it becomes too large to pass through. Roussel (1968) quotes Freud on man's prematurity at birth (1926a, pp. 154–155).

4e/97   "Quadrature" is puzzling and admits of several interpretations. Perhaps the ego as mediator between organism and environment buttresses its fictional role in an endless obsession with trying to keep things in place, a task as impossible as the squaring (quadrature) of the circle; perhaps the sense is that the task is as limitless as if the verifications were lifted to the fourth power (quadrature); in the astronomical sense, perhaps the ego would be in quadrature to the *Innenwelt* and *Umwelt*, raised above and observing both, as the half-moon is in quadrature, at a 90° angle from a line extending from the earth to the sun,

5a–c/   Lacan typically balances hysterical and obsessional
97–98   symptoms (e.g., 1977, pp. 46*b*, 89*f*–90*c*/254, 302–
304), and the linguistic techniques he refers to would
seem to be metaphor (the hysterical condensation)
and metonymy (the obsessional displacement). He
provides a more detailed treatment of the linguistic
mechanisms elsewhere (1977, pp. 156–160/505–511).

5*d*/98   Lacan's genetic order appears predicated on the
movement of the mirror stage: felt motor incoordina-
tion (later called the experience of *corps morcelé*) falls
under hysterical repression; the rise of the specular
ego institutes obsessional, fortifying defenses; and
captivation by the image of the other in transitivism
leads to paranoiac identification.

5*e*/98   Lacan provides references in *Écrits* (1966, p. 180). In
his later paper (1951) he says "transitivism" is a term
used by French psychiatrists in the discussion of paranoia (p. 16; the actual word used twice there is "trans-
ivitism," apparently a misprint, as is the later "body"
for "boy").

6*b*/98   For a careful elucidation of Freud's use of primary
(autistic) and secondary (object-withdrawn) narcissism, see Laplanche and Pontalis (1967, pp. 255–257).
Freud's paper, "On Narcissism" (1914a), is seen by
Schotte (1975) as the first of Freud's turning points, in
which he struggles ambivalently with "His Majesty
the Ego" as narcissistic love object (Freud, 1914a, p.
91; see also 1908, pp. 149–150, and 1917, pp. 138–
139). This, of course, sharply contrasts with Freud's
later exposition of the ego as the agency of consciousness that adapts the organism to reality. Laplanche
describes the ego as an object capable of passing itself
off as a desiring subject (1970, p. 66).

6*c*/98–99 Sartre's *Being and Nothingness* first appeared in France
in 1943; one section is titled "Existential Psychoanalysis."

6*f*/99   Lacan's view of the ego is in direct opposition to the view of the ego as a subject or agency facilitating adaptation to reality through rationality. The Lacanians see this emphasis on adaptation to "reality" made by the ego psychologists as the Americanization of Freud, the adapting of Freud to American life, much like the way the immigrant must adapt to his new environment, as nearly all of the ego psychologists did when they came here from Europe. In pointing this out, Mannoni (1968) states that the Americans have missed the ego's fictional, alienating, and distorting function (pp. 181–186).

     The ego's role in negation *(Verneinung)* is discussed by Lacan in his later paper (1951, pp. 11–12, 16) and in *Écrits* (1966, pp. 369–399). Lacan also makes clear his disquiet with any talk of "strengthening the ego" (1951, p. 16), and he tells us why: ". . . the ego is structured exactly like a symptom. Interior to the subject, it is only a privileged symptom. It is the human symptom *par excellence*, it is the mental malady of man" (1953–1954, p. 22). Leavy (1977) states that Lacan is not alone among analysts in taking a critical stance toward ego psychology.

7*a*/99   The "level of fatality" seems to allude broadly to the death drive, as well as to the ineluctable structures of the unconscious (and therefore of language).

7*f*/100   Lacan does not pretend to find in psychoanalysis a way of life as others do, e.g., Chrzanowski: "It is my thesis that psychoanalysis is not merely a particular form of psychotherapy; it is at all times also a philosophy of life" (1977, p. 175).

Chapter 2

Aggressivity in Psychoanalysis

Overview

This essay dates from mid-May 1948, when it was presented as a paper to the Eleventh Congress of the *Psychanalystes de langue française* (Brussels), in the form of a theoretical discussion of aggression following upon a more clinical discussion of the same theme. Composed, then, before the published version of the "Mirror Stage" essay, it is clearly complementary to the latter, for its principal theme is that the "notion of aggressivity" is a "correlative tension of the narcissistic structure" (1977, p. 22/116) with which the essay deals. In explaining this "correlative tension," Lacan introduces many subordinate themes, from which we shall try to disengage it, though for the sake of clarity we shall follow Lacan's own rather scholastic format: a short introduction followed by the exposition of five theses.

Lacan chooses as the starting point for his reflection the "aporia" that Freud was trying to deal with when, still attempting to understand man's experience "in the register of biology," he suggested the possibility of a "death instinct" (1977, p. 8/101). We recall the nature of that aporia: stubborn phenomena like the repetition compulsion, hatred, ambivalence, destructiveness toward self and others (e.g., masochism, sadism) were difficult — if not impossible — to explain by a monistic theory of instinct. Freud's suggestion, then, was that we conceive of two basic instincts in man, Eros and the destructive instinct: "The aim of the first of these basic instincts is to establish ever greater unities and to preserve them thus — in short, to bind together; the aim of the second is, on the contrary, to undo connections and so to destroy things. In the case of the destructive instinct we may suppose that its final aim is to lead what is living into an inorganic state. For this reason we also call it the *death instinct*" (1940, p. 148). The paradoxical notion of "death instinct" would remain a controversial issue among Freud's disciples, and it is to this controversy that Lacan returns by cojoining the problem of man's dis-integrating, destructive tendencies — and this is what we understand by "aggressivity" — with that of narcissism, at least as Lacan understands the term. This brings him to the formulation of his first thesis.

"Thesis I. *Aggressivity manifests itself in an experience that is subjective by its constitution.*"

Clearly the issue in the essay is aggressivity *in psychoanalysis*. However, this first thesis does not address the problem of aggressivity as such, but rather seems intended to establish the scientific respectability of any psychoanalytic theorizing at all. At the very outset of the essay, Lacan stated that his task was to prove "whether or not this notion [of aggressivity] can be developed into a concept capable of scientific use" (1977, p. 8/101), and in the first thesis he is at pains to explain how the psychoanalytic situation, although "subjective by its very constitution," i.e., a "dialectical grasp of meaning" through a "verbal communication" between two subjects, can nonetheless meet the methodological demands of a positive science if the experience is shown to be "verifiable by everyone" (1977, p. 9/103). He then suggests that this is indeed the case, since "this experience, constituted between two subjects one of whom plays in the dialogue the role of ideal impersonality . . . may, once it is completed, . . . be resumed by the other subject with a third subject" (1977, pp. 9–10/103). Lacan's claims of verifiability and replicability here may not appeal very much to hard-nosed positivists, but at least Lacan pays his dues to their demands, enabling him to settle down to serious business. The second thesis deals with serious business.

"Thesis II. *Aggressivity in experience is given to us as intended aggression and as an image of corporal dislocation, and it is in such forms that it shows itself to be efficient.*"

    Here Lacan begins at the periphery of the problem and moves slowly toward its center. More specifically, Lacan addresses the questions: How is the aggressivity of the patient manifested to the analyst? In what way is it effective? How is this effectiveness experienced by the subject?

    The patient's aggressivity is discernible to the analyst as an "intention" that is manifest in countless ways through his behavior. What is meant here by "intention"? Characteristically, Lacan does not explain. Etymologically, of course, the word signifies a "tending," or "inclination," toward some object, and in normal parlance it involves some kind of action, whether in the sense of a project to be executed or a goal to be achieved. For contemporary phenomenology, the word suggests a tending, or inclination (i.e., orientation), of consciousness toward an object of consciousness. Lacan probably uses it in the latter sense, broadening this sense, however, so that it may refer to an unconscious as well as conscious orientation of the psychic structure.

    What is the effect of such an intention, however unconscious, on the aggressive subject? Lacan sees it as influential on, even formative of, the subject — not to mention those dependent on the subject — no matter how constrained the subject's expression of aggressivity may be. This effect may be described in terms of "imprints" made on the psychic structure, imprints that may be referred to as "images" to the extent that they give a transient and superficial inflection to fundamental tendencies already shaped by what have previously been called *imagoes*, which as such constitute the so-called "instincts" (1977, p. 11/104).

Images characteristic of aggressive intentions are, according to Lacan, those that involve in one way or another fragmentation of the body (witness certain ritualistic practices, the fantasies of children, the imagery of a Hieronymus Bosch, certain archaic dream images, etc.). These imagoes coalesce into a certain gestalt proper to aggression (1977, p. 12/105) with which Lacan will now deal.

"Thesis III. *The springs of aggressivity decide the reasons that motivate the technique of analysis.*"

The task now is to determine more precisely the nature of this gestalt. Once more Lacan circles around the central issue, i.e., the "springs of aggressivity," by discussing the technique the analyst uses to discern this gestalt, i.e., the original imago out of which aggressivity rises as from a source.

This technique consists essentially of assuming an attitude by which the analyst becomes "as devoid as possible of individual characteristics," hence a "depersonalized" "ideal of impassibility" (1977, p. 13/106). The purpose is to elicit the patient's aggressivity because "these intentions form the negative transference that is the initial knot of the analytic drama" (1977, p. 14/107). The point is that aggressive intentions together with their intentional correlates reactualize some archaic imago in the subject which "has remained permanent at the level of symbolic overdetermination that we call the subject's unconscious" (1977, p. 14/108). This can be observed easily enough, for example, in cases of hysteria, obsessionalism, phobia, etc.

The hoped-for effect of the analyst's technique is to avoid offering to the patient an idea of the analyst's person that can be co-opted into the defensive maneuvers of the patient's ego. Ego here is, of course, to be understood not as the *perception-conscious-*

ness system of Freud's metapsychology but rather as "that nucleus given to consciousness, but opaque to reflexion, marked by all the ambiguities which, from self-satisfaction to 'bad faith' *(mauvaise foi)*, structure the experience of the passions in the human subject" (1977, p. 15/109). The approach is admittedly a roundabout one "that amounts in fact to inducing in the subject a controlled paranoia," i.e., a mechanism of projection that can be "properly checked" (1977, p. 15/109).

Lacan concludes by introducing the issue of the subject's experience of another subject like himself, an issue that brings us at last to the heart of the matter and that is treated in the following thesis.

"Thesis IV. *Aggressivity is the correlative tendency of a mode of identification that we call narcissistic, and which determines the formal structure of man's ego and of the register of entities characteristic of his world.*"

Finally, Lacan comes to the point. He proposes to seek out the "springs of aggressivity" but so far has dealt with that to which they give rise (namely, aggressive intentions) and the technique of searching for them. Hence the treatment of the problem so far has been more descriptive than theoretical. To speculate now about the ultimate *source* in the subject of these aggressive intentions is "to make the leap from the phenomenology of our experience"—understood in the loosest sense, to be sure—"to metapsychology" (1977, p. 16/110).

Lacan immediately tries to make this "leap" look less hazardous to the empirically minded in his audience by calling it a "requirement of thought"—the result of a need to propose a "formula of equivalence" when the passage from description to explanation proves impossible through a process of quantification. This is a critical point, of course, that Lacan slips blithely by: to what extent and in what way can *any* "formula of equivalence" that cannot be derived with mathematical rigor from empirical data be considered a "requirement of thought"? On the answer to such questions depends the validity of all metapsychology, not to mention Lacan's whole enterprise in particular. But the issue is too big for further comment here.

The thesis itself is fairly straightforward. We are already familiar (Chapter 1) with the *"mode of identification that we call narcissistic,"* i.e., the identification of the subject with the reflected (hence alienating) image of itself that *"determines the formal structure of man's ego"* (1977, p. 16/100). In other words, the "I is an other" (1977, p. 23/118). If anything is added here to the description of this "first stage of the dialectic of identifications," it is perhaps Lacan's emphasis on the affective aspect of it: "It is in this erotic relation, in which the human individual fixes upon himself an image that alienates him from himself, that are to be found the energy and form on which this organization of the passions [*passionnelle*] that he will call his ego is based" (1977, p. 19/113).

We recall, too, how Lacan understands this primal identification to determine "the register of entities characteristic of [man's] world," i.e., "things" as differentiated from both the ego and other subjects. In the "shifting field" of our experience certain gestalten emerge, to which are assigned the same "attributes of permanence, identity, and substantiality" that are assigned to the ego itself (1977, p. 17/111). The result is that the experience of objects is correlative with the experience of the ego. In itself this experience is dialectical, but the movement is frozen by the "formal fixation" of these attributes like a film that is "suddenly stopped in mid-action" (1977, p. 17/111).

By way of example, Lacan suggests how a series of paranoid states "in which we find all the successive envelopes of the biological and social status of the person, retains the original organization of the forms of the ego and of the object. . . experienced as events in a perspective of mirages, as affections with something stereotypical about them that suspends the workings of the ego/object dialectic" (1977, p. 17/111). In any case, Lacan sees this process of stagnation and fixation of both ego and object as "akin to the most general structure of human knowledge," and it is in this sense that he speaks of knowledge as "paranoiac" (1977, p. 17/111).

Now the core of Lacan's thesis is that aggressivity is the "correlative tendency" of this identification by which the ego (and its world) is constituted. He argues the point in two ways. According to the first argument, aggressivity arises when the ego encounters another subject like himself and there awakens in him a desire for the object of the other's desire (1977, p. 19/113)—a far-reaching Hegelian notion that will be treated more fully elsewhere. Prior to this moment, the infant, as the experiments of Charlotte Bühler and the Chicago school have shown (1977, pp. 17–18/111–112), experiences himself as "undifferentiated" from his counterpart, united to him in a confused identity, while internally there is a "conflictual tension" (is this what will later be called "need"?) that precedes the awakening of "desire." To illustrate, Lacan mentions a frequently cited example of aggressivity that he calls here "ambivalent" and that appears under the guise of "resentment." It is the incident mentioned by St. Augustine in which the infant, still unable to speak, shows clear signs of jealousy of his foster brother. Lacan designates aggressivity in this sense as "aggressive relativity," which marks the ego from its very origin, and he suggests that it is only to be expected that it will be manifest in "each great instinctual metamorphosis in the life of the individual" where the encounters with others that mark the "subject's history" will cross the path of the "unthinkable innateness of his desire" (1977, pp. 19–20/114). So aggressivity originates in the threat posed by the other in the triangular relationship of self-other-thing.

There appears to be a second way of conceiving primitive aggressivity, however, and it emerges as Lacan enlists the authority of Melanie Klein to corroborate his own position. Citing the fact that she shows us "the extreme archaism of the subjectification of a *kakon*," Lacan sees her as "push[ing] back the limits within which we can see the subjective function of identification operate" (1977, p. 21/115). This appears related to the early origin of the superego as self-critical agency. For the subject, the experience is one of depressive devaluation in the light of the ego as object of narcissistic identification. In this way we again see "the notion of an aggressivity linked to the narcissistic rela-tion" as such (1977, p. 21/115). We understand Lacan also to mean that when the unifying image of the ego integrates the "original organic disarray," the subject experiences a "peculiar satisfaction" that "must be conceived in the dimension of a vital dehiscence that is constitutive of man," i.e., a peculiar compen-sation for a radical gap, lack, or separation operative from birth (1977, p. 21/116). This "narcissistic passion" generates enor-mous energy in the ego. We infer — but here we go beyond the explicit text — that this energy converts into primitive aggressiv-ity whenever the integration — i.e., the fragile unity — of the ego is threatened. In this way, we take literally the assertion that ag-gressivity is "a correlative tension of the narcissistic structure" (1977, p. 22/116) and hypothesize that the aggressive imago of the *corps morcelé* (fragmentation) is the inversion of the gestalt of the ego (unification).

At this point Lacan moves on to certain corollaries of his thesis that permit him to take account of "all sorts of accidents and atypicalities" in the coming-to-be of the subject. First and most important is the relevance of the thesis for the develop-ment of the Oedipus complex.

The essentials of this development are familiar enough. We know that the infant experiences the parent of the same sex as a rival and resolves the rivalry by identifying with that parent (i.e., by "reshaping" himself according to the introjected imago of the parent) in what Freud calls a process of "sublimation" (1977, p. 22/117). However, Lacan claims that this "secondary identification" with the rival cannot be accounted for structural-ly unless "the way is prepared for it by a primary identification that structures the subject as a rival with himself" (1977, p. 22/117), as in the hypothesis of the ego as mirror image. Be that as it may, the rivalry is resolved by the "pacifying function" of the introjected imago, whereby the normal thrust of genital libido ("libidinal normativity"), which "operates as a supersession [*dé-passement*] . . . of the individual in favour of the species," is con-joined with an accommodation to the societal demands associated with the imago of the father ("cultural normativity"), thus accounting for the "cultural subordination" of man (1977, p. 24/118). This is indeed a "sublimation," but what is sublimated is precisely the aggression toward the parent. This is the significance Lacan sees in the primordial myth constructed by Freud in *Totem and Taboo* (1913).

"Thesis V. *Such a notion of aggressivity as one of the intentional co-ordinates of the human ego, especially relative to the category of space, allows us to conceive of its role in modern neurosis and in the 'discontents' of civilization.*"

Perhaps the importance of this final thesis simply consists in the fact that Lacan felt constrained to formulate it, as if to re-affirm his concern for the social dimension of man, even when dealing with the most elementary processes through which the individual is formed.

That the subject's experience of the reflected image of itself as ego is "especially relative" to its experience of space is evident enough, for the encounter with the image takes place within *reflected* space—whence a "spatial symmetry in man's narcissistic structure"—which is then expanded to include "the field of the other" and thereby "rejoins the objective space of reality" (1977, p. 27/122). But this reflected space is marked by the "imagery of the ego" and is to that extent *"kaleidoscopic"* (1977, p. 27/122), i.e., distorted in myriad ways. In any case, it is in this context, perhaps, that it is possible to see some correlation between the "instinct of self-preservation" and the "vertigo of the domination of space" (1977, p. 28/123)—we understand this to mean the struggle for "survival of the fittest"—in which Darwin saw the seeds of aggressivity.

Hegel, of course, saw the seeds of human aggressivity differently. For him, the basic human conflict is the struggle for recognition—struggle unto death—which is seen in paradigmatic form in the dialectical struggle between master and slave.

But however we understand the seeds of aggressivity philosophically, we face its consequences concretely when dealing with the "barbarism" of our age, which Lacan speaks of as the "modern neurosis," made up of many elements (1977, p. 26/121). One form of it is "psychotechnique," i.e., the domination of our lives by the machine — a "technical enterprise at the species scale" (1977, p. 27/122).

But if the enterprise is "at the species scale," then it is as wide as the "living space" of the species, which space is not that studied by physics but by psychoanalysis, insofar as it is structured by the mirror stage and is therefore distorted.

Be that as it may, we see human aggressivity adapting to the circumstances of this space on "the species scale" most dramatically in the phenomenon of war, which, curiously enough, seems to be "the midwife of all progress" (1977, p. 27/123). Yet war, to the extent that it is seen as a phenomenon of "species scale," is external to the individual and is made possible by the limitations of the individual — i.e., seeds of aggressivity that Melanie Klein speaks of as "internal bad objects" (1977, p. 28/123). These are projected in the category of space (1977, pp. 15, 28/109, 123). Corresponding to them in the category of time are different forms of anxiety, manifest in sundry ways (e.g., flight, inhibition) (1977, pp. 15, 28/109, 123). Where these two tensions intersect is that point in the human being where there is a primordial cleavage *(déchirement)*, the opening up of a gap (dehiscence) in him that is a sign of both the plenitude and finitude that Freud, in resorting to biological terminology, called the "death instinct" (1977, p. 28/124). As such, it is probably the deepest explanation we can find for the "barbarism" of the "modern neurosis."

Map of the Text

Introduction
  A. Aggressivity as a scientific notion
    1. can be used to objectify facts
    2. and establish a field where we can regard facts in co-varying relationships.

B. Psychoanalysis is our common field
1. as an open system
  a. whose gaps Freud expressed via the "death instinct,"
    i. which is central to the notion of aggressivity
  b. and is subject to ongoing discussion and elaboration.
C. Our responsibility to present-day psychology
1. lies in providing the categories implicitly used by behaviorists in the laboratory
2. and in providing the underlying notions for psychodrama and play therapies.

"Thesis I. *Aggressivity manifests itself in an experience that is subjective by its very constitution.*"

A. Psychoanalytic action grows out of verbal communication
1. i.e., "in a dialectical grasp of meaning."
  a. This dialectic presumes a subject manifesting himself to the intention of another
    i. despite the subject's pseudo-obsolescence in physics.
  b. A subject is necessary to understand meaning;
    i. conversely, a subject can be understood.
B. Psychoanalytic experience can form the basis of a positive science if:
1. the experience can be verified by everyone,
2. the experience is replicable,
3. and thus apparently universal.

"Thesis II. *Aggressivity in experience is given to us as intended aggression and as an image of corporal dislocation, and it is in such forms that it shows itself to be efficient.*"

A. In psychoanalytic experience we feel the pressure of intention.
1. We find it in symptoms, fantasies, dreams;
2. we measure it in the tone and gaps of discourse and behavior.

B. The efficacy of aggressive intention is obvious
   1. in its formative effect on subordinates,
      a. leading to castration and death
      b. and installing the image of the Punisher:
         i. images determine individual inflections of ten-
            dencies just as imagoes constitute matrices for
            "instincts."
C. Aggressive intentions are given "magical" efficacy by imagoes,
   1. specifically, imagoes of the fragmented body.
      a. Social practices reveal a specific relation between
         man and his body.
      b. Children's play expresses aggressive images.
      c. Bosch's work is an "atlas" of aggressive images.
      d. They appear in dreams during psychoanalysis.
   2. These all flow from the structure of aggressivity,
      a. with its symbolic and imaginary qualities
         i. whose effect on identification is lost by the be-
            haviorists.

"Thesis III. *The springs of aggressivity decide the reasons that motivate
the technique of analysis.*"

A. To the verbal dialectic Freud added:
   1. the rule of free association,
      a. allowing the analysand to progress in a blind inten-
         tionality;
   2. no predetermined duration;
   3. an impassive, depersonalized, apathetic listener,
      a. avoiding the trap of the patient's revenge.
B. But Freud's technique brings into play the subject's aggressivity toward us.
   1. In the negative transference, archaic imagoes are de-
      repressed.
   2. The aroused aggressive intention reactualizes the im-
      ago, i.e.,

    a. in hysteria;

    b. in obsessional neuroses and phobias.

  3. We operate without giving the aggressive intention any support through our elaborations.

C. Such aggressive reactions are characteristic of the ego,

  1. not the ego in Freud's perception-consciousness system,

  2. but the phenomenological essence he recognized in negation:

    a. the ego as opaque, ambiguous, pretentious, misunderstanding, and opposing the subject.

D. Rather than making a frontal attack, psychoanalysis detours from the ego

  1. by inducing in the subject a "controlled paranoia"

    a. in which bad internal objects are projected.

      i. This corresponds to the spatial dimension,

      ii. while anxiety corresponds to the temporal dimension.

  2 . The imago is revealed only if our stance is like a pure mirroring surface,

    a. but seeing in the analyst an exact replica of oneself, as in didactic analyses, can cause severe anxiety.

"Thesis IV. *Aggressivity is the correlative tendency of a mode of identification we call narcissistic, and which determines the formal structure of man's ego and of the register of entities characteristic of his world.*"

A. The aggressive tendency is fundamental to paranoia.

  1. Tendency is a metapsychological concept,

    a. allowing us to objectify aggressive reactions through the formula of libido.

  2. In tandem coordination the aggressive reaction, which reflects a particular form of paranoia, parallels the delusion representing a specific stage of mental genesis.

    a. Thus the aggressive reaction is arranged in a continuous series

b. that reveals earlier biological and social links,

c. as marked by earlier ego-object structures,

d. which are experienced as stereotyped mirages, thereby suspending the ego-object dialectical relationship in fixed moments of stagnation.

3. Human knowledge is paranoiac,

a. fixing the ego and objects as permanent,

b. introducing a gap between man and his environment

   i. through which he extends his power

      (a) by giving his objects multiple use and meaning;

      (b) by using his objects as defensive armor,

c. corresponding in its archaic forms to mental stages of objectifying identification.

B. States of identification in the child include:

1. undifferentiation from the other,

a. in which aggressivity serves not only exercise and exploration but also social relativity,

   i. on which occasions the child anticipates the functional unity of his body;

2. captation by the image of the other.

a. In the first stage, the image in the mirror

   i. is experienced as an ideal imago, salutary for the original distress of fragmentation and prematurity.

b. Thereafter the human form appears in transitivism,

   i. wherein children playing as actor and spectator, seducer and seduced, are identified with one another.

C. The ego's erotic relation to its image is a structural crossroads.

1. It is the source of the energy and the form of the ego as organization of erotic passion.

a. The form is crystallized in the conflicting tension internal to the subject (i.e., marking the subject as in conflict),

      i. and leads to desiring what the other desires,
         (a) eventuating in aggressive competitiveness
         (b) and the formal mapping of the triad of the other, the ego, and the object,
     ii. and which makes instinctual change in the individual a challenge to his delimitation (by the ego).
   b. The form of his ego can never be attained, even by the genius.
      i. The consequent depression engenders formal negations,
         (a) in which subject and other become confused in the ego's paranoiac structure.
     ii. In resentment is revealed our aggressivity toward the image of the other,
         (a) in whose absorption are reactivated images of primordial frustration.
   c. The cartography of Melanie Klein reveals
      i. the interior space of the mother's body;
     ii. imagoes of the father and siblings in rivalry with the subject;
    iii. the influence of bad internal objects
         (a) whereby the reevocation of inferiorities can disconcert the subject, fragmenting the ego.
    iv. In the primordiality of the "depressive position," we see the earliest formation of the superego.
2. Aggressivity is tied to the narcissistic relation and to the ego's systematic miscognition and objectification.
   a. In this relation a peculiar satisfaction comes from the integration of an original organic disorder.
      i. This satisfaction must be seen in the context of a vital gap constitutive of man.
         (a) This gap rules out any preformed environment
         (b) and is a kind of negative libido affirming the priority of discord to harmony.

      b. From the narcissistic passion the ego obtains the energy it places at the service of the reality principle.

      c. In his inheritance of the ego as perception-consciousness system, Freud failed to recognize the ego's distorting role in sensation and language.

      d. Aggressivity, in conclusion, appears to have its source in narcissism as it structures superego oppression and desire for recognition.

D. Aggressivity as "correlative tension of the narcissistic structure" sheds light on development.

  1. The Oedipus complex is a secondary identification reshaping the subject.

      a. This presupposes a primary identification that structures the subject as the rival of himself.

        i. The oedipal situation shapes the "instinct" in conformity with one's sex.

      b. It also has a pacifying function,

        i. linking individual development to cultural norms represented in the imago of the father.

        ii. In oedipal identification the subject transcends his primary aggressivity to affectively assume his neighbor.

  2. The original identification with the ego has misshaped the subject.

      a. All subjective activity is reduced to the being of the ego,

        i. denying the dialectical truth of "I is an other."

      b. Levels of the I are discordant.

      c. The ego resists the treatment of symptoms just as it excludes tendencies that are to be reintegrated.

      d. These tendencies bound up with oedipal failures are ego successes.

  3. Genital oblativity is not altruism.

      a. Genital libido subordinates the individual to the species,

      b. thus effecting sublimation and cultural subordination in the oedipal resolution:

      c. it thereby maintains the narcissistic structure in an
        aggressive tension.

      d. The problem of relating ego to other in "selfless" love
        is an old one.

   4. Aggressivity is involved in all regressions and libidinal
     transformations.

   5. Partial drives are ambivalent.

     a. They are hostile yet reach out to the other.

   6. The imago of one's own body has bearing on lateraliza-
     tion and inversions.

"Thesis V. *Such a notion of aggressivity as one of the intentional co-ordinates
of the human ego, especially relative to the category of space, enables us to conceive of its role in modern neurosis and the 'discontents' of civilization.*"

  A. The prominence of aggressivity in our culture is manifest
    in:

    1. its confusion in ordinary morality with the virtue of
      strength;

    2. its use, seen as a development of the ego, which use is
      regarded as indispensable

      a. in contrast to the practice of *yang* in Chinese morali-
        ty;

    3. the high regard for the idea of life struggle.

      a. In basing natural selection on the animal's conquest
        of space,

        i. Darwin simply projected Victorian imperialism
          and capitalism.

  B. Hegel saw aggressivity as basic to human ontology in
    these terms:

    1. Our history can be deduced from the master-slave
      conflict.

      a. The subject is nothing before the ultimate Master
        —death.

      b. The natural individual and natural values are to be
        negated

    c. and transformed in the struggle for the recognition of man by man,

    d. and therefore the satisfaction of human desire is possible only when mediated by the desire and work of the other.

C. Our barbarism is due to:
1. the relativization of society that comes with cross-cultural documentation,
    a. whereby we also destroy the cultures we study;
2. the absence of cultural forms and rituals;
3. the abolition of the polar male and female cosmic principles;
4. the promotion of the ego-individual leading to isolation;
5. our psychotechnology, which subordinates man to the machine.

D. Spatial symmetry lies in man's narcissistic structure
1. and is the basis for a psychological analysis of space,
    a. in terms of the animal's social mapping of space
    b. and the mirror experience of space
        i. wherein "the imagery of the ego develops,"
          (a) confounding the physicist's view of space.
2. War is man's tool for adapting to space
    a. and the internal space of bad objects adapts man to war.
    b. Spatial domination subordinates the preservation of life
    c. because the fear of death, the Master, is subordinate to the narcissistic fear of injury to one's own body.

E. The subjective tension in the dimension of space intersects with anxiety developed in the temporal dimension.
1. Here lies the relevance of Bergson and Kierkegaard to Darwinian naturalism and Hegelian dialectics.
2. At this intersection man assumes his original gap,
    a. but thereby founds his world in a suicide
    b. in the experience of the death instinct.

3. This gap or split in emancipated modern man reveals a neurosis of self-punishment with its personal and social hell.

NOTES TO THE TEXT

11*g*/105 The ogive and glass spheres appear to be details of Bosch's paintings. See, for example, his *Triptych of the Garden of Delights.*

12*b*/105 In "Some Reflections on the Ego" Lacan (1951, p. 13) states that these images appear in analysis at a particular phase of treatment, herald a very archaic phase of the transference, and lead to a marked decrease in the patient's deepest resistances.

12*h*/106 Encouraging analysts to shorten or lengthen each analytic session on their own judgment was a major source of friction within the International Psycho-Analytical Association (see Turkle, 1975, p. 338).

13*g*/107 The identity of this "establishment figure" *(tel grand patron)* is unknown to us.

14*b*/107 The sense seems to be that in the transference an imago acts to switch off behavior which formerly shielded the ego from a function or body part that constituted an aspect of the patient's unconscious identification (as in the following example of the girl with falling sickness).

15*a–c*/ 108–109 Lacan makes the same points in "Some Reflections on the Ego" (1951, pp. 11–12, 15).

15*d*/109 Readers unfamiliar with Melanie Klein will find a useful introduction and bibliography in Segal (1967).

16*a*/109 As noted in the previous essay, the double is an omen of death. The point may be that competitiveness becomes intensified, murderous rivalry becomes suicidal, when the mirroring presents an exact replica, thus recalling and threatening the original identification with the mirror image, which "structures the subject as a rival with himself," as Lacan will go on to say (1977, p. 22/117).

16*b*/110 Perhaps the oppressive action of bad internal objects is common to these states.

16*d*/110 Libido has quasi-mathematical symbolic utility, described by Freud as "a quantitative magnitude" but "not at present actually measurable" (Laplanche and Pontalis, 1967, p. 239).

17*b*/111 Lacan seems to say the aggressive reaction discloses an original costructuring of ego and object experienced as being in a stereotyped, frozen relationship.

17*d*/111 While in the case of animals objects have largely immediate salience for consumption, in man's case they are given a permanence that reflects the imputed stability of the ego, and have become part of instrumental and symbolic networks.

17*g*/111 See Chapter 1 for references (note 5*e*).

18*a–b*/ Lacan here acknowledges a substantial debt to Wal-
112 lon, who brought together themes of the unifying mirror image, identification, the category of space, the double, captation by the image of the other, and themes of domination and submission in the research of Charlotte Bühler (see Wallon, 1934, especially Part II, Chapter IV, "Le corps propre et son image exteroceptive," and Part III, Chapter II, "Sociabilité syncrétique"). Wallon views the children's motor behavior as expressions of "reciprocal stimulations" and "reciprocal attitudes" that form part of the structure of the situation in which the two children are identified with one another (pp. 192–193), rather than as acts of personal hostility.

19*è*/113 In the French text *organisation passionelle* has a more explicitly erotic ring than "organization of the passions."

19*d*/113 The origin of desire, the rise of competitiveness, and the forming of relationships involving ego, other, and objects are not clearly explained here. At bottom is the form of the ego, somehow "crystallizing" in internal conflict and tension: perhaps the division between subject and reflected image, perhaps the correlation between the unifying ego and the infant's bodily turbulence and fragmentation. If the latter can be called "need," Lacan may be referring to the development of desire from need (he takes this up in more detail in the next essay).

20c/114 As we saw earlier, identification is at the root of the paranoiac structure. Here ego and other become identified: whereas the first moment involved the denial of the subject's reality and the other's worth, now the subject's worth and the other's reality are negated. The *belle âme* represents a stage in Hegel's dialectic of self-consciousness in which internal disorder is projected onto the world and repudiated.

     Freud discusses the principal forms of paranoia as represented by contradictory variants of the proposition "I (a man) love him (a man)," and describes them as delusions of persecution, erotomania, and delusions of jealousy (1911c, pp. 63–64). Lacan appears to be referring to this text, since elsewhere (in the "Discourse at Rome") he mentions the "persecutory 'interpretation' " in which denied feeling emerges under the form of a negative verbalization (1977, p. 85/298).

20d/115 Augustine's observation also appears in "Some Reflections on the Ego" (1951, p. 16). The images of primordial frustration may include the separations of birth and weaning (as suggested in Lacan's article on the family [1938]).

21a/115 In contrast to acausal Humean associations, accidental associations in the subject's history are contingent but effective. They serve later on to disunify the subject by threatening the original identification.

21b/115 The oppressive superego operates by characterizing

the subject as ugly and evil *(kakon)*.

21*d*/116   The word "dehiscence" refers to "a bursting open," with biological and botanical references to: (a) "the opening of an organ along a suture or other definite line for the purpose of discharging its contents"; (b) "the bursting open of a capsule [or] pod...at maturity" (*Webster's New International Dictionary*, 1960, p. 690). In Lacan's use the emphasis seems to be on a rupture or gap, a kind of basic fault penetrating human existence. He later uses the notion of *béance* to express the gaping abyss linked with the origin of desire.

21*e*/116   We must keep in mind that when Lacan speaks of the "reality principle" he means the ego's distorting, negating, and oppositional manner of adjusting things to suit its own rigid style—especially its resistance to the growth of the subject.

23*c*/ 117–118   An "ara" is a macaw bird. The point seems to be that identity based on the stagnant, fixated ego has no room for dialectical truth in which dynamic relations between terms are posited in Hegelian fashion.

23*d*/118   The issue appears to be the confusion of the subject as spoken (i.e., the subject of the grammatical statement) and the subject as speaking, together with the tendency of different languages to persevere in this confusion.

24*a*/118   If, as Lacan has just said, "the Oedipal identification is that by which the subject transcends the aggressivity that is constitutive of the primary subjective individuation" (1977, p. 23/117), then the ego's aggressive exclusion, negation, and opposition to "tendencies" bound up with symptoms are the result of oedipal failure; on the other hand, they mark the success of the ego in resisting the inroads of "cultural normativity" and the reshaping of secondary identifications.

24*g*/119   The emphasis seems to be on the ego's aggressive resistance to growth and change, blocking the lifelong coming-into-being of the subject.

25*b*/120   Compare Sartre (1943, pp. 361–412).

25*c*/120   For a description of the classical "beautiful and good" ideal *(kalos kagathos)* see Jaeger (1939, p. 416, fn. 4, and elsewhere).

26*b–c*/ 121   The essential commentary on desire and the master-slave dialectic remains Kojève's first chapter (1939), which Wilden (1968) calls "especially influential" (p. 193). A brief summary, not a substitute, may send the reader to Kojève (and Hegel) for further clarification. Kojève stresses the role desire plays in bringing man back to himself (e.g., desire to eat something, a basic "I want," a basic affirmation of "I" in relation to "not-I"), as opposed to knowledge, where man is absorbed by what he knows and where only the object is revealed. Thus in desire the "I" is formed and revealed as a subject related to an object. Again, unlike the passivity of knowledge, desire leads to action, to consuming the object, destroying or assimilating it, basically negating its given nature. This negating action also transforms the subject into what it consumes (as in eating). The "I" as desire is empty; it becomes what it assimilates — thingish or animal, a natural "I," if it is directed only toward things.

     The mere "sentiment of life" (the awareness of being alive) of an animal must be distinguished from human self-consciousness, which, instead of being directed toward thingish or animal objects, must be directed toward a nonnatural entity, something that goes beyond the given. The only thing that goes beyond given reality is desire itself.

     Thus the only adequate object of human desire is another desire. To desire another desire is to desire to be the object of another desire, to be recognized by another desire as self-consciousness. Only another self-consciousness can recognize a self-consciousness as being what it is. To be itself, self-consciousness must go outside of itself and find itself in another.

To be truly human, however, really to transcend the merely animal concern for preservation of life, man must risk his animal life for the sake of his human desire. It is by this risk that man is given proofs of being essentially different from animal reality. This leads to the fight to the death for recognition, insofar as each seeks to impose himself as autonomous value on the other. Kojève describes it in this way:

> Man's humanity "comes to light" only in risking his life to satisfy his human Desire—that is, his Desire directed toward another Desire. Now, to desire a Desire is to want to substitute oneself for the value desired by this Desire. For without this substitution, one would desire the value, the desired object, and not the Desire itself. Therefore, to desire the Desire of another is in the final analysis to desire that the value that I am or that I "represent" be the value desired by the other: I want him to "recognize" my value as his value. I want him to "recognize" me as an autonomous value. In other words, all human, anthropogenetic Desire—the Desire that generates Self-Consciousness, the human reality—is, finally, a function of the desire for "recognition." And the risk of life by which the human reality "comes to light" is a risk for the sake of such a Desire. Therefore, to speak of the "origin" of Self-Consciousness is necessarily to speak of a fight to the death for "recognition" [1939, p. 7].

Here we see the place of Lacan's stress on the ego's aggressiveness, negation, and development through opposition. It is a fight to the death, then, in the effort to reject a thingish or animal mode of consciousness. Proving that the other is also willing to risk his life is to ensure that he is also truly human and is therefore capable of giving human recognition to one's self-consciousness. But killing the other or being killed would make recognition impossible. The resolution of the fight for recognition lies in working out a master-slave arrangement as a living solution to the master's desire for recognition as autonomous self-consciousness. The solution, however, is provisional, and the Hegelian dialectic moves on.

      Kojève's analysis is fundamental to a reading of Lacan and will appear more and more useful for clarifying later texts.

26d/121   If "Spartacus" is correctly suggested by "Spartacism," the sense would be that the rebellion of the worker is spawned by the Hegelian doctrine as transposed by Marx and Lenin. This finds support in Rosa Luxemburg's Spartacist party, a group of radical German socialists which became the German Communist Party in 1919 to promote the dictatorship of the workers.

27a/122   The reference to the hornet escapes us. "Original dereliction" is a reference to the Heideggarian notion of thrownness *(Geworfenheit)*.

27c/122   Lacan appears to be dealing with the way others and objects are discovered in the mirror as "the threshold of the visible world" (1977, p. 3/95), and with space as a social category, rather than as the Darwinian field for individual conquest. The "kaleidoscopic" quality suggests the "beautiful form" *(kalos eidos)* of the gestalt image perceived in the distorting mirror.

27d/   The once-simple space of physics has indeed yielded
122–123 to conceptions as wide-ranging as the classical cosmogonies.

28e/   The anxiety of bodily fragmentation (the intersection of
123–124 the spatial and temporal tensions?) is overcome by the identification with the mirror image, and this constitutes a negation of the subject, a kind of suicide, as well as the constitution of the world as having ego attributes.

Chapter 3

The Function and Field of
Speech and Language in Psychoanalysis

OVERVIEW

In September 1953, Lacan delivered the famous "Discourse at Rome." Originally it had been scheduled as a "theoretical report" by the president of the *Société psychanalytique de Paris* (SPP) to an annual congress of psychoanalysts. Traditionally, this congress included only analysts of the French tongue, but it was extended to include those of all the Romance languages— and of Dutch besides (1977, p. 30/237). In the previous June, however, Lacan had been forced to resign as president of the SPP, ostensibly because of the unorthodoxy of his treatment methods, but more profoundly because of his deep opposition to the rigidly formalistic training program then being developed for a new psychoanalytic institute in Paris. This institute, headed by Sacha Nacht, would presumably shape the future members of the SPP. Be that as it may, Lacan's resignation was followed by that of several other important members of the SPP (notably Daniel Lagache, who, as vice-president of the society, refused to succeed Lacan, the departing president). Thus the psychoanalysts who eventually met in Rome in September to hear Lacan were very much a splinter group, for which Lacan now became the acknowledged leader and spokesman. In any case, Lacan proceeded to deliver his "report" and seized the opportunity to make a full statement of his own views on the nature of psychoanalysis, with all that this implied for the training process of any psychoanalytic institute. Hence, the importance of the "Discourse" as the Magna Charta of the new movement in psychoanalysis; hence, too, its polemical tone.

The reader will notice a distinct difference in the tone and thematic of this essay from 1953 (1977, pp. 30–113/237–359) compared with the two previous ones from 1948 and 1949. Here for the first time Lacan insists on the centrality of language in his conception of the Freudian enterprise. No doubt the development of this preoccupation in Lacan was gradual, and we are led to assume that certain early papers of Lévi-Strauss made a profound impact on him. In Lacan's paper on the "Mirror Stage" from 1949, for example, he speaks of the formative power of the *imagoes* "whose veiled faces it is our privilege to see in outline. . . in the penumbra of symbolic efficacity" (1977, p. 3/95). Lacan refers here explicitly to Lévi-Strauss' essay "The Effectiveness of Symbols," also published in 1949, in which Lévi-Strauss proposes to understand language as the unconscious structure of society. Again in the present essay from 1953, Lacan remarks, "Isn't it striking that Lévi-Strauss, in suggesting the implication of the structures of language with that part of the social laws that regulate marriage ties and kinship, is already conquering the very terrain in which Freud situates the unconscious?" (1977, p. 73/285). And he once again refers explicitly to Lévi-Strauss, to his paper "Language and the Analysis of Social Laws" (1951). The influence of Lévi-Strauss on Lacan at this time thus appears to have been decisive in helping him articulate his own conception of the correlation between the Freudian unconscious and the laws of language. That correlation will become apparent in the second section of the "Discourse."

Lacan begins with a brief introduction, the purpose of which is to state his fundamental theme: the importance of speech and language in the psychoanalytic process as such. The direction of contemporary psychoanalysis, he claims, has turned more and more away from its true center, i.e., the function of speech and the field of language. An examination of the current literature on the subject reveals three areas of special interest: (1) the function of what Lacan calls "the imaginary," i.e., the role of fantasies and images in psychoanalytic experience as manifest particularly in the fantasies of children; (2) the conception of object relations on the libidinal level; and (3) the role of countertransference in psychoanalysis, and hence the necessity of training for psychoanalysis. All three of these fall victim to the same temptation of overlooking the fact that the foundation of the whole experience is speech itself—an area in which the analyst ought to be a "past master" (1977, p. 36/244).

But since Freud, this field of investigation has "been left fallow"—and even he discerned it in experience more than he explored it theoretically. As for his followers, they have been caught up in issues of technique passed on to others in the most ritualistic fashion. In America particularly, Lacan claims, this tradition has been distorted by the cultural milieu, deeply marked as it is by communications theory, behavioral psychology, and the alleged national experience of self-achievement through adaptation to the milieu.

Whatever may be said about Lacan's assessment of the American mind, it is clear that Freud's technique can be understood and applied only to the extent that the concepts on which it is based are understood. Lacan takes as his task in this essay "to demonstrate that these concepts take on their full meaning only when oriented in a field of language, only when ordered in relation to the function of speech" (1977, p. 39/246). This program suggests in reverse order the outline of the essay that follows (an outline also suggested by its title): the first section deals with the function of speech; the second with the field of lan-

guage; the third specifically with the consequences of the preceding as they affect the issue of technique.

I

Empty speech and full speech in the
psychoanalytic realization of the subject

What is at stake in the essay is the "realization of the subject" through the mediation of psychoanalytic discourse. Lacan
does not define "subject" for us, and at this point we know more
what he does not mean by it (i.e., it is not simply the "ego," an
alienated reflection of the subject) than what it is. The subject is
"realized" to the extent that it achieves its truth. The question
here is: How can the psychoanalytic interchange facilitate this
process? In the simplest terms, by helping the subject pass from
the use of "empty" speech (*parole vide*) to "full" speech (*parole pleine*),
where "speech," or "word," has the sense Saussure (1916) gave it
in distinguishing "speech" from "language": an individual, conscious act of expression. What determines whether or not it is
called "empty" or "full"? Precisely the extent to which it impedes
or facilitates the realization of the truth of the subject (Lacan,
1953–1954, p. 61).

Lacan begins with the nature of "empty" speech, "where
the subject seems to be talking in vain about someone who,
even if he were his spitting image, can never become one with
the assumption of his desire" (1977, p. 45/254). In other words,
the subject speaks of himself as if he were an other, as if his own
ego were alienated from the deeper subjectivity that properly
assumes "his desire." In a different context, Lacan describes that
speech as "empty" that is "caught up in the 'here and now' with
the analyst, where the subject wanders about in the machina-
tions of the language system, in the labyrinth of a system of reference offered him by his cultural context" (1953–1954, p. 61;
our translation).

The analyst may collude with this misapprehension by the
subject of his true self in many ways, which in their essence consist in the analyst's own failure to distinguish between the ego

and the subjectivity of his client. This may happen first of all through his own failure to be a true "auditor" of the word spoken in silence by the subject (1977, p. 40/247). The analyst may fail to recognize that the appropriate response may be silence in return. Instead, he may respond as if this "silent" word were a sheer void (as much in himself as in the analysand), a void that must be filled by some reality "beyond speech," such as an analysis of behavior. To be sure, this is done by words that elicit other words—all of them jamming the true word (uttered in silence) and in that sense profoundly empty.

Is the solution, then, "introspection"? Not at all. "Introspection" all too often finds only the alienated ego in its empty monologue. Instead, the process of analysis involves the difficult task of "working through" the consequences of the subject's initial alienation essentially through the subject's "free association." This process may involve different stages, commonly referred to as frustration, aggressivity, and regression. How are these to be understood?

Frustration in the analysand does not derive from the analyst's silent refusal to confirm the subject's empty speech, but rather from the subject's painful recognition that his ego, which he has hitherto taken to be identical with his own "being," is nothing more than a "construct in the imaginary" (1977, p. 42/249), i.e., a mirrorlike image of his true self. The recognition of his ego as an alienation of himself is, indeed, "frustration in its essence" (1977, p. 42/250). The aggressivity that the subject experiences at such a moment, then, is the intense reaction of the slave in the face of the profound futility of his labor, i.e., of the ego experiencing the disintegration of its very stability as, for example, when its defenses are slowly dismantled (1977, p. 42/250). In such a context, regression may be seen to be the successive moments in the decomposition of the ego in which the ego finds compensation in a series of fantasy relationships (1977, p. 44/252).

Through all of this, the first task of the analyst is to avoid being seduced. He does this not only by responding appropriately to the analysand's silence, but by trying to pace the patient's recognition of his own ego structures according to his capacity to integrate this recognition. "Nothing must be read into [any here-and-now situation] concerning the ego of the subject that cannot be reassumed by him in the form of the 'I,' that is, in the first person" (1977, p. 43/251). This assumption by the subject of his own "mirages" is achieved in and through the analytic discourse as such. The analyst does not address himself to some "object beyond the subject's speech." Rather, the patient must remain for him at all times a subject. The patient's speech is a "musical score" that the analyst simply tries to punctuate as with a metric beat. Even the termination of the analytic session is a form of such punctuation. And if the analyst seeks "supervision" of his work (so that he himself is now a subject in the patient's stead vis-à-vis the supervisor), the purpose is to learn to discern the multiple registers of the subject's musical score (1977, p. 45/253).

What, then, is achieved, by all of this? Eventually, to be sure, the "full" word. But more precisely, how? Not essentially by an examination of the "here and now" or by the analysis of resistances. Rather, above all, it is achieved through the "anamnesis," through the recollection by the patient of his own past in dialogue with the analyst. Both aspects of the process need to be stressed.

What is recollected is what the subject has been (Heidegger would say *gewesend*), i.e., his personal history as he experiences it, for "the effect of full speech is to reorder past contingencies by conferring on them the sense of necessities to come" (1977, p. 48/256). Hence, "it is not a question of reality, but of truth" that is at stake — though the notion of "truth" here needs further elaboration.

In this regard, it is important that the recollection is *articulated* to another (Anna O. called Freud's method the "talking cure"). The process is "the birth of truth in speech." It is precisely the articulation that renders the past *present* in the analysis. "For it is present speech that bears witness to the truth of this revelation in present reality, and which grounds it in the name of that reality. Yet in that reality, only speech bears witness to that portion of the powers of the past that has been thrust aside at each crossroads where the event has made its choice" (1977, p. 47/256).

Moreover, psychoanalytic speech is addressed to an *other*. The process is essentially *inter*subjective and the subject's speech must include the response of his interlocutor (1977, p. 49/258). Thus, the assumption of his history by the subject, insofar as it is constituted by the speech addressed to the other, forms the ground of the new method that Freud called "psychoanalysis." The means of psychoanalysis "are those of speech," for it is speech that "confers a meaning on the functions of the individual." The operations involved "are those of history, in so far as history constitutes the emergence of truth in the real." And the domain of psychoanalysis is the realm of "concrete discourse, in so far as this is the field of the transindividual reality of the subject" (1977, p. 49/257).

By "transindividual" here Lacan seems to mean that dimension of the subject that lies beyond the compass of his individual consciousness, i.e., that "is not at the disposal of the subject in re-establishing the continuity of his conscious discourse" (1977, p. 49/258). It is therefore "other" than conscious discourse, and it is what Lacan understands Freud to mean by the "unconscious." The unconscious "is that chapter of my history that is marked by a blank"—the "censored chapter" that nonetheless can somehow be deciphered. It is discernible, for example:

> —in monuments: this is my body. That is to say, the hysterical nucleus of the neurosis in which the hysterical symptom reveals the structure of a language, and is deciphered like an inscription which, once recovered, can without serious loss be destroyed;
> —in archival documents: these are my childhood memories, just as impenetrable as are such documents when I do not know their provenance;

— in semantic evolution: this corresponds to the stock of
words and acceptations of my own particular vocabulary,
as it does to my style of life and to my character;
— in traditions [oral traditions and natural languages], too,
and even in the legends [myths] which, in a heroicized
form, bear my history;
— and, lastly, in the traces that are inevitably preserved by
the distortions necessitated by the linking of the adulter-
ated chapter [of my own life] to the chapters surrounding
it, and whose meaning will be re-established by my exegesis [1977, p. 50/259].

Note that this catalogue includes some items that are proper to
the individual (e.g., childhood memories) and some that have a
much wider base in general human experience (e.g., traditions,
legends, semantic evolution, etc.). What is most important at the
moment, however, is that the conception of the unconscious is
foreign to any interpretation that would identify it with sheer instinctual urges or drives (1977, p. 54/264), whose development in
the individual may be traced through a series of maturational
stages (1977, p. 53/262).

　　Rather, a proper understanding of the unconscious obliges
us to consider it in terms not of instincts, but of history. "What
we teach the subject to recognize as his unconscious is his history" (1977, p. 52/261). Lacan speaks of "primary historization,"
implying apparently a "secondary historization" as well. By "primary" historization we understand him to mean the process that
engenders events themselves, the "facts" of history that have
been "recognized in one particular sense or censored in a certain
order." Accordingly, a "secondary" historization would consist
in the effort through analytic discourse "to perfect the present
historization of the facts that have already determined a certain
number of the historical 'turning points' in [the subject's] existence" (1977, p. 52/261). In this context, the classical stages of
psychosexual development belong to "primary" historization
and the reconstitution of them with the help of the analyst to
"secondary" historization. In either case, however, they are
radically intersubjective in character (1977, p. 53/262).

Be that as it may, what is clear for Lacan is that the "subjectivity" of the subject includes more than what has been experienced "subjectively," i.e., consciously by him. That is why the "truth of his history is not all contained in his [consciously discernible] script" (1977, p. 55/265). There is a larger text that supports his discourse, although he himself may know "only his own lines." The larger text Lacan calls "the discourse of the other," "the unconscious" in its strictest sense. It is to the nature of this larger text, not speech but language, that he now turns.

II
Symbol and language as structure and limit
of the psychoanalytic field

Lacan proposes to explore the larger text, "other" than individual consciousness, within which the psychoanalytic exchange takes place, and he speaks of it as the "psychoanalytic field." His thesis will be that this field is essentially the structure of language itself, the limits of which define the limits of psychoanalysis in the sense that outside of this field psychoanalysis cannot function. As for the correlation between language and symbol that is thematized here, we recall once more that during these years the influence of Lévi-Strauss appears to have been particularly strong.

Again Lacan declares his intention to "rediscover the sense of [the psychoanalytic] experience" by returning to the work of Freud (1977, p. 57/267). Three works in particular he finds especially significant, insofar as they suggest how profoundly Freud's insight was marked by an awareness of the importance of language. The first of these is *The Interpretation of Dreams* (1900a), where Freud teaches us that "the dream has the structure of a sentence" (1977, p. 57/267), and the "oneiric discourse" is elaborated by all the devices of rhetoric (1977, p. 58/268). Moreover, as the analysis progresses, the patient's dreams come to function more and more simply as the elements of a dialogue, the dialogue of analysis.

In Freud's *The Psychopathology of Everyday Life* (1901), "every unsuccessful act is a successful, not to say 'well turned,' discourse" (1977, p. 58/268). Moreover, pathological symptoms are "structured like a language," for (as Lacan tells us elsewhere) they have the structure of metaphor insofar as in the symptom one signifier (with all its associations) replaces another signifier (with all of its associations) (1977, p. 166/518). The symptom is resolved when the proper word is uttered revealing the substitution.

Finally, in Freud's *Jokes and Their Relation to the Unconscious* (1905b), Lacan's distinction between the conscious intention of the individual and the field of language to which the subject is exposed finds strong confirmation, for there must "have been something foreign to me in what I found for me to take pleasure in [the joke]" (1977, p. 60/271). Lacan finds in the wealth of language that makes it possible for jokes to emerge further evidence for Freud's appreciation of the linguistic nature of the unconscious. Thus "it was certainly the Word *(verbe)* that was in the beginning, and we live in its creation, but it is the action of our spirit that continues this creation by constantly renewing it" (1977, p. 61/271).

At this point Lacan begins to elaborate his conception of the field of language to which the subject on the unconscious level is exposed. In its most basic form, it is conceived as the law that governs all human interchange. "No man is actually ignorant of it, since the law of man has been the law of language since the first words of recognition presided over the first gifts" (1977, p. 61/272). But these gifts themselves are essentially symbols— "signifiers [useless in themselves] of the pact that they constitute as signified." The law governing the exchange of gifts is one of symbolic interchange and the order it establishes is the "symbolic order."

The autonomous character of this order is important to note here, for it is this that distinguishes language as a system of signs from the set of signals that are evident in the animal kingdom and that can be simulated in conditioning experiments. (In

this regard, Lacan cites the findings reported by Jules Masser-
mann.) Every sign is composed of both a "signifier" and a "signified" and in language each of these elements is located within a
mesh of similar elements with regard to which it assumes its
specific character. Thus,

> what defines any element whatever of a language *(langue)*
> as belonging to language, is that, for all users of this lan-
> guage *(langue)*, this element is distinguished as such in the
> ensemble supposedly constituted of homologous elements.
>
> The result is that the particular effects of this element
> of language are bound up with the existence of this ensem-
> ble, anterior to any possible link with any particular expe-
> rience of the subject. And to consider this last link [as in
> the case of conditioning signals] independently of any ref-
> erence to the first is simply to deny in this element the
> function proper to language [1977, pp. 63–64/274].

This conception of an autonomous order of symbols is essential to Freud's entire insight, Lacan maintains. "For Freud's
discovery was that of the field of the effects in the nature of man
of his relations to the symbolic order and the tracing of their
meaning right back to the most radical agencies of symbolization in being. To ignore this symbolic order is to condemn the
discovery to oblivion, and the experience to ruin" (1977, p. 64/
275).

Much will be made of this notion of "symbolic order" as
Lacan's thought develops. Here it suffices to see that the symbolic order, conceived now as "law," governs not only the order
of language, but the logic of mathematical combination, and indeed, the whole pattern of social relatedness that emerges under
the guise of marriage ties and kinship relationships, superim-
posing "the kingdom of culture on that of a nature abandoned to
the law of mating" (1977, p. 66/277). Thus, "Symbols in fact en-
velop the life of man in a network so total that they join together, before he comes into the world, those who are going to en-
gender him 'by flesh and blood' " (1977, p. 68/279). In a similar

vein, Rabelais speaks of the Great Debt whose economy "extended to the stars themselves" (1977, p. 67/278). Characteristic of Lacan, however, is the designation of this order as the "law of the father": "It is in the *name of the father* that we must recognize the support of the symbolic function which, from the dawn of history, has identified his person with the figure of the law" (1977, p. 67/278). This law is all-pervasive, then, providing man with both servitude and grandeur "in which the living being would be annihilated, if desire did not preserve its part in the interferences and pulsations that the cycles of language cause to converge on him" (1977, p. 68/279).

If all this is to be said of language, how are we to understand the nature of speech, i.e., "the word"? Lacan's answer here is enigmatic: It is a "presence made of absence"—and he alludes to the famous anecdote that Freud recounts in "Beyond the Pleasure Principle":

> This good little boy...had an occasional disturbing habit of taking any small objects he could get hold of and throwing them away from him into a corner, under the bed, and so on, so that hunting for his toys and picking them up was often quite a business. As he did this he gave vent to a loud, long-drawn-out 'o-o-o-o', accompanied by an expression of interest and satisfaction. His mother and the writer of the present account were agreed in thinking that this was not a mere interjection but represented the German word *fort* ['gone']. I eventually realized that it was a game, and that the only use he made of any of his toys was to play 'gone' with them. One day I made an observation which confirmed my view. The child had a wooden reel with a piece of string tied round it. It never occurred to him to pull it along the floor behind him, for instance, and play at its being a carriage. What he did was to hold the reel by the string and very skilfully throw it over the edge of the curtained cot, so that it disappeared into it, at the same time uttering his expressive 'o-o-o-o'. He then pulled the reel out of the cot again by the string and hailed its reappearance

with a joyful *'da'* ['here']. This, then, was the complete game—disappearance and return [1920, pp. 14–15].

The sense of this passage for Lacan is that the child, by modulating the phonemes "o-o-o-o" and "da" in this game of "disappearance and return," strove to make the mother present in her absence. For the child, it is the inchoation of the spoken word; for Lacan, the paradigm of all speech. For he accepts from the testimony of the linguists (1977, p. 73/284–285) the principle that the elementary particles of speech are the phonemes that may be divided according to a system of bipolar opposition into 12 sets of binary pairs "out of which each language makes its own selection" (Jakobson and Halle, 1956, p. 29). Lacan sees the *Fort! Da!* as such a pairing of phonemes. When the child first activates the experience of them that he has assimilated from the community into which he is born, he is initiated into "the world of meaning of [his] particular language in which the world of things will come to be arranged" (1977, p. 65/276). Thereafter, "it is the world of words that creates the world of things" in the sense that it renders them present—i.e., meaning-ful—in their absence.

With this much said about the fundamental relationship between language and speech, Lacan proceeds to discuss the tensions between them. He first looks at various forms of pathology in the subject and designates three "paradoxes": (1) In psychosis, the subject is "objectified," so to speak, in a "language without dialectic," i.e., he is "spoken" by language (rather than speaking it) through stereotypes, "petrified forms" of the unconscious, etc. (1977, p. 69/280). (2) In neurosis (classically characterized by symptoms, inhibitions, and anxiety), the speech of the subject is excluded from the individual's conscious discourse, but it finds expression in other forms (e.g., in symptoms). In its fullest sense, then, it includes the "discourse of the other," and it was precisely through deciphering this speech that Freud discovered the "other," i.e., the unconscious (1977, p. 69/281). (3) In "normal" inauthenticity, the subject "loses his meaning in the objectivizations of discourse" (1977, p. 70/281).

Captivated by the fascinations of the scientific milieu in which we live, the subject takes himself to be an object like the rest and thereby forgets his subjectivity. Thus he becomes blocked from true speech (the full word) by being caught behind a "language barrier" of empty words, whose thickness is measurable "by the statistically determined total of pounds of printed paper, miles of record grooves, and hours of radio broadcasting that the said culture produces per head" (1977, p. 71/282).

Yet the situation is not quite as bleak as all this may sound. Subjectivity in our own day remains creative and "has not ceased in its struggle to renew the never-exhausted power of symbols in the human exchange" (1977, p. 71/283). Psychoanalysis has made a contribution to this struggle, and its task now is to bring its own efforts into line with the thrust of modern science so as to assure itself of a legitimate place in it. This is all the more possible because the psychoanalyst is a "practitioner of the symbolic function," and this function lies at the heart of the movement (i.e., structuralism) that is establishing a new order of the sciences in our day. This new order is based on the principle that the "conjectural" sciences are no less rigorous than the "exact" sciences, for "exactitude is to be distinguished from truth" (1977, p. 74/286). The science of linguistics, which lies at the basis of contemporary anthropology and (as already indicated) plays an essential role in Lacan's conception of the symbolic order, is a case in point (1977, p. 73/284–285).

At any rate, the physical sciences, for all their vaunted exactitude, are not without their limitations. "Our physics," for example, "is simply a mental fabrication whose instrument is the mathematical symbol" that serves as the "measurement it introduces into the real" (1977, p. 74/286). This can be seen in the case of the measurement of time. But mathematics can also symbolize another kind of time, namely, the "intersubjective" time that structures such human actions as are considered in a purely conjectural science like game-theory (1977, p. 75/287). Such formalizations as these have their place in psychoanalytic conjecture, too, in order "to ensure its own rigour" (1977, p. 75/287).

Yet the real test of psychoanalysis is to deal with the time that counts as the subject's history. Here the ideal will be "an identification of the subjectivity of the historian [in this case the subject himself] with the constituting subjectivity of the primary historization in which the event is humanized [i.e., his own past, not only conscious but unconscious]" (1977, p. 75/287). This is made possible by the historicity of the subject himself, by reason of which genuine progress may be made through recollecting the past in the present.

If what has been said so far has any validity, then the consequences for the training of the psychoanalyst must be drawn. Not only must we include in the curriculum Freud's comprehensive catalogue of subjects (in addition to psychology and sexology, "the history of civilization, mythology, the psychology of religions and the science of literature") (Freud, 1926b, p. 246), but a new awareness of the importance of language in the process suggests the inclusion of several cognate subjects as well ("rhetoric, dialectic in the technical sense that this term assumes in the *Topics* of Aristotle, grammar, and, that supreme pinnacle of the aesthetics of language, poetics, which would include the neglected technique of the witticism") (1977, p. 76/288). All in all, a formidable task!

III

*The resonances of interpretation
and the time of the subject
in psychoanalytic technique*

In this third section Lacan draws the consequences of the preceding for psychoanalytic technique. He concludes by extending the analysis to a consideration of the subject's temporality. This lies at the basis of the historization process, the full acknowledgment of which is essential to achieving the full word. Accordingly, Part III falls conveniently into two sections: (1) the resonances of interpretation and (2) the time of the subject in psychoanalytic technique.

The resonances of interpretation

The problem of technique is this: How help the subject, exposed as he is to the whole field of language, achieve full speech (1977, p. 88/302)? To begin with the negative, this is not done by the analysis of resistances (1977, p. 78/290). Freud's example in this regard is instructive. In the case of the Rat Man (1909b), for example, he tolerates the resistances as long as he can use them to involve the subject in the articulation of his own message (1977, p. 79/291). It is obviously the message that is important here.

Nor is full speech brought about by any form of interpretation that permits the subject to be objectified. As we have seen, this may occur if the analyst fails to distinguish between the subjectivity of the subject and his ego, taking the ego as "identical with the presence that is speaking" (1977, p. 90/304). It is all too easy to fall into such an error if one takes ego to mean "the perception-consciousness system" and then makes the easy transition to considering it as the "function of the real." Soon psychoanalysis becomes a relationship between two bodies, in which "the analyst teaches the subject to apprehend himself as an object" (1977, p. 91/304), as he is for the analyst. Accordingly, if the task is for the subject's *id* to be conformed to an *ego*, as Freud's famous dictum is improperly taken to suggest, then this conformity is to the analyst's ego rather than to the analysand's.

It is in terms of such an objectivization that Lacan understands many a theoretical formulation of the "splitting of the *ego*" in analysis. In other words, "Half of the subject's *ego* passes over to the other side of the wall that separates the analysand from the analyst, then half of that half, and so on, in an asymptotic procession" (1977, p. 91/305). The wall is the wall of words — empty words — that constitute a "language barrier" between the analyst and the subject. Behind the wall resides the "reality" of the subject that the analyst feels he must analyze. Experiencing himself in corresponding fashion, the subject feels that the analyst on the other side of the wall already knows in advance the truth about him—and therefore is all the more inclined to be "wide open to [the analyst's] objectifying intervention" (1977, p. 94/308).

More positively, the principles that govern Freud's own technique are those that determine "the dialectic of the consciousness-of-self, as realized from Socrates to Hegel" (1977, pp. 79–80/292). Freud's specific contribution was to see that the subject as a self has an other center than consciousness and in that sense is "de-centered." It is because of Freud's insistence that the self has this "other" center, i.e., the unconscious, that the subject warrants the Hegelian description of an "identity" of the particular (i.e., consciousness) and the universal (i.e., the unconscious).

It is this "identity" of the particular and universal (of consciousness and the unconscious) in both the subject and the analyst that enters into the psychoanalytic dialogue. And in its essence, this interchange is "a communication in which the sender [i.e., the subject] receives his own message back from the receiver [i.e., the analyst] in an inverted form" (1977, p. 85/298). We take this to mean that the speech of the subject always "includes its own reply" in the sense that the *lacunae* among the spoken words (consciousness) are already filled in by the subject's unconscious dimension, and the analyst's response (quite "particular" to the subject [1977, p. 79/291]) is such as to bring the unconscious dimension of the subject's speech into his awareness. The effectiveness of the analyst's response will be in proportion, of course, to his own attunement to the unconscious within himself, but it is the subject's *own message* (not the analyst's) that is received back from him now in "inverted" form. Thus it is the function of the analyst's own utterance "not to inform [the subject about himself] but to evoke" (1977, p. 86/299)—i.e., to evoke the resonances, conscious and especially unconscious, in the subject's own discourse as if it were a piece of polyphonic music: "analysis consists in playing in all the many staves of the score that speech constitutes in the registers of language and on which depends the overdetermination of the symptom" (1977, p. 79/291).

The symptom is "overdetermined" in that it results from the coalescence of several (or at least more than one) contributing factors — in Lacanian terms, from the constellation of several signifiers, or "symbols." We take "symbols" here in the structuralist sense as the elements of the "symbolic function/order." As the translator notes: "The symbols referred to . . . are not icons, stylized figurations, but signifiers, . . . differential elements, in themselves without meaning, which acquire value only in their mutual relations" (Sheridan, 1977, p. ix), the basic pattern of which is correlative with the law of human interchange already described.

In order to relieve the symptom, then, the analyst must, by the evocative style that encourages "free association" — and sometimes "communicates what it does not actually say" (1977, p. 82/295) — help the subject to disengage the various signifiers that constitute the symptom. This the analyst does by introducing the subject "into the *primary language* in which, beyond what he tells us of himself, he is already talking to us unknown to himself, and, in the first place, in the symbols of the symptom" (1977, p. 81/293). In what sense this primary language is also the "language of his desire" is a problem that need not concern us at the moment. Let it suffice to say that it is "primary" because it is the language into which the *in-fans* is first introduced when he begins to speak — universal in the sense that it has a character "that would be understood in all other languages," yet because it structures *his* subjectivity, "it is absolutely particular to the subject" (1977, p. 81/293).

In other words, primary — not "primitive" — language is the language of the *subject's* unconscious, of "identity" of the particular and universal. This is the language that Freud deciphered, whose "essential field" Ernest Jones (1916) delineated by reducing the thousands of "symbols" (in the sense now that the term is normally understood in analysis) to five: those referring "to one's own body, to kinship relations, to birth, to life, and to death" (1977, p. 82/294). These typify the resonances that the analyst's response may evoke. "There is therefore no doubt that the analyst can play on the power of the symbol by evoking it in a carefully calculated fashion in the semantic resonances of his remarks" (1977, p. 82/294).

Yet as Lacan uses the word "symbol," the "primary" character of these symbols goes deeper still and "brings them close to those [prime] numbers out of which all the others are composed." We take this to mean that the "primary" character of symbols for him consists in the signifiers in their most radical form — even down to the level of the phonemes? — out of which all meaningful articulation is composed. Be that as it may, if symbols are understood in the most radical manner possible, "we shall be able to restore to speech its full value of evocation by a discreet search for their interferences" (1977, p. 82/295). This may make heavy demands on the literary and linguistic erudition of the analyst, but at least it lets us see how far Lacan is willing to go in insisting on the necessity for a "renewed technique of interpretation in analysis" (1977, p. 82/294).

But we must not forget that this "renewed technique" is a function of the basic principle of psychoanalysis, i.e., the principle of dialectical exchange. What is sought in the exchange is the response — not the "reaction" — of the other (1977, p. 86/299–300). Whatever is addressed to the dialogue partner engages not only the speaker but the partner, for "speech commits its author by investing the person to whom it is addressed with a new reality" (1977, p. 85/298), thereby effecting some kind of "transformation" in him (1977, p. 83/296). From the analyst's point of view, this transformation may consist merely in awakening in the subject a sense of his own subjectivity: "if I call the person to whom I am speaking by whatever name I choose to give him, I intimate to him the subjective function that he will take on again in order to reply to me, even if it is to repudiate this function" (1977, pp. 86–87/300). Yet when all is said and done, the "decisive function" in any response that the analyst makes to the subject is "to recognize him" — the alternative is "to abolish him" as subject. "Such is the nature of the analyst's *responsibility* whenever he intervenes by means of speech" (1977,

p. 87/300). The vagaries of Freud's own efforts at such a dialectical exchange may be seen, for example, in the case of the Rat Man (Freud, 1909b), where it succeeds (1977, pp. 88–89/302–303), and in the case of Dora (Freud, 1905a), where it does not (1977, pp. 91–92/305–306).

However (and this brings us back to an earlier theme), in order for the analyst to "recognize" the subject appropriately, he must first of all discern the place where the subject's ego is, so that he may know "through whom and for whom the subject poses *his question*" (1977, p. 89/303). Typically, for example, the hysteric will experience his ego quite differently from the obsessional. Hence, it is "always in the relation between the subject's ego *(moi)* and the 'I' *(je)* of his discourse that you must understand the meaning of the discourse if you are to achieve the de-alienation of the subject" (1977, p. 90/304). It is the failure to do this that leads to the evils of objectivization (see above) and, in effect, to "abolishing" the subject as a subject (1977, p. 87/300).

If all this leaves much to be explained, the general sense of it remains fairly clear: the technique of psychoanalysis is based on a principle of dialectical exchange achieved through the medium of language articulated through speech. That is the essential. Lacan includes certain digressions and extrapolations that enrich our appreciation of the importance of language in the process without clarifying very much our understanding of it. After dealing with the issue in Part II, Lacan tells us again that language, as it is structured by the symbolic order, is a specifically human phenomenon that differs radically from the signal system of animals (e.g., the "wagging dance" of bees). The signals in the animal's system are in a nonarbitrary one-to-one relation of signifier to signified according to a fixed coding, whereas in language this relation is arbitrary and both signifier and signified derive their meaning from a whole network of lexical and other relationships in which they find their place (1977, p. 84/297). In the case of the bees, there is no retransmission of the message, so that the message serves only as a relay of the action without any *subject* detaching it from the action and using it as a symbol of communication to another subject.

Moreover, Lacan finds different ways to celebrate the power of language in psychoanalytic discourse. Sometimes it is by sardonic comment on those who fail to recognize it. For example, he scoffs at the analyst who fails to appreciate the difference between the words "need" and "demand" in terms of their symbolizing effect on the subject (1977, p. 83/296). He is only slightly more benign toward any analyst who experiences a "guilty conscience about the miracle operated by his speech. He interprets the symbol and, lo and behold, the symptom, which inscribes the symbol in letters of suffering in the subject's flesh, disappears" (1977, p. 92/306).

Sometimes he is more positive, as when he describes the intimate relation between words and the embodiment of symptoms. "Words are trapped in all the corporeal images that captivate the subject. . . . [They] can undergo symbolic lesions and accomplish imaginary acts of which the patient is the subject" (1977, p. 87/301). Accordingly, the discourse itself may sometimes become eroticized and take on a "phallic-urethral, anal-erotic, or even an oral-sadistic function" (1977, p. 88/301). But here speech itself becomes an "imaginary, or even real object in the subject" and ceases to fulfill its function as an articulation of the symbolic order, the proper locus of language.

Introduction of the terms "imaginary" and "real" as distinct from "symbolic" at this point calls our attention to a specifically Lacanian terminology. From the "Mirror Stage" paper, we have some sense of what Lacan means by the "imaginary": it is the sphere of the *imago* — "the world, the register, the dimension of images, conscious or unconscious, perceived or imagined" (Sheridan, 1977, p. ix) where there is "a sort of coalescence of the signifier and signified" (Laplanche and Pontalis, 1967, p. 210). From the present essay we have some sense of what Lacan means by the "symbolic": it is the comprehensive structure whose discrete elements operate as signifiers related only arbitrarily to a signified(s) (in the sense already explained), or, more generally, the orders to which such structures belong, or, finally, the law (i.e., fundamental pattern) on which this order is based. What, then, does he mean by the "real"? The "real" for Lacan seems to be the order of brute fact. As the translator notes: "What is prior to the assumption of the symbolic, the real in its 'raw' state (in the case of the subject, for instance, the organism and its biological needs), may only be supposed, it is an algebraic x" (Sheridan, 1977, p. x). In contrast to the "substitutions" in the symbolic order and the "variations" in the imaginary, the real is a point of constancy, before which the imaginary "falters" and over which the symbolic "stumbles" — the "ineliminable residue of all articulation" (Sheridan, 1977, p. x).

Although these notions are far from clear at this point, their emergence in the exposé leads Lacan to raise the question of how the dimension of the real enters into the psychoanalytic discourse. If we understand the word "reality" here to mean "real" in the sense just described — at least, most generally, as the order of fact that is neither symbolic nor imaginary — then "reality" enters into the analytic process in the sheer *fact* of the analyst's response, whether this is in the form of "active intervention" or "abstention, [in] his refusal to reply" (1977, p. 95/ 309–310). In the latter case, if the "abstention" is an appropriately resonating silence that serves to elicit from the subject full speech, then it really lies at the junction of the real and the symbolic, for it makes its own contribution to the "dialectical punctuation" of the analytic discourse.

Be this as it may, another way in which the symbolic and the real come together for Lacan is in the function of *time*. And this brings us to the second section of Part III.

The time of the subject in psychoanalytic technique

There are several ways in which time plays a significant role in the psychoanalytic process. In the first place, the time for the entire analysis (i.e., its length) must be experienced by the patient as indefinite, partly because there is no legitimate way to predict what the patient's "time for understanding" will be, partly because predicting the coming–to–term of the subject's exploration of his truth implies that this truth is "already there" some-how in the analyst, thus confirming the subject's "original mir-age" of the analyst's omniscience and, in effect, leaving "the sub-ject in the alienation of his truth" (1977, p. 96/310–311). The unhappy results of such an illusion Lacan finds exemplified in Freud's (1918) account of the Wolf Man case.

There is another way in which time, as a mode of reality, plays an important role in the psychoanalytic process — in terms of the duration of each session and the terminal point that marks the end of it. We have already mentioned that for Lacan all interventions by the analyst serve as punctuation of the dis-course. This is most especially true for the termination of the session. "The suspension of a session cannot *not* be experienced by the subject as a punctuation in his progress" (1977, p. 98/313). Hence the termination is a privileged intervention that must be used judiciously by the analyst, with the result that ses-sions will be of varying duration. For if it is true that "the un-conscious needs time to reveal itself," it is also true that the "time" of the unconscious is not measured by "clock" time.

Flexibility in regard to the length of the session will have an effect on the analyst as well as on the subject, for when the ana-lyst departs from the observation of the "standard time limit" set by his peers, his whole function as an analyst is put into ques-tion (1977, p. 97/312). On the other hand, the "neutrality" he alleges in following the "standard time limit" is challenged as simple "non-action," which may in its own way take on an "ob-sessive value" that lends itself to the "connivance of the subject" (1977, p. 99/314). For the patient is all too ready to make the "standard time limit" serve his own powers of resistance. Thus, if we take Hegel's dialectic of master and slave to be the para-digm for the relationship between therapist and patient (more of this later), the patient is quite capable of using the "standard time limit" of the ordinary session — for that matter, any fixed, predictable time limit — as a maneuver to wait out the master's death. At any rate, this is the rationale for Lacan's well-known use of "short sessions," for which he has often been criticized

(1977, p. 100/315). What has to be underlined here, it seems, is the conception of the termination of the session as an essential form of punctuating it as discourse. As in the study of manuscripts, where the absence of punctuation may be a source of ambiguity: "The punctuation, once inserted, fixes the meaning; changing the punctuation renews or upsets it; and a faulty punctuation amounts to a change for the worse" (1977, p. 99/313–314).

But there is a still more profound way in which time affects the analytic process, insofar as time is an index of the intrinsic finitude of the human subject. It is with this theme, together with its complex and far-reaching implications for the function of speech, that Lacan brings his long discussion to a close.

Lacan's transition to the theme of finitude is interesting, for it passes by way of reference to Freud's hypothesis of a "death instinct." Lacan comes to this after acknowledging that whatever the astuteness of the analyst, he is never entirely "master" of the analytic situation—he is always prey to what Freud called the "negative therapeutic reaction" (1977, p. 101/316). We know that it was precisely to deal with the negative therapeutic reaction that Freud was led to his notion of a "death instinct."

It is perhaps worth recalling the thrust of Freud's argument. We understand well enough that a "negative therapeutic reaction" is an aggravation of symptoms as a result of therapeutic efforts rather than an alleviation of them, as if the subject preferred suffering to being cured. Eventually, Freud theorized that this reaction was grounded in a form of masochism—not necessarily in the strict sense of sexual perversion (by which sexual gratification is gained through suffering and humiliation), but at least in the "moral" sense of the inclination of a subject, because of an unconscious sense of guilt, to seek out the position of victim (Freud, 1924a, p. 161). But masochism itself Freud eventually grounded in what, after 1920, he referred to as the "death instincts"—a basic category of instincts (whatever the paradoxes of the term [1977, pp. 101–102/316–317]) that tend to lead the living organism back to the inorganic state from which (presumably) it arose, i.e., toward death (Freud, 1940, p. 148). Thus it is referred to as the "destructive instinct" (Freud, 1924a, p. 163) and, according to Freud, may account not only for the phenomenon of moral masochism, i.e., destructiveness of self, but also for the tenaciousness of symptoms so often observed under the guise of the "compulsion to repeat" (Freud, 1920, p. 44), i.e., the tendency of the subject to place himself repeatedly in disadvantageous situations and thus reenact an earlier experience without being aware of the prototype.

For Lacan, this evolution of Freud's thought was perfectly consistent with its beginnings—a consistency marked by an abiding fascination with nature. At the beginning of Freud's career stood nature according to Goethe, for it was during a public reading of the poet's "Hymn to Nature," Freud tells us, that he received his vocation to medicine (Freud, 1925a, p. 8). At the close of Freud's career stood nature according to Empedocles, the pre-Socratic philosopher, for whom nature (not yet distinguished from mind) was a dynamic process in which the coming to be and passing away of sensible reality through the intermingling of the four elements (earth, air, fire, water) was governed by two dominating forces: love *(Philia)*, principle of attraction, and discord *(Neikos)*, principle of separation and disintegration (1977, pp. 102–103/318). Here Freud found in an ancient wisdom welcome affirmation of his own conception of the dual principle of Eros and Thanatos.

Be that as it may, it is not to Empedocles that Lacan turns in order to elucidate further Freud's insight into the meaning of a death instinct, but rather to the contemporary philosopher Martin Heidegger, whose celebrated analysis (1927) of human *Dasein* (i.e., existence, or ek-sistence, in a sense of radical openness to Being) as Being-unto-*death* follows from a philosophical conception of the human being that is profoundly different from Freud's. Lacan's transition to the Heideggerean conception is by way of the notion of historicity he comes to when speaking of the repetition compulsion. Freud suggests that this compulsion is best dealt with by searching out the prototypic experience that the subject compulsively repeats through a careful analysis of the transference, i.e., "in replacing his ordinary neurosis by a 'transference-neurosis' of which he can be cured by the therapeutic work" (Freud, 1914b, p. 154). Now this process Lacan describes by a non-Freudian formula—"the historizing temporality of the experience of transference"—adding immediately that in similar fashion "the death instinct essentially express[es] the limit of the historical function of the subject. This limit is death" (1977, p. 103/318)—and there we are, knee-deep in Heidegger.

Heidegger indeed comes to a discussion of death as the first step in analyzing the specifically temporal (hence historical) character of *Dasein*. For our present purposes, it suffices to recall that death in Heidegger's analysis—which places a heavy emphasis on the *finite* aspect of human existence—is the most dramatic form of limit that defines this existence from the beginning. As such, death is the ultimate seal of human finitude, for it is within the limit set by death that one's existence "takes on all the meaning it has" (1977, p. 105/320). We take Lacan to mean, then, that what Freud attempted to deal with in terms of the death instinct may be understood better if transposed into terms of human finitude, as discerned in Heidegger's conception of *Dasein*'s (for Lacan, the "subject's") Being-unto-limit-death (1977, p. 103/318).

Now Lacan tells us that "this limit is at every instant present in what history possesses as achieved. This limit represents the past in its real form, that is to say, . . . the past which reveals itself reversed in repetition" (1977, p. 103/318). In this context we take him to intend "repetition" to be taken in a Heideggerean sense. For Heidegger, repetition *(Wiederholung)* is *Dasein*'s "explicit handing over to itself" of the past; it is "the return upon possibilities of *Dasein*" as it has been up to the present (1927, p. 385). The past would "reveal itself reversed in repetition," then, insofar as the "subject," in what Heidegger calls "advancing resolve," is extended authentically toward a future that advances through its past.

Having thus joined Freud and Heidegger (whether successfully or not remains to be seen), Lacan proceeds to capitalize on his achievement. "There is therefore no further need," he writes, "to have recourse to the outworn notion of primordial masochism in order to understand the reason for the repetitive games in which subjectivity brings together a mastery of its dereliction and the birth of the symbol" (1977, p. 103/318). The "repetitive games" here, of course, are not the "repetition compulsion" of Freud but the *Fort! Da!* experience described above. Through these "games of occultation," the child masters his "dereliction" (presumably Heidegger's "thrownness" [*Geworfenheit*]). In other words, in this case, the child masters the absence of the mother through the inchoative exercise of speech, which is "the birth of the symbol" in the child. "Repetition" of this kind is not to be explained by an "outworn notion of primordial masochism." Rather, it is to be explained in terms of the child's first — but radical — experience of *limit* (i.e., finitude, death) as experienced through separation from (hence, negation of) the mother.

We have already seen in what way the child is thus "born into language," having previously received the first phonemes of his speech from "the concrete discourse of the environment" (1977, p. 103/319). More important here is the fact that this first experience of separation/limit/death is also the moment in which "desire becomes human." We take this to mean, at the very least, that this is the moment in which the child first experiences "desire" as distinct from the "need" that has characterized the quasi-symbiotic tie with the mother up to this time. In other words, the child now experiences the otherness of the mother and with that not only his own "lack of being," but a desire for the mother which, in the Hegelian schema, becomes a desire to be desired by her in turn, i.e., to be the "object" of the mother's desire (1977, p. 104/319). Moreover, this desire in the child, since it is born out of the rupture of a bond with the mother that was a quasi-identity up to that moment, has this quasi-identity as its paradigm. Hence, in the separation that follows, desire is essentially insatiable — and in that sense somehow infinite or "eternal-

94 LACAN AND LANGUAGE

ized." Furthermore, desire is diverted through channels that now become available to the child by reason of the symbolic power of speech in the same way the primordial phonemes substitute for the absence and presence of the mother in the *Fort! Da!* experience.

In any case, the replacement of the mother by a symbol may be considered equivalent to the "death" of the mother, so that "the symbol manifests itself first of all as the murder of the thing, and this death constitutes in the subject the eternalization of his desire" (1977, p. 104/319). There are several ways, then, in which death may be seen as ingredient to the first experience of language: as radical limit, it is "death" that the child experiences when the rupture of the symbiotic bond with the mother reveals the child's own "lack of being," i.e., finitude (1977, p. 105/320); as negation of the thing, it is "death" that the child imposes on things by substituting for them the symbols of speech. It is no wonder, then, that the theme of death is so closely intertwined with the entire humanizing process, as is manifest in countless ways in our culture, history, and philosophy.

Philosophically, death plays an essential role not only in the thought of Heidegger but in that of Hegel, too, and allusions to the latter in the text are plentiful. In fact, for Lacan the philosophical conceptions of the nature of man in both these philosophers seem to blend in the work of the analyst: "the undertaking of the psychoanalyst acts in our time as a mediator between the man of care [i.e., man according to Heidegger] and the subject of absolute knowledge [i.e., man according to Hegel]" (1977, p. 105/321). For a philosopher, this might take a bit of doing, but for Lacan the difficulties of such a synthesis simply underline the "loftiness" of the analyst's undertaking. It emphasizes, too, the need for the "long subjective ascesis" in his training that helps him learn not only the skills of his trade, but the full meaning of his own historicity. It is by reason of the latter that the analyst can "rejoin at its horizon the subjectivity of his time" (1977, p. 105/321), that he can share the cultural experience of his fellows — "well acquainted with the whorl into which his period draws him in the continued enterprise of Babel" (1977, p. 106/321) as he fulfills his function "as interpreter in the discord of languages."

Thus Lacan reaches the conclusion of his long discourse by coming full circle back to this starting point: the issue of appropriate training for the psychoanalyst in the light of the essential nature of psychoanalysis, whose true center is the function of speech and the field of language (1977, p. 106/322). He finishes with a flourish. With a bow to both West ("the imperative of the Word as the law that has formed [man] in its image" [1977, p. 106/322]) and East (the story of Prajapâti from the Upanishads), he addresses his readers head on: "If the domain defined by this gift of speech is to be sufficient for your action as also for your knowledge, it will also be sufficient for your devotion. For it offers a privileged field" (1977, p. 106/322).

Map of the Text

Preface.
  A. Historical background has import for our concerns,
  B. just as the reexamination of the history of Freud's concepts has import for their use.
Introduction.
  A. The power of the word is such that we turn away from it
    1. and alter our technique
      a. with undue emphasis on resistance.
    2. Our "scientific" literature instead deals with:
      a. the function of fantasies in development,
      b. libidinal object relations,
      c. countertransference and training of the analyst.
        i. But all three risk abandoning the foundation of the word.
    3. Even Freud did not venture too far afield in his discoveries.
    4. Formalism and miscognition have led to a deterioration of analytic discourse.

B. The American group especially has obscured Freud's inspiration,
   1. in its ahistorical bent for "communication" and behaviorism,
   2. and in its emphasis on social adaptation, human relations, and human engineering.
C. Freudian technique cannot be understood or correctly applied if we ignore the concepts on which it is based.
   1. The concepts, in turn, take on full meaning when related to the field of language and the function of the word.

I. *Empty speech and full speech in the psychoanalytic realization of the subject.*
   A. The empty word marks the initial period of analysis.
      1. Psychoanalysis has one medium: the word.
         a. There is no word without a reply:
            i. silence is a reply;
            ii. so is the void within the analyst,
               (a) which he seeks to fill by analyzing behavior
               (b) and from which the subject seeks to seduce the other.
      2. The mirage of introspective monologue is opposed to the labor of free association.
         a. This labor involves "working through," and meets with:
            i. Frustration—not from the analyst's silence, but from the alienated *ego.*
            ii. Aggressivity—due not to frustrated desire, but to the slave's frustrated labor.
               (a) Hence the aggressive response to analysis of resistances,
               (b) and the danger of objectification by the analyst's focus on gestures.
                  (i) But even empty silence bears witness to the word,

(ii) and even the ending of a session punctuates its discourse.

iii. Regression — not as a real relation, but as an ego-activated fantasy relation.

(a) Thus the analyst cannot be guided by supposedly "real contact" with the subject,

(i) nor is it needed in supervision.

(ii) Instead he filters the musical score of the subject's discourse.

3. The empty word is ego-focused.

B. The full word

1. has the following characteristics:

a. anamnesis versus analysis of the here and now,

b. intersubjectivity versus intrasubjectivity,

c. symbolic interpretation versus analysis of resistance.

2. Anamnesis and the "talking cure" are not a function of consciousness.

a. Verbalization in hysteria and hypnosis relates the past to the present as necessities to come.

b. It is not a question of reality in recollection, but of truth,

i. as, for example, in Freud's treatment of the Wolf Man.

c. The subject's assumption of his history in dialogue is the ground of psychoanalysis.

3. The "talking cure" is intersubjective,

a. and the intersubjective continuity of the discourse aims to restore continuity in the subject's motivations.

4. Discontinuities in discourse mark the place of the unconscious as transindividual.

a. The unconscious participates in thought,

b. whose truth is inscribed in:

i. monuments of the body qua hysterical symptoms,

           ii. archival memories,

          iii. characterological and semantic evolution,

          iv. family legends,

          v. distortions in the continuity of experience.

     c. It is recovered in secondary historization,

          i. which reveals the subjective sense of instinctual stages

          ii. and not their analogical meaning.

  5. Even Freud made the theory of instincts subordinate to the historization of the subject in the word.

     a. The subject is not reducible to subjective experience,

     b. for his unconscious is structured by a discourse that is other to him.

II. *Symbol and language as structure and limit of the psychoanalytic field.*

  A. Psychoanalytic experience has a narrower focus than does common experience.

    1. Much of the patient's mode of experiencing remains unknown to us,

    2. which falsely leads us to seek "real contact" with patients.

  B. We return to Freud to rediscover the meaning of psychoanalytic experience as manifest particularly in:

    1. *The Interpretation of Dreams.*

     a. The dream is structured like a sentence,

          i. which is elaborated in its rhetoric of syntactical displacements and semantic condensations,

     b. and is the expression of dialectical desire.

    2. *The Psychopathology of Everyday Life.*

     a. Every parapraxis is a successful discourse.

     b. The symptom has the structure of language.

     c. The apparent chance combination of numbers reflects this structure.

    3. *Jokes and Their Relation to the Unconscious.*

     a. In the witticism the spirit shows reality to be

subordinated to the nonsensical.

    b. The point of wit always strikes the listener unexpectedly,

    c. implying an other that goes beyond the individual.

    d. In neglecting the language of symbols, psychoanalysis has changed its object.

C. The nature of fundamental discourse: the law of man is the law of language,

    1. originating in the exchange of gifts.

       a. Symbolic gifts signify a pact as signified,

       b. because as gifts their functional utility is neutralized.

       c. We see the origins of symbolic behavior in animals,

          i. but not in animal research that is ignorant of the nature of the sign.

             (a) The sign consists of the relation of the signifier to the signified,

             (b) and has distinctiveness and effectiveness as an element of language only in relation to the whole ensemble.

    2. The concept completes the symbol and makes language of it,

       a. freeing it from the here and now,

       b. producing a word that is a presence made of absence.

       c. Through the word, absence names itself,

          i. as in Freud's example of the *Fort! Da!*,

       d. giving birth to a particular language's universe of sense in which the universe of things is arranged.

       e. In this way the concept engenders the thing,

          i. and the world of words creates the universe of things.

          ii. Speech and the human world itself are made possible by the symbol.

D. The law of exchange governs the system of family ties,
   1. governing the exchange of women and gifts,
      a. according to an order which, like language, is imperative but unconscious in its structure.
   2. The Oedipus complex marks the limits of awareness of our unconscious participation in the primordial law.
      a. This law, in regulating matrimonial alliances, superimposes the kingdom of culture on the kingdom of nature.
   3. This law is the same as an order of language,
      a. making kinship nominations possible and weaving the yarn of lineage.
   4. The figure of the law is identified with the father.
      a. The symbolic father, expressed in the "name of the father," must be distinguished from the imaginary and the real father.
   5. The law is also expressed in the Great Debt, guaranteeing the exchange of wives and goods.
   6. This law is pervasive, precedes and follows man, and would be inexorable if desire did not introduce interferences.
E. The relation between the law of language and speech has negative and positive consequences.
   1. Negatively, three paradoxes result:
      a. In madness speech no longer tries to make itself recognizable;
         i. in delusions the subject is objectified in a language without dialectic,
         ii. so that he no longer speaks but is, rather, spoken.
      b. In the symptoms, inhibitions, and anxiety of neuroses, the word is driven out of conscious discourse,
         i. but finds support in organic stimuli or in images,

    ii. so that the symptom becomes the signifier of a signified repressed from consciousness,
        (a) and thus participates in language
        (b) that includes the discourse of the other.
    iii. In deciphering this word, Freud revealed the primary language of symbols.
    iv. Our exegesis resolves these hermetic elements by liberating the imprisoned meaning.
  c. In the objectifications of discourse, the subject loses his meaning.
    i. The subject is alienated in "scientific" civilization, forgetting his own existence and his death.
    ii. We meet this alienation when he talks to us about himself as ego.
    iii. We add to it when we talk of ego, superego, and id.
    iv. The thickness of this language barrier, which is opposed to speech, is measured in tons of print, miles of record grooves, etc.
2. Positively, the symbolic character of creative subjectivity has never been more manifest:
  a. in a revised conception of science as conjectural,
  b. with linguistics as a basic scientific model,
    i. yielding discoveries in ethnography and anthropology,
  c. and in a semiotic reorganization of the sciences.
    i. The symbolic function is a double movement within the subject in which action and knowledge alternate.
    ii. The opposition between the exact sciences and the conjectural sciences is erased,
        (a) for exactitude is distinguished from truth
        (b) and conjecture does not rule out rigor.
    iii. Even physics has a problematic relation to nature.

         (a) Experimental science is not defined by the quantitative nature of its object, but by its mode of measuring it.

            (i) The clock, operating by gravity, was used to measure the acceleration due to gravity.

      iv. Mathematics can also be applied to intersubjective time,

         (a) providing psychoanalytic conjecture with rigor.

      v. History sets an example for us.

      vi. Linguistics can help psychoanalytic practice.

      vii. Rhetoric, grammar, and poetics should be added to the "liberal arts" curriculum of the analyst in training.

III. *The resonances of interpretation and the time of the subject in psychoanalytic technique.*

  A. *The resonances of interpretation.*

    1. Psychoanalysis must return to the word and language as its base,

      a. rather than to the principles of the analysis of resistances,

        i. which lead to an ever greater miscognition of the subject,

        ii. and which principles Freud ignored in treating the Rat Man,

           (a) making instead a symbolic gift of the word.

      b. We choose instead to resonate with the word of the subject,

        i. so that analysis consists in sounding all the multiple keys of the musical score which the word constitutes in the registers of language.

    2. To understand the effect of Freud's word, we turn to its principles, not its terms.

      a. These principles are the dialectic of self-consciousness,

    b. but require a decentering from consciousness of self.

    c. Psychoanalysis reveals the unconscious as a universal structure disjunctive of the subject.

3. To free the word, we introduce the subject to the language of his desire, the primary language of symbols and symptoms.

    a. This language is both universal and particular.

        i. Freud deciphered it in our dreams;

        ii. Jones defined its essential field in reference to the body, kinship, birth, life, death.

    b. The symbol, though repressed, has its full effects by being heard;

    c. the analyst evokes its power by resonance.

        i. The Hindu tradition teaches us that the word can make understood what it does not say.

    d. Like prime numbers out of which all others are composed, symbols are the stuff of language.

    e. We restore the word's evocative power by using metaphor as a guide.

        i. Therefore we must assimilate, as Freud did, literature, poetics, folklore, etc.,

        ii. and we must do more than just attend to the "wording."

4. In its symbolizing function, the word transforms the subject addressed.

    a. We must distinguish symbol and signal.

        i. The dance of bees is a signal, not a language, because of the fixed correlation of sign to reality,

        ii. whereas linguistic signs acquire value from their relations to each other.

        iii. In addition, the bee's message is never retransmitted, but remains fixed as a relay of the action.

    b. Language is intersubjective.

    i. It invests the person addressed with a new
       reality.

   ii. The word always subjectively includes its
       own reply,
       (a) wherein what is unconscious becomes
           conscious.

  iii. As language becomes just information, "re-
       dundancies" become apparent.
       (a) These "redundancies" are precisely what
           does duty as the resonance of the word.

   iv. To be evocative rather than informative is
       the central function of language.
       (a) In the word, I seek the response of the
           other.
           (i) In calling the other person by what-
              ever name, I intimate to him his
              subjective function.
       (b) In his reply to the subject, the analyst
           either recognizes or abolishes the subject
           as subject.
           (i) All spoken interventions have a
              structuring function.

5. Language is a subtle body:
  a. words can be trapped in corporeal images,
  b. and suffer physical wounds;
  c. the discourse as a whole can be eroticized;
  d. the word can lose its status as symbol and be-
    come an imaginary or real object.

6. The advent of a true word and the subject's realization of his history remain the only goal of analysis.
  a. This is opposed to any objectifying orientation as
    seen in the aberrations of new tendencies in
    analysis.
  b. Freud even takes liberties with facts in order to
    reach the subject's truth.
    i. His treatment of the Rat Man gives abun-
      dant examples of this.

7. Responding to the analysand requires knowing where his ego is,
    a. that is, knowing through whom and for whom the patient poses *his* question.
        i. The hysterical subject is identified with an external spectacle.
        ii. The obsessional masters an internal stage.
    b. "Ego" must be distinguished from "I" if the subject's alienation is to be overcome.
        i. This is possible only in giving up the idea that the subject's ego is identical with the presence speaking.
        ii. This error is promoted by the psychoanalytic correlation of ego and reality in the topology of ego, id, and superego,
            (a) and leads to the subject's apprehending himself as an object.
            (b) In more and more refined splitting, he is expected to conform to the analyst's ego.
                (i) Such analysis of resistance leads to a negative transference, as in the case of Dora.
8. The present emphasis on analysis of resistance stems from the analyst's guilt about the power of the word.
    a. We deny responsibility for it by imputing magical thinking to the patient.
    b. We achieve distance through condescension.
    c. We fail to see the cunning of reason in both our scientific discourse and symbolic exchange.
    d. In attending to the un-said in the gaps of discourse, we should not listen as if someone were knocking on the other side of a wall,
        i. for in attempting to translate nonlinguistic sounds we must look to the patient to confirm our understanding.
        ii. In illusion we are led to seek his reality be-

yond the wall of language,

   iii. just as he believes his truth is given to us in advance and thus he remains vulnerable to objectification at our hands,

      (a) wherein the effects of the transference are constituted.

  9. In distinguishing the symbolic, the imaginary, and the real, we see that there are reality factors in the analysis:

    a. in the transference there are real feelings responding to our person as real factor;

    b. reality is encountered in both the analyst's interventions and his abstention;

    c. in his punctuating reply to the subject's true word.

    d. There is also a junction of the symbolic and the real in the pure negativity of the analyst's silence as well as in the function of time.

B. *The time of the subject in psychoanalytic technique.*

  1. The duration of the analysis must remain indefinite.

    a. We cannot predict the subject's "time for understanding."

    b. To fix a date is to alienate the subject and act as if he can place his truth in us,

      i. as occurred in Freud's treatment of the Wolf Man.

  2. The duration of the session is often obsessionally fixed by the analyst,

    a. whereas as gatherer of the lasting word and witness of his sincerity, the analyst punctuates the subject's discourse in ending the session.

      i. In manuscripts and symbolic writing, punctuation removes ambiguity and fixes the meaning.

    b. A fixed hour lends itself to connivance in the obsessional subject,

      i. who in his forced labor waits for the master's death,

       ii. and is alienated, living as he does in the fu-
          ture and identifying himself with the dead
          master.
       iii. His "working through," then, is a seduction
          of the analyst.
    c. The use of short sessions breaks the discourse in
       order to give birth to speech.
3. Beyond the wall of language lies the outer darkness
   of death.
    a. Freud's "death instinct" is rejected by those who
       share an erroneous view of the ego and of speech.
    b. The ironic conjunction of "death" and "instinct"
       expresses the polar relation of life and death at
       the heart of life,
       i. whose resonances must be approached in the
          poetics of the Freudian work.
    c. The death instinct expresses the limit of Heideg-
       gerean man as Being-unto-death.
4. The profound relationship uniting the notion of the
   death instinct to the problems of the word makes the
   notion of primordial masochism unnecessary.
    a. In the repetitive game of *Fort! Da!* we see speech
       develop as separation is faced.
    b. In this moment of inchoative speech desire be-
       comes human.
    c. In mastering absence the verbal action becomes
       its own object to itself.
    d. In the child's solitude his desire becomes the
       desire of an other.
5. As the symbol negates the object of desire, desire
   becomes eternalized.
    a. The tomb is the first symbol of man's presence.
    b. Death is the intermediary between man and his-
       tory.
       i. Among animals the individual death passes
          into the species, while among men suicidal

death as symbolic passes into history.

   c. Man's freedom is inscribed within the borders of death as threat, self-sacrifice, and negation of the other as master.

   d. It is from death that the subject's existence takes on its meaning.

6. The meaning of death shows absence to be the heart of speech.

   a. The circularity of the torus exemplifies the death-bounded dialectic of analysis,

      i. a dialectic that is not individualistic,

      ii. and has implications for the training of the analyst.

   b. Humanity is formed by the law of the word.

      i. It is in the gift of the word that the effects of psychoanalysis reside.

      ii. All reality comes to man by this gift,

      iii. whose domain is enough for our action, knowledge, and devotion.

NOTES TO THE TEXT

30/237   Additional historical background to the "Discourse at Rome" is provided by Turkle (1975, pp. 336–337; 1978, pp. 97–118). Wilden (1968) also provides important background information and highlights the spirit of the "Discourse" (pp. xxiii–xxvi). In addition, the reader is directed to his 65 pages of notes to the text, some further reference to which will be made below.

35a/242   The "subject" in this case appears to refer to the analyst, whose alibi for loss of effectiveness is the patient's resistance. At times the "subject" can refer to either the patient or analyst and sometimes both at once.

37g/245   The "c factor" remains a conundrum for us (but see note 106b below).

40*d–e*/
248

In failing to realize that his silence is a reply, the analyst experiences it as a void to be filled with speech about behavior. His word is then rendered suspect since it is a reply only to the felt failure of his own silence in the face of (the English text misreads "in the fact of") his own echoing void.

The analyst's move parallels the patient's lifelong attempt to overcome his own gap or dehiscence (now called *béance*) by means of the narcissistic and imaginary constructs of his ego through which he strives for the other's recognition.

The reference to "humbler needs" *(besoins)* would seem to be taken up later (p. 46*a*/254) under the rubric of "the individual psycho-physiological factors" which are excluded from the analytic relation, i.e., physical needs which place the primary emphasis on the "real" as opposed to the symbolic (verbal) contact between the patient and analyst.

42*b*/
249–250

As Lacan indicates in his footnote (1977, p. 107, n. 10/250, n. 1), these "theorists" include *notre ami* Michael Balint, who writes of "the analytical cure of *ejaculatio praecox*...because the ego has been strengthened" (1938, p. 196).

43*c*/251

Since progress lies in "an ever-growing dispossession" of the ego as "his construct in the imaginary" (p. 42*a*/249), teaching the subject *what* he has been leads only to greater objectification.

43*g*/251

In his excellent note to this paragraph, Wilden (1968, pp. 101–102) brings together *tessera* as password, object of pottery used for recognition, and *symbolon* and also specifics the text from Mallarmé.

45*b*/253

Lacan often compares discourse to a polyphonic musical score (e.g., 1977, p. 154*d*/503), suggesting multiple levels of ongoing signification.

46*f*/255

Aufhebung is the rich Hegelian term with a loose meaning of an "overcoming" or "negating" whereby what is overcome is integrated.

48*d*/257   Wilden again provides a very helpful note here:

> Lacan's analysis of this sophism is concerned with the psychological and temporal process involved between three hypothetical prisoners of which the first to discover whether he is wearing a black or white patch on his back has been offered his freedom by the prison governor. The prisoners are not allowed to communicate directly. The governor has shown them three white patches and two black patches and has fixed a white patch on each man's back.
>
> Lacan analyzes the intersubjective process in which each man has to put himself in the place of the others and to gauge the correctness of his deductions through their actions in time, from the *instant du regard* to the *moment de conclure*. The first moment of the *temps pour comprendre* is a wait (which tells each man that no one can see two black patches), followed by a decision by each that he is white ('If I were black, one of the others would have *already* concluded that he is white, because nobody has yet started for the door.') Then they all set off towards the door and all hesitate in a retrospective moment of doubt. The fact that they *all* stop sets them going again. This hesitation will only be repeated twice (in this hypothetically ideal case), before all three leave the prison cell together [1968, pp. 105–106].

He refers to Lacan's paper in *Écrits* (1966, pp. 197–213).

55*c*/264   As Wilden writes, " '*Une vérité de La Palice*' is a self-evident truth, a truism" (1968, p. 110). The identical note appears in Sheridan's translation (Lacan, 1977, p. 108).

55*e*/265   The now-classic phrase, "the unconscious of the subject is the discourse of the other," refers to the trans-individual, universal structure of language as the domain in which gaps in conscious discourse are experienced as foreign by the individual subject; in addition, but not secondarily, it refers to the way desire (for the other and for recognition by the other) is signified through the operations of metaphor and metonymy, i.e., through unconscious condensation and displacement or linguistic substitution and combination.

56*b*/265   The third term is the "other."

56/266   The Gospel text admits of several translations, including "What I have told you all along" (New English Bible New Testament), "Why do I talk to you at all" (Oxford Annotated Bible, Revised Standard Version), and "What I have told you from the outset" (Jerusalem Bible). Lacan may have read the translation from the Vulgate, "I am the Beginning who speaks to you," now seen as grammatically impossible. See his later reference, "it was certainly the Word *(verbe)* that was in the beginning" (1977, p. 61*d*/271).

58*a*/268   The first broad division, "the syntactical displacements," group together linguistic mechanisms in which the deliberate alteration of word order appears to be the common element, e.g.:

> *Ellipsis* involves the omission of understood words.
> *Pleonasm* refers to a redundancy or fullness of language, as in "with my own eyes I saw..."
> *Hyperbaton* is the inverting of word order, as in "echoed the hills."
> *Syllepsis* uses one word to govern two while agreeing with only one in gender, case, or number, or uses one word in the same grammatical relation to two adjacent words, one metaphorical and one literal, as in "taunts more cutting than knives."
> *Apposition* sets a second word beside the first with

the same referent and grammatical place (as in "the River Tiber") or a second phrase beside the first in a loose attribution (as in "to kill the prisoners — a barbarous act").

The second group, the "semantic condensations," appears to rely on the use of one word in place of another, e.g.:

Metaphor uses a word literally denoting one thing in place of another, often to suggest some sort of likeness between them.

Catachresis involves the incorrect use of one word for another, as "demean" for "debase," or a forced or paradoxical usage, as in "blind mouths."

Antonomasia substitutes an epithet, such as proper title for proper name, or vice versa, as in "Solomon" or "His Majesty." (The English text misprints "autonomasis.")

Allegory describes one thing under the guise of another in a prolonged metaphor.

Metonymy operates according to the principle of contiguity, designating an attribute of a thing or something closely related to it for the thing itself it suggests, as the effect for the cause, the container for the contained, the geographical name for the event or function.

Synecdoche uses the part to designate the whole or the whole for the part, the species for the genus (or the genus for the species), or the material for the thing made, as in "thirty sail" for "thirty ships," "the smiling year" for "spring," "boards" for "stage," etc.

(The above was drawn from *Webster's New International Dictionary* [1960] and *Webster's New Collegiate Dictionary* [1974].)

It would be consistent to relate the first group to Jakobson's axis of combination and Lacan's description of the "word-to-word connexion" while the second group illustrates the axis of substitution and Lacan's "one word for another." Lacan isn't consistent in this way, however, since the "word-to-word connexion" he associates with metonymy, which appears in the second group. There is further discussion of these figures of speech and Lacan's definitions in "The Agency of the Letter in the Unconscious" (1977, pp. 156–164, 169/505–516, 521).

58*b*/268   One way to read this might be that the dream's law comes *d'autrui*, from the place of the other, thus from a place other than Freud's own conscious processes.

59*b*/269   The French text is more intelligible here in saying that "the symptom resolves itself entirely in an analysis of language, because it [the symptom] is itself structured like a language, because it [the symptom] is language from which speech [*la parole*] must be set free" ("le symptôme se résout tout entier dans une analyse de langage, parce qu'il est lui-même structuré comme un langage, qu'il est langage dont la parole doit être délivrée"). The symptom is structured or "knotted" by the nodal points *(les noeuds)* which are signifiers that function as coordinates for the network of associations. Lacan elsewhere (1977, p. 154/503) calls them *points de capiton,* upholstery buttons, which bind together from below the mass of associative material. Tracking the associations to these nodal points and resonating with the key words (switch-words) liberates the words, thus resolving the symptom.

Ferenczi (1912) gives the example of a woman patient whose dream he interprets as expressing a desire for a better-educated husband, more beautiful clothes, etc:

At this moment the patient's attention was deflected from the analysis by the sudden onset of toothache. She begged me to give her something to ease the pain, or at least to get her a glass of water. Instead of doing so, I explained to the patient that by the toothache she was perhaps only expressing in a metaphorical way the Hungarian saying "My tooth is aching for these good things." I said this not at all in a confident tone, nor had she any idea that I expected the pain to cease after the communication. Yet, quite spontaneously and very astonished, she declared that the toothache had suddenly ceased. [p. 167].

In Lacanian terms we can read this as an instance of how a new signifier (toothache) is substituted for the original signifier (*Fájrá a fogam*, "My tooth aches for it") and thereby the symptom becomes structured as a metaphor. Ferenczi is able to suggest to the patient the importance of this substitution and by interpreting the symptom linguistically (i.e., as a metaphor) the symptom is relieved by the power of the spoken word itself (rather than by taking some other action).

    This is the first time in these essays that Lacan explicitly presents the tension between language *(langage)* and speech *(la parole)*, a theme he dwells on later in this section (see 1977, p. 68/279).

60*c–d*/270   The Freudian texts are specified in the notes to the English translation (1977, pp. 108–109) and again they parallel Wilden's notes (1968, p. 117).

61*d*/271   The effort to reflect back on the originative action of the unconscious prompts the creation of a new verbal expression, as Lacan's example itself illustrates.

61*f*/272   The Argonauts were a group of 50 Greek heroes led by Jason. They sailed the Aegean and Black Seas (in the first long ship, the Argo) on their way to obtain the Golden Fleece and return it to Greece. The French

Danaën appears to be the generic term for Greeks and the reference would be to the Trojan horse.

63a/273 The reference is to C. V. Hudgins (1933). This is described as a "celebrated experiment" in *Carmichael's Manual of Child Psychology* (Mussen, 1970, p. 951).

65d/276 The play of the child is, of course, the *Fort! Da!* episode. Its relation to presence and absence and the birth of speech was discussed earlier by us (pp. 18–23) and is taken up again by Lacan (see below, 1977, p. 103d/318).

65f/276 One implication seems to be that language differentiates things just as the child's rudimentary phonemes enable him to differentiate from his mother.

66a/276 The law of symbolic exchange, in which the neutralization of the signifier and the law of language are revealed (see above, 1977, pp. 61–62/272), determines the symbolic equivalence of the gift of a woman and the gift of a thigh of an elephant. Wilden (1968, p. 126) notes that the proverb is the epigraph to Lévi-Strauss' *Elementary Structures of Kinship* (1949b). A note to the English text does the same without reference to Wilden. This repetition occurs so frequently that no further alert will be given to the reader and discretionary use of Wilden's notes will continue.

68c/279 The salvific import of "being-for-death" is missing in Heidegger.

68d/279 The precise sense of *les cycles du langage* and of *les ordres* is unclear; perhaps Lacan means that language is diachronic and thus has cycles, and is calling attention to the symbolic, imaginary, and real orders—all related to the expression of desire.

69e/280 Wilden's note on the role of illness (supplied by Hyppolite) makes reference to the Hegelian texts (1968, p. 130).

70d/280 The unified gestalt of the idealized ego-image hides the experience of fragmentation just as the pretensions of the *belle âme* cover its projection of internal disorder onto the world.

71*c*/282   The "sectors A, B, and C" may echo the "*c* factor" (1977, p. 37/245).

71*d*/283   The implication seems to be that the more the psycho-analyst demands "true" speech as opposed to empty talk after the manner of "the precautions against verbalism that are a theme of the discourse of the 'normal' man in our culture" (p. 71*b*/282), the more he appears to reinforce the thickness of the wall of language. This is clearly a logical snare, to be denounced in the same way that Hegel, abstract idealist philosopher that he was, denounced "the philosophy of the cranium," i.e., phrenology, and Pascal spoke of the ironies of madness.

72*f*/284   The movement, of course, was and is structuralism.

73*e*–*f*/ 284–285   The reference is to the work of Jakobson and Halle (1956).

75*d*–*e*/ 287   See our note (Wilden's actually) to p. 48*d*.

76*d*/288   The epistemological triangle he describes is unclear to us.

80*a*/292   Lacan sees Freud's corrective to Hegel in his discovery of the unconscious, which requires a decentering from ego-consciousness. (The ex-centric or decentered subject is a major theme in "The Agency of the Letter in the Unconscious" [1977, pp. 165–166/516–517].)

80*c*–*d*/ 292   The unconscious as discourse of the other provides the locus for the identity of the particular (in terms of the subject's desire as expressed in his own signifying chains of metaphor and metonymy) with the universal (in terms of the transindividual structure of language). Such an unconscious, defined earlier as "that part of the concrete discourse. . . not at the disposal of the subject in re-establishing the continuity of his conscious discourse" (1977, p. 49/258) is disjunctive of the subject, prohibiting any description of him as *individuum*.

81*a*/293   It is typical of Lacan to arch broadly and obscurely across philosophical history from Plato to Kierkegaard. We can take a few tentative steps toward understanding by suggesting that the Platonic *skopia*, a vision of the whole as well as underlying pattern, provides a model for Lacan, but with the following corrective: whereas Plato's vision is grounded in the recollection of eternal essences and Kierkegaard's in the repetition anticipated in an eternal future, Lacan places himself in-between and thereby accents here the temporality and historicity of the subject and of truth.

81*b*/293   The dialogue in Lewis Carroll is as follows:

> ". . . there are three hundred and sixty-four days when you might get un-birthday presents—"
>
> "Certainly," said Alice.
>
> "And only *one* for birthday presents, you know. There's glory for you!"
>
> "I don't know what you mean by 'glory,' " Alice said.
>
> Humpty Dumpty smiled contemptuously. "Of course you don't—till I tell you. I mean 'there's a nice knock-down argument for you!' "
>
> "But 'glory' doesn't mean a 'nice knock-down argument,' " Alice objected.
>
> "When I use a word," Humpty Dumpty said in rather a scornful tone, "it means just what I choose it to mean—neither more nor less."
>
> "The question is," said Alice, "whether you *can* make words mean so many different things."
>
> "The question is," said Humpty Dumpty, "which is to be master—that's all" [1923, p. 246].

81*d*/   There are hints here of an individuating principle
293–294   whereby the moment of differentiation from the mother

is achieved when the infant's desire for her presence is articulated and embedded in universal discourse by means of its idiosyncratic rudimentary speech (in the *Fort! Da!* experience). What remains obscure is the relationship between the elementary phonemes and the symbolism of primary language.

81*e*/294 Jean Francois Champollion deciphered hieroglyphics in 1821 and thereby merited being called the founder of Egyptology.

82*e*/294 Wilden's note offers a definition of *dhvani* that stresses the word's power to convey a sense different from its primary or secondary meaning (1968, p. 142).

82*h*/295 This is an especially tricky paragraph. Lacan does *not* appear to be saying that symbols are the ultimate signifieds for all the words of a language, but rather that they are subjacent to *(sous-jacents à)* all the meaning-units of language, with a relationship to them closely analogous to (but not identical with) the relationship between prime numbers and composite integers. "A prime number is an integer $p > 1$ divisible only by 1 and p; the first few primes are 2, 3, 5, 7, 11, 13, 17, and 19. Integers that have other divisors are called composite; examples are 4, 6, 8, 9, 10, 12, . . ." (Harris and Levey, 1975, p. 1978). Composites, therefore, are the products of prime numbers. In a sense symbols, therefore, are the "stuff" of units of meaning, causing a kind of multiplying static by their presence. By using the thread of metaphor, with its substitute signifier tuning in to the secondary associative chains of the displaced signifier, we can search for their presence and thereby restore to the word its full evocative power by resonating with them.

84*d*/297 A more recent description of the waggle dance (not exactly Lacan's) can be found in Wilson (1975, pp. 177–178).

85*b–c*/ What is *la forme, la forme essentielle* which is at stake
298   here? Judging by Lacan's examples, it would seem to

be the second-person singular and as such indicating the opening of a domain inclusive of the other in so radical a fashion that to address another in any way (not just with the solemnity of vows) is to invest him with a new reality, a new role, minimally the role of respondent.

94e/309 Buddhist references to love (passion, attachment), hate (aversion, aggression), and ignorance (delusion, confusion) are common; for example, the saviors "promote the virtues of the faithful, help to remove greed, hate, and delusion" (Conze, 1951, p. 152).

95e/ The point may be that the analyst's abstention, when
309–310 it is based on the principle that all that occurs in the work on the unconscious level is accessible as the discourse of the other (and thus he remains silent to let the other speak), combines the elements of both a real intervention and a symbolic reply.

102c/317 Wilden's useful note (1968, pp. 151–152) discusses the phrase's transferred sense in relation to the theory of *dhvani* or suggestion (see also note 82e above).

102e/318 The two principles governing all change, as formulated by Empedocles (of Acragas, now Agrigento, Sicily), are specified (in 103c) as love and strife. See Kirk and Raven (1957) for further information. Freud makes a lengthy comparison between the views of Empedocles and his own (1937, pp. 244–247).

103a/318 See Heidegger (1927, p. 250). Heidegger doesn't speak of a *subject* in this way, but rather of *Dasein*. What Heidegger means by *Dasein* is a specific existential-ontological structure. What Lacan means by *subject* is highly problematic. A preliminary effort to relate Lacan's notion of the subject to Heidegger's *Dasein* may be found in Richardson (1978–1979).

Earlier Lacan spoke of "recollection" (1977, p. 48/256) and suggested a Heideggerean context for it

(1977, p. 47/255); moreover, he repudiates a Nietzschean interpretation (1977, p. 112, n. 112/318).

103d/318   The *Fort! Da!* experience, discussed earlier, is Lacan's focus for the next six paragraphs.

103f/319   In mastering desire through language (i.e., by mastering the mother's presence and absence in the words repeated now for their own sake), the child's desire is fragmented, multiplied, squared (raised to a second power) as it becomes articulated through the endless signifying chain. Now present somehow in words (i.e., symbolically — the whole mystery of language) the object is "destroyed" in its reality: thus Lacan goes on to say that "the symbol manifests itself first of all as the murder of the thing" (p. 104c/319). In this experience of differentiation and distance from the mother, the child experiences his own separate, limited reality (against that background of the ultimate horizon of limit, death) and seeks to be recognized by her, i.e., desires to be the object of her desire (the dialectic of self-consciousness begins). For a Husserlian analysis of presence and absence in language, see Sokolowski (1978).

104b/319   The child here seems to be engaged in the *Fort! Da!* or peek-a-boo game with another.

104c/319   Now trapped in the symbolic order, desire is never fulfilled but achieves a kind of eternalization in language (a familiar theme in poetry).

105a/320   An exact illustration is offered by the death of the patient Billy Bibbitt in *One Flew Over the Cuckoo's Nest* (Kesey, 1962).

105b/320   Death is the limit, the boundary that de-fines man and the point from which he begins to be. To speak of "desire for death" in this Heideggerean context can only mean, as Lacan says three paragraphs later, that it is "in the full assumption of his being-for-death," that is, in authentically accepting his ownmost possibilities, that he can affirm himself for others. Anything short of this, such as narcissistically identifying with the other or struggling to be the object of the other's desire is to be caught up in the imaginary structures of the ego.

105c–d/
320–321

We take the phrase "mortal meaning" to suggest again that the "meaning" of the subject, de-fined as "mortal" (i.e., by death) through speech, has a "centre exterior to language" in the sense that its center, as individual, is other than the transindividual center of language itself. As for the topological allusions here, they anticipate a later period in the development of Lacan's thought and require for an understanding of them an exposition that is broader and more comprehensive than the present one. We defer a discussion of these issues, then, to a later day.

106b/321

Wilden's note (1968, p. 156) quotes Freud (1905a): "It is a rule of psychoanalytic technique that an internal connection which is still undisclosed will announce its presence by means of a contiguity — a temporal proximity — of associations; just as in writing, if 'a' and 'b' are put side by side, it means that the syllable 'ab' is to be formed out of them" (p. 39).

The factors b for biology and c for culture may shed light on the previous two references (see 37g, where "the c factor" belongs to culture, and 71c, where culture includes the sectors A, B, and C).

106f–i/
322

Eliot's *The Waste Land* (1922) ends:

> Datta Dayadhvam Damyata
> Shantih Shantih Shantih

In his notes to the poem, Eliot translates these as "Give, sympathize, control" and refers to the Brihadaranyaka-Upanishad, 5, 1 for the fable of the meaning of the thunder. Lacan also gives the same reference: "lisons-nous au premier Brâhmana de la

cinquième leçon du Bhrad-âranyaka Upanishad."
Wilden (1968), however, in his translation writes,
"so we read in the second Brahmana of the fifth les-
son" and in his English text Sheridan (1977) follows
Wilden.

Chapter 4

The Freudian Thing,
or the Meaning of the Return to Freud
in Psychoanalysis

Overview

Lacan refers to this essay as an "amplification" of a lecture he gave at the Neuropsychiatric Clinic in Vienna on November 7, 1955, a little more than two years after his "Discourse at Rome." We find that language remains fixed in the central place given to it at Rome, while ego psychology comes under severe attack as Lacan attempts to delineate authentic Freudian psychoanalysis according to his re-reading of Freud.

The use of *thing (la chose Freudienne)* in his title here allows Lacan to make a number of points. Mannoni (1971) remarks that the Lacanians found it was necessary to work on Freud's theory "like a thing," an expression Freud himself used in a letter to Fliess (1887–1902, pp. 129, 133). In French, *la chose Freudienne* also refers more generally to "the Freudian matter" or "the Freudian business." In this essay it more specifically indicates the transpersonal but material agency of language from which "it speaks" in the unconscious. Concretely, in this essay Lacan does make a thing speak. His style here is a bit more flamboyant, even theatrical, as he presents, in this operatic city, truth speaking from center stage, protagonists, a talking desk, an interlude, and the mythical figures of Actaeon and his hunting dogs in pursuit of Diana, representing truth in her nakedness.

The essay is divided into 13 sections (we have given them a numbered sequence), each with its own title. Some are suggestive of the romantic novel ("The adversary," "[The] imaginary passion") or silent film captions ("Resistance to the resisters"). While the titles appear loosely to punctuate the flow of thought, some broad divisions are offered to provide further unification. The first section is Lacan's *mise en scène*, positing as the essay's central theme that as a result of Freud's discovery "the very centre of the human being was no longer to be found at the place assigned to it by a whole humanist tradition" (1977, p. 114/ 401). The next five sections deal with the relations between truth and the signifier. Section VII is titled "Interlude," and as the longest section it can be seen as the turning point of the essay, putting into question the place of the ego and of consciousness in relation to meaning. The outcome of such questioning leads Lacan to assert that the ego is no different from the nearby desk as far as discourse is concerned. The five sections following the Interlude deal with the distinction between the ego and the Other, "between the field of the ego and that of the unconscious" (1977, p. 142/433). The final section is an exhortation regarding the role language should play in the formation of analysts. There is a balance, then, in the essay's structure (1-5-1-5-1) which is not evident at first.

I

Situation in time and place of this exercise

In 1955 Austria (and Vienna) achieved reunification with neutral status after the post-World War II division into four zones of occupation. Lacan appears to allude to this when he

speaks of Vienna making itself heard once again through its op-
era and thereby "resuming what had always been its mission,
namely, to create harmony at this point of cultural convergence
as only it knew how" (1977, p. 114/401). Lacan has come to this
"eternal city of Freud's discovery" to herald the return to Freud.
Such heralding is not without conflict, however, for Lacan is
quick to note the failure of the International Psycho-Analytical
Association to commemorate the house where Freud worked.
He also launches, almost immediately, into his usual criticism
of American psychoanalysis. The same war that divided Vienna
drove emigrants to the United States, where "a cultural ahis-
toricism" (1977, p. 115/402) prevails in defining the kind of assimilation required in order to achieve status–recognition. The
European psychoanalysts had to assimilate by gaining status-
recognition for differences vis-à-vis patients (who were quick to
demand such differences) according to "the reactionary principle operant in the duality of the sick and the healer" (1977, p.
115/403). In their way of adapting to American society they fall
under Lacan's criticism for forgetting history and its function in
analysis. What has become of psychoanalytic theory since Freud's
death, moreover, shows what psychoanalysis is not, and in
urging a return to Freud, Lacan seeks to revitalize what has
continued to sustain psychoanalytic practice.

Freud's work is a coherent effort to maintain a "primary
rigour" amid different stages and changes in direction. It not
only answers the questions it poses, but even goes beyond this
to provide answers to present questions. The systematic study
of Freud's texts yields genuine discoveries of unused concepts, clinical details, and methodology that transform clinical
practice.

II

The adversary

Lacan insists that the "meaning of a return to Freud is a
return to the meaning of Freud" (1977, p. 117/405), a meaning

addressed to all of us, for Freud put the truth into question, and the truth personally concerns each of us. It should especially concern psychoanalysts since analysis rediscovers the power of truth in the analysis of symptoms and of defenses against unconscious tendencies. The peace that follows the recognition of such tendencies signals the truth. This signal is rendered questionable, however, by a theory that views the ego's defenses as unconscious and even goes so far as to identify mechanisms of defense with the dynamics of the unconscious. Haven't we gone too far "when we admit that the drive itself may be led to consciousness by the defence in order to prevent the subject from recognizing [himself in] it"? (1977, p. 118/406). Lacan's obvious concern here is to keep the field of the ego distinct from the processes of the unconscious, although he doesn't spell out the latter, referring rather to "tendency" *(tendance)* and "drive" *(pulsion)*. To do justice to "these mysteries" Lacan must resort to another kind of duality, one that sustains the words of the discourse. This can only be the signifier-signified couple to be defined in Section V.

Lacan responds to critics who charge him with being an overly philosophical ideologist by stating that the criterion for truth is intrinsic to the psychoanalytic situation for "Psychoanalysis is the science of the mirages that appear within this field" (1977, p. 119/407). As a "unique" and "abject" experience, it is useful "to those who wish to be introduced to the principle of man's follies, for, by revealing itself as akin to a whole gamut of disorders, it throws light upon them" (1977, p. 119/407). For Lacan it is absurd to claim that analytic practice is strictly tied to unalterable forms discovered by chance and that analysis leads reductionistically only to ahistorical, preoedipal realities (oral and anal) that provide the illusion of truth. Analysis was situated by Freud in the oedipal framework and thus it opens onto "all the fields of creation" (i.e., the entire symbolic order). It began with a particular truth, an "unveiling" (this usually has reference to the phallus), with the result that after Freud "reality is no longer the same for us as it was before" (1977, p. 120/408). For the most part, however, truth is so easily confused with its surrounding reality that it is in her nakedness that truth best attracts our attention (although she subsequently suffers at our hands) and it is in death that she is best preserved (a notion of death involving the ego and the analyst that will be taken up later).

III
The thing speaks of itself

Rather than identifying the criterion for truth, Lacan has truth herself promise: "I will teach you by what sign you will recognize me" (1977, p. 121/409). The discourse of error and Hegel's notion of "the cunning of reason" are suggested as approaches, but it is rather the unintended mistake, "the unsuccessful" act, the dream and the joke that are the signs of truth. For this reason, the "trade route of truth no longer passes through thought," truth is no longer a function of consciousness or the ego. Rather, the way lies through things. "[Rebus,] it is through you that I communicate," says truth, echoing Freud's work on the riddle of the dream (1977, p. 122/410). Lacan also echoes Heidegger by situating truth in being rather than in the fortress of consciousness. The things which are signs of "the truth who speaks" are linguistic signs, material taken up by language, like Cleopatra's nose in Pascal's aphorism. And if reason's cunning were somehow made consciously intelligible, truth would become deceit, for her ways pass through the dream, the mediocre, the absurd. Truth, in short, is contradictory for the logic of natural consciousness.

IV
Parade

This title invokes images of display, pageantry, and exhibition; it is the term used to refer to male courting rituals among animals. This most theatrical section begins with truth disappearing into the shadows or the underworld of death, signaling

a search for the murderer, the one hiding the truth, the speaker
— the three seem to be the same. The blame falls on the ego in
this "drama of knowledge," but the scene shifts and we now see
the protagonist Freud as Actaeon pursuing the goddess of truth.
She offers him "the quasi-mystical limit of the most rational discourse in the world," the limit suggesting a barrier, where "the
symbol is substituted for death" (recall the link between language, limit, and death [Chapter 3, p. 94]) and the symbol operates "in order to take possession of the first swelling of life" (the
moment when desire becomes part of the signifying chain)
(1977, p. 124/412). In other words, the truth is that every discourse is bound by a limiting factor constituted in the way the
word is "a presence made of absence" or "the murder of the thing,"
originating from the first moment of separation (limit) from the
mother. This is the moment of first human desire, signified by
the phallus that the child desires to be for the mother but later
must forgo in the oedipal resolution — the symbolic castration
which is the price paid to enter the symbolic order.

All of this, Lacan assures us, is beyond the reach of Freud's
disciples, whom he tries to reorient with the words spoken by
truth: "I speak" and "There is no speech that is not language."
We have mistakenly emphasized the "I" rather than the speech.
Language, moreover, is an order constituted by laws, not natural expression, code, or information; in this order one properly
says, following Freud, that *it speaks*, and it does so "where it is
least expected, namely, where there is pain" (1977, p. 125/413).
To know more, we must follow Saussure.

V

Order of the thing

In this section we approach the heart of the Lacanian re-
reading of Freud. We begin with the signifier-signified distinction of Saussure. Lacan here associates the signifier with language material (phonemes) and the order of synchrony, that is,
the coexisting ensemble of distinctive phonemic features, each

identified solely by its relation of difference from all the others present in the existing language structure. The network of the signified Lacan associates with "concretely pronounced discourses" (i.e., speech) and the order of diachrony, that is, the actual words sequentially chained to produce a meaningful statement. The statement's coherence or "unity of signification" is never resolved in a "pure indication of the real" (does not get its meaning from "real" objects) but always "refers back to another signification," i.e., the signifier refers not to a given signified but to another signifier. Ultimately we must affirm that we stand in a kind of circle of understanding in which "the signification is realized only on the basis of a grasp of things in their totality" (1977, p. 126/414). This grasp is a function of the signifier which "alone guarantees the theoretical coherence of the whole as a whole." The signification, furthermore, cannot be reduced to the level of information, for speech implies more than what is said.

These are the bases that distinguish language from mere signs (Lacan made this point in the "Discourse at Rome" [1977, p. 84/297]). These linguistic bases put the notion of dialectic in a new light. The illustration of the dialectic chosen by Lacan is Hegel's critique of the "beautiful soul," a particular stage in the dialectic of self-consciousness in which individual conscience (earlier called "the law of the heart") becomes the ultimate criterion for condemning the behavior of others. This leads eventually to the condition described by Lauer (1976): "Since *doing* anything runs the risk of sullying its purity, for the 'beautiful soul' *saying* the right thing becomes all important." As moral critic, the beautiful soul "wants to impose on the man of action the obligation of justifying himself in words, with the result that everything is levelled off, and the very distinction between good and evil becomes a matter of words." When the other admits he has done wrong, the beautiful soul "does not admit the same in regard to himself; as critic he is not subject to criticism" (pp. 226–227). In this way the self-centeredness becomes apparent so that (in Heidegger's description of the day-to-day ontic level of being) the glib talk of the beautiful soul partakes of the same fallenness as the disordered behavior that is criticized. Thus Lacan can speak of "the tauto-ontic of the *belle âme* as mediation, unrecognized by itself, of that disorder as primary in being" (1977, p. 126/415).

Recognition by law is the basis given by Hegel for the dignity of the "person," and Lacan equates this with the "I" of consciousness (this equation is open to question). He can then play off Freud against Hegel in making this "I" (ego) "responsible for the manifest disorder to be found in the most enclosed field of the real being," i.e., in the imaginary "pseudo-totality" of this organism (1977, p. 127/415). The basis of the disorder is prior to the mirror stage, in the congenital gap (*béance*) of prematurity at birth, and in the later return in discourse of imaginary (bodily) elements that appear fragmented (*morcelés*) in this gap. In other words, the defensive self-righteousness of the ego arises to cover the gap and overcome the fear of fragmentation, and this internal disorder is in turn denounced in the other, who is seen as a threat to the ego.

But this genesis is not required to demonstrate the signifying structure of the symptom, for the symptom is a signifier and can be deciphered in a sequence of signification to reveal the omnipresence of the signifying function for the human being. This function determines the meaning of exchange to the extent that society is not a collection of individuals but an "immixture of subjects" mutually transformed by the symbolic order. Such transformation places the incidence of truth as cause at the level of the subject, and thus introduces inherent heterogeneity. Lacan may be referring here to the truth-perception of one class of men in conflict with another, so central to the Marxist dialectic, whose resistance to psychoanalysis is therefore unwarranted since "its ethic is not an individualist one" (1977, p. 127/416), the American example of individualistic success notwithstanding.

Lacan now turns to his main theme: that the subject, "the legatee of recognized truth," "the true subject of the unconscious," is not the ego of consciousness, "constituted in its nucleus by a series of alienating identifications" (1977, p. 128/417). He proceeds to re-read Freud's (1933) formula *"Wo Es war, soll Ich werden,"* not as it has entered English, "Where the id was, there the ego shall be," in the sense that the ego supplants the id. Lacan's lucid analysis leads him to conclude that Freud's formula signifies: " 'There where it was' *('Là où c'était'),* I would like it to be understood, 'it is my duty that I should come to being' " (1977, p. 129/417–418). What is at stake is not a grammatical conception of how the "I" *(le je)* and the ego *(le moi)* relate, but a process somehow on the level of being, rather than ego consciousness, whereby the "I" as subject comes to being in the unconscious, comes to "emerge. . . from this very locus in so far as it is a locus of being" (1977, p. 128/417). All of this affects analytic practice, especially the handling of transference and resistance, to which Lacan now turns.

VI
Resistance to the resisters

Now that the argument has gained momentum, this title exhorts us not to be sidetracked. After the previous section's emphasis on the centrality of language and the symbolic order, the warning is needed, for we must "remember that the first resistance with which analysis has to deal is that of the discourse itself," insofar as "it is first a discourse of opinion" (1977, p. 130/419). In the last chapter we saw that analysis begins with the period of the "empty word" in which the discourse, Lacan now tells us, at first *(d'abord)* consists of mere opinion (ego reflection) and not truth (echoing the Platonic distinction between *doxa* [opinion] and *episteme* [knowledge]). There is danger of resistance, furthermore, because "all psychological objectification will prove to be bound up with this discourse" (1977, p. 130/148). Lacan also warned of the dangers of objectification in the previous essay when he called attention to the "third paradox of the relation of language to speech," namely, "that of the subject who loses his meaning in the objectifications of discourse" (1977, p. 70/281). The analysis of resistances thus leads to "a reinforcement of the objectifying position in the subject," and by maintaining "the subject in a state of observation" (the observing ego?) we enter "a circle of misunderstanding that nothing in analysis, or in criticism, will be able to break" (1977, p. 130/419).

What is even more treacherous, however, is the effect on the analyst, who cannot proceed to objectify the subject and yet speak to him as he should. In its essence, objectification falls under "a law of misunderstanding" *(méconnaissance)* which rules the subject not just as observed (the objectified) but also as observer (the objectifier). The analyst should not speak about the subject, "for he can do this himself," but about another thing *(autre chose)*, "something other [*chose autre*] than that which is in question when he speaks of himself" (1977, p. 130/419). This "something other" is "the thing [*la chose*] that speaks to you," which would remain inaccessible under conditions of objectification. As a word addressed to the analyst, this "thing" is capable of evoking *(évoquer)* its own response. The analyst hears the message "under this inverted form" and by returning it gives the subject the satisfaction of having recognized its truth. This is what the analysts of the '20s stopped achieving because they were caught in the objectifying analysis of resistances, rendered unable to recognize the response evoked in them, and thus unable to hear the inverted (unconscious) form of the subject's message and return it to him. The "thing that speaks" appears, then, to be the unconscious as it moves into the analytic discourse. If truth is to be considered in terms of adequacy, it is *this* "thing" which must be its norm, "this thing that speaks to us, which speaks within us, . . . even in escaping behind the discourse that says nothing but to make us speak" (1977, p. 131/420). But how do we speak about it?

VII
Interlude

When we turn to what other psychoanalysts are concerned with, we find they speak of the ego — as a synthesis of functions,

a function of synthesis, as autonomous, as an operational notion. It is this preoccupation, obstructing the presence of the
"thing," which Lacan now sets out to demolish. He begins
boldly by asking if the notion of the ego in analysis differs operationally from any other thing—for instance, this desk (or
reading stand [*pupitre*]) close at hand. He then undertakes "to
show that the discourses concerning the ego and the desk (and
that is what is at stake) coincide point by point" (1977, p.
132/421). The desk, like the ego, "is dependent on the signifier,"
for the word is responsible for the fact that it is not just a piece of
wood. Moreover, the chain of signifiers conjoined to the desk,
to which the desk refers (such as papers, wills, and other
documents), are as "dignified" in their human status as the
things and signifiers to which the ego devotes its interest and attention in its discourse—indeed, the ego finds itself subordinated to the desk's documents in the form of legal contracts,
etc. Furthermore, to lend a human voice to the desk would
enable it to speak of its individual existence and its history (easily documented) which is, like us, prey to fatality. One of us,
lastly, may dream that he is this desk, which then becomes a
signifier of desire in a chain of significations to which the consciousness of this desk will have given its interest—and here,
Lacan says, we touch on "the preconscious of this desk" (1977,
p. 133/423).

Before he attempts to clarify his last remark, Lacan notes
the protest from the quarter of phenomenology-psychiatry: consciousness belongs not to the desk, but to ourselves; it is we who
"perceive the desk and give it its meaning" (1977, p. 134/423).
Whatever truth may be conceded here, consciousness cannot
encompass "the high form which, however weak we may be in
the universe, guarantees us an imprescriptible dignity in it"
(1977, p. 134/423), i.e., conscious reflection cannot comprehend our own meaning, as Pascal saw. Reflection, in fact, does
not connote interiority but mirage, rendering the desk no different from the observer when placed with one of us between two
parallel mirrors. For in this position of reflection both ego and

desk are scrutinized by an other, from which they receive back endlessly their distorted images.

Having attacked the priority assumed by consciousness in perceiving meaning, Lacan now comes back to his remark about what might be called "the preconscious of this desk." His clarification consists in defining perception as unconscious and as reflecting the essence of the object perceived. It is this "essence" that appears to include, "potentially or actually," "affectations" (e.g., attributions of this desk) that are hardly separable from "the preconscious," for these attributes adjust themselves exactly to my "affections" and come to consciousness with them. He grants that the ego, not the desk, "is the seat of perceptions but in being so it reflects the essence of the objects it perceives and not its own, in so far as consciousness is its privilege, since these perceptions are very largely unconscious" (1977, p. 134/424). He appears to be saying that affective qualities have their ontological basis in beings, not in consciousness. He then takes a swipe at the arguments of "bastard forms of phenomenology" for diverting us from the fact that the desk does not talk.

VIII
The discourse of the other

Once the symbolic order is given its due recognition, the desk begins to speak and challenges the notion that the ego treated in analysis is "better than the desk that I am" (1977, p. 135/425). For the health of the ego is conceived in a way that ultimately reduces it to conformity with the analyst's ego, whose task it is to strengthen the patient's ego by bringing it into conformity with the analyst's perception of reality. Seeing the patient's neurosis as due to "the weakness of the ego" (1977, p. 136/425), the analyst tries to talk to the patient in "his own language," even to the ludicrous point of talking "babyish" as a parent does to a child to get him to comply. The desk now claims to be the ideal patient, because less troublesome, since "it is simply a question of substituting your discourse for mine" (1977, p. 136/426).

The desk itself remains a word, not an ego, "a means that I have employed in my discourse," says Lacan. Yet if we examine its role in analysis, the ego, too, is a means comparable to the desk. The desk has the advantage of not being a means of resistance, even though it "will soon be torn to pieces" *(morceaux)* by Lacan's audience for use as a weapon *(arme)* to attack the speaker for saying these outrageous things (1977, p. 136/426). Lacan uses these same terms to describe the ego, but in reverse, for the ego is a "means of the speech addressed to you from the subject's unconscious, a weapon [*arme*] to resist its recognition, it is fragmented [*morcelé*] in that it bears speech [as articulated, discrete signifiers] and whole in that it helps in not hearing it [as an obstacle to hearing]" (1977, p. 137/426–427). We've been given signals, again, about the mirror stage, and before Lacan deals with it in the next section, he links the imaginary with the symbolic order, telling us "it is in the disintegration [*désagrégation*] of the imaginary unity constituted by the ego that the subject finds the signifying material of his symptoms" (1977, p. 137/427). The order of signification itself is subject to the ego's narcissistic use, for "it is from the sort of interest aroused in him by the ego that the significations that turn his discourse away from those symptoms proceed" (1977, p. 137/427).

IX
[*The*] imaginary passion

This interest of the ego is none other than the passion of self-love, known to moralists but needing psychoanalysis to relate it to one's body image. This image is represented by the other, and I become so dependent on it as a result of the "signification that interests me so much" that it "links all the objects of my desires more closely to the desire of the other than to the desire that they arouse in me" (1977, p. 137/427). In other words, I become identified with the other in image and desire. The objects of desire, in turn, become modeled on the ego, after the fashion of paranoiac knowledge discussed earlier (Chapters 1 and 2).

All of this, of course, is the result of the mirror stage, which Lacan proceeds to describe. One consequence is that the anxiety of the fragmented body experience provokes aggressivity in response to the threat posed by the image of the other. Through "an appeal to the power of the image in which the honeymoon of the mirror so delighted" (1977, p. 138/428), the anxiety is quelled, i.e., through the pseudo-unification of the ego. The model of this synthesizing function of the ego is the notary or functionary mastering reality by treating objects as functional images of himself. But it is in the captivating relation to another ego that the alienation constituting the ego decisively appears, for as the ego identifies with the other in a "dual relation of ego to ego," there occurs a mutual distribution of master-slave roles (paralleled in each subject by the original relation of mastery of ego image to fragmented body), not unlike the complementary roles between notary and client. This results in a permanent war of *toi ou moi* involving the struggle for survival of the notary (the masterful ego) in each of the subjects.

In this framework of a two-ego analysis, the language of the ego is reduced to repetitive command, aggressive echo, or delusional flourish, hardly propitious for the analysis of defenses, despite the appearances of corroboration in the "object relation" (1977, p. 139/429). We have to do with neither a "two body psychology" nor the "two ego analysis" it shelters.

X
Analytic action

What we do in analysis is more complicated, for "we teach that there are not only two subjects present in the analytic situation, but two subjects each provided with two objects, the ego and the other *(autre)*, this other being indicated by a small *o*" (1977, p. 139/429). But when a pair of subjects (*S* and *O*) meet, one of those "objects" drops out in accordance with a "relation of exclusion" between the "other" of *S* and the "other" of *O*. While this remains obscure, perhaps reflecting our inadequacy with "a

dialectical mathematics with which we must familiarize ourselves" (1977, p. 139/429), we can attempt an understanding
based on the transitivist identification just discussed in the preceding section, where reference was made to "the relation of exclusion that . . . structures the dual relation of ego to ego" (1977,
p. 138/428). In this relation, there is an "identification precipitated from the ego to the other in the subject" — that is, in the
other subject — and it would seem that it is because of this identification that the ego of one becomes "the other" of another. In
other words, the ego of S becomes the other of O, while O's ego
becomes the "other" of S, leaving us with "four players," S and its
aspect of being "the other" for O, and O with its aspect of being
"the other" for S.

Lacan's language supports this interpretation as he vigor-
ously argues for a radical distinction between the level of the
"Other," with a capital O, and the level of the "other" with a
small o, where we see "the respective effects of the symbolic and
the imaginary" (1977, p. 140/430). The analyst must "be thor-
oughly imbued with the radical difference between the Other
[l'Autre] to which his speech must be addressed, and that second
other [autre] who is the individual that he sees before him" (1977,
p. 140/430). In practice, this means that he conducts analysis
"by pretending he is dead . . . either by his silence when he is the
Other with a capital O [l'Autre avec un grand A], or by annulling
his own resistance when he is the other with a small 'o' [l'autre
avec un petit a]" (1977, p. 140/430), that is, when he functions
from the place of the ego, the source of his resistance as analyst.
He does this in order to be "the good listener" and thereby facilitate "the acceptance of a word," a word "which constitutes a
pact, whether admitted or not, between the two subjects, a pact
that is situated in each case beyond the reasons of the argument"
(1977, p. 140/430), that is, situated beyond conscious discourse
in the Other. The rational logic of conscious discourse "is never
more than a body of rules that were laboriously drawn up," and
this leads Lacan to say what we've experienced all along: "I shall
expect nothing . . . of those rules except the good faith of the

Other, and, as a last resort, will make use of them if I think fit
or if I am forced to, only to amuse bad faith" (1977, p. 140/431).
What, then, is the Other?

XI
The locus of speech

Lacan begins by describing the Other as "the locus in which
is constituted the I who speaks [with] him who hears," a locus
that "extends as far into the subject as the laws of speech, that is
to say, well beyond the discourse that takes its orders from the
ego." Lacan tell us that we've known about this other level of
linguistic operations "ever since Freud discovered its unconscious field and the laws that structure it" (1977, p. 141/431).
The remainder of this section contrasts the field of the unconscious with the "concrete field of individual preservation" (1977,
p. 142/432), i.e., the field of the ego.

These unconscious linguistic processes account for the fact
that certain symptoms are analyzable. This is because they
structure the symptoms, not because the symptoms contain an
"indestructible" infantile desire or because desires are fixated or
regressed in relation to an object. On the contrary, as Freud described in a letter to Fliess (see note 201*b*), the repression inherent to a symptom has to do with a signifier that has been repressed and that can subsequently be recollected and recognized.
These "laws of recollection and symbolic recognition" are different from "the laws of imaginary reminiscence," which have to do
with "the echo of feeling or instinctual imprint," although the
latter can provide material for the signifying structures of the
former (as, for example, images which operate as signifiers in
the dream-rebus). Lacan adds a critical note to the process of
repression, transference, and symptom formation when he
stresses that in these processes what dominates "the desire to be
recognized" is "the desire of recognition" so that the signifier of
the desire is preserved "as such until it is recognized" (1977, p.
141/431).

In the Freudian unconscious only a signifier can be repressed, for the unconscious is determined by "the symbolic law," i.e., the laws of language. That is why when Freud established "the Oedipus Complex as the central motivation of the unconscious, he recognized this unconscious as the agency of the laws on which marriage alliance and kinship are based" (1977, p. 142/432) — and, according to Lévi-Strauss, these laws are essentially linguistic in nature. The centrality of the Oedipus complex, moreover, determines why "the motives of the unconscious are limited . . . to sexual desire," and why "the other great generic desire, that of hunger, is not represented, as Freud always maintained, in what the unconscious preserves in order to gain recognition for it" (1977, p. 142/432–433).

The "concrete field of individual preservation," on the other hand, is "structured in this dialectic of master and slave, in which we can recognize the symbolic emergence of the imaginary struggle to the death in which we earlier defined the essential structure of the ego" (1977, p. 142/432). This field is linked not to the division of labor (thus discounting a simple Marxist view of alienation), but to the division of desire and labor. The point seems to be that "from the first transformation introducing into food its human signification to the most developed forms of the production of consumer goods" (1977, p. 142/432), the satisfaction of needs has been caught up in the desire and the struggle for recognition in an ego-to-ego relationship of domination and servitude. Thus hunger, an aspect of the ego field rather than the unconscious, is not represented "in what the unconscious preserves in order to gain recognition for it." Freud, moreover, intended a rigorous separation, "even in their unconscious interference, between the field of the ego and that of the unconscious." We have lost this sense of rigor and our focus has shifted from the significations of guilt in the subject's action to his "affective frustration, instinctual deprivation, and imaginary dependence" — i.e., a shift from the symbolic to the imaginary order. This shift in psychoanalysis, according to Lacan, has fostered a "general infantilization" and "social mystification" characteristic of our age (1977, p. 142/433).

XII
Symbolic debt

This section stresses the debt we owe to language, whose truth analytic practice is in danger of repressing. We are forgetful of the truth that Freud showed us with the Rat Man, namely, that "it is out of the forfeits and vain oaths, lapses in speech and unconsidered words. . . that is moulded the stone guest who comes, in symptoms, to disturb the banquet of one's desires" (1977, p. 143/433). The speech of parents, betraying nothingness and despair, can affect children more than deprivation. It is from the gaps of the symbolic order itself that arises the "ferocious figure" of the superego, for two reasons: (1) the child's grasp of the law, prior to speech, is a misapprehension; (2) the law's presentation by the parental figure is often hypocritical. This leads to "the broken link of the symbolic chain" that opens up the field of the imaginary (1977, p. 143/434).

Analytic practice that is based on the imaginary field of "dual complicity" can have value only if it reduces the resistance of the ego to "the speech that is avowed at that moment of the analysis that is the analytic moment." It is in "the avowal of this speech" that "the analysis must rediscover its centre and its gravity" (1977, p. 143/434). If we take seriously "the symbolic debt for which the subject as subject of speech is responsible" (1977, p. 144/434), then the traditional definition of truth, *"Adaequatio rei et intellectus,"* turns out to have an additional meaning, hinging on the word *reus*, with a metaphorical meaning of "he who is in debt for something." Truth then becomes the correspondence between the intellect and the subject's status as one in debt to the symbolic order.

XIII
The training of the analysts of the future

By returning to "the structures of language so manifestly recognizable in the earliest discovered mechanisms of the un-

conscious," we will find "the modes in which speech is able to recover the debt that it engenders" (1977, p. 144/435). We recall
that these mechanisms are parapraxes, jokes, dreams, and symptoms, in which we recognize the structures of metaphor and
metonymy. The modes of debt recovery include the study of
languages and institutions, the resonances of literature, and the
significations of art, all "necessary to an understanding of the
text of our experience." Freud's own example shows that "he derived his inspiration, his ways of thinking and his technical
weapons from just such a study" (1977, p. 144/435), and he regarded it as a necessary condition for the teaching of psychoanalysis. Its neglect is linked to the present state of analysis, and
if a new generation is to recover the meaning of the Freudian
experience and preserve themselves from psychosociological objectification, they must be initiated into the methods of linguistics, history, mathematics, and other "sciences of intersubjectivity" (1977, p. 145/435). This will require innovative teaching,
for "the pact instituting the analytic experience must take account of the fact that this experience establishes the very effects
that capture it in order to separate it from the subject" (1977, p.
145/435–436), i.e., we must make intelligible how analysis generates a dialectic of signification that develops a life of its own
beyond both parties and accounts for the power of words to al-
ter symptoms. We are uneasy about this power, denounce
magical thinking in others, and make excuses for the fact that
our practice is sustained by language and its link with truth.
Because truth, however, like the subject, holds a place on the
margin, Freud tells us that "it is impossible to keep to three un-
dertakings: to educate, to govern, and to psychoanalyse"
(1977, p. 145/436). Presumably a similar dialectic of speech
develops in each of these endeavors, revealing that truth is
complex, humble, alien, "stubborn to the choice of sex [be-
cause of its link to the signifier of the phallus?], akin to death,
and, all in all, rather inhuman," much like Diana (1977, p.
145/436).

Map of the Text

I.   *Situation in time and place of this exercise*
   A.   Vienna is the place of Freud's Copernican revolution.
      1.   But this place has been neglected by psychoanalysis,
         a.   so that a return to Freud is seen as a reversal.
   B.   Post-war emigrés spread psychoanalysis to the United States,
      1.   where ahistoricism defines assimilation,
         a.   to which the emigrants responded by seeking recognition for what differentiated them as healers and wise men from their patients as sick and ignorant,
      2.   effacing Europe along with their bad memories.
   C.   Our return to Freud shows how psychoanalysis has been distorted since his death.
      1.   Studying Freud's texts yields genuine discoveries,
         a.   with obvious transformative effects on practice.

II.   *The adversary*
   A.   "The meaning of a return to Freud is a return to the meaning of Freud."
      1.   Such a return is a challenge to everyone insofar as it puts truth into question.
         a.   Truth is at the heart of analytic practice,
            i.   through which we constantly rediscover the power of the truth in our flesh,
            ii.   and in which we recognize the unconscious in the subject's defenses against it.
            iii.   The peace following such recognition comes from the truth,
            iv.   but we have distorted Freud in identifying unconscious and defense.
   B.   The adversary accuses us of bringing in Plato and Hegel.
      1.   But Freud's method introduces us to the principle of human folly,
         a.   and is not absurdly reductionistic or due to chance.

      b. But it began with a particular truth,

      c. which has become confused with surrounding reality,

      d. and must again be surprised in its nakedness.

III. *The thing speaks of itself*

    A. Truth vanishes as soon as she appears

      1. to men who are phantoms.

      2. The discourse of error bears witness to her,

      3. as well as Hegel's cunning of reason.

      4. Truth wanders about in parapraxes, dreams, jokes.

      5. The road of truth no longer goes through thought, but through things as the signs of her speech.

IV. *Parade*

    A. "Who is speaking?"

      1. Libido, ego, or "the golem of narcissism"?

        a. In the moment of truth the phallus enters.

      2. Truth says "I speak," and "There is no other speech but language."

        a. Objections come from the nonverbal sphere.

    B. It speaks, Freud discovered,

      1. where there is pain,

      2. in an order of language constituted by laws

        a. differing from natural expression and not a code,

        b. as Ferdinand de Saussure indicated.

V. *Order of the thing*

    A. Saussure distinguished signifier and signified.

      1. The network of the signifier is the ensemble of phonemes in a language.

      2. The network of the signified is the diachronic set of the spoken discourses,

        a. whose signification always refers to other signifiers, not to specific things, and

        b. whose signification is realized only on the basis of a grasp of things in their totality.

      3. Thus language is distinguished from the sign,

        a. for it is only through signifiers that we can comprehend the whole.

B. Hegel's "beautiful soul" falls prey to the dialectic of language,
   1. in which the I is defined as a legal being,
   2. whom Freud made responsible for internal disorder.
   3. This disorder is made possible by a congenital gap and fragmentation.
C. For the human being, the symbolic function is omnipresent:
   1. in the signifying structures of symptoms imprinted on the flesh;
   2. in the exchange of gifts;
   3. in the commingling of subjects constituting society,
   4. where the incidence of truth as cause requires a revision of causality to include subjectivity,
   5. so that even Marxism must give up resistance to Freud.
      a. For the psychoanalytic ethic is not individualistic,
         i. despite the misunderstanding of it in America.
   6. Analytic experience is rooted in the general structure of semantics.
D. The subject is not the ego.
   1. At the level of the unconscious the true subject is bequeathed recognized truth.
   2. The nucleus of the ego is made up of an alienating sequence of identifications,
   3. thus necessitating a re-reading of *"Wo Es war, soll Ich werden,"*
      a. in which Freud discovered subjectivity in its radical ex-centricity.
E. Linguistics teaches us to view the symptom as a signifier,
   1. appearing in a context of significations in the analytic dialogue,
   2. thus dissipating many ambiguities in the concepts of transference and resistance.

VI. *Resistance to the resisters*
  A. The first resistance with which analysis must deal is the discourse itself,
    1. as opinion and objectification.
  B. But analysis of resistance reinforces the subject's objectifications,
    1. and misunderstanding increases with emphasis on the observing state.
    2. The analyst cannot proceed to objectify the subject and still speak to him as he should,
      a. for it is not about him that the analyst must speak to him;
      b. rather, the analyst must respond by recognizing the other "thing" in what he says.
      c. Since the thing speaks to us even in escaping behind the discourse,
      d. the traditional definition of truth has a literal sense, i.e., correspondence *(adaequatio)* between intellect and thing.
VII. *Interlude*
  A. But what about the ego?
    1. As a function, as synthesis, as autonomous, as part of general psychology?
    2. As an operational notion?
  B. The ego is no different from this desk operationally (i.e., in discourse).
    1. The desk, as much as the ego, depends on the signifier.
    2. The significations of the desk are no less dignified than the ego's.
    3. If I lent my voice to the desk, it could speak of its existence and history as evidenced in documents.
    4. The desk can be a signifier in dreams, revealing a preconscious.
    5. But phenomenologists protest that the preconscious and consciousness belong to ourselves, not the desk.

        a. It is we who perceive the desk and bestow its meaning,

            i. but we do not give ourselves meaning.

        b. The desk and the observer are no different (with regard to consciousness) when they are placed between mirrors,

            i. since the image of each is other for the observer.

        c. In the same way the mirage of consciousness consists of an endless series of false reflections.

        d. "Preconscious" cannot be separated from the desk's affective qualities which enter consciousness in adjusting to my affections.

        e. The ego's perceptions of objects are largely unconscious and reflect their essence, not its own.

    6. But we avoid discussing the fact that the desk does not speak.

VIII. *The discourse of the other*

    A. "How is the ego better than I am?" asks the desk.

        1. The ego's health is defined by its adaptation to reality, but in fact is distinguished by identification with the analyst's ego.

        2. We infantilize the subject's speech as we equate neurosis with ego weakness.

        3. The desk is an ideal patient since the analyst can simply substitute his own discourse and ego.

    B. In truth, the desk is "I" as grammatical subject, not an ego.

        1. However, as means in the discourse, the desk can be compared to the ego as means in analysis;

        a. but the desk shows less resistance than the ego.

        b. The ego is a defensive weapon used to resist recognition of the unconscious.

        c. The ego is an imaginary unity,

            i. in whose disintegration the subject discovers the signifying material of his symptoms,

       ii. from which his discourse is turned away by the ego.

IX. *Imaginary passion*

  A. The interest of the ego is the passion of self-love.

    1. Psychoanalysis has analyzed its relation to one's own body image,

      a. which is represented by one's fellow-man.

    2. This passion makes me so dependent on this image that all the objects of desire are linked to the desire of the other.

      a. These objects appear in a space structured by vision and the mirror experience.

  B. The mirror stage is a consequence of man's prematurity at birth,

    1. in which the infant jubilantly identifies with the total human form,

    2. whose unity is threatened by the image of another.

    3. According to the paranoiac principle of human knowledge, objects are an imaginary reduplication of the ego.

    4. The alienation that constitutes the ego in identification with the other leads to the transitivist quarrel.

    5. The language of the ego is reduced to reactive aggressivity,

      a. in which we locate the analysis of defense,

      b. and whose outcome is judged to be a function of the object relation so that a "two body psychology" shelters a "two ego analysis."

X. *Analytic action*

  A. In the analytic situation there are not two but four players.

    1. Each subject has two objects, ego and other.

      a. But these are merged in the Subject-Other relationship.

    2. The analyst's silence makes death present.

      a. He must distinguish the symbolic register of the

Other from the imaginary register of the other.

    i. This is based on the radical difference between the Other to whom his speech is addressed and the second other whom he sees.

B. Every discourse is addressed to the good listener for the acceptance of a word which constitutes a pact situated beyond reasons.

    1. And we expect nothing from rules of logic except the good faith of the Other,

        a. so that we make use of them only to beguile bad faith.

XI. *The locus of speech*

A. The Other is the foundation of all dialogue.

    1. This realm reaches into the subject as far as the laws of speech do,

        a. beyond the ego's discourse.

        b. Freud discovered it as the field of the unconscious, together with the laws structuring it.

B. These unconscious laws determine the analyzable symptoms,

    1. not because infantile desires are indestructible,

    2. but because they are permanently recollected in a repressed signifier that seeks to be recognized.

        a. The laws of such recollection and symbolic recognition are different from the laws of feeling or instinct.

    3. This unconscious is the agency of laws governing marriage, kinship, and exchange.

        a. It is in this sense that the motives of the unconscious are expressed in terms of sexual desire.

C. The field of the ego's survival is structured in the dialectic of master and slave,

    1. where we find Hegel's "struggle to the death" which defines the essential structure of the ego.

        a. Freud intended a rigorous separation between the ego's field and that of the unconscious,

    i. whose recognition the ego resists by its own significations in speech.

     (a) As a result, we are now led away from dealing with the significations of guilt to encouraging infantilization and ideology.

XII. *Symbolic debt*

 A. Analytic practice risks repressing the very truth it bears in its exercise,

  1. which haunts us in the lapses of our discourse.

  2. Parental speech has more effect on the child than deprivation.

   a. The misunderstood law gives rise to the ferocious superego.

 B. Analysis which is reduced to a mobilization of defenses is to be criticized,

  1. because it is disordered in practice as well as principle,

  2. while its striving for success has value only in reducing the resistance of the ego to the word.

  3. Analysis must rediscover its center in the acknowledgment of this word actualized in the transference,

   a. so that the intellect can be adequate to the symbolic debt for which the subject is responsible as subject of the word.

XIII. *The training of the analysts of the future*

 A. We return to the language structures recognizable in unconscious mechanisms.

  1. Freud believed the history of language and literature was necessary for understanding the text of our experience and for teaching psychoanalysis,

   a. but this insight has been ignored.

  2. Training a new generation of analysts will require initiation into the methods of the linguist, the historian, and the mathematician,

a. thereby warding off the psychosociological objectification in which uncertain analysts have looked
   for substance.
b. This reform requires communicating with disci-
   plines defined as sciences of intersubjectivity, or
   "conjectural sciences,"
   i. turning about what is implied by "human
      sciences,"
c. and it requires innovative teaching.
   i. For truth is complex, humble, marginal,
      akin to death, and rather inhuman.

Notes to the Text

115*a*/402   A misprint in the English text reads "have not reached"
             instead of "have now reached."

116*f*/404   The French text ends this paragraph with *questions de
             l'actuel*, more sharply translated as "questions of the
             present" than "questions of the real." To allow a text
             bound up in tradition to speak to us (who are also
             bound up in tradition) is precisely the task of herme-
             neutics, "that discipline of commentary."

118*c*/406   Since the French text reads "pour éviter que.le sujet
             s'y reconaisse," we translate: "in order to prevent the
             subject from recognizing himself in it," rather than
             ". . . from recognizing it."

118*d*/406   The image of the bandit shape lurking behind every
             tree suggests a familiar diatribe against symbol-
             hunting, the reification of the signified in a fixed (an-
             alogic) relation to the signifier (see, e.g., 1977, p.
             160/510). It is not clear what is "this little, then,
             which can become everything on occasion," unless it
             refers back to the little it takes to believe that one is
             in the forest of Bondy, where truth consists of fixed
             one-to-one relationships between the signifier and
             the signified.

119d/407 Balthazar Gracian (1601–1658) was a Spanish Jesuit philosopher, novelist, and epigrammatist. La Rochefoucauld (1613–1680) is best known for his moral maxims and polished epigrams (Lacan quoted him earlier [1977, p. 54d/264]). Madeleine de Scudéry (1607–1701) was a novelist who had one of the chief literary salons of Paris. Freud joined this circle apparently by setting the tradition of moral casuistry onto the terrain of sexuality, whose literary map, when properly oriented, still serves as guide for the psychoanalyst in his office.

119e–
120a/407 The translation is in question here. In the zealot's opinion, regarding the forms governing psychoanalytic practice, "elles détiennent l'accès à une réalité transcendante aux aspects de l'histoire," i.e., "they confine access to a reality transcending aspects of history," and therefore the taste for order and love of beauty have their permanent (and ahistorical) foundation in toileting. Lacan has already told us (1977, p. 53/262) "the anal stage is no less purely historical when it is actually experienced than when it is reconstituted in thought."

120b/407 The French is a bit stronger in stating that regarding the analytic relation Freud was only satisfied with having situated it in the position of the Oedipus complex.

The preoedipal (object relations) theorists narrow the analytic relation as much as the experimental psychologists restrict the scope of discovery by their methodology.

120d/408 Diogenes, the Greek Cynic philosopher, went about in daylight with a lantern, "looking for an honest man." The light held aloft in the proverbial symbol of the search for truth also appears to have broad general reference. The mention of the well may be related to the French phrase "la vérité est au fond du

puits" ("truth lies at the bottom of a well"). The cas-
ket (perhaps another reference) suggests a later theme,
namely, truth's relationship to death (see 1977, p.
124*c*/412, Diana and "the smooth surface of death,"
and p. 145*e*/436, where truth is "akin to death").

121*c*/409   In Hegel, reason's cunning operates by means of
contradiction, impasse, deceptive appearance, and
frustration in order to forward the dialectic to its
grand conclusion: self-consciousness aware of itself
as absolute spirit.

122*b*/410   The sentence "All the same. . ." *(Quand même)* begins
better with "Even though," thus subordinating this
clause to "you will not get off so lightly." The next
sentence might read ". . . to see me escape (by situating me not in you yourselves but in being itself) first
from the dungeon of the fortress in which you are so
sure you have me secured." The "most far-fetched
conceit" translates *la pointe la plus gongorique.*

Luis de Gongora y Argote (1561–1627) has
been called Spain's greatest poet. His style yields the
term "Gongorism" and is characterized by innovative use of metaphor, classical and mythological allusion, and latinization of vocabulary. Lacan has referred to himself as the Gongora of psychoanalysis
(1966, p. 467). Who would dispute the point?

122*c*/410   Fichte (1762–1814) spearheaded post-Kantian German idealism with his notion of the absolute Ego.

The choice of "riddle" in English loses the force
of *rébus* in French, referring to Freud's (1900a) illustration that the dream is like a rebus, a picture-puzzle linguistically structured. The Latin dative and
ablative plural form for "things" is *rebus.*

123*a*/411   Pascal (1670) wrote: "Cleopatra's nose, had it been
shorter, the whole face of the world would have been
changed" (#162).

123*c*/411   *"Parade"*: in "The Agency of the Letter in the Unconscious" Lacan writes of "the fascinating display of mating...ritual" (1977, p. 172/525); the French is even more explicit: *l'érection fascinante de la parade*.

124*a*/412   Schreber fell victim to the divine rays which spoke, i.e., to the signifier (see 1977, p. 185*a*/538).

124*c*/412   In classical myth Actaeon, the hunter, came upon Diana, the virgin huntress (Artemis to the Greeks), bathing in a stream. Because he saw her naked she turned him into a stag, whereupon his own dogs, no longer recognizing him, tore him to pieces. Freud, unlike Actaeon and unlike the analyst who becomes "the prey of the dogs of his thoughts" (1977, p. 124*d*/ 412), has given the slip to the dogs who from the beginning have been thrown off their scent (not "tracked down" as in the English). Freud tries to draw them back into pursuit (these thinkers who pursue the truth), but he cannot slow down his own pace.

124*d*/412   Giordano Bruno (1548–1600) stressed the relativity of perception in the dialectical pursuit of truth. He had a major influence on Spinoza and Leibniz.

125*d*/413   Rather than turn to the ego, we should turn to the ridges (better than "angle of intersection" for *arêtes*) of speech, i.e., to the slopes of the sliding of the signified under the signifier, namely, metaphor and metonymy (see 1977, pp. 154–160/503–511).

Stalin's bull is explained by Lacan's note in "The Agency of the Letter in the Unconscious":

> We may recall that the discussion of the need for a new language in communist society did in fact take place, and Stalin, much to the relief of those who adhered to his philosophy, put an end to it with the following formulation: language is not a superstructure [1977, p. 176/ 496].

126*a*/414   The use of "non-overlapping networks" to translate *qui ne se recouvrent pas* is misleading; the networks do not cover one another, but they may overlap.

126*b–c*/ 414
The next chapter presents Saussure's ideas in more detail. For the moment is should be said that Lacan is embellishing Saussure's elementary relationship of signifier as sound-image to signified as concept.

126*d*/414
The antecedents of "it" (signification? redundancy?) are also ambiguous in the French. The point seems to be that we cannot base the meaning of a sentence solely on the information contained in the sentence (for there is no one-to-one connection between words and things, and speech always says more than it says). Redundancy (in Lacan's view of information theory) is "precisely that which does duty as resonance in speech" (1977, p. 86*c*/299).

126*h*/415
Rather than "which he erects," we translate "which it erects," referring to the infatuated "I."

127*d*/415
The text should read: "Deciphered, it [the symptom] is self-evident and shows, imprinted on the flesh, the omnipresence for the human being of the symbolic function" ("Déchiffrée, elle est patente et montre imprimée sur la chair, l'omniprésence pour l'être humain de la fonction symbolique").

127*f*/ 415–416
The French text speaks of "the incidence of truth" (*l'incidence de la vérité*) and "the heterogeneity of this incidence," not "effects" as in the English.

128*c*/416
The alpha-omega distinction is at first confusing. The sense seems to be that the distinction between subject and ego emerges in the early Freud (point alpha) as the distinction between unconscious and preconscious, but in the later Freud (point omega) as the distinction between *Es* and *Ich* in the famous formula. We prefer to translate: "separated by an abyss from (*des*) preconscious functions" rather than "of." Lacan writes in "The Agency of the Letter in the Unconscious": "a large number of psychical effects that are quite legitimately designated as unconscious, in the

sense of excluding the characteristic of consciousness, are nonetheless without any relation whatever
to the unconscious in the Freudian sense" (1977, p.
163/514).

128e/417   The narcissistic shift from "this am I" to "it is me" was
noted earlier in the "Discourse at Rome" when La-
can pointed out that "the 'ce-suis-je' of the time of Vil-
lon has become reversed in the 'c'est moi' of modern
man" (1977, p. 70/281).

129a/417   The theme of radical ex-centricity (not "eccentricity")
as noted earlier will be developed in "The Agency of
the Letter in the Unconscious" (1977, p. 165e/517;
171g/524). The English text omits Lacan's development of the neologism s'être: "There where it was (Là
où c'était), one can say 'là où s'était'. . ."

130a/419   The French text has "recognize the truth" (la vérité),
not "recognize the fact" as in the English.

131a/420   See the earlier discussion (p. 83) of the sender receiving his message back from the receiver in an inverted form.

131b/420   Lacan may be utilizing an ambiguity in the French
verb for "knowing": "Cette vérité que nous connais-
sons ainsi ne pouvons-nous donc la connaître?"
("This truth that we know in this way, can we therefore know it?"). The first knowing consists of a response evoked by the "other thing," a hearing of the
message "in this inverted form" and returning it to
the sender. Not the result of perception-consciousness as much as a mutual coming-to-presence through
a kind of birth, this form of knowing suggests Claudel and his formula, "Toute naissance est une co-
naissance" ("Every birth is a co-birth, a knowing").
Lacan refers to Claudel at the end of the Selection
(1977, p. 324/827).

Adaequatio rei et intellectus is the classic definition of
truth seen as a conformity of the intellect with what is.

131d/420   Chosisme is one of the terms used to characterize the

French anti-novel, typified in the work of Robbe-Grillet and Sarraute. It also refers to a philosophical stance loosely called "concretism."

131e/420   The French text begins "What other thing are you going to look for" ("Qu'allez-vous chercher autre chose"), so that *chose* is repeated anew and appears to be the "pirouette" in the preceding line. The irony of the analyst willing to objectify the ego but eschewing its being taken as a thing is expressed in the "delicate shoes" replacing the "big clogs" which hide the truth (1977, p. 119a/406).

131f/420   The "thirty-five years" refers to "Beyond the Pleasure Principle" (Freud, 1920), in which the distinction between ego instincts and sexual instincts was changed from qualitative to topographical.

132a/421   That the inventor of the autonomous ego (probably a reference to Heinz Hartmann) should receive praise for bringing psychoanalysis into general psychology appears to be as ironical as if the wealthy Aga Khan, noted for his interest in horse breeding and racing, were to be praised for teaching his followers how to bet on his horses.

132c/421   Instead of the simple misprint, the English text should read *chosisme*.

132d/421   Rather than "Of so little use" for *en si peu de chose*, we translate "In so little a way (is it distinguished). . ."

132f/422   The English omits a word Lacan will repeat, namely, that the ego *intéresse*, "gives its interest to," significations. Later (1977, p. 133c/423) the consciousness of the desk inspires the dreamer's interest in significations. We would also translate: "it is from the sort of interest which the ego arouses in the subject that come the significations which divert his discourse" (1977, p. 137b/427); "This interest *of* the ego is a passion" whose nature was glimpsed by the moralists (1977, p. 137c/427); and this passion brings to every relation with the body image "a signification that interests me" (1977, p. 137c/427). Lastly, evidence for Lacan's deliberate usage comes from his ironic satisfaction that his audience will find what he says "interesting" and from his wondering whether what he says happens to "interest" them (1977, p. 136e–f/ 426); he even seizes the moment to make the point that what is "interesting" euphemistically designates what is of only moderate interest (as befits the ego?), while "speculations of universal interest are called 'disinterested' " (1977, p. 136e/426). The point of all this is to suggest that there is a narcissistic relation between the ego and certain significations, i.e., the ego can cluster speech (significations) to serve defensively its own imaginary ends. For an "interesting" analogy in Heidegger, see his *What Is Called Thinking* (1952, p. 5).

133b/422 The desk as "intersign" of fatalities suggests its mediating role for the documentation of wills, death records, etc.

133c/422 Again, the English has "riddle" for *rébus* in the French.

134a/423 The reference is to man as "a thinking reed" in Pascal's *Pensées* (1670, #347–348).

134d/424 The dispositions of pure exteriority, immoderately spread by man, which condition ego consciousness, may be statues, monuments, photographs, automobiles, and other narcissistic artifacts.

135a/424 Karl Jaspers is a handy target for Lacan both as philosopher and psychopathologist.

135d/425 This paragraph begins with the imputation of a *petitio principii,* a mode of attack used elsewhere by Lacan (see, e.g., 1977, p. 120b/407).

136a/425 The sense seems to be that the patient, presumed to have a weak ego, is treated in a condescending manner by the analyst just as even well-informed parents resort to baby-talk to seduce infants into conforming to their intentions. The irony is that "talking in his own language" becomes condescending whereas it

should serve as the guiding principle promoting resonance with the word.

136*f*/426   The pleonasm is in the "look and see" while the antonomasia appears to be in the substitution of the desk
for his person, about to be attacked by the audience.

137*a*/427   The French for "bears speech" is *porte la parole*, suggesting *porte-parole* ("mouthpiece" or "spokesman"), a
role that splits the ego from the subject's unconscious. The ego is also fragmented insofar as
speech must be articulated, but is whole insofar as it
blocks or stands in the way of hearing what is said.

137*c*/427   As indicated above, *Cet intérêt du moi* is better translated as "This interest of the ego" rather than "in the
ego." This section draws heavily on themes discussed
in Chapters 1 and 2. In the French "my fellow-man"
is *mon semblable*, also translated as "my counterpart,"
referring to the other as experienced in the confused
identification of ego and other in transitivism. The
role of the other in determining the objects of desire
is described by Kojève (1939):

> Desire directed toward a natural object is hu-
> man only to the extent that it is "mediated" by
> the Desire of another directed toward the same
> object: it is human to desire what others desire,
> because they desire it. Thus, an object perfectly
> useless from the biological point of view (such
> as a medal, or the enemy's flag) can be desired
> because it is the object of other desires [p. 6].

137*e*/427   The English would be more readable with commas:
"from which results, at the time indicated, the jubilant identification. . . ."

138*a*/428   Again, the English can be rendered more readable:
"an operation which, . . . [and] being of much the same
kind as the 'aha!'. . . ., does not fail to bring. . . ."

138*b*/428   The notary or solicitor *(notaire)* executes deeds, han-
dles real estate transactions, successions, marriage

contracts, etc.

138d/428 The English text has "coadaptation" for "coaptation," a stronger word, for "coaptation" means a fitting together and making fast, indicative of a captivating identification with the other. Some discussion of "transitivism" appeared earlier (Chapter 1).

139a/429 This paragraph may be read as describing the discoursing environment of the young child whose speech consists of the Aha! experience of Köhler's chimps, the repetition of parental commands upon playthings and to oneself, and aggressive mimicry, while parental speech consists of rote descriptions of objects and frenzied *ritornello* (a short, recurrent instrumental passage in a vocal composition) — this forms the reductive basis of the ego's language.

140e/430 Rather than "to whom it brings its salvation," the English becomes more comprehensible in using another meaning of *salut*: "to whom it brings its greeting."

141a/431 The I speaks *with (avec)* "him who hears," not *to* him.

142a/432 We recall Lacan's discussion of the law of exchange in the "Discourse at Rome" (1977, pp. 65–66/276–277).

143c/434 The second sentence reads: "Will we divert our study *of* what will come *from* the law [*de ce qu'il advient de la loi*] . . . and *from* the imperative [*et de l-imperatif*] . . . : that is to say, *from* the springs [*c'est-à-dire des ressorts*]. . . ." The law's content is misunderstood before it is known, its compelling quality is challenged before it is discerned: these are the springs from which arises, out of such gaps in the symbolic order, the imaginary figure of the superego, reimposing what was misunderstood or challenged in the course of development.

Chapter 5

The Agency of the Letter in the Unconscious or Reason Since Freud

Overview

This essay deserves a special place among the papers selected for this collection, partly because it articulates, more fully than any other single essay available to us here, Lacan's fundamental thesis that the unconscious is "structured like a language," partly because it is slightly more readable than the rest. The reason for this (and Lacan almost apologizes for the fact) is that in its present form it finds a place midway between the genre of the spoken word and the genre of the written text.

Generally speaking, the genre of the spoken word for Lacan is more easily comprehensible by the auditor than the genre of the written text, which is intended to be read rather than heard. Editing the latter permits a "kind of tightening up" that Lacan likes "in order to leave the reader no other way out than the way in"—a way that Lacan prefers "to be difficult" (1977, p. 146/493). In this much, at least, he succeeds admirably! The

160

present essay, though written down after it was delivered, happily escapes such strenuous redaction and retains some of the original rhythms *(mesures)* of the spoken word essential to shaping the response Lacan intends.

At any rate, the invitation to address the *Fédération des étudiants ès lettres* offers an especially appropriate occasion to discuss the role of the *letter* in the unconscious. For the commitment of these students to the world of letters (i.e., literature) recalls the primary place that Freud assigned to literature in the formation of the psychoanalyst—an insistence that is overlooked by many present-day analysts. Yet how can they fail to recognize its importance when their "whole experience must find in speech alone its instrument, its content, its material, and even the background noise of its uncertainties" (1977, p. 147/494)?

I
The meaning of the letter

Lacan's purpose in these pages is to discuss the function *(instance)* of the letter in structuring the unconscious—a conception that challenges, of course, the notion of the unconscious as "seat of the instincts." How is "letter" to be understood here? Quite "literally" as "that material support that concrete discourse borrows from language" (1977, p. 147/495), where "concrete discourse" is taken to be the "speech" of an individual subject and "language" the universal structure that preexists "the moment at which each subject at a certain point in his mental development makes his entry into it" (1977, p. 148/495). Language, thus understood as structure, precedes and founds the social patterns of a community as well as its historical "discourse." This structure, Lacan admits, is discernible through the methods of scientific linguistics as these have developed under the inspiration of Ferdinand de Saussure. Saussure's fundamental position is that a language is made up of signs, in which the signifying component (e.g., acoustic image) and signified component (e.g., mental concept) are related only arbitrarily (i.e., not necessarily).

But the import of "this primordial distinction [between signifier and signified] goes well beyond the discussion concerning
the arbitrariness of the sign" (1977, p. 149/497), so much so that
the bar that separates signifier and signified in the formula S/s
may be conceived as "a barrier resisting signification" (1977, p.
149/497). What Lacan seems to be insisting on is that not only
is the relation between signifier and signified arbitrary, but
there is no one-to-one correspondence between them at all (as
the logical positivists would like to maintain) — still less between
the signifier and the "thing" referred to. The hard fact is that "no
signification can be sustained other than by reference to another
signification" (1977, p. 150/498).

To exemplify this Lacan introduces an example of his own
invention: two different signifiers ("Ladies" and "Gentlemen")
are located respectively above two separate doors — each signifier referring to essentially the same signified (a water closet).
What differentiates these two signifiers, then, is not the content
of the signified, which is common to both, but rather the chains
of associative signifiers that history, culture, and social mores
have assigned separately and reciprocally to the sexual differentiation implied in them.

More precisely, what is the structure of the signifier? Basically, it is composed of "ultimate differential elements" that
then are combined "according to the laws of a closed order"
(1977, p. 152/501). These basic units are the phonemes that,
when divided into 12 sets of binary pairs ("differential coup-
lings"), account for "the discernment of sounds in [any] given
language" (1977, p. 153/501), as Jakobson and Halle (1956)
have shown. It is when these sounds find written form that they
constitute, in the strictest sense, the "letter" with which the
whole essay deals, i.e., the rudimentary and "essentially local-
ized structure of the signifier" (1977, p. 153/501).

As for the combination of these elements "according to the
laws of a closed order," these laws (e.g., of grammar and lexicol-
ogy) function in different ways that interlink with one another
to form what Lacan calls the "signifying chain": "rings of a neck-

lace that is a ring in another necklace made of rings" (1977, p. 153/502). Yet the capacity of signifiers to convey meaning is not restricted by such laws. A signifier, for example, can "anticipate" meaning "by unfolding its dimension before it" as happens in the pregnant interruption or in the adroitly adversative "but. . ." That is why "we can say that it is in the chain of the signifier that the meaning 'insists' but that none of its elements 'consists' in the signification of which it is at the moment capable," so that we "are forced. . . to accept the notion of an incessant sliding of the signified under the signifier" (1977, pp. 153–154/502).

The relation between signifier and signified is not purely linear, as if a single voice were articulating the signifiers in temporal sequence. Rather, signifiers relate to one another "vertically" as well as "horizontally," clinging together in clusters ("anchoring points") of sounds that in effect produce a polyphonic effect that can be "aligned along the several staves of a [musical] score" (1977, p. 154/503). Hence: "There is in effect no signifying chain that does not have, as if attached to the punctuation of each of its units, a whole articulation of relevant contexts suspended 'vertically', as it were, from that point" (1977, p. 154/503).

Lacan proceeds to discuss through the remainder of this first section two fundamental ways in which clusters of signifiers coalesce: through processes that the linguistic tradition calls "metonymy" on the one hand and "metaphor" on the other. Each of these processes is illustrated by an example.

Lacan introduces his treatment of metonymy by an elaborate example of the signifier "tree," in which he recalls some of the complexities of its polyphonic resonances, beginning with the simple matter of "vowels and consonants," then extending the associations to "symbolic contexts." There are two points to make here: in the first place, the richness of association belongs to the signifier "tree" quite independently of any subject who uses it in speech, and such trans-subjective wealth permits the subject, "precisely in so far as [the subject has] this language in common with other subjects, that is to say, in so far as it exists as a [natural] language, to use it in order to signify *something quite other* than what it says" (1977, p. 155/505). Second, the associative richness of the signifier "tree" accrues to it by virtue of a kind of *"word-to-word* connexion" with other signifiers, and this is what Lacan understands by metonymy.

For Lacan, then, metonymy is "the one side *(versant)* of the effective field constituted by the signifier, so that meaning can emerge there. The other side is *metaphor*" (1977, p. 156/506). What characterizes metaphor is not the connection of one word to another but the substitution of *"one word for another"* (1977, p. 157/507). The critical example here is taken from Victor Hugo's (1859) poem about "Sleeping Booz": *"His sheaf was neither miserly nor spiteful."* "Sheaf" is the signifier that is substituted for another, namely, Booz himself. The connection between the two is indicated here by the word "his," thus emphasizing what is true for every metaphor, namely, that "the occulted signifier [remains] present through its (metonymic) connexion with the rest of the chain" (1977, p. 157/507). Thus, "the munificence of the sheaf" is attributed to Booz by virtue of his "accession to paternity," and it is in this attribution that the "creative spark" of this particular metaphor consists—it is here that "sense emerges from non-sense" (1977, p. 158/508). Such, then, is the other side "of the effective field constituted by the signifier, so that meaning can emerge there."

After this general treatment of metonymy and metaphor, Lacan says a word about the function of metonymy in the development of the subject. The matter is far from clear, but let it suffice for the moment to say that the dynamic of desire will find in metonymy (among other things) "the power to circumvent the obstacles of social censure" (1977, p. 158/508).

In conclusion, Lacan alludes to the classic adage, "the letter killeth while the spirit giveth life," conceding a certain basic truth in it but adding "we should also like to know how the spirit could live without the letter," for the letter "produces all the effects of truth in man without involving the spirit at all" (1977, p. 158/509). This takes us to the heart of Freud's experience of the unconscious as Lacan understands it, and introduces the whole problem of the "decentered" self, which becomes thematic in the second section of the essay.

II
The letter in the unconscious

In this section Lacan comes to the heart of the matter: the function of the "letter" in the "unconscious" as Freud reveals it to us. But first some precisions. To begin with, the "unconscious" for Freud (hence, at issue here) does not necessarily coincide, we are told, with the "psychical" unconscious, i.e., "psychical effects" that exclude the characteristic of consciousness. Rather, at issue is the "topography" *(topique)* of the unconscious — we take this to mean the unconscious as a fundamental structure that for Lacan can ideally be formalized in algorithms (1977, p. 163/514). Second, "letter" here refers not only to the strict sense of that term mentioned above, i.e., the written form of the phonemes, but to the broad sense according to which it is taken to be the underlying structure of signification as such. Thus, Freud's conception of the unconscious is modeled on his experience of the dream as a "rebus" — a notion that Lacan (with Freud) insists must be taken literally *(à la lettre)*:

> This derives from the agency in the dream of that same literal (or phonematic) structure in which the signifier is articulated and analysed in discourse. So the unnatural images of the boat on the roof, or the man with a comma for a head, which are specifically mentioned by Freud, are examples of dream-images that are to be taken only for their value as signifiers, that is to say, in so far as they allow us to spell out the 'proverb' presented by the rebus of the dream. The linguistic structure that enables us to read dreams is the very principle of the 'significance of the dream', the *Traumdeutung* [1977, p. 159/510].

Dream-images, then, are signifiers, and signifiers are letters that "spell out" the message of the dream. Accordingly, the "letter" in question here is "the same literal (or phonematic) structure in which the signifier is articulated and analysed in discourse." Such is the fundamental principle of Freud's *Interpretation of Dreams* (1900a), and Freud "staked the whole of his discovery on this essential expression of his message" (1977, p. 159/509). That is why hieroglyphics were so suggestive to him —a set of images that are essentially signifiers of meaning that has nothing to do with what the images themselves pictorially represent. Hence, the discernment of meaning contained in them (and, by analogy, in a dream) resembles far less the "decoding" of a message, i.e., the conversion of an artificial convention into "natural" language, than the "deciphering" of a cryptogram, i.e., the translation of one "natural" language that (like hieroglyphics) has been lost into another (1977, p. 150/ 510–511).

In any case, what Freud describes as "dream-work" follows the laws by which signifiers relate to each other: "distortion" *(Entstellung)* is the "sliding of the signified under the signifier"; "condensation" *(Verdichtung)* "is the structure of the superimposition of the signifiers, which metaphor takes as its field"; "displacement" *(Verschiebung)* "is closer to the idea of that veering off of signification that we see in metonymy" (1977, p. 160/511). And the "subtle processes" by which "such logical articulations as causality, contradiction, hypothesis, etc." find expression "are the object of a special study in Freud in which we see once more confirmed that the dream-work follows the laws of the signifier" (1977, p. 161/512).

But the crucially important function of the signifier in this conception of the unconscious was overlooked by Freud's early followers, partly because his formalization of the nature of the unconscious preceded the "formalizations of linguistics for which one could no doubt show that it paved the way by the sheer weight of its truth" (1977, p. 162/513), partly because psychoanalysts "were fascinated exclusively by the significations revealed in the unconscious" without realizing that the "secret attraction" of these significations was derived from a "dialectic that seemed to be immanent in them" but in fact was rooted more profoundly in the still unthematized nature of the signifier itself (1977, p. 162/513). In any case, it is the nature of the unconscious with its intrinsic relationship to the law of the signifier that accounts for the "absolute coherence" between Freud's "technique" of free association and his "discovery" of the unconscious — whether this be considered "in the normal person or in the neurotic" (1977, p. 163/514).

At this point Lacan turns to the topography *(topique)* of the unconscious, elaborating a series of formalizations that transpose Saussure's original formula S/*s* into algorithms that transcribe this relationship when the signifier refers directly to other signifiers under the guise either of metonymy (word-to-word relationships) or of metaphor (word-for-word substitution) (1977, p. 164/515). In either case, the question arises as to the place of the subject. At stake is the relationship between the unconscious as transindividual structure and the individual subject of our normal experience.

Good Frenchman that he is, Lacan begins all over again with Descartes. It is a commonplace, of course, that Descartes found his "unshakable foundation of truth" in the subject's awareness of himself in the very process of his own thinking/doubt: "I think, therefore I am." A philosophical analysis of this procedure, as well as the historical record of how it was subsequently embroidered with such terminology as "transcendental" and "existential," need not concern us here. Let it suffice to say simply that, taken at face value, the formula suggests that consciousness and subjectivity are coterminous.

But this is precisely what Freud with his own version of the Copernican revolution challenges, and Lacan poses the neuralgic question thus: "Is the place that I occupy as the subject of a signifier concentric or excentric, in relation to the place I occupy as subject of the signified?" (1977, p. 165/517). The expected answer is, of course, "excentric," for excentric circles, as opposed to concentric ones, are those that have different centers. The sense is that the subject occupies different "places," one the center of conscious discourse (signifiers), another the center of unconscious discourse, governed by "signifying mechanisms" that shape the signified and are quite legitimately designated as "thought" (1977, p. 165/517). This double polarity permits Lacan to relish a series of paradoxes such as: "I think [i.e., on the unconscious level] where I am not [i.e., consciously], therefore I am where I do not think" (1977, p. 166/517). The heart of the matter is that "the S and the *s* of the Saussurian algorithm are not on the same level" (1977, p. 166/518)—and this was the secret of Freud's great discovery.

The secret penetrates to the very "dimension of being [of the subject]: *Kern unseres Wesen* are Freud's own terms" (1977, p. 166/518). It is on this level that neuroses (as also myths) find their roots: "whether phobic, hysterical, or obsessive, the neurosis is a question that being poses for the subject 'from where it was before the subject came into the world' (Freud's phrase, which he used in explaining the Oedipal complex to little Hans)" (1977, p. 168/520). How "being" is to be understood here is not terribly clear, still less is any possible distinction between the unconscious, the "other scene" (1977, p. 167/519), and the "being" of the self, but the term reappears in the title of the third section of the essay and we shall return to it below.

More important for the present argument is to see how the law of the signifier functions on the level of psychopathology. The mode of metaphor, for example, gives structure to the symptom, insofar as "flesh or function is taken as a signifying element" that substitutes for the "enigmatic signifier of the sexual trauma." Between the two "there passes the spark that fixes in a symptom the signification inaccessible to the conscious subject in which that symptom may be resolved" (1977, p. 166/518).

The mode of metonymy, for its part, functions through the processes of desire. The nature of desire itself is treated elsewhere and it is not practical to delay over it now. Here it is important only to see that desire, the residue of a lost paradise, seeks its term by "eternally stretching forth towards the *desire for something else*" (1977, p. 167/518), where the "something else" is related to a previous "something else" by means of metonymy.

But the thrust of desire is a "dialectic of return" to some lost paradise, hence essentially a "recollection." This movement of return marked the development of Freud himself in his dogged fidelity to the "humble but inflexible consequences of the 'talking cure' " (1977, p. 167/519). But, for our present purposes, it is perhaps more important to note how Freud, in the case of Little Hans (1909a), treated the boy's pathology by helping him, through the mediation of the boy's father, to develop, "around the signifying crystal of his phobia, all the permutations possible on a limited number of signifiers" (1977, p. 168/520). In fact, then, if not in theory, Freud dealt with this patient's unconscious according to the law of the signifier that governs it.

What of the patient's ego in all of this? Lacan introduces it apparently out of the blue and refers again to the analysis we have already seen (Chapters 1 and 2), according to which the ego is an alienating projection and its defenses essentially "imaginary inertias that it concentrates against the message of the unconscious." What he adds here is that these defenses (as Fenichel, for example, describes them) are themselves simply "the reverse side of the mechanisms of the unconscious," which have the form of figures of speech that are "the active principle of the rhetoric of the discourse" that is ultimately determined by the laws of the signifier (1977, p. 169/521).

If Lacan's thesis is taken seriously, then the analyst must accept certain austere consequences. In the first place, the analyst must renounce any pretension to omniscience, for "the simplest (and even sickest)...[may seem] to know as much as [the analyst]" about what ought to be made of a given discourse (1977, p. 169/521), since he has equal access to the law of the signifier in the unconscious. Again, as analysts we must strive to become, as Freud was, "an encyclopedia of the arts and muses," and be content "to be antidotes to trifles" in spending time on the "allusions, quotations, puns, and equivocations" of the patient's discourse (1977, pp. 169–170/521). Examples of

Freud's own practice abound in what may be called his three "canonical" books on the unconscious: *The Interpretation of Dreams* (1900a), *The Psychopathology of Everyday Life* (1901), and *Jokes and Their Relation to the Unconscious* (1905b). There we see the early Freud in full possession of (and by) his insight, and it is instructive to note how a much more mature Freud, for example in his article on "Fetishism" (1927), follows the same form of analysis (1977, p. 170/522).

All of this adds up to a highly different conception of the Freudian unconscious from the one most readers are used to. But Lacan's position is unequivocal: "The unconscious is neither primordial nor instinctual; what it knows about the elementary is no more than the elements of the signifier" (1977, p. 170/522). In fact, as Lacan sees it, the "intolerable scandal" of Freud's discovery was not the emphasis on man's sexuality, but rather the fact that it was so " 'intellectual' " (1977, p. 171/523) — as such a conception of the unconscious implies. For Lacan, the infallible sign of "bad psychoanalysts," then, is that they deprecate with the term "intellectualization" "all technical or theoretical research that carries forward the Freudian experience along its authentic lines," as, presumably, Lacan's own does (1977, p. 171/523).

III
The letter, being and the other

The English translation of this title loses completely the musical assonance of the French: *La lettre, l'être et l'autre*, which has to be heard rather than read to be appreciated. The aural contiguity of these three signifiers shows (through metonymy) the interconnectedness and the mutual complementarity of what is signified by them. This signified is a complex unity that, like a musical chord, attempts to sound the interior harmony of all that has been said so far. To summarize this section we shall separate out the different elements of this chord according to the sequence of signifiers in the title.

The letter

As to how "letter" is to be understood at this point we already have some idea: it is that "same literal (or phonematic) structure in which the signifier is articulated and analysed in discourse" (1977, p. 159/510) — in other words, the law of language. What is strummed out here is how central language and its laws are to all human intercourse. It is only with the appearance of language, for example, "that the dimension of truth emerges" (1977, p. 172/524), since without language even a lie would be impossible. Similarly, it is language that makes possible all questioning (1977, p. 172/525); all negotiations between human agents that reach beyond sheer behavior presuppose this "third locus which is neither my speech nor my interlocutor" — "the locus of signifying convention" (1977, p. 173/525).

But the profound role that language plays in the entire human enterprise may be seen most strikingly, perhaps, in the example of a scholar such as Erasmus when we realize that the impact he had on "the revolution of a Reformation" derived from the fact that "the slightest alteration in the relation between man and the signifier, in this case in the procedures of exegesis, changes the whole course of history by modifying the moorings that anchor his being" (1977, p. 174/527). This suggests that the real reason why Freud himself has had such an earth-shaking effect, not just on the human sciences but on all aspects of contemporary Western culture, is that he, too, "is seen to have founded an intangible but radical revolution" of a very similar kind (1977, p. 174/527).

Being

So be it: "the slightest alteration in the relation between man and the signifier" modifies "the moorings that anchor [man's] being." The laws of language, then, anchor man's being: that is why the unconscious for Freud reaches down to the "*Kern unseres Wesen,* the nucleus of our being" (1977, p. 173/526). To be sure, this dimension cannot be an "object of knowledge," but "we bear witness to it as much and more in our whims, our aberrations, our phobias and fetishes, as in our more or less civilized personalities" (1977, p. 174/526). To the extent that such a testimony can still be called "scientific," Lacan can say that "Freud brought within the circle of science the boundary between the object and being that seemed to mark its outer limit" (1977, p. 175/527).

That this mode of expression has echoes of Heidegger, Lacan is ready to admit, not by way of resorting to some "ready-made mental jetsam" by which "one excuses oneself from any real thought" but by "the effort to leave the speech he proffers us its sovereign significance" (1977, p. 175/528). But what is that "sovereign significance" for Lacan? What is clear is that Heidegger's talk of "being" bears some deep affinity with the Freudian unconscious with its languagelike structure; what is not clear is how the two are to be differentiated. In any case, the dimension of being, as also of the unconscious, is a center that is "other" than the center of conscious thought and constitutes "the self's radical ex-centricity to itself" (1977, p. 171/524). But this brings us to the third element of the essay's closing chord: "the other."

The other

Lacan poses the question sharply: referring to the paradox mentioned above ("I think where I am not," etc.), he asks, "is what thinks in my place, then, another [ego]?" (1977, p. 171/523). Certainly not, if this means a "split personality" of some sort. Well, then, who "is this other to whom I am more attached than to myself, since, at the heart of my assent to my own identity it is still he who agitates me" (1977, p. 172/524)? Evidently it is not an "other" subject, nor is it discovered through an " 'awareness of others' " (1977, p. 173/526). In terms of other subjects, the "other" in question here "can be understood only at a second degree of otherness," through which it is in a "position of mediating" between me and other subjects (1977, p. 172/525). As such, it is the "guarantor of the truth" (1977, p. 172/524) and of "Good Faith" (1977, p. 173/522).

That is why Lacan capitalizes it: "If I have said that the unconscious is the discourse of the Other (with a capital O) it is in order to indicate the [dimension] beyond [individual subjects]" (1977, p. 172/524). If he adds here that in this dimension "the recognition of desire is bound up with the desire for recognition," this introduces the whole problem of the nature of desire which is not otherwise thematized in this essay. We defer a discussion of this formula, then, to later. In any case, it is the otherness of *this* other that constitutes the "radical heteronomy that Freud's discovery shows gaping within man" (1977, p. 172/524).

Such, then, is the "self's radical ex-centricity to itself." What is the subject's task in the face of all this? Freud himself suggests the formula: *"Wo Es war, soll Ich werden"* (There where it was, I must come to pass) (1977, p. 171/524). But this does not so much engage us to seek to " 'Know thyself' " on the psychological level as to reconsider the ways that lead us back to this original "where" that Freud has shown us (1977, p. 174/526). To the extent that we succeed, the result is "one of reintegration and harmony, I could even say of reconciliation *(Versöhnung)"* (1977, p. 171/524).

The closing chord is resolved with one final word that brings us back to the principal issue of the entire essay, namely, that the laws of language in the unconscious are grounded in being itself: "if the symptom is a metaphor, it is not a metaphor to say so, any more than to say that man's desire is a metonymy. For the symptom *is* a metaphor whether one likes it or not, as desire *is* a metonymy, however funny people may find the idea" (1977, p. 175/528).

Map of the Text

Introduction.
    A. This reworking of a lecture to liberal arts students falls
    . between writing and speech.
        1. Writing makes possible a tightening of discourse so that the reader has no way out but the way in.
        2. Speech has different rhythms "essential to the formative effect" that is sought.

B. Literary training was designated by Freud as requisite
for analysts,

   1. but in the psychoanalytic journals we observe novice concerns with symbolization and language.

   2. How can today's psychoanalyst fail to recognize that
"speech is the key to [the] truth"?

      a. For from it his experience receives its instru-
ment, framework, material, and even the static
of its uncertainties.

I.   *The meaning of the letter.*

  A. Language is distinguished from speech.

    1. In the unconscious, psychoanalysis discovers the
entire structure of language,

      a. whose letter is to be taken literally

         i. in the sense of the phonemes of language
used by a speaker.

    2. Language exists prior to the moment the subject
speaks and should not be confused with speech's
psychical and somatic functions.

      a. The aphasias distribute their deficits according
to the two slopes of the signifier (as Jakobson
shows).

      b. The subject is the serf of language and of a dis-
course in which he is already located at birth.

         i. This discourse establishes tradition, which
sets down the basic structures of culture,

            (a) and whose laws governing exchange are
a function of language.

      c. Even dialectical materialism does not view lan-
guage as a superstructure.

  B. The science of linguistics has achieved objectivity through
its algorithm: S/s — "the signifier over the signified."

    1. This Saussurian formula expresses the primordial
distinction between two orders separated by a barrier that resists signification.

      a. It presumes the arbitrariness of the sign,

2. thus demonstrating that every signification depends on its reference to another signification.
   a. Language covers the entire field of the signified,
      i. constituting objects through concepts.
   b. It is an illusion to think that the signifier serves to represent the signified.
C. A diagram from the sexual field replaces Saussure's illustration of S/*s*.
   1. In this example we see how the signifier becomes physically part of the signified (the sign over separate doors).
   2. In the example of the children at the railway station, the bar is materialized in the rails,
      a. whose form suggests that its resistance may not be dialectical.
D. The signifying domain has an articulated structure.
   1. Its units are subject to a double condition:
      a. that of "being reducible to ultimate differential elements,"
         i. which are the phonemes;
      b. that of being combined "according to the laws of a closed order"
         i. to form signifying chains.
         ii. These are laws of grammar and lexicology.
   2. Meaning does not reign supreme beyond this closed order,
      a. for the signifier foreshadows meaning, sketching its dimension as the chain unfolds,
         i. as is illustrated by the use of adverbs and conjunctions.
         ii. Hence, it is only in the signifying chain that meaning "insists," for meaning is not constituted by the single element of the chain.
   3. There is imposed, then, the notion of a continual "sliding of the signified under the signifier,"
      a. which is illustrated by Saussure's image of lines

connecting corresponding segments of the Waters of *Genesis*.

   b. A linear conception of the way the chain of discourse is constituted has merit only in the direction of time.

   c. Our experience instead suggests the image of
"anchoring points."

   d. Poetry reveals a polyphony like that of a musical
score,

      i. for every signifying chain has, suspended
vertically from its units, whole contexts of
association,

        (a) as illustrated by the word "tree."

      ii. For the signifier to operate, it is not neces-
sary that it be present in the subject,

        (a) for it has become part of the linguistic
tradition.

E. This structure of the signifying chain allows me to use
it "to signify *something quite other* than what it says."

  1. The figure of style through which I can do this is
called metonymy,

    a. as in the example "thirty sails."

    b. It is based on the word-to-word connection, not
on any part-to-whole relation.

  2. The other slope of the effective field of the signifier
is called metaphor,

    a. as in *"His sheaf was neither miserly nor spiteful."*

    b. Its formula is *"one word for another,"* where one sig-
nifier takes the place of the other in the signifying
chain.

    c. Metaphor occurs precisely where "sense emerges
from non-sense."

  3. In metonymy we find the means of evading censor-
ship.

    a. We are now getting warm in our investigation of
Freudian truth.

II. *The letter in the unconscious.*
   A. In *The Interpretation of Dreams,* Freud deals with "the letter of the discourse."
     1. As a rebus, the dream has the same literal and phonematic structure in which the signifier is articulated in discourse.
       a. The signifier's image has nothing to do with its signification.
       b. Only the linguistically untrained favor a symbolism derived from natural analogy.
       c. Today's analyst must learn to decipher, not decode.
     2. The general precondition for the functioning of the dream is *distortion* or *Entstellung.*
       a. This is "the sliding of the signified under the signifier."
       b. It is always present in discourse,
       c. but this action is unconscious.
     3. The two slopes of the incidence of the signifier over the signified are also found in the functioning of the dream.
       a. *Condensation* or *Verdichtung* involves "the superimposition of the signifiers":
         i. metaphor is its field;
         ii. its mechanism is "connatural with poetry" *(Dichtung).*
       b. *Displacement* or *Verschiebung* is the "veering off of signification,"
         i. which is demonstrated in metonymy,
         ii. and is the most appropriate device the unconscious uses to elude censorship.
     4. These two mechanisms are distinguished from their homologous role in discourse only in a regard to the means of representation.
       a. This is a limit, imposed on the signifying material, that functions interior to the discourse,

      i. and does not reduce it to mere pictorial dis-
        play.
   b. Like charades, the dream lacks the precise
     meaning to represent subordinate clauses.
   c. The rest of the dream-elaboration consists of sec-
     ondary fantasies, like daydreams, which func-
     tion in wish fulfillment.

5. The constitutive role of the signifier suffered a general misunderstanding from the beginning,
   a. because *The Interpretation of Dreams* appeared
     before the formalizations of linguistics,
   b. and because psychoanalysts were bewitched by
     unconscious symbolism.
      i. Freud changed his tack to counteract this
        bias,
      ii. while maintaining the dignity of the object of
        his discovery.
   c. Theory and practice are no longer integrated, as
     they were in Freud.

6. In analyzing dreams, Freud intends to demonstrate
   the laws of the unconscious.
   a. Dreams of the normal person or the neurotic
     reveal the same laws.
   b. This unconscious is not synonymous with the
     psychological order,
      i. for many psychical effects that exclude
        consciousness have nothing to do with the
        Freudian unconscious.
      ii. And the Freudian unconscious can have
        somatic effects.
   c. The topography of the unconscious is defined by
     the algorithm S/s,
      i. whose formula can be applied to metonymy
        and metaphor.

B. The function of the subject is crucial to our discussion.
  1. The Cartesian *cogito* is the historical peak of the
    epistemology of science.

      a. Simply criticizing it evades the notion of the sub-
ject,
         i. which is necessary even for a science of strat-
egy.
        ii. It also keeps us from recognizing Freud's
Copernican revolution,
          (a) which questioned the centrality of the
place man assigns himself in the universe.
  2. Is my place as subject of a signifier concentric or
excentric in regard to my place as subject of the
signified?
    a. It is not a matter of knowing whether my self-
description conforms to my reality,
      i. but instead of knowing whether I as speaker
am identical with myself as spoken about.
    b. The Cartesian *cogito* is central to the mirage that
makes modern man so sure he is himself even
when he has doubts about himself.
    c. The signifying game of metonymy and meta-
phor goes on without my awareness.
    d. In this way I can say, "I think where I am not,
therefore I am where I do not think."
C. The unconscious is the kernel of our being.
  1. The symptom is a metaphor in which flesh or function becomes the signifying element,
    a. whose signification is not accessible to the con-
scious subject.
  2. Desire is channeled by metonymy,
    a. in an endless series of substitute objects.
  3. Myths, the sexual theories of the child, neurotic
compulsions, all respond to the same necessities.
D. The ego was defined by Freud according to its particular resistances.
  1. These are of an imaginary nature, lures reducible to
the narcissistic relation as developed in the mirror
stage.

      a. In synthesizing sensorimotor selections, the ego answers for reality, a reality suspended from duty along with the ego.

2. The ego concentrates imaginary inertias to resist the message of the unconscious.

3. Its disguises operate through a resistance that is intrinsic to discourse.

      a. Thus the defense mechanisms are inversions of unconscious mechanisms,

          i. whose most proper labels are Quintilian's figures of speech.

      b. Psychoanalysts of today mistakenly describe resistance in terms of a fixed emotional state, thus losing one of Freud's truths.

          i. Because we must make our way into the truth, it is disturbing and we repress it.

          ii. The scientist, seer, or quack wants to be the only one to know the truth.

E. As Freud shows, knowledge of art and literature helps in interpreting the unconscious,

1. for the unconscious does not consist of instincts but of signifiers.

      a. Freud's early works give a web of examples involving the two axes of language: connection and substitution.

2. The incident of the "shine on the nose" discloses the nature of unconscious thought.

3. The abyss opened by the idea of unconscious thought, and not sexuality, provoked early resistance to psychoanalysis.

      a. Sexuality, after all, always prevailed in literature.

      b. Ironically, recent psychoanalysis has turned sexuality into a moral affair.

      c. Before Freudian sexuality was sanctified it was a scandal because it was so "intellectual."

      d. Today all research forwarding the authentic Freudian experience is condemned as "intellectu-alization."

III. *The letter, being and the other (La lettre, l'être et l'autre).*

  A. To account for unconscious thought, are we postulating another ego? Do we have psychological Manichaeism?

    1. This is not a matter of split personality,

      a. but rather a goal: *Wo Es war, soll Ich werden,*

      b. a goal of reintegration and harmony, even of reconciliation.

    2. We cannot ignore "the self's radical ex-centricity to itself," i.e., the truth Freud discovered,

      a. or else psychoanalysis becomes a compromise tactic.

      b. Nor can we speak of the "total personality."

      c. The gap in man caused by this radical heterono-my can be covered over only dishonestly.

      d. Who is this other who wags me and "to whom I am more attached than to myself"?

  B. "The unconscious is the discourse of the Other,"

    1. as the region where the desire that seeks to be recog-nized is the desire for recognition.

    2. The Other is "the locus of signifying convention," "the guarantor of Good Faith."

      a. The dimension of truth emerges with the appear-ance of language.

      b. Every question presupposes language.

        i. This goes beyond the signal systems found among animals.

        ii. This also goes beyond "an awareness of others."

      c. The other challenges our truth, as in Gide's case.

  C. Freud shows us the ways that lead to "the nucleus of our being," *Kern unseres Wesen,*

    1. not as what we know objectively, but rather as that which makes our being.

      a. We bear witness to it in whims, phobias, fetishes,

   as well as in our civilized personalities.
   b. Madness and reason both serve the Logos.
2. Our being's moorings are modified by the slightest
   change in the relation between us and the signifier,
   as is seen when exegesis shifts its approach.
   a. Here lies Freud's revolution, affecting everything.
      i. This is not a matter of technique based on
         categories of psychology,
      ii. or on the vulgar concepts in which its prac-
          tice recommends itself.
3. Freud brought into science the relationship between
   being and the object.
   a. This is not to be dismissed as a case of neo-
      Heideggereanism.
4. We refer to being and the letter and differentiate the
   other from the Other,
   a. in order to deal with the effects of resistance and
      transference.
   b. For it is not a metaphor to say that the symptom
      is a metaphor,
      i. because "the symptom *is* a metaphor,"
      ii. just as "desire *is* a metonymy."

NOTES TO THE TEXT

146/493   The translation of *l'instance* as "agency" suggests the
          active nature of the letter in the unconscious, but not
          the quality of this action. In the first English transla-
          tion of this essay, Miel (1966) uses "insistence," con-
          veying the autonomous quality of this agency. (Miel's
          translation is one we have drawn on, as Sheridan
          apparently also has in his translation of *Écrits: A
          Selection.*) In French, *l'instance* means "entreaty," "soli-
          citation," "urgency," "earnestness," and "instance,"
          with the last strengthened by the notion of the "in-
          stand-ing" or persistence of the letter.

146d/494 Speech has different meters *(mesures)*—not "techniques"—which are essential to the formative effect.

147*g*/495   The French word for "meaning" is *sens,* connoting both "sense" and "direction" or "way."

148*b*/495   For "the two sides of the signifying effect," the French text has *les deux versants de l'effet signifiant.* We prefer to translate *versants* as "slopes," to be more congruous with later expressions regarding the sliding *(glissement)* of the signified under the signifier. The reference is to the twofold character of language, the axis of selection (metaphor) and the axis of combination (metonymy) as delineated by Jakobson (1956). They view aphasia as a linguistic problem involving two basic types of speech disturbance: a deficiency in verbal selection and substitution based on similarity or a deficiency in combination and contexture based on contiguity.

149*b*/497   Saussure writes: "The linguistic sign unites, not a thing and a name, but a concept and a sound-image. . . . I propose to retain the word *sign* [*signe*] to designate the whole and to replace *concept* and *sound-image* respectively by *signified* [*signifié*] and *signifier* [*signifiant*]" (1916, pp. 66–67).

150*b*/498   The point seems to be that the signified (the concept) is itself not a *thing,* but an aspect of language, whose meaning lies in words, other signifiers. Language, then, covers the field and in doing so it can answer or correspond to every need that can be articulated.

The example of the word *chose* ("thing") appears in Saussure (1916, p. 95) to illustrate the change from its Latin origin *causa* ("cause," "reason," "case," or "point"). Lacan elaborates to suggest the inherent contradiction implied in any attempt to chart a univocal connection between "things" and individual words.

Lacan's note refers to his seminar dealing with St. Augustine's "De locutionis significatione" ("On the signification of speech") as reported in Volume I of *Le Séminaire* (1953–1954), in which he says:

> The fundamental phenomenon of the analytic revelation is this relationship of one discourse to another on which it is propped. We find manifested there this fundamental principle of semantics, that every semanteme refers to the whole of the semantic system, to the polyvalence of its uses. Furthermore, for all that is properly of language, insofar as it is human, that is to say, utilizable in speech, there is never any univocal quality to the symbol. Every semanteme always has several senses... every signification only refers to another signification... language is not made to designate things [p. 272; our translation].

He goes on to speak, following Augustine, of how "it is impossible to handle language by referring the sign to the thing on a word-by-word basis" (p. 277).

151*b*/500 The nominalist debate refers to the classical discussion, ancient in origin but of special importance to medieval thinkers, concerning the philosophical status of universal terms such as "man," which seem to refer both to a class and to individual members of that class. Does such a term refer to some ontological absolute? Or to some construct of the mind? Or to nothing at all beyond the term or name *(nomen)* itself, since only individuals exist? The nominalist position holds the last of these and retains its importance for contemporary thought.

152*b*/500 The rails separate the two orders of signifier (Ladies/ Gentlemen) and signified (the children as sexual beings). Later the rails suggest the incessant veering off of meaning found in metonymy in which desire is caught "eternally stretching forth towards the *desire for something else*" (1977, p. 167/518).

152*d*/501   In *Gulliver's Travels,* Jonathan Swift (1726) describes
how the prolonged war between the two kingdoms of
Lilliput and Blefuscu originated in a dispute over
whether eggs should be broken at the larger or small-
er end (p. 53).

153*a*/501   Claude Garamond (1480–1561) designed a roman
type which was influential in establishing the roman
letter as standard. The Didot family spans 250 years
of printing history.

153*d*/502   In his discussion of St. Augustine, Lacan states:

> *If* is a conjunction of subordination. But in the
> sentence "the *if* displeases me," this word is used
> as a noun. St. Augustine proceeds with all the
> rigor and analytic spirit of a modern linguist,
> and he shows that it is the usage in the sentence
> which defines the qualification of a word as part
> of the discourse [1953–1954, p. 274; our trans-
> lation].

153*g*/502   The Miel translation (1966) provides a helpful note:
"The allusions are to the 'I am black, but comely...'
of the *Song of Solomon,* and to the nineteenth century
cliché of the 'poor but honest woman'" (p. 111). The
identical note, with no reference to Miel, appears in
Sheridan's translation (Lacan, 1977, p. 176).

154*a*/502   Saussure's illustration appears in his discussion of
the relation between thought and language (1916):

> Psychologically our thought — apart from its ex-
> pression in words — is only a shapeless and in-
> distinct mass. Philosophers and linguists have
> always agreed in recognizing that without lan-
> guage, thought is a vague, uncharted nebula.
> There are no pre-existing ideas, and nothing is
> distinct before the appearance of language [p.
> 111].

For Saussure, the sounds that go to make up phonemes are as shapeless as thought and the "mysterious fact" is that both thought and sound come together in an arbitrary manner in working out reciprocally differentiated units of language (i.e., words). He goes on to say:

> In addition, . . . to consider a term as simply the union of a certain sound with a certain concept is grossly misleading. To define it in this way would isolate the term from its system; it would mean assuming that one can start from the terms and construct the system by adding them together when, on the contrary, it is from the interdependent whole that one must start and through analysis obtain its elements. . . .
>
> Language is a system of interdependent terms in which the value of each term results solely from the simultaneous presence of the others [pp. 113–114].

For a recent critique of Saussure on linguistic grounds, see the review essay by Marie-Laure Ryan (1979).

154c/503   It is unclear to us why the inversion of the terms "Peter hits Paul" would reverse the time of the action rather than the direction of intentionality.

155a/504   The French text has Ἐν-Πάντα. The allusion here (and later, p. 168e/520) is to Heraclitus' *Logos* and Heidegger's (1951) interpretation, "Logos" (which Lacan [1956] translated, as he tells us near the end of this essay, making it available in *La Psychanalyse*).

> Heidegger claims that Heraclitus' formula Ἐν-Πάντα (one-in-many [-beings]) describes the manner in which Λογος functions. As Ἐν, Λογος is the One, the Only, that unifies all beings in themselves, insofar as it gathers them into themselves, letting them lie forth in non-concealment as themselves. Because Λογος is Ἐν,

it may be called the utterly Simple. Ἐν is likened to a lightning-bolt, by reason of which beings are lit up in their Being [Richardson, 1963, pp. 492–493].

155*d*/504   The "level of the signified" is the "whole articulation of relevant contexts suspended 'vertically' " (1977, p. 154/503)—the polyphony that resonates with the signifier, i.e., the richness of language itself, going beyond the individual subject and certainly going beyond conscious awareness.

155*f*/505   Lemaire (1970) writes of metaphor and metonymy as "the two linguistic phenomena responsible for the autonomy of the signifier, or for the supremacy of the signifier over the signified in language. This supremacy of the signifier was defined by language's peculiar aptitude for signifying something other than what it is literally saying" (p. 191). Lacan later elaborates the role of metaphor and metonymy as slopes for the sliding of the signified under the signifier, and thereby accounts for the nature of dream distortion (1977, p. 160/511). These language processes operate unconsciously, thus raising the question about the place of the subject, which he takes up again later.

156*f*/506   The Loewenstein (1956) article referred to in Lacan's note (1977, p. 177/506) contains a "personal communication" footnote mentioning Jakobson.

156*h*/506   Both the French text and Sheridan's citation in footnote 21 contain an error; *n'était pas* should read *n'était point* (Hugo, 1859). See *Écrits* (1966, p. 892), for additional commentary by Lacan in which he makes explicit the link between "His sheaf" and the phallus.

158*d*/508   The non-sense of the sheaf being neither miserly nor spiteful makes sense only because the subject, Booz, has gone underground to the level of the signified, displaced by the new signifier, "the sheaf"; in jokes there is an irruption of non-sense "from below" that disrupts the sense of the conscious discourse.

158*f*/508 This book by Strauss (1952), a political philosopher, is also discussed by Gadamer (1960) in the context of how to understand a text:

> Is not conscious distortion, camouflage and concealment of the proper meaning in fact the rare extreme case of a frequent, even normal situation? — just as persecution (whether by civil authority or the church, the inquisition etc) is only an extreme case when compared with the intentional or unintentional pressure that society and public opinion exercise on human thought. Only if we are conscious of the uninterrupted transition from one to the other are we able to estimate the hermeneutic difficulty of Strauss' problem. How are we able to establish clearly that a distortion has taken place? Thus, in my opinion, it is by no means clear that, when we find contradictory statements in a writer, it is correct to take the hidden meaning — as Strauss thinks — for the true one. There is an unconscious conformism of the human mind to considering what is universally obvious as really true. And there is, against this, an unconscious tendency to try extreme possibilities, even if they cannot always be combined into a coherent whole. The experimental extremism of Nietzsche bears irrefutable witness to this. Contradictions are an excellent criterion of truth but, unfortunately, they are not an unambiguous criterion when we are dealing with hermeneutics [p. 488].

158*h*/509 Lacan begins his *Écrits* (1966) with "The Seminar on [Poe's] 'The Purloined Letter.' " This has been translated by Mehlman (1972b).

159*c*/509   There is a discrepancy between the letters cited in the French text (107 and 119) and in Miel's (1966) translation (107 and 109); the latter are repeated in the *Selection* (1977). The letters appear in Freud's *The Origins of Psychoanalysis: Letters to Wilhelm Fliess, Drafts and Notes* (1887–1902). In letter 107, Freud wrote, "I cannot afford to keep to myself the finest — and probably the only lasting — discovery that I have made" (p. 281); in letter 119: "The climax of my achievements in dream interpretation comes in this installment" (p. 299).

159*d*/510   In his first sentence Freud does not mention the word "rebus" but states that by using his procedure "every dream reveals itself as a psychical structure which has a meaning" ("jeder Traum sich als ein sinnvolles psychisches Gebilde herausstellt") (1900a, p. 1; 1900b, p. 1). The rebus appears at the beginning of Chapter VI, in a context buzzing with linguistic referents: the dream-thoughts and dream-content are like two different languages *(Sprachen)*, the dream-content "seems like a transcript [*Übertragung*, 'transference'] of the dream-thoughts into another mode of expression [*Ausdrucksweise*, 'style'], whose characters [*Zeichen*, 'signs'] and syntactic laws [*Fügungsgesetze*] it is our business to discover by comparing the original and the translation [*Übersetzung*]. . . .The dream-content. . . is expressed as it were in a pictographic script [*Bilderschrift*], the characters of which [*deren Zeichen*] have to be transposed [*zu übertragen sind*] individually into the language [*die Sprache*] of the dream-thoughts" (1900a, p. 277; 1900b, p. 283–284). He goes on to say we would be led into error if we tried to read *(lesen)* these signs *(Zeichen)* as pictures instead of according to their symbolic relation *(nach ihrer Zeichenbeziehung*, "according to their character as signs"). An example of a rebus, a picture-puzzle, is then given, and Freud instructs us to "try to replace each separate element by a syllable or word [*eine Silbe oder ein Wort*] that can be represented by that element in some way or other. The words [*Die Worte*] which are put together in this way are no longer nonsensical [*sind nicht mehr sinnlos*] but may form a poetical phrase [*Dichterspruch*] of the greatest beauty and significance" (1900a, p. 278; 1900b, p. 284).

For a careful analysis of the role of language, especially in Freud's early works, see Forrester (1980), whose book is presented, in part, as a prolegomena to understanding Lacan's reading of Freud.

160*b*/510   In discussing representation by symbols, Freud wrote: "I should like to utter an express warning against over-estimating the importance of symbols [*Symbole*] in dream-interpretation, against restricting the work of translating dreams merely to translating symbols and against abandoning the technique of making use of the dreamer's associations" (1900a, pp. 359–360).

160*f*/511   We prefer the translation, "the two slopes of the incidence of the signifier" *(les deux versants de l'incidence du signifiant).*

161*b*/512   Freud's Chapter VI, Section I deals with secondary revision (1900a, pp. 488ff.).

162*g*/513   The "hieroglyphic aviary" appears to refer back to the "ornithological specimens" (1977, p. 159/510), whose role as signifiers is overlooked.

164*a–b*/
515   These difficult formulas we shall attempt to illustrate by Lacan's own example of the fetish (1977, p. 170/ 522), in which the patient had to see a "shine on the nose *(Glanz auf der Nase)*" to obtain sexual satisfaction. *Glanz* (shine) in the patient's original English was "glance." The contiguity of sound establishes a metonymic link between *Glanz/glance at the nose*, while the similarity of shape establishes a metaphoric link between the nose and phallus. In the metonymy

desire is chained from the original glance at the mother in sexual curiosity to the shine *(Glanz)* needed for sexual satisfaction, both words forming part of the word-to-word chain "glance *(Glanz)* at the nose." The intervals between words concretize (and actually allow for the chaining of) the gap, the want-to-be *(manque à être)* out of which desire originates and which the chain of signifiers perpetuates (since the discourse never fills or closes the gap but only conceals it). The bar is not crossed in metonymy (i.e., the signified is never attained) since there is a continual veering off of meaning. In this example the meaning emerges only in the metaphoric structure in which "nose" is a substitute signifier for "phallus," the primary signifier of desire, now the signified which has crossed the bar.

164c/516 Earlier (1977, p. 153f/505), Lacan touched on the role of the subject in language's ability to signify something other than what it says; it is not a matter of the subject deliberately disguising his thought, but of an unconscious chain of signifiers set up by metaphor. Laplanche and Leclaire (1960) quote Lacan: "Metaphor must be defined as the implantation, into a chain of signifiers, of another signifier, by dint of which the one it replaces falls to the rank of signified, and, as latent signifier, perpetuates the interval onto which another chain of signifiers can be grafted" (p. 156). The subject as conscious thinker has no place in this process of associative chaining.

165a/516 The Latin phrase reads: "Where I think 'I think, therefore I am,' there I am." Lacan counters this with: "I think where I am not, therefore I am where I do not think" (1977, p. 166/517).

165c/516 The problem is the relationship between the conscious subject and thought. This problem would be of special interest to Lacan's university audience, seated in the Descartes Amphitheatre of the Sorbonne (1977, p. 176, n. 3/494, n. 1). Lacoue-Labarthe and Nancy (1973, p. 19) call attention to Lacan's address as being his first *intervention véritable* in a university.

165*d*/516 In his paper "A Difficulty in the Path of Psycho-Analysis" (1917), Freud describes how humanity's narcissism has "suffered three severe blows" (p. 139), first, from Copernicus' challenge to the earth's central place in the universe (the cosmological blow), second, from Darwin's challenge to man's presumption of superiority to other animals (the biological blow), and, third, from the challenge of the Freudian unconscious to the ego's mastery in its own house (the psychological blow).

166*c*/517 Desire is split in the unconscious processes of metonymy (related to a lack of being in the gaps of the chain of the signifiers) and metaphor (related to a refusal or denial of the signifier repressed below the bar).

167*f*/519 These allusions all appear to relate to the earlier discussions of what the subject's "desire has been in his history." Hölderlin's *nostos* refers to his poem "Homecoming/To the Kinsmen," suggestive of nostalgia (and perhaps Lacan is also alluding to Heidegger's [1943] meditation on Hölderlin and a view of temporality as the future coming through the past). On the other hand, the notion of repetition in Kierkegaard (1843) is forward-looking (see Nordentoft, 1972, p. 106). Lacan seems to be saying that Freud, ever-faithful to the basically linguistic nature of his discovery, was able to discern in the history of the subject the movement of desire (made apparent in symptoms, dreams, and parapraxes) as structured by unconscious signifiers and by radical finitude. Regarding *Logos*, see note 155*a* and the end of the Overview in Chapter 8 (discussing Lacan's reference to *Logos* on p. 291/695). Empedocles was discussed earlier (see note 102*e*).

168*d*/520 Freud's phrase is "Long before he was in the world" (1909a, p. 42).

169*a*/520 The translation should read, "Freud seems to abound in the delegation which is traditionally made to it [the ego] of answering for reality" ("Freud...paraisse abonder dans la délégation qui lui est faite tradition-ellement de répondre de la réalité"). Suspension *(le suspens)* connotes being suspended from duty (like a priest or policeman); when the ego is so treated, its "reality" of perceptual synthesis is also suspended.

169*b*/520 The subject is a displacement at least in the sense that he becomes caught up in the signifying chain and subject to the metonymy of desire.

169*c*/521 To the earlier definitions (note 58*a*) of some of these terms, we now add these:

> *Periphrasis* uses a longer phrasing in place of a possible shorter expression.
> *Suspension* defers the principal idea to the end of a sentence or paragraph.
> *Litotes* emphasizes by understatement, by indicating the negative of its opposite ("not many" for "a few").
> *Hypotyposis* is a vivid, picturesque description.

(The above was drawn from *Webster's New International Dictionary* [1960] and *Webster's New Collegiate Dictionary* [1974]).

170*e*/522 After describing the fetish (see note 164*a–b*), Freud (1927) wrote:

> When now I announce that the fetish is a substi-tute for the penis, I shall certainly create disap-pointment; so I hasten to add that it is not a substitute for any chance penis, but for a partic-ular and quite special penis that had been ex-

tremely important in early childhood but had later been lost. That is to say, it should normally have been given up, but the fetish is precisely designed to preserve it from extinction. To put it more plainly: the fetish is a substitute for the woman's (the mother's) penis that the little boy once believed in and — for reasons familiar to us — does not want to give up.

What happened, therefore, was that the boy refused to take cognizance of the fact of his having perceived that a woman does not possess a penis. No, that could not be true: for if a woman had been castrated, then his own possession of a penis was in danger; and against that there rose in rebellion the portion of his narcissism which Nature has, as a precaution, attached to that particular organ [pp. 152–153].

171c/523   To minimize ambiguity, since the French has *un autre moi*, we translate, "Is what thinks in my place, then, another ego?"

172f/524   The relation between the recognition of desire and the desire for recognition is a repeated theme (see 1977, pp. 141d/431, 260c–d/623).

173d/525   In *The Praise of Folly*, Erasmus makes reference to Midas in his second paragraph (1509, p. 43). Dionysus gave King Midas the power to turn everything he touched into gold because he had befriended Silenus, the oldest of the satyrs. When even his food was affected, he begged to be relieved of his power. He was also given ass's ears by Apollo for preferring the music of Pan to that of Apollo. Midas hid his shame under a high cap so that only his barber knew. The secret, however, was uttered into a hole in the ground whence reeds grew, and whenever the wind blew they voiced his secret folly.

There also appears to be a dig at Husserlian phenomenology. See Husserl's Fifth Meditation in his *Cartesian Meditations,* where the question is posed: "*How* can my ego, within his peculiar ownness, constitute under the name, 'experience of something other,' precisely something *other*" (1929, p. 94).

Chapter 6

On a Question Preliminary to Any Possible Treatment of Psychosis

Overview

This essay first appeared as an article in *La Psychanalyse* (1958b), and summarizes the work of the first two terms of the seminar of 1955–1956. Though its composition follows that of "The Agency of the Letter in the Unconscious" (Chapter 5), its thought represents a slightly earlier level of development. As such, it is Lacan's most direct address to the problem of psychosis, where paranoia is taken to be the paradigm of psychosis and Daniel Paul Schreber's account of his personal experience (1903a) to be the paradigmatic case of paranoia. Reduced to its simplest terms, this essay attempts to explain the origin of psychosis in the light of Lacan's general theory of the linguistic structure of the unconscious. In his explanation, Lacan designates a mechanism distinct from "repression," which he calls (with textual warrant from Freud) "foreclosure," i.e., "repudiation" *(Verwerfung)* of a fundamental signifier. The essay gravitates toward this notion as toward its principal pole.

196

I
Towards Freud

The essay begins with an introductory section that takes a global swipe at traditional approaches to the problem: "Half a century of Freudianism applied to psychosis leaves its problem still to be rethought, in other words, at the *status quo ante*" (1977, p. 179/531). Before Freud, Lacan claims, psychology was victimized by a heritage of scholasticism, which left it trammeled in "an abstract theory of the faculties of the subject" (1977, p. 179/531). Under the circumstances, this theory could not be counterbalanced by subordinate attention to affect. At best, it settled for a naive conception of the perceiving subject *(percipiens)* and implied a naive conception of the perceived object *(perceptum)* as well, "for even if the alternations of identity of the *percipiens* are admitted, its function in the constitution of the unity of the *perceptum* is not discussed" (1977, p. 180/532).

With this allusion to the role of the perceiving subject in "constituting" the unity of the perceived object, we are reminded of a language (at least) and a conception (perhaps) that Merleau-Ponty developed in his *Phenomenology of Perception* (1945). For whatever value it may have in trying to find a sense in Lacan's text, let us recall the drift of Merleau-Ponty's discussion. Starting from the phenomenology of the late Husserl, with its focus on the world of lived experience *(Lebenswelt)*, Merleau-Ponty analyzes our presence in the world through the mediation of our perceiving body. Thus, our embodied consciousness and the world of our experience are seen to be intimately correlated with each other. "The thing, and the world, are given to me along with the parts of my body, not by any 'natural geometry', but in a living connection comparable, or rather identical, with that existing between parts of my body itself" (1945, p. 205). Accordingly, one might say that the thing is not so much "*given* in perception" as "internally taken up by us, reconstituted and experienced by us in so far as it is bound up with a world, the basic structures of which we carry with us, and of which it is merely one of many possible concrete forms" (1945, p. 326).

Thus, Merleau-Ponty can speak of a genuine "communion" between man and what he perceives:

> As I contemplate the blue of the sky I am not *set over against it* as an acosmic subject; I do not possess it in thought, or spread out towards it some idea of blue such as might reveal the secret of it, I abandon myself to it and plunge into its mystery, 'it thinks itself within me'. . . . Every perception takes place in an atmosphere of generality and is presented to us anonymously. . . . So, if I wanted to render precisely the perceptual experience, I ought to say that *one* perceives in me, and not that I perceive [1945, pp. 214–215].

This pre-predicative communion with the things encountered in the world is characteristic of the psychotic as well as of the normal person, and Merleau-Ponty is, of course, well aware of the need to account for the difference between hallucination and "true" perception (1945, pp. 334–345). How Merleau-Ponty deals with this issue is another matter, which need not concern us here, so let us be content with this much recollection of his thought and return to Lacan's text itself.

Whether or not Lacan is suggesting a phenomenological solution to the problem of polarity between subject and object in perception is not at all clear. What is clear is that he challenges the simplistic notion of a subject-object dichotomy that lies at the base of so many theories of psychotic hallucination. "All of them, ingenious as they are in declaring, in the name of a manifest fact that a hallucination is a *perceptum* without an object end up asking the *percipiens* the reason for this *perceptum,* without anyone realizing that in this request, a step has been skipped, the step of asking oneself whether the *perceptum* itself bequeathed a univocal sense to the *percipiens* here required to explain it" (1977, p. 180/532). Lacan seems to be suggesting, then, that, given the conception of hallucination as a "*perceptum* without an object," there may be another dimension to consider in explain-

ing it beyond the mere projective power of the perceiving subject.

This becomes apparent when we consider auditory hallucinations. To begin with, it is clear that the *perceptum* itself has
not "bequeathed a univocal sense to the *percipiens*" when we realize that "the act of hearing is not the same, according to whether
it aims at the coherence of the verbal chain. . . or according to
whether it accommodates itself in speech to sound modulation"
(1977, p. 180/532). Yet the sense is not determined by an "ob-
jectivizing" function of the perceiving subject either. "For it is at
the level at which subjective 'synthesis' confers its full meaning
on speech that the subject reveals all the paradoxes of which he
is the patient" (1977, p. 181/533). One of these paradoxes begins to appear, for example, when the subject engages in dialogue with the other, "for simply by entering the other's auditory
field, the subject falls under the sway of a suggestion from which
he can escape only by reducing the other to being no more than
the spokesman of a discourse that is not [the other's] own" (1977,
p. 181/533). The paradox, then, is that while the subjective
"synthesis" seems to proceed from the perceiving subject, it is
determined somehow by something other than itself.

But this is even more obvious when the subject attends to
his own speech. The essential here is not simply that it is impossible for the subject to speak without hearing what he says, but
rather that, "the *sensorium* being indifferent to the production of
a signifying chain, . . . this signifying chain imposes itself, by itself, on the subject in its vocal dimension" (1977, p. 181/533).
In short, what Lacan seems to be saying by all this is that aside
from the projective power of the perceiving subject in the "constitution" of the hallucinatory perception, there is another element that enters into the patterning of it, which is independent
of the conscious subject.

At this point, Lacan offers a clinical vignette to exemplify
this process. A woman patient, bound to her mother in an "affective binary relation," suffered jointly with the mother from a
defensive delusion of being intruded upon and spied upon. The

daughter recounts how in the corridor of her dwelling place she met a man (the rather inconsequential lover of a neighbor with whom both mother and daughter had had a falling out). This man, she thought, called after her the offensive word "Sow!" A simplistic interpretation no doubt would claim that this *percep-* *tum* was merely projected by the perceiving subject by reason of her own impulse to call him "Pig!" But Lacan is not satisfied with this and presses her to say what she, for her part, murmured in the man's presence immediately prior to his alleged epithet. Her reply: " 'I've just been to the pork butcher's...' " (1977, p. 182/534). Aha!

What is the import of this apparently innocuous remark? We are told that the woman had recently separated from her husband and his family (her mother had disapproved of the marriage anyway). She was convinced that her in-laws were going to "cut her into pieces." But this is precisely what happens to the poor unfortunate things that end up at the pork butcher's! Her remark reflects, then, the anxiety about being "cut into pieces" (like a sow) at the butcher's. This remark is uttered in the man's presence as a kind of strophe, to which (after a hiatus that waits for a response) the antistrophe is heard: "Sow!"

Now it is important to note that the patient herself, though she was aware that her remark was "allusive," was "perplexed as to which of the two present [herself or the man] or the one absent person [the mother] was being alluded to" (1977, p. 182/535). The remark in itself, then, had a certain ambiguous anonymity to it, indicated by the subject "I," functioning here as a "shifter," at least until the disparaging antistrophe gave determination to the discourse, which thus "came to realize its intention as rejection in hallucination" (1977, p. 183/535). Of course, this opens up enormous questions to which we must return, but the point for now seems to be that much more goes into the constitution of the hallucination here than the projective activity of the "unifying subject" (1977, p. 183/536). Some elemental pattern gives structure to the discourse, determines its antiphonal format, correlates the signifiers of the strophe (pork butcher's) and antistrophe ("Sow!"), etc. — and all this goes on *independently* of the conscious, speaking subject.

It is clear, then, that if we are to understand the nature of psychosis, we must begin by understanding the relation between the subject and the signifier. Such, at least, has been the way that Lacan himself has taken: in the beginning, his doctoral thesis on paranoia (1932) led him to "the threshold of psychoanalysis" (1977, p. 184/536); more recently, in his seminar of 1955–1956, he followed Freud's (1911c) advice to reexamine the Schreber case, and his structural analysis of the phenomena of Schreber's *Memoirs* (1903a) led him back once more to the same issue (1977, p. 183/536). All of this, then, "makes it incumbent on us to define this process [of psychosis] by the most radical determinants of the relation of man to the signifier" (1977, p. 184/537).

The advantage of the Schreber case as paradigm for the study of psychosis is that it makes an examination of the psychotic process in these terms possible. "But we do not have to have reached that stage to be interested in the variety of verbal hallucinations to be found in Schreber's *Memoirs*" (1977, p. 184/537), for quite clearly they do not fit into the categories according to which they are " 'classically' classified," in terms of their "involvement in the *percipiens.*" Rather, we recognize their relation to the *perceptum*, i.e., "the differences that derive from their speech structure, in so far as this structure is already in the *perceptum*" (1977, p. 184/537).

Now to speak in linguistic terms: "Simply by considering the text of the hallucinations, a distinction arises...between code phenomena and message phenomena" (1977, p. 184/537). The code phenomena are those elements of the hallucinatory text that are so interrelated as to form a linguistic system to which Schreber can give the name " 'basic language' " *(Grundsprache),* "specified in expressions that are neological in form... and usage" (1977, p. 184/537). This system is not only self-contained but self-promulgating: "Hallucinations inform the subject of the forms and usages [of] the neo-code" (1977, p. 184/

537), where the "forms and usages" communicated are essentially a set of signifiers rather than something signified. Thus,
"these messages are regarded as being supported by beings
whose relations they themselves state in modes that prove to be
very similar to the connexions of the signifier" (1977, pp. 184–
185/538): "Do not forget," writes Schreber, "that the nature of
the rays is that they must speak" (1903a, p. 130).[1] In other
words, the *Nervenanhang* (annexation of nerves) and the *Gottesstrahlen* (rays of God) "are simply the joining together of the
words *(paroles)* that they support," with the result that "there is
the relation here of the system to its own constitution as signifier" (1977, p. 185/538). Such, then, are the code phenomena to
which Lacan refers.

But there are message phenomena, too, i.e., "interrupted
messages, by which a relation is sustained between the subject
and his divine interlocutor, a relation to which the messages
give the form of a challenge or endurance test" (1977, p. 186/
539). Thus Schreber tells us:

> My nerves are influenced by the rays to vibrate corre-
> sponding to certain human words; their choice therefore is
> not subject to my own will, but is due to an influence ex-
> erted on me from without. From the beginning the *system of
> not-finishing-a-sentence* prevailed, that is to say the vibrations
> caused in my nerves and the words so produced contain
> not mainly finished thoughts, but unfinished ideas, or only
> fragments of ideas, which my nerves have to supplement to
> make up the sense. It is in the nature of nerves that if un-
> connected words or started phrases are thrown into them,
> they automatically attempt to complete them to finished
> thoughts satisfactory to the human mind [1903a, pp. 216–
> 217].

For example, the fragment "now I will . . . myself . . ." elicits
the complementary phrase "face the fact that I am an idiot"

---

[1] Citations from the *Memoirs* are keyed to the original German pagination,
which is indicated in the English translation.

(1977, p. 186/539–540). Lacan points out that the interruption occurs "at the point at which the group of words that one might call index-terms [or shifters] ends," i.e., those terms in the code that indicate the position of the subject on the basis of the message itself, "after which, the properly lexical part of the sentence, in other words that which comprises the words that the code defines by their use. . . , remains elided" (1977, p. 186/540).

What is the import of all this? Apparently to call our attention to the essentially linguistic structure that underlies Schreber's hallucinatory text and thereby underscore the importance of exploring carefully "the relation of man to the signifier." Thus, Lacan concludes this part of his discussion by observing that one is struck "by the predominance of the function of the signifier in these two orders [i.e., code and message] of the phenomena, not to say urged to seek what lies at the bottom of the association that they constitute[:] of a code constituted by messages [about] the code, and of a message reduced to that in the code which indicates the message" (1977, pp. 186–187/540). As the section concludes, it is important to note only that it was the Freudian experience that led Lacan in the direction indicated here, and he proposes to examine what that experience introduces into the question.

II
After Freud

Yet if we look at the record of what theorizing has been done about the problem of psychosis since Freud's contribution, it has all followed a single fundamental scheme, "namely, how can the internal be transmitted to the external?" The answer (uncritical enough): through the "all-powerful" capacity of the *percipiens* for "affective projection" (1977, p. 187/541) — even though the objections to such an explanation are "overwhelming" (1977, p. 188/541). And this, despite the fact that Freud (1911c, pp. 62–66), in exploring — à propos of Schreber — the different ways of "presenting the switching of the relation to the

other in psychosis," by using "the form of a grammatical deduc-
tion," "namely, the different ways of denying the proposition, 'I
love him,' " "expressly dismisses the mechanism of projection as
insufficient to account for the problem, and enters at that point
on a very long, detailed and subtle discussion of repression"
(1977, p. 188/541-542).

Later texts of Freud, according to Lacan, have been mis-
used to support a theory of affective projection by the *percipiens*.
For example, his essay "On Narcissism" (1914a) is interpreted
to suggest that the *percipiens* is "entitled to inflate and deflate a
dummy reality" (1977, p. 188/542). With the structural theory
of the '20s and the emergence of a conception of the ego as agency of adaptation, mediating between conflicting demands of id,
superego, and external world, one found it still easier to conceive of the ego as a *percipiens* with a "synthesizing function," and
psychosis as somehow the failure of the ego in its task of adaptation. Psychosis, then, would result from a *"loss of reality"* on the
part of the ego (1977, p. 188/542), leaving the ego under the
sway of the id. Little did it matter that in his essay "The Loss of
Reality in Neurosis and Psychosis" (1924b), Freud called "attention to the fact that the problem lies not in the reality that is lost,
but in that which takes its place" (1977, pp. 188-189/542). The
common interpretation prevailed: "the store of accessories is inside, and they are taken out as required" (1977, p. 189/542). It
is thus that Katan (1950), for example, can interpret Schreber's
hallucinatory phantasmagoria as a "curtain interposed by the
operation of the *percipiens* between the tendency [of instinctual
temptation] and its real stimulant" (1977, p. 189/542).

To be sure, "the structures revealed by Freud continue to
sustain, not only in their plausibility, but also in the way they
are manipulated, the would-be dynamic forces with which psychoanalysis today claims to direct its flow" (1977, p. 190/544).
But this does not mean that the structures (and the notions involved in them) are easily — or correctly — understood. Here Lacan refers to the following notions: "the equivalence...of the
imaginary function of the phallus in both sexes..., the castra-

tion complex found as a normative phase of the assumption by
the subject of his own sex, the myth of the murder of the father
rendered necessary by the constituent presence of the Oedipus
complex in every personal history, . . . the profoundly dissident
character of the notion of drive in Freud" (including the disjunction between tendency, direction, and object) with all that this
implies for the "conceptual systematic" that began with Freud's
"sexual theories of childhood" (1977, pp. 189–190/543). Easily
understood or not, however, nothing is to be gained by sacrificing such notions in favor of "an educative naturism that has no
other principle than the notion of gratification and its obverse,
frustration" (1977, p. 190/544).

But let us be more precise and consider one commentator
on the Schreber case in particular, Ida Macalpine, whose work
deserves attention, if only because her "critique of the cliché that
is confined in the factor of the repression of a homosexual drive
. . . to explain psychosis, is masterly," pointing out, as she does,
that homosexuality is less a "determinant" of paranoia than a
"symptom" of it (1977, p. 190/544). She overlooks the fact,
though, that if Freud places an emphasis on homosexuality, it is
first of all to show that homosexuality conditions grandiosity in
delusion and, even more essentially, to indicate the "mode of
otherness in accordance with which the metamorphosis of the
subject operates, in other words, the place in which his delusional 'transferences' succeed one another" (1977, p. 190/544).
But to acknowledge this would be to recognize the importance
for Freud of the Oedipus complex in the paranoiac process,
something that Macalpine refuses to admit.

The point is crucial. Instead of appealing to the Oedipus
complex for an explanation of the genesis of psychosis, Macalpine appeals to a nonoedipal "phantasy of procreation, which is
observed in children of both sexes, even in the form of phantasies involving pregnancy" (1977, p. 191/545). Her argument in
brief is this:

> [Schreber's psychosis is] a reactivation of unconscious ar-
> chaic procreation fantasies concerning life, death, immor-

tality, rebirth, creation, including self-impregnation, and accompanied by absolute ambisexuality expressed in doubt and uncertainty about his sex. Homosexual anxieties were secondary to the primary fantasy of having to be transformed into a woman to be able to procreate. These fantasies are best described as somatic hallucinations and hypochondriacal delusions. They led to Schreber's system centering on creation and the origin of life, whether by God or the sun, sexually or parthenogenetically [Macalpine and Hunter, 1955, p. 395].

Now Macalpine feels the need "to link this phantasy to a symbolic structure" (1977, p. 191/545). But she looks for this structure in a set of "ethnographical references" rather than in the "symbolic articulation that Freud discovered at the same time as the unconscious, and which, for him, is, in effect, consubstantial with it: it is the need for this articulation that he signifies for us in his methodological reference to the Oedipus complex" (1977, p. 91/546). Without such a linkage between fantasy and symbolic structure, the fantasy remains in the purely imaginary order, isolated and alone. For "no imaginary formation is specific, none is determinant either in the structure, or in the dynamics of [the] process" (1977, p. 191/546).

This neglect of the role of the symbolic order in the psychotic process is not unique to Macalpine. On the contrary, it continues to grow in psychoanalysis as analysts continue to explain the difference between neurosis and psychosis in terms of the ego's relation to reality. Now, one issue serves "as the bridge across the frontier of the two domains" (1977, p. 192/546). What is this issue? The text here is ambiguous but we take it to be the relation to the other. After all, it is this that lies at the basis of the whole phenomenon of transference. In the neurotic, early conflicts in relationships with the other are conceived of as reemerging through the process of transference, so much so that the ability to form a transference (and thereby relate in some way to the other) is taken to be characteristic of the neurotic and a confirmation of the earlier conflicts. In the psychotic, conflicts in relationships with the other are conceived of as so early or so severe that the patient withdraws his libidinal interest from the outside world and directs it narcissistically to himself. Thus arises the notion of the psychotic as withdrawing from an unbearable world and of "loss of reality" as the hallmark of psychosis (see Macalpine and Hunter, 1955, pp. 20–21). That is why the formation of a transference in the psychotic would be, according to this hypothesis, impossible. Now, if psychoanalysis is conceived as essentially the analysis of the transference, and if the formation of a transference is impossible for the psychotic, then obviously "psychoanalysts claim to be able to cure psychosis in all cases where a psychosis is not involved" (1977, p. 192/547).

However, if "'[i]t is clear that psychoanalysis is possible only with a subject for whom there is [an other]' " (1977, p. 192/527), then there is indeed a bridge possible between the psychotic patient and the psychoanalyst. But what does this bridge cross over? Certainly not a wasteland, but rather the great "river" (1977, p. 192/547) of the unconscious, which we take to be the symbolic order as Freud experienced it.

III
With Freud

We come here to a more precise disengagement of the nature of Freud's experience. Essentially it is an experience of "thought" processes that affect us but lie beyond the thought processes we are normally conscious of as thought. Indeed, it is striking that this "dimension. . . should never have been thought" (1977, p. 192/547) to the extent of being appropriately put into words before Freud, even though there has always been ample evidence (e.g., the experience of desire, boredom, confinement, revolt, prayer, sleeplessness, panic, and the like) to testify to its influence not only on the individual but also on the social level of human life. But perhaps the grandiosity of conscious thought that feels sufficient unto itself would have been "unable to tolerate this possible competition" (1977, p. 193/548).

In any case, this is the dimension "in which Freud discovered that, without thinking about it, and without anyone being able to think he thinks about it better than anyone else therefore, it thinks (*ça pense*)" (1977, p. 193/548). It is in these terms that Freud "announces the unconscious to us: thoughts which, if their laws are not quite the same as those of our everyday thoughts, . . . are [nonetheless] perfectly articulated" (1977, p. 193/548). This "dimension," or "Other Place" ("Elsewhere": *Ailleurs*), Freud calls, taking the term from Fechner, *ein anderer Schauplatz*, "another scene" (1900a, p. 48; 1900b, pp. 50–51; see also 1887–1902, p. 244), and Lacan calls simply the "Other" (1977, p. 193/548).

How does it function in relation to the subject? As a kind of discourse, bits of which emerge into our conscious life "in certain privileged moments, in dreams, in slips of the tongue or pen, in flashes of wit" "whose syntax Freud first sought to define" (1977, p. 193/549). Lacan situates this syntax in his "schema L" (presented in this essay as a simplification of the earlier version that appeared in "The Seminar on the Purloined Letter" [1966, p. 53]). The French editor of the *Écrits* calls attention to how the dual relation between the ego and its objects (which reflect its form) creates an obstacle between the subject (S) and "the locus of its signifying determination [i.e., the Other]" (1977, p. 332/904). The Other, then, would be "the locus from which the question of [the subject's] existence may be presented to him" (1977, p. 194/549). For the question that the Other poses is indeed about the subject's existence (polarized, to be sure, by questioning about "his sex and his contingency in being"). The analyst discerns this question in "the tensions, the lapses, the phantasies" of the patient's conscious discourse, and it is precisely "by means of elements of the particular discourse" that the "question is articulated in the Other." "It is because these phenomena [of the conscious discourse] are ordered in the figures of this discourse [of the Other] that they have the fixity of symptoms, are legible and can be resolved when deciphered" (1977,

p. 194/549). We take this to mean that symptoms experienced on the level of the conscious subject are to be relieved by discerning their place as signifiers within the structures of the discourse of the Other.

The question as it emerges from the Other is a genuine putting of the subject into question. It arises from the discrete arrangement of unconscious signifiers in a way that is most unlikely — yet at the same time most likely, too: "most unlikely, since their chain is found to survive [*subsister*] in an alterity in relation to the subject as radical as that of as yet undecipherable hieroglyphics in the solitude of the desert"; yet "most likely, because there alone their function of inducing the signification into the signified by imposing their structure on it may appear quite unambiguously" (1977, p. 194/550).

Freud's experience of this unconscious Other is altogether different from that of Jung. For Jung, the Other finds expression in "protomorphic proliferations of the image," i.e., a series of images that remain on the level of fantasy (hence in the order of the imaginary), to be interpreted by a kind of divination (i.e., "mantic") on the part of the analyst. What Freud found wanting in this kind of divination was "the directing function of a signifying articulation" (1977, p. 195/550) following the spare pattern of its own internal law. In ther words, Jung's conception of the Other, according to Lacan, remained too much bound to the order of the imaginary; it took too little account of the symbolic order as such. But it is *this*, the symbolic order, that specifically characterizes man as man.

Let us come, now, to a closer examination of the "questioning of the subject in his existence" by the Other, which follows the basic pattern of schema L. This schema has a "combinatory structure" (i.e., implies many elements that may be considered in varying combinations), which is seen in greater detail in schema R. The latter schema, then, is an expanded version of the former.

The text here is extremely obscure, and the interpretation of it that we offer is, at best, only plausible. The posing of the question by the Other implies "the three signifiers in which the Other may be identified in the Oedipus complex" (1977, pp. 195–196/551), i.e., the ego ideal, mother, and father. These are the signifiers of relation (between the child and mother), of love (mother), and of procreation (father), or, according to schema R, the triad I-M-F. The fourth term, then, is the subject who is being questioned, but who is separated from this polarity in the Other by the bar that splits the subject into conscious and unconscious fields. This occurs "in the mode of death," because (we assume) this splitting takes place through the event of castration, which in its own way is a kind of death, insofar as it defines the subject's limits as Being-unto-death. The subject becomes "the true subject to the extent that this play of the signifiers will make [him] signify" (1977, p. 196/551), i.e., fill up the lacunae in his conscious discourse.

This play of the signifier is not inert but dynamic, since it is animated by the figures of the subject's past "that the denomination of signifying Others involves in the contemporaneity of the Subject" (1977, p. 196/551). And the subject enters into this play, marked, indeed, by the sign of death and is in that sense a "dummy *(mort)*, but it is as a living being that he plays [the game out]; it is in his [everyday] life that he must take up the suit *(couleur)* that he may bid" (1977, p. 196/552).

So far, so good—but now we come to schema R. It looks innocent enough: two complementary right triangles form a square—one triangle (the lower) representing the symbolic order, the other (upper) triangle representing the imaginary order, with a shaded area intruding upon the latter and indicating the order of reality. Without going any further, we notice that one-half of the square is given to the symbolic order while the remaining half is composed of the order of the imaginary and reality, suggesting the close narcissistic connections between reality and the imaginary as well as their subordination to the symbolic order.

Fair enough! But now Lacan packs into the diagram all the complex relationships of his entire system, including elements of it that he has not yet explained in the texts he has selected for the consumption of English-speaking readers. Patience! Let us try to gain a general sense of it, trusting that Lacan's use of it in interpreting Schreber's *Memoirs* will warrant the tortuous effort to understand the diagram now. We follow here the French editor's explanatory note (1977, pp. 333–334/905–906):

1. Triangle *I* is bound by the ego *(e)* and specular image *(i)* together with the subject's (S) identification with the phallus as imaginary object (ϕ — small phi, *not* capital phi as in the English translation); this constitutes the register of the imaginary.

2. Triangle *S*, the register of the symbolic, is bound by the signifier of the primordial object, the mother (M); by the Name-of-the-Father (F) in the locus of the Other (O); and by the ego ideal (I), where the child is marked through symbolic identification.

3. The field of reality *(R)* (*champ de la réalité* [1966, p. 553]), framed by both the imaginary and the symbolic, includes the solid line (*i*-M) where objects *(o)* are found, and the dotted line (*e*-I) where imaginary identifications are situated *(o′)*.

With this said, two final remarks about the schema are in order. First, for all its condensation of elements that precede the resolution of the oedipal situation, the relations shown by the schema strictly speaking should not be called "preoedipal" but at most "pregenital," because it is only in the "retroaction of the Oedipus complex," i.e., by reason of the Oedipus complex's being already resolved, that they can be talked about at all (1977, p. 197/554). Second, the "phallocentrism" suggested by the schema need not alarm us. For the phallus is not a physical organ in this conception, but rather an image that functions as the signifier of desire, playing a role for the subject insofar as he is "entirely conditioned by the intrusion of the signifier" (1977, p. 198/555). Such an understanding of the phallus throws a new light on the old question about the "primary or secondary nature of the phallic phase" (1977, p. 198/555).

However that may be, "Freud revealed this imaginary function of the phallus . . . to be the pivot of the symbolic process that completes *in both sexes* the questioning of the sex [on the level of conscious discourse] by the castration complex [as it emerges through the discourse of the Other]" (1977, p. 198/555). But this symbolic process implies a signification that rests upon a metaphor, "in particular, the paternal metaphor" (1977, p. 198/555), according to which the signifier, the Name-of-the-Father, serves as metaphor for the symbolic order.

The point here seems to be that whereas Macalpine, in making her case against the Oedipus complex as decisive for the genesis of psychosis, considers the critical factor to be a non-oedipal fantasy of procreation "in which the procreative function of the father would be eluded" (1977, p. 198/555), Lacan, for his part, insists that the paternal function (and by implication the whole Oedipus complex) is indeed crucial for an understanding of psychosis but through a *symbolic* paternity, i.e., in the notion of paternity as embedded in the symbolic order itself. In other words, even in those cultures where the role of the real father may have been misunderstood, there is still a place assigned to the *function* of a father. "It is certainly this that demonstrates that the attribution of procreation to the father can only be the effect of a pure signifier, of a recognition, not of a real father, but of what religion has taught us to refer to as the Name-of-the-Father" (1977, p. 199/556).

"Of course, there is no need of a signifier to be a father, any more than to be dead, but without a signifier, no one would ever know anything about either state of being" (1977, p. 199/556). It is only through signifiers that these states enter into the discourse that characterizes properly human life. And the allusion to death here is not without its import, for, according to Freud, the symbolic father that establishes the Law is the mythical father slain by his sons, so that "the symbolic Father is, in so far as he signifies this Law, the dead Father" (1977, p. 199/556). At any rate, it is with this symbolic father that the Oedipus complex is concerned, and in reference to this father that the phallus plays its own symbolic role.

IV
Schreber's way

And it is by taking the role of the symbolic father as a starting point that Lacan undertakes now to explain the nature of Schreber's psychosis. For the symbolic father plays a crucial role in structuring normal development, and it is in contrast to this that the psychotic process is to be explained.

Lacan sees the role of the symbolic father in the development of the subject as essentially metaphorical in nature — hence, the formula: "paternal metaphor" (1977, p. 199/557). For metaphor involves substitution, i.e., of one signifier (S) for another (S′) in which the suppressed signifier (S′) comports its own signification (x). The result is that the substitute S gains a new, far richer signification, beyond what it has originally, by reason of a compound suppression of which it is now the signifier.

Now the "paternal metaphor" also involves a substitution, for normally when the subject arrives at the oedipal stage, the symbolic father (i.e., the "Law" or "Name-of-the-Father") intervenes in the mother-infant dyad in such a way as to replace (i.e., substitute for) the infant's desire of the mother. This desire of the mother comports in turn its own signified for the subject, i.e., being the phallus for the mother. Hence, the Name-of-the-Father involves the suppression of the desire of the mother and the phallus as signifier of this desire in the subject's unconscious (O). (We recall, in French *nom* and *non* are homophones.)

This is the pattern of normal development. But what if for some reason the Name-of-the-Father is in default and there is an "inadequacy of the signifier itself" (1977, p. 200/557)? Freud (1925b), for his part, speaks of a fundamental affirmation *(Bejahung)* that precedes and makes possible all negation *(Verneinung)*, since negation implies something already somehow affirmed in order for it to be denied. The "inadequacy of the signifier" in Lacan's terms would consist in the default of precisely this fundamental affirmation. It is this default that he calls "foreclosure," thus translating Freud's term *Verwerfung*. "We will take *Verwer-*

fung, then, to be the *foreclosure* of the signifier" (1977, p. 201/558), where the "signifier" is the Name-of-the-Father. The result is a "mere hole" in the Other, the symbolic order, "which, by the inadequacy of the metaphoric effect will provoke a corresponding hole at the place of the phallic signification" (1977, p. 201/558), i.e., in the signifying function of the phallus in the unconscious.

It is only in terms of such a conception as this that it is possible to conceptualize Schreber's psychosis. This is what Lacan will try to show in terms of "the most advanced form of delusion of which [Schreber's] book is an expression" (1977, p. 201/559).

Now, the most striking thing about Schreber's delusional system is the fact that it is based on "the power of creation attributed to speech, of which the divine rays *(Gottesstrahlen)* are the hypostasis" (1977, p. 202/559). Given Schreber's own intellectual background, this is a paradox indeed — all the more reason for him to believe "that something must have happened that does not proceed from his own mind" (1977, p. 202/560).

If we follow the sequence of phenomena described by Schreber in Chapter XV (1903a, pp. 204–215), we can see how some of these phenomena (e.g., the "miraculous creations") may be conceived as a kind of "fringe effect" of the signifier which has "remained silent" in the subject (i.e., the "Name-of-the-Father" as foreclosed), but which "projects from its darkness a gleam of signification on to the surface of the real" (1977, p. 203/561), i.e., the "imaginary real" — the real as the subject fantasizes it. Here there emerges an interesting trio that warrants closer scrutiny: Creator (i.e., God), Creature (i.e., the hallucinated creations), and Created (i.e., the subject, Schreber).

We have already said a word about the Creature. Let it suffice for the moment — we shall return to the matter below. As to the Creator, "this God. . .lowers himself into beings who appropriate disconnected identities" (1977, p. 203/561), yet "withdraws ever further. . .[by] a withdrawal that can be intuited from the increasing slowness of his speech" (1977, p. 204/562). Indeed, we could regard such a God as "suited above all for emptying the places. . .in which the murmur of words is deployed, if Schreber did not take care to inform us in addition that this God is foreclosed from any other aspect of the exchange" (1977, p. 204/562). In other words, Schreber's God, his "unique Other," is related to the Created (subject) essentially by means of *speech*. As to the Created (subject), he in turn resorts to "words" "to elude. . . the traps set by the alarming inanity of his Lord," and thus "prevents his fall only by the support of his Word *(verbe)* and by his faith in speech" (1977, p. 205/563). The subject's relation to God, then, is likewise achieved through means of *speech*.

How, then, can we conceptualize the relation between these three members of the trio, using, for example, the parameters of schema R? Let us suppose that the Created subject holds the place of I (the ego ideal) and assumes the position F left vacant by the absence of the Law, i.e., by default of the Name-of-the-Father. Where, then, would we locate the Creator? Presumably at point M, the primordial symbolization of the mother, where the divine *liegen-lassen* would take place through the absence that opens up by reason of the foreclosure of the symbolic father, i.e., through a kind of "hole dug in the field of the signifier" (1977, p. 205/563).

And what of the Creatures of speech? For Lacan, they occupy the place of the child that Schreber so much wanted but was denied. As such, they may be conceived as "circumventing" this "hole dug in the field of the signifier." "It is around this hole, in which the support of the signifying chain is lacking in the subject. . . that the whole struggle in which the subject reconstructed [himself] took place" (1977, p. 205/564).

But all this concerns the symbolic order. A word should be said now about the imaginary order, for already with the "hole dug in the field of the signifier" "there had opened up for him in the field of the imaginary the gap that corresponded in it to the defect of the symbolic metaphor" (1977, p. 206/564). This gap could be filled only through the process of *Entmannung* (emasculation) — a notion that seems to make Ida Macalpine uncomfortable. To be sure, there is a certain ambiguity involved in regarding "the transformation of the subject into a woman *(Verweiblichung)*" as the equivalent of castration and Macalpine is perfectly right in calling attention to the fact (1977, p. 206/564). But she fails to see that this ambiguity is grounded in the structure of the subject as such. For on the imaginary level the very thing that leads the subject to accept transformation into a woman is precisely what makes him forfeit the inheritance of his virility: the vocation to become the spouse of God, the object of God's desire — in other words, the phallus for God. That is why Lacan can say that "it is not by being foreclosed from the penis, but by having to be the phallus [for God] that the patient is [dedicated] to become a woman" (1977, p. 207/565). After all, the problem of being/having a phallus is, for Lacan, as proper to a woman as to a man.

It is curious — is it not? — that "it was in his mother's apartment, where he had taken refuge, that the subject had his first attack of anxious confusion with suicidal raptus" (1977, p. 207/ 566). This suggests that his psychotic regression is intimately related to the fact that "the identification. . . by which the subject assumed the desire of the mother" is somehow or other "shaken" (1977, p. 207/565). As a result, "incapable as he is of being the phallus that the mother lacks, he is left with the solution of being the woman that men lack" (1977, p. 207/566). We take this to mean that by becoming the spouse of God, through whom the salvation of men will be mediated, he eventually becomes the woman that mankind lacks. This, then, would be the meaning of the famous fantasy that is usually seen "as belonging to the incubation period of his second illness, namely the idea 'that it would be beautiful being a woman submitting to copulation' " (1977, p. 207/566).

Does all this add up to homosexuality in Schreber? In point of fact, the *Menschenspielerei* (" 'Men's little games' ") that one would expect to follow from such an attitude never materialized for Schreber, since in his fantasy world other men became "as divested as him of any phallus" (1977, p. 207/566). There is no evidence, then, of any homosexual "acting out" on Schreber's part. On the contrary, he came to conceive of his feminization as a form of *Versöhnung* ("expiation," "propitiation") that should be understood more radically, perhaps, in the sense of *Sühne*, i.e., of "sacrifice" for the sake of his destiny to save mankind (1977, p. 208/566). What deserves emphasis, it would seem, is not homosexuality but the megalomania manifest in Schreber's delusion.

For Freud, "the reconciliation" in question was an intra-psychic accommodation within Schreber himself, according to which Schreber's "ego found compensation in his megalomania while his feminine wishful phantasy made its way through and became acceptable" (1911c, p. 48). But this interpretation, where megalomania is seen as a balm to homosexual wishes, seems to run counter to what Freud says later in the same study, where paranoia is taken to be basically a "fixation at the stage of narcissism" (1911c, p. 72), i.e., infantile megalomania—developmentally before the stage of homosexual wishes. The discrepancy is to be explained, no doubt, by the fact that Freud's subsequent precisions about the nature of narcissism (1914a) were at this point still in a stage of gestation.

Delusion apart, what is to be said of the subject himself through all of this? The fact is that he underwent a kind of death. He tells us that, in a state described in the clinical records as "catatonic stupor," he recalled even having read his own obituary in a newspaper. Other phenomena that he describes, such as "a 'leprous corpse [escorting] another leprous corpse,'" suggest a duality that implies "the subject's regression . . . to the mirror stage" overcast by the shadow of death. There is even a suggestion of his body as dis-integrated, "a sort of sump for fragments detached from the identities of his persecutors" (1977, p. 209/568). The relevance of all this for the problem of homosexuality is admittedly beyond question, but the matter must be explored very cautiously, for "the use of this term in interpretation may produce serious damage, if it is not illuminated with the symbolic relations that . . . were determinant here" (1977, p. 209/568).

What, indeed, are the "symbolic relations that . . . were determinant here"? They are manifest, we are told, "in the form in which the imaginary structure is restored" (1977, p. 209/568). Recall that when the triadic relationship that normally characterizes the symbolic order (according to schema R) has been disrupted by the "hole dug in the signifier," there is a corresponding disruption in the triadic relationship that characterizes the imaginary order, i.e., between the mother, the infant (ego ideal), and the phallus as signifier of desire. In Schreber's case, as we have already seen, this disruption consisted in the fact that the "identification. . . by which the subject assumed the desire of the mother" was somehow "shaken" with the result that instead of being the phallus that the mother lacked he had to become "the woman that men lack" (1977, p. 207/566).

Now, this shattered structure is "restored" under two aspects that Freud himself distinguished. The first of these aspects is Schreber's transsexualist experience before the mirror, where "nothing, he says, in the upper part of his body, seems to him incapable of convincing any possible lover of the female bust" (1977, p. 210/569). The second of these two aspects is the fantasy of a correlation between this "feminization" of the subject and "divine copulation" (1977, p. 210/569). In the latter, Freud saw somehow an allusion to the notion of death, for the German suggests that the " 'soul-pleasure' " *(Seelenwollust)* of the feminized subject bears some relationship to the " 'bliss' " of souls after death *(Seligkeit)*, inasmuch as there appears to be a semantic affinity between the two words involved. For his part, Lacan, though admitting, of course, that "the letter manifests itself in the unconscious" (1977, p. 210/569), suggests that the "agency" of the letter in the unconscious "is much less etymological. . . than homophonic," since the unconscious "is concerned more with the signifier than with the signified" (1977, p. 210/570). But this is a digression.

To be sure, the "act of divine fecundation" would not take place by means of "an obscure passage through the organs" but "through a spiritual operation" by which a "new spiritual humanity" may be engendered and the "creature of the future" redeemed. The fantasy emerges as a kind of parody of a situation in which two "ultimate survivors" of "some human catastrophe," capable of repopulating the earth, would face the enormity of their procreative power.

Such fantasies are the way in which the disruption in the imaginary order is "restored," situated as they are around a "hole" there, where the "soul-murder" that the subject has undergone through the foreclosure of the symbolic order has "installed" his symbolic "death" (1977, p. 211/570). Is the "hole" thus conceived simply "the effect in the imaginary order of the vain appeal made in the symbolic order to the paternal metaphor" (1977, p. 211/571)? Or is it more like the subject's scrambling effort to cancel the "elision" of the phallus that has taken place, by somehow reintroducing it into the gap that is opened up in "the subject's regression. . . to the mirror stage" mentioned above (1977, p. 211/571)? In any case, the phallus is at stake here in the relationship between the infant and his mother as the primordial Other.

Lacan tries to schematize the complex process that transpires here with a diagram (schema I), which admittedly suffers from the limitations endemic to any effort to "formalize the intuitive" (1977, p. 212/571). We take it for what it is worth, realizing that, like the other schemata, it is less important than "the analysis on which it is based" (1977, p. 214/574).

The essential here is to realize that schema I is merely a magnification of schema R after it has been distorted by psychotic disorganization. In terms of the symbolic order, we have already seen that in the foreclosure of the (Name-of-the) Father a "hole" is dug in the field of the signifier (represented in schema I by the hyperbola). Around this hole, on one side, the ideal of the subject's ego begins to slide toward the place of the absent symbolic father so as to take the place of the Other, with resultant "alienation of speech." Around the other side of the hole (hyperbola), the mother's primordial place is preempted by the creative power of God ("the divine other"). Corresponding to this in the field of the imaginary there is another hole (hyperbola) that is dug when the phallus is "elided"—not simply repressed as signifier of desire but eliminated, so to speak, yet nonetheless somehow reintroduced in disguised form around the edge of the hole. This occurs under the guise of the subject's transvestite *jouissance*, by which the subject contemplates himself in his specular image as his own primary love object on the one hand, and, on the other, under the guise of the "future of the creature," i.e., the feminization by which he becomes the phallus for God. Stretched between these two hyperbolas is the field that may be called the subject's "reality" (1977, p. 213/573). (As for details of schema I, the reader will find some help in the Notes.)

Remark here how Lacan sees all of this polarized around the function of language. As Lacan sees it, Freud's whole effort to interpret Schreber's *Memoirs*, relying as he does only on a written document (not simply as a record of the case but as a specimen of its terminal state), suggests that for him the only thing that matters—"the only organicity that is essentially relevant to this process"—is whatever "motivates the structure of signification" (1977, p. 213/572). Thus, in terms of schema I, as soon as the ego ideal preempts the place of the Other in the absence of the symbolic father, the result is "alienation of speech" (1977, p. 212/572), which has an "effect," as by "induction," on the imaginary order (1977, p. 213/572). One specimen of this might be the instance where the lower God's hallucinated epithet, *Luder!*, may be taken to suggest "lure," a kind of "impertinent" commentary by the Other on the siren quality of the imaginary order.

Through all of this the subject has his own criteria for "reality," but two forms of the "real" to which he clearly relates are his wife, whom he continues to love through his psychosis, and the readers for whom he writes his monograph. It follows, then, that the subject's relation to certain others conceivably may be quite normal even though his relation to the Other may be unbalanced—a kind of anomaly that has been called (with some warrant) "partial delusion" (1977, p. 214/574).

The heart of the matter, then, remains the function of the

signifier, for "it is in man's relation to the signifier that this drama [of madness] is situated" (1977, p. 214/574). When all is said and done, our task is to "listen to the speaker, when it is a question of a message that does not come from a subject beyond language, but from speech beyond the subject" (1977, p. 214/574). For it is in such speech that "the very law of the signifier is articulated: . . .'All Nonsense [i.e., the irrational] is abolished!' " (1977, p. 214/574). It is because of man's exposure in his very being to this law that Lacan can say that "it would not be man's being if it did not bear madness within itself as the limit of his freedom" (1977, p. 215/575).

V

Post-scriptum

Lacan brings his paper to a close with a summation that restates his thesis. His purpose is clear enough: as the title suggests, it is to address the "question preliminary to any possible treatment of psychosis," namely, how to designate "the defect that gives psychosis its essential condition, and the structure that separates it from neurosis" (1977, p. 215/575). As we have seen, that defect for Lacan consists in the "foreclosure of the Name-of-the-Father in the place of the Other, and [thereby] the failure of the paternal metaphor" (1977, p. 215/575). This foreclosure is the result of some "accident" in the register of the Other. This Other is the locus of what Freud called the "unconscious" — a "memory" whose nature remained for Freud an open question to the end. Lacan suggests an answer to that question, namely, that this "memory" is the "signifying chain" (into which the infant is initiated through the *Fort! Da!* experience) that "develops in accordance with logical links whose grasp on that which is to be signified. . . operates through the effects of the signifier, [described by Lacan] as metaphor and metonymy" (1977, p. 215/575) — in other words, the symbolic order.

Before proceeding, Lacan cannot forgo the opportunity for a few polemical thrusts. After pointing out the nonmystical quality of Schreber's relationship with God, he refuses to accept the allegedly "ineffable nature of lived experience" as a reason offered by "science" for not talking about it. For how is it "ineffable" if "it *(ça)*" i.e., the Other, speaks in any "lived experience"? And the structure of subjectivity is indeed discernible if only we realize that "what is analysed is identical with what is articulated" (1977, p. 216/576). Furthermore, the conception of psychosis suggested here is perfectly compatible with "what is called good order," without going so far as the psychiatrist (or even psychoanalyst) does who trusts "his own compatibility with that order to the extent of believing that he is in possession of an adequate idea of the *reality* to which his patient appears to be unequal" (1977, p. 216/576). This sort of thing, after all, does not tell us very much about the "foundations of psychosis." Nor is an appeal to the "transference mechanism" very illuminating either, for no matter how skillfully the theory is elaborated, in practice it is conceived "as a relation that is purely dual in its terms" (1977, p. 216/577), i.e., without any reference to the Other. And if transference is taken as "a phenomenon of repetition," what is being repeated in paranoid persecution? It is too easy to say: some kind of "paternal inadequacy," and then go scrambling through an abundance of biographical material in clinical cases to confirm such a hypothesis (1977, p. 217/577).

No, the question must be approached in "structural terms." The heart of the matter is this:

> For the psychosis to be triggered off, the Name-of-the-Father, *verworfen*, foreclosed, that is to say, never having attained the place of the Other, must be called into symbolic opposition to the subject.
>
> It is the lack of the Name-of-the-Father in that place which, by the hole that it opens up in the signified, sets off the cascade of reshapings of the signifier from which the increasing disaster of the imaginary proceeds, to the point at which the level is reached at which signifier and signified are stabilized in the delusional metaphor [1977, p. 217/577].

But how in fact can the Name-of-the-Father be called by a

subject to a place "in which it has never been" (1977, p. 217/ 578)? By an encounter with some specific concrete father-figure, denoted by Lacan as simply "A-father." The essential, though, is that the Name-of-the-Father "constitutes the law of the signifier" (1977, p. 217/578). It would be a mistake, then, to be distracted by the so-called "environmental co-ordinates of psychosis" either in terms of the mother ("from the frustrating mother to the smothering mother") or of the father (his "paternal inadequacy," etc.). It is all too easy to reduce such matters "to the rivalry between the two parents in the subject's imaginary order" (1977, p. 218/578). Rather, what is significant with regard to the mother is "not only... the way in which [she] accommodates herself to the person of the father, but also... the place that she reserves for the Name-of-the-Father in the promulgation of the law" (1977, p. 218/579). And reciprocally, the father's role in the family constellation must be understood in terms of *his* relation to the law: "The father's relation to this law must be considered in itself" (1977, p. 218/579), independently of any personal characteristics he may have in the concrete.

This, then, is the way that Lacan—in contrast to all the rest of "the most inspired authors" who have commented on Freud's analysis of the Schreber case—interprets "the pre-eminence that [Freud] accords to the transference of the relation to the father in the genesis of psychosis" (1977, p. 219/580). The contrast is particularly sharp in the case of Niederland (1951). The latter properly calls attention to the "delusional genealogy, constructed with the names of Schreber's real ancestors..., to show in their convergence on the name of God *(Gott)* an important symbolic chain by which the function of the father can be manifested in the delusion" (1977, p. 219/580). But Niederland fails to discern "the agency of the Name-of-the-Father" here and thus misses the true import of the delusion. When he then tries to explain "the role of the paternal function in the triggering off of delusion," he focuses his attention on what for Lacan is "the subject, rather than the signifier" (1977, p. 220/580).

It does not work. For Niederland sees the occasion of Schreber's psychosis to be his "assumption of paternity," i.e., "when

Schreber is called upon to assume a prominent 'father' role as *Senätspräsident*, the conflicts of libidinal and aggressive origin that had been repressed for 32 years break through, and he falls ill on the very date his father died" (Niederland, 1974, p. 111). The fact is, however, that there was at the same time a *nonas-sumption* of paternity, i.e., the failure of Schreber's effort to beget a physical child—a situation that found its parallel in the precipitating factor of Schreber's first illness, i.e., a nonassumption of "paternity" in the form of "the failure of his candidature for the Reichstag" (1977, p. 220/581). Niederland's thesis is inconsistent, then. The problem is that it focuses on Schreber as *subject* in his relation to paternity, whereas, if Niederland had shifted the focus instead to the "signifier of paternity" as such, i.e., the Name-of-the-Father in the locus of the Other, the inconsistency would have dissolved. This is precisely what Lacan, with his thesis about "primordial foreclosure *(Verwerfung)* that dominates everything with its problem" (1977, p. 220/581), has done.

At any rate, when, through foreclosure, the hole dug in the field of the signifier finally opened up for Schreber, Flechsig was not big enough to fill it—such, at least, is the way that Freud understands how the subject was precipitated into psychosis (1977, p. 221/582). This hole in the signifier consisted in the bankruptcy of the Name-of-the-Father, i.e., the bankruptcy of that signifier which "in the Other, as locus of the signifier, is the signifier of the Other as locus of the law" (1977, p. 221/582).

If all this sounds novel, the fact is that such a conceptualization of psychosis in no way goes "beyond Freud" but rather attempts to do no more "than to restore access to the experience that Freud [himself] discovered" (1977, p. 221/582).

MAP OF THE TEXT[2]

I. *Towards Freud.*

   A. The application of Freudianism has not advanced our thinking regarding psychosis.

---

[2] In Chapters 6 and 7, Lacan has indicated subdivisions in his major sections by a series of Arabic numerals. Our subdivisions A, B, etc., correspond to Lacan's numbers 1, 2, etc.

1. Before Freud the psychological discussion of psychosis was founded in scholastic philosophy.
2. Contemporary science is free from this metaphysical concoction,
   a. but we practitioners are not.
3. Our theory of knowledge is fixed in theoretical abstractions of faculties,
   a. which remain deaf to pleas for concreteness,
   b. and uncorrected by a recourse to affect,
      i. since we retain an univocal idea of the subject.
B. We have retained a simplistic view of the relations between the perceiver and the perceived.
   1. In this view variations in the perceived are correlated with differences in sense registers of the perceiver.
      a. This diversity of register is overcome as long as the perceiver is a match for reality.
      b. In the same way we approach insanity by relying on scholastic categories.
   2. Most psychological positions look inside the perceiver to explain hallucinations,
      a. and thereby overlook whether the perceived in a hallucination structures meaning for the perceiver.
   3. The verbal hallucination is not reducible to a particular *sensorium,* nor to a perceiver who might give unity to it.
      a. The verbal hallucination is not intrinsically auditory,
      b. nor is the act of hearing itself a single register,
         i. since it can attend to either meaning or sound.
      c. It doesn't help to view the hallucination as an objectification of the perceiver,
         i. since he is subject to the influence of the other,
         ii. especially in paranoid projection.

4. The crucial point is that consciousness does not account for a hallucinated statement because:
   a. the chain forces itself on the subject,
   b. with the reality of temporal duration,
   c. in an equivocal manner, thus challenging a supposedly unifying consciousness.

C. A clinical example of a *folie-à-deux* illustrates these aspects of the verbal hallucination.
   1. The hallucinated response "Sow!" from a man follows the patient's comment, "I've just been to the pork butcher's . . ."
      a. The man represents the angry camp of her husband's family
         i. who threatened to chop her to pieces.
      b. Her anxiety about the fragmented body experience remains beyond awareness
      c. and finds its confirmation in the angry retort,
         i. which offers her as object for the butcher's knife.

D. The irruption of the signifier into the real is most clearly seen in the case of the broken signifying chain.
   1. The ambiguity of the perceived signifier awakens an otherness in the perceiver,
      a. which the classical view of the unifying subject reduces to imaginary effects,
      b. so that we must learn about hallucinations from the text of a madman.

E. If we avoid reducing the perceived to qualities of the perceiver, we find in the structure of the perceived a linguistic distinction between code and message.
   1. In Schreber's *Memoirs* the code includes the voices using the *Grundsprache*
      a. in neologistic expressions
      b. and in messages called autonyms, which are self-reflexive,
         i. and which challenge the notion of a distinct "metalanguage."

      c. The anticipatory effect of the signifier has nothing to do with intuition,
         i. and is reduced to mere repetition when the voices deal with thoughts and feelings (that is, with variations in the perceiver).
    2. Messages are interrupted in a challenging manner
      a. at the point where code-terms define the position of the subject,
      b. while the content of the message is elided.
    3. The signifiers function in such a way that code and messages are reflexively related.
      a. This gives rise to a topology of the subject as structured by the signifier,
      b. which must form the basis of any neurological investigation,
         i. following Freud's influential work on dreams.

II. *After Freud.*

  A. The contribution Freud made regarding psychosis has ended in a decline.
    1. Current conceptions boil down to a simplistic question: How to make the internal pass into the external?
      a. The subject is treated as an indestructible perceiver in psychosis,
         i. rather than including an unconscious register.
      b. The perceiver is viewed as determining his perception (assumed to represent reality)
         i. by means of affective projection.
    2. The mechanism of projection is used in an uncritical way,
      a. which fails to distinguish, e.g., between types of jealousy.
      b. Freud presents the shifting of the relation to the other in psychosis by means of the substitution of signifiers,

       i. and sets aside projection as not sufficient to account for the problem,

      ii. while hinting at the notion of foreclosure.

B. Even Freud's paper on narcissism has been used to reinforce the notion of the perceiver constructing the perceived.

    1. This construction operates by means of investing or deinvesting objects with libido.

      a. Freud's view of unconscious identifications with the other as constituting the ego is taken as support for its synthesizing function,

      b. and has led to the promotion of the idea of *"loss of reality,"*

         i. although Freud's concern was with what takes its place.

    2. The view persists that what is inside is placed outside as needed.

      a. Thus Katan views Schreber's hallucinations as following the defense against instinctual temptation.

C. Projection of a tendency is viewed as a response to regression.

    1. The withdrawal of a tendency from its object is called regression,

      a. without distinguishing types of regression.

    2. The very mention of Freud's concepts causes bewilderment

      a. to those who view psychoanalysis as reeducation.

D. Only those who stand outside this group are rigorous, like Macalpine.

    1. She rightly criticizes the cliché of repressed homosexuality as the explanation for paranoia.

      a. In Schreber the idea began in an earlier waking thought about being a woman.

         i. The form of this thought reveals that it was narcissistically enhancing.

      2. But she ignores how Freud related the homosexual issue to grandiosity and to transference figures,

        a. and how he referred to the Oedipus complex.

      3. She replaces it with a fantasy of procreation,

        a. which she links to a symbolic structure

        b. based on anthropological evidence.

      4. But an image has no impact except as part of a signifying articulation,

        a. which Freud designates by the Oedipus complex.

  E. Macalpine cannot be blamed for this misunderstanding of the symbolic order.

      1. This misunderstanding flourishes among psychoanalysts

        a. who separate neurosis from psychosis in terms of the ego's "responsibility for reality."

        b. A bridge between the two appears is the notion of transference,

          i. but without an appreciation of the meaning of the "other."

III. *With Freud.*

  A. It is striking that thinkers have not been able to articulate the structure of the unconscious.

      1. Its effects have become necessary parts of collective organizations,

        a. and are evident in dream-thoughts.

  B. Schema L signifies the relation between the subject and the Other.

      1. The Other here is the discourse of the unconscious,

        a. and the origin of questioning regarding the sex and existence of the subject.

  C. This questioning is articulated in discrete signifiers.

      1. The signifying chain exists as radically other to the subject,

        a. but also as imposing an unambiguous signification.

      2. The separations opened in the real world by the signifier follow gaps in the world

      a. to such an extent that we wonder if in this case the signifier follows the law of the signified.

      b. This is not true at the level where the existence of the subject or of the world is questioned.

D. Our experience of the unconscious Other, according to Freud, is not a function of natural forms.

  1. The Jungian school appears to rely on these forms,

      a. but they are useful only for disclosing imaginary relations.

  2. Freud rejected this position because it neglected the structure of the signifying chain.

      a. This chain follows its own internal law,

      b. which structures the material phonemes

      c. and without which man could not even sustain himself in the imaginary order.

E. Schema L leads to a structure governed by varying combinations of terms.

  1. This structure is composed of a tetrad and two trinities.

      a. The tetrad consists of the subject and three signifiers (relation, love, procreation)

         i. The subject enters their play as dead (barred).

         ii. The signifiers structure the three agencies of ego, reality, and superego.

      b. The imaginary triad of specular image, fragmented body, and phallus corresponds to the symbolic triad of mother, child (or ego ideal), and Name-of-the-Father.

  2. The imaginary order opens up a gap which allows the subject to imagine himself as mortal,

      a. but his "symbiosis with the symbolic" makes this action possible,

      b. and the "symbiosis with the symbolic," in turn, could not take place without this gap.

F. Schema R is a conceptual visualization of this double triad.

    1. The lines conditioning the object in the field of reality are also indicated by a quadrangle.
        a. One of its corners gives meaning to the object relations approach by viewing the ego ideal in terms of the child as desired object of the mother.
        b. This has reference not to a preoedipal but to a pregenital stage,
            i. in which the child identifies himself as his mother's phallus,
            ii. and which was much debated in terms of the phallic phase.
G. For Freud, the phallus completes the symbolic process wherein castration situates sex.
    1. Our culture mystifies this symbol so that it is even obscured in psychoanalytic circles,
        a. and has become a part-object.
    2. Its signification is evoked only by the paternal metaphor.
    3. By resorting to heliolithism, Macalpine situates procreation in a preoedipal culture,
        a. and thereby evades the paternal function.
        b. But however paternity is attributed, it is always as a function of recognizing the signifier of paternity.
        c. This signifier is linked to death.
IV. *Schreber's way.*
A. The paternal metaphor evokes the signification of the phallus.
    1. The structure of metaphor induces a new signification.
    2. In the metaphor of the Name-of-the-Father this new signification is the repressed phallus.
    3. In psychosis an inadequate signifier responds to the appeal to the Name-of-the-Father.
    4. Freud referred to this inadequacy as foreclosure.
        a. It involves the absence of the judgment of attribution.

      b. So that where the Name-of-the-Father is called
        for there is only a hole,
          i. with a corresponding hole below the bar in
            the metaphor.
          ii. This hole or damage Schreber relates to
            "soul-murder,"
          iii. and the suggestion of incest is a sign of the
            failure of the paternal metaphor, the Oedi-
            pus complex, the symbolic order.

B. Recognition of the unconscious brings with it surprise.
   1. We are struck by how Schreber's delusion attributes
     creative powers to speech,
     a. although creation from nothing is shocking to
       thought.
   2. Schreber's thoughts sharply contrast with his cul-
     tured background,
     a. and their intrusiveness is proof for Schreber that
       they do not come from his own mind,
         i. contrary to what psychiatrists say about pro-
           jection.

C. We can now follow the sequence of themes in
   Schreber's Chapter XV.
   1. Schreber's hand is kept in the game of forced think-
     ing by a dramatic stake,
     a. which is the threat of God's abandonment.
   2. When his replies cease in "thinking-nothing," bel-
     lowing and the call for help occur,
     a. showing his subjective tearing from God and
       from the signifying chain from which he hangs
       suspended.
     b. The appearance of sounds and miraculous crea-
       tions show his effort to illuminate the real through
       representations.
     c. These hallucinations suggest "the trio of Creator,
       Creature, and Created."

D. The Creator is one-in-many and many-in-one.

    1. He enters beings who steal "disconnected identities,"
      a. and their capture in Schreber's body threatens
         God's integrity.
      b. Yet God lets them expand despite their inane
         speech,
         i. whose homophones are striking.
    2. God's withdrawal is reflected in his speech
      a. and in his aloofness from men.
      b. With the abolition of personal identity, only ver-
         biage will survive.
    3. The miraculous creatures are not messengers of the
      symbolic order but imaginary representations.
      a. Schreber prevails not through representations
         but through his words and the order of the world.
E. We can resituate the subject in schema I in terms of the
    symbolic triad of schema R (I-M-F).
    1. The Created I is located in F,
      a. now empty of the Law of the Father,
      b. and is defined solely in relation to the mother in
         M,
         i. since the symbolic father has been foreclosed,
         ii. and the Creator takes a "let-lie" position.
    2. By stretching point I of schema R back to the now
      foreclosed point F, schema I is developed.
      a. The line I to M culminates in the Creatures of
         speech,
         i. who occupy the place of Schreber's unborn
           child, the point I of schema R,
         ii. and this line skirts the hole in the field of the
           signifier made by the foreclosing of the
           Name-of-the-Father.
    3. Schreber's struggle is around this hole
      a. where he lacks the support of the signifying chain,
      b. and where his imaginary sexualization is ironi-
         cally recognized.

F. The gap in the imaginary order that corresponds to the defect in the symbolic order can only find its resolution in emasculation.
  1. The acceptance of this emasculation goes through different stages in Schreber,
    a. although the term is not acceptable to Macalpine,
      i. who seems to shy away from castration, as if real castration were at stake.
      ii. But she rightly notices the ambiguity of equating becoming a woman with castration.
  2. The ambiguity of subjective structure confounds being and having the phallus.
    a. Thus Schreber is dedicated to become a woman in order to be the phallus,
      i. along the lines of the symbolic parity between *Mädchen* (girl) and phallus,
        (a) which is based on their function in social and symbolic exchange.
G. When the identification with his mother (as her phallus) is shaken, Schreber moves toward becoming a woman.
  1. Here lies the meaning of his intercourse fantasy,
    a. and not in having intercourse with imagined figures of men.
  2. He becomes reconciled to becoming a woman,
    a. in the service of grandiosity,
    b. and not of homosexuality, as Freud incorrectly states.
H. Freud would have grasped the true cause of the reversal in Schreber if he had realized that Schreber as subject had died.
  1. There is external evidence supporting this,
    a. in the form of a topographical regression to the mirror stage.
  2. The homosexuality must be seen in terms of symbolic relations.

I. The symbolic determination of the homosexuality is spelled out in the restored imaginary structure.
   1. This structure has two aspects.
      a. Transvestism is linked with feminization,
      b. as also is divine copulation and eventual fecundation.
   2. Schema R can be redrawn as schema I in order to depict the psychotic outcome.
      a. From the image of the creature Schreber (between *i* and *e*), there curves a line to transvestite (narcissistic) pleasure and to anticipated identification as God's spouse.
         i. This line skirts a hole, the absent phallus where soul-murder installs the death of the subject.
      b. The asymptotic line between the two curves joins the delusional ego at *e* to the divine other (who takes the place of his mother) at M.
         i. The real lies between the narcissistic image at *i* and the ego ideal at I
            (a) which takes the place of the Other and thereby alienates speech.
      c. The schema materializes how the signifier induces in the imaginary the overturning of the subject,
         i. as illustrated in the end-of-the-world experience,
         ii. and as suggested by the hallucinated expression *Luder!*,
            (a) which includes the notion of "lure," or imaginary capture.
      d. The field *R* of reality is restored for the subject as an islet of consistency,
         i. but it has a subordinate role as both cause and effect,

          ii. and is rendered habitable only because the imaginary and symbolic orders have been reshaped.

    e. The discussion of our place in o and the role of loving husband in o' remains undeveloped,

        i. except to note that such relations are compatible with an unbalanced relation to the Other.

  3. Macalpine's position would be strengthened by a misunderstanding of the symbolic order's role in schema I.

    a. Reason is right to study madness,

        i. for this drama is situated in the human being's relation to the signifier,

        ii. involves a word beyond the subject,

        iii. and is the limit of human freedom.

V. *Post-scriptum.*

  A. The Other is the unconscious locus of a memory which is the object of a question.

    1. To this question responds the signifying chain,

      a. which begins in the *Fort! Da!* experience,

      b. and which grasps the being of beings

      c. through metaphor and metonymy.

    2. The essential defect of psychosis is an accident in this register,

      a. which is termed "foreclosure"

      b. and involves the failure of the paternal metaphor.

  B. The signifier of the Other is absent in the *Memoirs.*

    1. The intimate form of address is absent in Schreber's relationship to God,

      a. which appears as a mixture rather than a union of being to being,

      b. and which shows none of the joy and presence of the mystical experience.

    2. Science and contemporary thought decline to say anything about mysticism,

    a. but in stressing the ineffable they ignore the fact that it (*ça*) speaks,

    b. while science too shares in social psychosis,

      i. despite the psychiatrist's notion of reality.

C. The psychosis is set in motion when the foreclosed Name-of-the-Father is summoned "into symbolic opposition to the subject."

  1. The hole created by the lack of this signifier attracts a cascade of images

    a. until the signifier-signified relations are restabilized in the delusion.

  2. The Name-of-the-Father is summoned by A-father,

    a. who takes up a third position relative to the ego (*o*) and objects (*o'*).

D. In the principle of this foreclosure, the Name-of-the-Father stands for the symbolic triangle, since it constitutes the law of the signifier.

  1. In psychosis the key family variable is not the mother but her respect for the father's word,

    a. although his own relation to the law is also important.

  2. What matters is the Name-of-the-Father as signifier in relation to the symbolic order,

    a. and not specific names as such,

    b. nor the mere assumption of paternity.

  3. To Schreber, his father was an unacceptable representative of the law,

    a. and Flechsig failed to fill the void of the foreclosure,

      i. which was the precipitating transference factor.

    b. The result is an angry, eroticized condemnation of the paternal signifier,

      i. and a symbol of our age.

  4. In all of this we are not trying to go beyond Freud,

    a. but rather to get back to his discovery.

NOTES TO THE TEXT

179*b*/531   The Latin text reads: "With care I dedicate this, which I have taken pains with for thirty-three years in the same place, to Saint Anne, the guardian spirit of the place, and to the youth who followed after me there." The reference is to Saint Anne's Hospital in Paris where Lacan trained and continued to conduct clinical teaching.

179*e*/531   A Greek term with a long history, *physis* essentially means nature, natural objects, or the law of nature; *antiphysis*, therefore, is what is over against nature.

179*f*/531   A useful overview of the kind of baggage that psychology still carries is provided by Kurt Lewin in "The Conflict between Aristotelian and Galileian Modes of Thought in Contemporary Psychology" (1931).

180*b*/532   In his session of January 11, 1956, of his seminar on the psychoses, Lacan makes reference to Merleau-Ponty's *Phenomenology of Perception* (1945), and specifically to his chapter on "The Thing and the Natural World."

182*a*/534   Lacan discussed this type of *folie-à-deux* in his 1932 doctoral dissertation.

182*f*/535   For a discussion of shifters, index-terms, and autonyms, see Barthes (1964, pp. 22–23).

183*a*/535   The allusiveness of " 'I've just been to the pork butcher's. . .' " consists in its implicating the daughter as victim (without the speaking ego's awareness), the man as representative of the husband's murderous camp, and the mother as delusional protector—the phrase "oscillates" among them until it conjures up the retort "Sow!," which definitively fixes the meaning with rhythmic finality.

     The unspeakable object that is rejected "in the real" appears to be the *corps morcelé*, the patient's body in bits and pieces. The word "Sow!" comes in its place, detached from *her* (*elle,* not from "it"). Rather than the "cursing" of the strophe, the French *maugrément* can be translated as "fretting," more congruent with the patient's statement, especially if it is viewed as unconsciously expressing anxiety about bodily fragmentation.

183*b*/535 The symbol "irrealizes" by transposing things from the real to the symbolic order, by rendering their brute facticity absent and enabling us to deal with their symbolic presence. Compare related expressions, such as "the symbol manifests itself first of all as the murder of the thing" (1977, p. 104/319).

183*c*/536 The signifier conveys meaning on both conscious and unconscious levels and, when the perceiver assents to it, he resonates with it on many levels.

184*a*/536 Instead of "But his departure from the phenomenon" for *mais ce départ du phénomène,* we translate "But a start from the phenomenon."

184*d*/537 Instead of "or rather, the differences," the French reads, *à savoir bien plutôt les différences,* "namely, [to recognize] indeed rather the differences."

185*b*/538 Barthes (1964) defines metalanguage as "a system whose plane of content is itself constituted by a signifying system" (p. 90), that is, its message is another code.

185*c*/538 The signifier *Nervenanhang* serves as a specific example: its initially enigmatic meaning of "nerve-annexation" is a void replaced by the significance of this meaning as chain of signifiers, "simply the joining together of the words" noted in the earlier paragraph 185*a*.

185*d*/538 There is a curious process here: to the extent that the voices concern themselves with variations in the *percipiens,* they become inane and repetitive, like Schreber's consciousness.

185*e*/539   Schreber (1903a) discusses the memory-thoughts in
             Chapter XII (p. 165).

186*f*/539   A misprint in the English text has "he will pause" in-
             stead of "we will pause" *(nous nous arrêterons).*

186*g*/540   Eco (1976) writes: "Pierce defined the index as a type
             of sign causally connected with its object" (p. 115); in
             this case, the pronouns get their meaning from the
             speaker speaking them, but it is the message that in-
             forms us of the meaning.

187*a*/540   Instead of a semicolon, the French text has a colon
             after "the association that they constitute," with what
             follows clearly defining this association; in addition,
             "messages on the code" is clumsier than "messages
             about the code" *(messages sur le code).*

187*c*/540   The "neuraxis" is the cerebrospinal axis.

187*h*/541   Possibly misleading connotations are suggested by
             the English translation's use of "an opaque id" for *un
             Ça opaque* which is perhaps best left as "an opaque
             Ça." The frequent use of *ça parle* by Lacan for the ut-
             terance of the unconscious makes clear that he is re-
             ferring here to the complex structure of the uncon-
             scious (which a notion of subject as ego fails to take
             into account when we are dealing with psychosis).
                 The perceiver's correlative is, strictly speaking,
             the perceived, the *perceptum* assumed to be the repre-
             sentation of reality.

188*b*/   To present the shifts in the relation to others, Freud's
541–542   exposition relies on the effect of the substitution of
             signifiers, rather than on a simple projection of "in-
             ner" feelings "outside."

188*c*/542   The "toothing stones" appear to include the notion of
             foreclosure, implied in Freud's text: "It was incorrect
             to say that the perception which was suppressed inter-
             nally is projected outwards; the truth is rather, as we
             now see, that what was abolished internally [*innerlich
             Aufgehobene*] returns from without" (1911c, p. 71).

189*c*/543   Schreber's literary creation, as in the case of the *per-ceptum*, follows certain laws of language and therefore cannot be accounted for simply as a projection.

189*d*/543   Instead of "what problem would he still erect," we prefer the impersonal "what problem would still be erected" to translate *quel problème ferait-il encore*. The "couple" seems to be the junction of a tendency and its object, the withdrawal of the tendency to be regression, and the projection of the tendency "in reality" to be a response to the regression (*répond de la régression*, not "is a response from the regression").

189*e*/543   The poles of "nature and nurture" are suggested by "development and entourage." The English text fails to say "the mention of features" (*la seule mention des traits*). The references to the phallus are elaborated in Chapter 8 of Lacan (1977). The French *l'effet de dédoublement* is better translated as "the effect of splitting," rather than "the effect of duplication." Last but not least, rather than "the disjunction of principle," we prefer "the disjunction in principle" for *la disjonction de principe*.

190*b*/543   We can note how Freud encloses in quotes his use of "frustration" (*Versagung*) (1911c, p. 62; 1911d, p. 298).

190*f*/544   The French text does not say "This process began at an early stage" but rather "This process was engaged for a long time ("Ce procès est dès longtemps engagé"). The hypnopompic lies on the threshold of sleep and wakefulness; a tomography is a plane x-ray. The narcissistically enhancing quality of the idea lies in its being "beautiful."

190*g*/544   Lacan is stating that for Freud the homosexuality was integral to the grandiosity of being God's spouse, and also reflects a relationship to the transference figures of Flechsig and God, his brother and his father.

190*h*/544   Glover (1932) has written: "Nevertheless in the Schreber paper [of Freud] no direct mention was made of the aggressive impulses and the mechanism of paranoia was described mainly in terms of libidinal conflict and related to repression of the inverted Oedipus situation" (p. 302). Macalpine and Hunter (1955), who elsewhere refer to Glover's paper (p. 371), write that Freud interpreted Schreber's illness as being the result of conflict over unconscious homosexuality, "having its origin in the boy's inverted Oedipus situations, i.e., his homosexual attachment to a father figure" (p. 10).

191*b*/545 The patient was an obsessional (1977, p. 100/315).

191*e*/545 Macapline and Hunter (1955) believe "that the primary disturbance is not interpersonal but intrapersonal" (p. 22); their clinical discussion regarding the interpretation of homosexuality follows on pp. 23–26, 410–411.

191*f*/546 Hysteria is denounced by Macalpine and Hunter (1955), who write: "It is doubtful whether hysteria or anxiety hysteria is an adequate diagnosis today, other than as a non-specific assessment of temperament and omnibus label for milder cases of mental disturbance" (p. 385).

191*g*/546 Rather than "This is because no..." (for *C'est qu'aucune*), we translate "The fact is that no...." Anxiety about one's sex reinforces the place of the Oedipus complex which is a result "opposite" to the one Macalpine sought.

192*d*/547 The river is a reference to the Other. Regarding Midas, see note 173*d* in Chapter 5.

192*f*/547 The relationship between conscious thinking and unconscious thought is a frequent theme in the *Écrits* (e.g., 1977, p. 166/517–518). The reference to the *Odyssey* appears to allude to Telemachus, son of Odysseus and Penelope, thinking in his father's absence of his mother's unwelcome suitors consuming their supplies.

193c/548   The pun encompasses a great deal: Baudelaire is viewed as the founder of the symbolist movement in poetry; *Les Fleurs du mal* (1857) was condemned as obscene.

194a/549   It is the form of the ego that is reflected in objects, as in paranoiac knowledge (discussed earlier [1977, p. 17/111]).

194b/549   Lacan again makes his basic distinction between the level of the *percipiens* (the anxious ego) and that of the *perceptum* (the articulated question).

194d-e/
550   There are gaps between discrete signifiers in the signifying chain, and here Lacan appears to wonder if they are patterned after the gaps in the world created when objects are named and transposed into the symbolic order as individual identifiable entities — gaps between objects, between different experiences of the same objects, between different orders in the world — living and nonliving; human and natural; the imaginary, the symbolic, and the real. In any case, the world cannot provide the pattern for the kind of questioning that extends to the existence of the world itself and even beyond its order.

195b-c/
550   In the next essay (1977, p. 233/593), Lacan equates Jung's approach with that of Boehme as an attempt to read the *signatura rerum*, as if nature as articulable were the foundation for the symbolic order. These imaginary forms, says Lacan, are useful only in divining (as a "mantic") structures of the ego. See Jung's *Symbols of Transformation* (1912).

195g/551   Rather than "if he is taken away," we prefer "if it is taken away," referring to the place of the Other *(Car ôtez-l'en)*; without the symbolic order, man could not even live in the imaginary order. Whether animals (who do live in the imaginary order of seduction and captivation) also relate to the Other is unclear, since our principal means of access to the Other is through the "sporadic sketches of neurosis" (limited to the human condition). Thus, rather than "but only that it appears otherwise than in the sporadic sketches of neurosis," we translate "but only that it [i.e., the relation to the Other] does not appear to us except in the sporadic sketches of neurosis," for "mais seulement qu'elle ne nous apparaît pas autrement que dans de sporadiques ébauches de névrose."

195*h*/551   Although the precise meaning is uncertain, we prefer as a translation not "in its position as fourth term in the topology," but rather "in its topology as tetrad" for *dans sa topologie de quaternaire.*

196*a–b*/ 551   The tetradic structure of schema L (transformed now into the more detailed schema R) consists of three signifiers, each of which may belong to a corner of the schema: "relation" belonging with I, the child or ego ideal; "love" with M, the mother as primordial object; and "procreation" with F, the Name-of-the-Father (the French text does not use quotation marks). The fourth term, the subject, enters only as barred, as signified, as absence in words — "the mode of death." He becomes "the true subject" when he speaks and enters the play of the signifiers, which make him signify (not "make it signify," for *va le faire signifier*).

196*c*/551   Rather than "in each particular part," for *dans chaque partie particulière*, we translate "in each particular case," and again later "over and above each case," for *au-delà de chaque partie.*

196*d*/552   Since there is apparently only one symbolic triad (I-M-F), the plural "symbolic triads" is a misleading translation of *le ternaire symbolique.*

197*b*/552   Instead of "rather than merely depending on them," it seems to make more sense to see these lines which circumscribe the field of reality as "indeed far from merely depending on it," that is, on reality *(bien loin* *d'en seulement dépendre).*

197*d*/553   In the extremities of the segment going from the subject (S) to the primordial object (M) are others the
subject desires to have (the first of whom, in the imaginary order, is the reflection in the mirror), while
in the extremities of the segment going from the subject (S) to the ego ideal (I) are others the subject desires to be like (again, the first of whom is the ego).
Their "reality" is in large measure a function of how
much or how little the subject is identified with the
imaginary phallus. It may be helpful to visualize the
dynamic interrelations among the four terms (at
each corner of schema R) by means of arrows: (1) beginning at the upper left corner going from the subject to the mother, with the subject desiring to be the
object of her desire, and from the mother to the phallus as object of her desire; (2) from the phallus to the
ego ideal as imaginary identification; (3) from the
symbolic father to the ego ideal as symbolic identification; (4) from the father to the mother as object of
his desire and from the mother to the symbolic
father, affirming the place of "the Name-of-the-
Father" and thereby making the symbolic identification possible. Without the relationships expressed in
(3) and (4) the conditions of possibility for psychosis
are established.

198*c*/155   For additional details, see the Notes to the Text of
Chapter 8 (p. 283/687).

199*i*/557   The paternal metaphor, in which the Name-of-the-
Father is substituted for the desire of the mother,
gives the phallus its status of repressed signifier of the
other's desire, and gives the subject the capacity to
imagine himself as independent. De Waelhens
(1972) writes:

> . . . the subject cannot abandon himself to or be
> swallowed up in the lack *that he is*. He will there-
> fore imagine himself as being that which fills up

all lack, and particularly the lack of the mother, that is to say, the phallus. *To be* that which annuls the lack of the mother protects the subject from all abandonment, from all separation from his mother, to the point of making abandonment or separation (imaginarily) impossible. This is what the psychoanalytic language means when it speaks of the child as the penis of the mother.

However, it is all too clear that such an identification, no matter how advantageous at the start, must eventually be surmounted, under penalty of the most radical failure. For how else could that which fills up all lack succeed in recognizing itself as subject of lack, a lack which is the only entry into negativity and desire? For, as long as he remains in the position just described, the subject cannot accede to either negativity or desire, since desire is recognition of lack and an appeal to the other to be recognized by him as subject of this lack [p. 126].

200*a*/557   The *x* is the putting-into-question of the meaning of the original signifier as it now relates to the substitute signifier. The *s* is the added meaning that results, the product of the relation of signifiers. A more detailed attempt to explicate Lacan's notion of metaphor (including the "paternal metaphor") appears in Muller (1979).

200*b*/557   The "O" stands for "Other" (in French, "A" for *Autre*). We understand that the phallus, with whom the infant identifies as the object of the mother's desire, has been barred so that, with primary repression established, it is now an unconscious signifier of the desire of the other.

200*c*/557   Since later (p. 201*c*/558) the Name-of-the-Father is "called for" *(est appelé)*, we translate not "the appeal of" but "the appeal to the Name-of-the-Father" *(l'appel du Nom-du-Père).*

200e/558   For a definition and references to foreclosure in Freud, see Laplanche and Pontalis (1967, pp. 166–169).

201a/558   In his paper on "Negation," Freud (1925b) wrote:

> Thus the content of a repressed image or idea can make its way into consciousness, on condition that it is *negated.* Negation is a way of taking cognizance of what is repressed; indeed it is already a lifting of the repression, though not, of course, an acceptance of what is repressed. . . .
>
> The function of judgement is concerned in the main with two sorts of decisions. It affirms or disaffirms the possession by a thing of a particular attribute; and it asserts or disputes that a presentation has an existence in reality [pp. 235–236].

201b/558   Freud (1887–1902) writes: "Thus what is essentially new in my theory is the thesis that memory is present not once but several times over, that it is registered in various species of 'signs' " (p. 173). The transcription of perceptual signs *(Pcpt.-s)* is "the first registration of the perceptions" (p. 174). He goes on to say: "A failure of translation" from one registration to another "is what we know clinically as 'repression' " (p. 175).

But *foreclosure* is another matter entirely, Lacan stresses, and he gives us a clue when he writes: "It is on the signifier, then, that the primordial *Bejahung* bears. . . . We will take *Verwerfung,* then, to be *foreclosure* of the signifier" (1977, p. 201/558). Lacan provides a more detailed discussion in his as yet untranslated 1954 essay "Response to the Commentary of Jean Hippolyte" (1966, pp. 381–399), where he writes of the effect of foreclosure as "a symbolic abolition" (p. 386) which is precisely "opposed to the primordial *Bejahung* and constitutes as such that which is eliminated" (p. 387; our translation). Foreclosure "cuts short" from manifestation in the symbolic order what would otherwise be affirmed in the *Bejahung* that is "the primordial condition for something in the real to come to offer itself to the revelation of being, or, to use the language of Heidegger, to be let-be" (p. 388). This "inaugural affirmation" that lets-be, Lacan states, is the meaning of Freud's *Einbeziehung ins Ich* (as discussed in his paper on "Negation" [1925b]) while the correlative *Ausstossung aus dem Ich* "constitutes the real as the domain of what subsists outside of symbolization" (p. 388). This is why castration, in the case of the Wolf Man, foreclosed "from the very limits of the possible," comes to appear "in the real," in the hallucination of the nearly severed finger (p. 388).

In all of this Lacan appears to be positing (with warrant from Freud's texts), an epistemology radically based on semiotics. He writes that "it is only through the symbolic articulations entangling it to an entire world that perception receives its character of reality" (p. 392). Perception, as Freud wrote to Fliess, is registered in memory under the species of "signs" *(Zeichen)*; thus for Lacan it is "the symbolic text that constitutes the register of recollection" (p. 392). Secondary repression presumes the unconscious symbolic text that has already been established through affirmation *(Bejahung)*: it is the absence of this affirmation in foreclosure that results in a "hole," a "symbolic abolition," a failure symbolically to register the import of castration.

201*c*/558 The hole "at the place of the phallic signification" appears to be the absence of the repressed phallus as unconscious signifier, the failure of the Name-of-the-

Father to intervene and lead to the oedipal shift from imaginary identification with the phallus to its going below the bar (as depicted in the final term of the paternal metaphor on p. 200/557).

202*f*/560   The comma after "misunderstanding" is a misprint.

202*g*/560   Schreber's being as subject hangs suspended from his efforts to reply and thereby prevent God from withdrawing. The text omits "which" before "certainly seems to be" *(qui semble bien être)*. The "unspeakable void" in (a) would then be God's absence and the subject's own concomitant annihilation.

203*a*/560   Schreber's "subjective tearing" *(le déchirement subjectif)* is from God or from the signifying chain from which he hangs suspended as subject. The sounds of the signifiers, and perhaps the shape of the mouth involved in making them, suggest the gaping abyss of separation.

203*b*/560   A misprint has "or manifestations" for "of manifestations" *(de manifestations)*.

203*d*/561   It would seem that the delusional representations are not signifiers but anticipations of meaning, desperate attempts to make the real accessible on the part of the subject identified with the phallus and for whom the Name-of-the-Father is foreclosed. Neither the phallus nor the Name-of-the-Father (the symbolic order itself) functions in a truly signifying manner, so that what illumination arises on the level of the real comes from the imaginary order, and is therefore ephemeral.

     Instead of "both times" we read "the two times" for *les deux temps*, referring to the events described in the preceding (c) and (d).

203*f*/561   Instead of "which subjectively creates it," we prefer "who . . .," referring to Schreber.

203*h*/561   Schreber (1903a) writes that "the filaments aiming at my head and apparently originating from the sun or other distant stars do *not* come towards me in a straight line but in a kind of circle or parabola" (p. 315). The cited text is in Section IV, not V, of the Postscripts.

203*i*/561   The English text has an omission: "God lets the field of nonintelligent beings extend ever farther" *(s'étendre toujours plus loin).*

205*b*/563   In his notion of continuous creation, the French philosopher, Nicolas Malebranche (1638–1715), conceived of God as the only true cause and creative agent, who wills that things happen in accordance with so-called natural causes; this active willing is continuous, and is therefore a continuous creation of what takes place. His Augustinian brand of Platonism was criticized by the empiricist Locke. These two tendencies — idealism and empiricism — constitute, of course, one of the classic polarities in the history of philosophy.

205*f*/563   The "place in F" is not vacated *by* the Law, but is rather "left empty of the Law" *(laissée vacante de la Loi).* Rather than saying the absence "appears to be denuded," we prefer "appears to be laid bare" *(paraît se dénuder).* In the absence of the Law of the Father, the ego ideal is shaped solely in reference to the desire of the mother.

205*g*/563   The line does not "end" but rather "would culminate" *(culminerait)* in the Creatures of speech where it balloons out from its ends in I and M in schema I (1977, p. 212/571). The child is not "rejected in the hopes" of Schreber, but rather "denied to" his hopes *(refusé aux espoirs).*

206*a*/564   In antiphrasis the contrary of what is meant is said.

206*b*/564   The absence (due to foreclosure) of symbolic castration by the Law of the Father leads Schreber to repeat, in the real, the castration involved in the delusional *Entmannung,* but without the salutary effect of symbolic castration, for he does it in order to *be* the phallus, which is incompatible with *having* it.

206*c*/564   Lacan's use of "reasonable compromise" *(un compromis raisonnable)* can be based, not on *vernünftig*, which doesn't appear in our German text, but on *aus Vernunftgründen* (out of a basis of reason) (Schreber, 1903b, p. 177), that is, on an "a priori" basis (since the World-order demanded the *Entmannung*) Schreber felt he must be "reconciled" to the thought of being transformed into a woman ("mich mit dem Gedanken der Verwandlung in ein Weib zu befreunden").

206*e*/565   The first-century work *The Satyricon*, attributed to Petronius, is viewed by some as a take-off on Homeric themes from the *Odyssey*, but here the hero Encolpius ("the Crotch") is relentlessly pursued by Priapus (the phallic divinity) into struggles with lust and impotence. After one impotent episode Encolpius exclaims: "I no longer recognize myself at all. That part of my body with which I once was an Achilles is dead and buried" (p. 157). He then rejects the razor in favor of a verbal rebuke of the offending organ, for being "cold as ice," "too scared," having "screwed [its] crinkled length against my crotch, so cramped along my gut, so furled and small, I could not see to cut at all" (pp. 162–164). This passage is echoed by Schreber's words in the beginning of Chapter XIII, when he notices the portentous changes in his body: "In the immediately preceding nights, my male sexual organ might actually have been retracted had I not resolutely set my will against it" (1903a, p. 176). Lacan quotes *The Satyricon* at the beginning of Part III of the "Discourse at Rome" (1977, p. 77/289), using the same quote with which Eliot (1922) begins *The Waste Land.*

206*f*/565   Rather than "never a question," the text should read: "Or will she believe perhaps that it was ever a question of real castration. . . ?" ("Ou croirait-elle peut-être qu'il se soit agi jamais d'une castration réelle. . . ?").

206*g*/565 The clause following the colon in the second sentence should read: "which requires that that which borders at the imaginary level on the transformation of the subject into a woman must be precisely that which makes him forfeit any inheritance from which he could legitimately expect the attribution of a penis to his person" ("laquelle comporte que cela qui confine au niveau imaginaire à la transformation du sujet en femme, soit justement ceci qui le fasse déchoir de toute hoirie d'où il puisse légitimement attendre l'affectation d'un pénis à sa personne").

207*b*/565 The patient is not "doomed" but rather "dedicated" to become a woman *(voué à devenir une femme).*

207*c*/565 Fenichel (1949) wrote of one of his patients, a male transvestite: "In his perverse practices this patient represented not only a phallic girl but also a phallus pure and simple. . . . The equations, 'I am a girl' and 'my whole body is a penis' are here condensed into the idea: 'I = my whole body = a girl = the little one = the penis' " (p. 304).

The English text should read: "to whom [Fenichel] it [the symbolic parity] gives the theme for an essay of some merit" ("à qui elle donne le thème d'un essai méritoire").

207*f–h*/
566 The solution can also be read as being the woman "mankind" lacks *(qui manque aux hommes).* Lacan appears to posit an intermediate stage in which Schreber's feminization involves sexual contact with men who, however, turn out to be penisless, so that Schreber then saves the day by becoming reconciled to the status of being God's spouse. In his *Memoirs,* however, Schreber indicates no overt interest in sexual contact with men but stresses, early in Chapter XIII: "Nothing of course could be envisaged as a fur-

ther consequence of unmanning but fertilization by divine rays for the purpose of creating new human beings" (1903a, p. 177). The meaning of the fantasy, then, would lie not in an assumed reference to sexual contact with men, but in its anticipation of fertilization by God. The transition would then go from being his mother's phallus to being the phallus for mankind to being God's phallus.

Bartlett (1882) offers "the bridge of asses" as a quote from Euclid's *Elements* (Book 1, Proposition 5), and defines it as "Pons asinorum (i.e., too difficult for asses, or stupid boys, to get over)" (p. 103).

The line of the drawing is not parallel to the face but to the figure *(leur figure)*, as can be seen in Little Hans's drawing of the horse (Freud, 1909a, p. 13).

208a/566 Niederland (1974) points out that *hinmachen* means not only "make" but also "defecate," and he stresses the anal-sadistic nature of Schreber's concerns (p. 45).

208c/567 The French text has "compromise of reason" *(compromis de raison)*, and refers back to the earlier discussion (see note 206c).

208d/567 Rather than "an alliance of nature," we prefer "an alliance likely to satisfy" *(une alliance de nature à satisfaire)*.

208e–f/ 567 In developing the theme of the homosexual wish, Freud (1911c) writes:

> It was impossible for Schreber to become reconciled to playing the part of a female wanton towards his doctor; but the task of providing God Himself with the voluptuous sensations that He required called up no such resistance on the part of his ego. Emasculation was now no longer a disgrace. . . . By this means an outlet was provided which would satisfy both the contending forces. His ego found compensation in his

megalomania, while his feminine wishful phantasy made its way through and became acceptable. The struggle and the illness could cease [p. 48].

Freud goes on to say, however, after his discussion of repression and projection, that in conjunction with "the sexual overvaluation of the ego" (p. 65), "the majority of cases of paranoia exhibit traces of megalomania, and that megalomania can by itself constitute a paranoia. From this it may be concluded that in paranoia the liberated libido becomes attached to the ego, and is used for the aggrandizement of the ego" (p. 72). Freud describes this as a return to the stage of narcissism "in which a person's only sexual object is his own ego" (p. 72).

In his "On Narcissism: An Introduction," Freud (1914a) unequivocally gives the pivotal focus to the ego as narcissistic love object (pp. 74–75). This early narcissistic phase is apparent in the overvaluation parents show toward " 'His Majesty the Baby' " — the "centre and core of creation," "as we once fancied ourselves" (p. 91). Narcissism later appears as displaced onto the ego ideal: "This ideal ego is now the target of the self-love which was enjoyed in childhood by the actual ego. . . . What he projects before him as his ideal is the substitute for the lost narcissism of his childhood in which he was his own ideal" (p. 94). It would seem, then, that for Schreber, becoming the spouse of God plays the pivotal role as his ego ideal, and that the homosexual concerns are subordinate.

208g/567   The sense is that after writing his 1914 paper on narcissism, Freud would not have missed (n'eût-il pas. . . manqué) the real basis of the change in Schreber from indignation to acceptance of the Entmannung. The basis was that between these two phases the subject was dead, thereby giving a free hand to the narcissistic elaborations of the imaginary order, culminating in the grandiose delusion of becoming God's spouse.

209c/568   Rather than "as a 'leprous corpse leading to another leprous corpse,' " we translate "as a 'leprous corpse escorting another leprous corpse' " ("comme d'un 'cadavre lépreux conduisant un autre cadavre lépreux' ").

For another approach to the relationship between bodily fragmentation and psychotic discourse, see Deleuze's (1979) comparison of the work of Antonin Artaud and Lewis Carroll.

209g/568   The "imaginary structure" to be restored appears to be the same one which dissolves in his mother's apartment (see 1977, p. 207e/565–566), namely, "the imaginary tripod" of schema R (I-ϕ-M, which encloses e-ϕ-i). It is restored by being transformed into schema I (p. 212/571) with coordinates at i (the specular image of his transvestite activity) and at e (the anticipated feminization and fecundation, which serve to unify and dispel the images of the fragmented body). Some clarification is needed regarding the difference between e and I and since the text gives only hints we must make an attempt to distinguish them. Clearly e ("m" in the French text for moi) stands for "ego," and is described as such (p. 197c/553; p. 212d/572); clearly I stands for "ego ideal" (l'Idéal du moi, p. 572b) and is described as such (p. 197c–d/553; p. 212e/572). The problem is that "the future of the creature" appears on schema I (p. 212/571) at point e, and was described earlier as "the feminization of the subject" linked to divine copulation (p. 210d/569) and as "the ideal identification" (p. 211e/570), so that we would expect it, instead, to be at point I. A resolution may be found by viewing both e and I as being on the same axis (which they are in schema R and schema I), the axis of the ego. Point *e*, then, is determined with reference to point *i* and is that unification of the fragmented body which is accomplished by the installation of the specular image as idealized form (the first identification), which is how the ego is defined, while point I is determined with reference to point M or F, depending on whether the Name-of-the-Father is foreclosed or not, and consists of the later symbolic or imaginary identifications through which the ego is refashioned. See the French editor's discussion of this schema (1977, p. 334/906–907).

210*f*/569   The relevant passage in Freud (1911c) occurs on page 30, not page 3, as in Sheridan's note (1977, p. 224).

211*a*/570   Rather than "we are here beyond the world," which is misleading, we translate "we are here in a beyond-the-world" ("nous sommes ici dans un au-delà du monde").

211*b*/570   Rather than "in which" for *dont*, we translate "about which, of course, God could not commit himself. . ."

211*e*/570   This paragraph describes the left curved line of schema I, branching from "the image of the creature" (i.e., Schreber) to the specular image at *i* and the ego at *e*, circumventing the hole in the imaginary where the signifier of the phallus is foreclosed (this parallels Lacan's earlier description of the right curve on p. 205/563). The hole depicts the death of the subject as foreclosed from the symbolic order. The transformation of schema R into schema I can be pictured by cutting out the opposite corners ($\phi[S]$ and F[O]) (the phallus/subject and Father/Other referents of schema R) and stretching points *i* and *e* to the left while also stretching points M and I to the right.

211*f*/571   Rather than "in order to resolve it," we prefer "in order to cancel it [the elision]," for *pour la résoudre*. The phallus is reintroduced as a lack insofar as the subject identifies himself as the phallus (and therefore as *not* having it). He cannot utilize the phallus as signifier but identifies with it in an imaginary manner as is concretized in his alienating absorption with his transvestite mirror image. What he was for his mother he will now try to be for God.

212*d*/ 571–572   The graphics of schema I in the French text are much clearer: the interior is marked by vertical lines, so that the diagonal line of the double asymptote from *e* to M stands out sharply; also point *o (a)* ("is addressed to us") is clearly over to the right near M, and is therefore consistent with schema R. The asymptotic line (which is approached but never touched by either curve) and the structure of the hyperbola have mathematical properties we will leave for the mathematicians to explore. Freud's (1911c) use of "asymptotic" occurs on p. 48.

212*g*/572   The sense is that Freud caught the role of the signifier by using only a written document, which was the evidential witness to, as well as the product of, the terminal state of psychosis.

213*b*/572   The "induction effects" may refer to the process whereby, for example, a magnetizable object becomes magnetized when in a magnetic field, or other similar electromotive and electromagnetic effects of one field on another. The foreclosed signifier of the Name-of-the-Father brings about a corresponding overturning of the subject, the gap in one system corresponds to the gap in the other.

213*f*/573   *The Compact Edition of the Oxford English Dictionary* (1971), offers as derivation for "lure," *leure, lewre, luer,* and *lewer*; reference is made to the Old French *leurre, loerre,* and *loire.* The word is probably of Teutonic origin, and the reader is referred to the Middle High

German *luoder* and the Modern German *luder*, whose meaning includes "bait" or "lure."

213*g*/573   It is not just the "staggered shift," but the "unwedging" *(décalage)* of the fields of the imaginary and the symbolic that distorts reality.

214*c*/574   The French text describing the relation to the other "in so far as it is similar to him" is *en tant qu'à son semblable,* indicating the other as "counterpart," which is the word used in earlier essays with reference to aggressive and competitive relations (see Chapters 1 and 2).

215*a*/575   It is our exposure to (and therefore possible foreclosure of) the symbolic order that defines both our being and our potential for madness.

215*b*/575   The French text does not say "the being and the existent," but rather "the being of the existent" *(l'être de l'étant),* or even, to be more explicitly Heideggerean, "the being of the being."

215*f*/575   Rather than "the mark of negative features," the French text reads "marks it with negative features" *(la marque de traits négatifs).* The "opposition" is between Schreber's experience marked by voracity, disgust, and complicity, and mystical experience, illuminated by presence and joy. Schatzman (1974) misses the point when he compares Schreber's experience with shamanistic mysticism (p. 5).

216*a*/576   Instead of "to disarm the effort that it expends," the French text says the exact opposite: "to disarm the effort from which it excuses itself" ("pour désarmer l'effort dont elle se dispense").

216*b*/576   In the lengthy sentence, "I will not deny . . . ," Lacan says he has seen enough to question by what criteria this modern man would dissuade Lacan from situating him in social psychosis. The Pascal quote appears in an earlier chapter (1977, p. 71/283).

217*d*/577   The absence of the Name-of-the-Father "sets off" the cascade, but the French is more precise in saying it "lures" or "entices" *(amorce)* the cascade of reshaped signifiers.

217*e*/577   The French for "A-father" is *Un-père.*

217*f*/577   Rather than "in some relation based on the imaginary dyad," we translate "in some relation which has as base the imaginary couple" ("dans quelque relation qui ait pour base le couple imaginaire"). This suggests the triad of schema R (*o-o'*-O) (1977, p. 197/553) in which A-father would be situated at F. The phrase "eroticized aggression" or its equivalent is repeatedly used to describe the axis S-M (p. 197*d*/553, p. 219*f*/580) and suggests the combination of narcissistic love object and rivalrous identification with the other that the mirror stage gives rise to (some discussion of this appears in Chapters 1 and 2). The English translation inverts "reality-ideal" (for *idéal-réalité*) while the French (and the English follows here) appears to invert the relation between *o'* and *o (le couple imaginaire a-a')*; *o'* would correspond on schema R with the axis on which ego *(e)* and ego ideal (I) are located, while *o* would be on the axis of love object (*i* and M) and reality (the solid line linking *i* and M, the segment denoting objects). The translation, rather than "that interests the subject in the field of eroticized aggression that it induces," can read "who interests the subject in the field of eroticized aggression that he induces," referring back to A-father.

218*a*/578   In the French, "environmental" is in quotes.

218*b*/578   The question, "Whom do you love most. . . ?" is used by Freud in his discussion of the Rat Man (1909b, p. 238).

218*d*/579   The meaning of "the other way around," that is, the love and respect of the father by which he puts the mother in her place, may refer to how the Name-of-the-Father intervenes between child and mother to

put an end to the imaginary dyad in which one is
phallus for the other.

218*e*/579 De Waelhens (1972) gives a clear illustration of how
a mother fails to reserve such a place. Speaking of
mothers of psychotic patients, he writes, drawing on
the work of Aulagnier-Spairani (1964): "These wom-
en neither recognize nor comprehend the law as
such. That which replaces the law — for themselves
and for the others upon whom they attempt to impose it — is their own caprice" (p. 63). De Waelhens
then presents Aulagnier's analogy of a card game.
These mothers understand only a form of "solitaire,"
which is played without partners and without rules.

> The cards which are normally only symbolic in-
> struments through which a game can be played
> between myself and others, a game in which the
> very fact of cheating means that I understand
> the rules, become in this case an end in them-
> selves. One no longer needs to know, in order
> to play, that the King is higher than the Queen,
> nor that the established order determines the
> value: to play such "solitaire" there is no need to
> understand the symbolic value of the signs — the
> signs by themselves suffice, and one can, in
> each instance, make a new law. It is a law which
> has no need of any symbolic support, and which
> only depends on the arbitrary choice of the one
> who plays [p. 63].

This suggests the "fundamental absence of law in the
arena in which these subjects [the mothers] locate
themselves" (p. 63).

219*b*/579 The dishonest behavior is transparent to the children.
219*c*/580 Referring to his own work, Lacan says the consequences that may be expected "from it in [not "in
their"] investigation and technique are to be judged

elsewhere" ("Les suites qu'on en peut attendre dans l'examen et la technique...").

219d/580   An excellent summary of the Schreber material is provided by Meissner (1976).

219f/580   Rather than "grasping in it the chain," we translate "grasping there the chain" (d'y saisir la chaîne).

219g/580   Schreber wrote:

> I want to say by way of introduction that the leading roles in the genesis of this development, the first beginnings of which go back perhaps as far as the eighteenth century, were played on the one hand by the names of Flechsig and Schreber (probably not specifying any individual member of these families), and on the other by the concept of *soul murder* [1903a, p. 22].

Lacan appears to be calling attention to the names as signifiers, the Name-of-the-Father in particular, and the link between the foreclosed signifier and the hole in the signified (the meaning of soul-murder?), so that Flechsig's name stands for his father's and reveals the void of the foreclosure. Lacan might have added Schreber's reference to *Hamlet* ("in Hamlet's words, *there is something rotten in the state of Denmark* — that is to say, in the relationship between God and mankind") (1903a, p. 203). Actually — a minor point — the words were spoken by Marcellus (in Act I, Scene iv). Indeed, Lacan (1959) does provide us with an analysis of *Hamlet*, in which he discusses the inverse of foreclosure, namely the hole in the real caused by someone's death, and sees mourning, like psychosis, triggering a swarm of images to fill the hole. The original mourned object is the phallus, given up in the resolution of the Oedipus complex: "Indeed, the 'something rotten' with which poor Hamlet is confronted is most closely connected with the position of the subject with regard to the phallus" (p. 49). For further elaboration, see Muller (1980).

220*d*/581 Rather than "the third position, to which the signifier of paternity is called," we read "the third position, where the signifier of paternity is called for" ("la position tierce où le signifiant de la paternité est appelé").

For clinical examples of the role of the father in psychosis, see Schneiderman (1980, pp. 171–194). For a glimpse of Lacan's mode of discourse with a psychotic patient, see the interview presented in Schneiderman (1980, pp. 19–41).

220*e*/581 The French text says the exact opposite: "the preceding considerations do not leave me here unprepared" ("les considérations qui précèdent ne nous laissant ici sans vert").

220*f*/581 Jacques Prévert (1900–1977) was a popular French writer of poems, screenplays, and plays, and was also involved in radio, television, and documentary films. Lacan quotes him earlier (1977, p. 64/275).

221*e*/583 The first words of the sentence appear to be elided, so that we read: "This is the term in which" *(Terme où).* The English translation omits a pronoun, so that we read: "the failure of the signifier which in the Other" *(c'est-à-dire du signifiant qui dans l'Autre).*

Chapter 7

The Direction of the Treatment
and the Principles of Its Power

OVERVIEW

The present essay, edited 14 months after "The Agency of the Letter in the Unconscious" (Chapter 5), was composed as a report to be delivered at an international symposium sponsored by the *Société française de psychanalyse* (Royaumont, July 1958). In its own right a self-contained text, it may be presumed to continue the line of thought already evident in the previous essay. It unquestionably crystallizes many of the themes that Lacan was discussing in his seminars at that time.

In question is the nature of psychoanalysis as a treatment process or, more specifically, what path is to be followed in the development of the treatment and how. The first part of the question finds its response in the notion of "direction," where what is at stake is obviously not the "direction" of the *patient* in the sense of "guidance," "instruction" or "control" by the analyst (1977, p. 227/586) but rather the direction of the *treatment*, where the issue is the sequence or emphasis to be given to the various elements found within it: interpretation, transference, and the rectification of the subject's relationship to the real (1977, p. 237/598). As to the *how* of the process, this is addressed under the guise of the "principles of its power." Freud himself believed that the principle of his power lay in the transference (1977, p. 226/585), but the reserves with which this is to be understood are subject to discussion in this essay.

I
Who analyses today?

The word "today" in the heading of this first section suggests that we are in for a polemic against certain contemporary conceptions of the analytic process that are foreign to Lacan's own. Thus the opening paragraph strikes a subtly derisive tone toward certain themes popularized chiefly in *La Psychanalyse d'aujourd'hui*. These themes include the stress on the importance of the analyst's person (1977, pp. 226, 228/585, 587), and hence the role of countertransference in the treatment (1977, pp. 226, 229/585, 589); the insistence that the heart of the treatment is an "emotional re-education of the patient" (1977, p. 226/585); the focus on the fact that the analytic situation involves "two persons" (1977, p. 228/588); the emphasis on the treatment's proceeding "from within," etc. (1977, p. 229/588). But the central difficulty that Lacan finds fault with, permeating in one way or another all of these themes, seems to be the conception of the ego as an agency of adaptation both in the patient and in the analyst, with any interaction between them to be understood in these terms. Hence, the question "Who analyses today?" is by implication a question about the nature and function of the analyst — for that matter, of psychoanalysis itself.

Lacan's approach to the problem is hardly direct. He begins by referring to the notion of "direction" that is the theme of the entire essay. Granted that the direction in question is not of the patient but of the treatment, who, then, supplies it? The analyst, of course, but *how*? The analyst's first task is to make the subject follow the analytic rule (1977, p. 227/586). The analyst thus starts by instructing the patient up to the limits of his own (perhaps deficient) understanding of the rule. Given the differences among analysts even on this level, it is clear that "from the initial directives on, the problem of direction cannot be formulated in an univocal communication" (1977, p. 227/586).

But the analyst's involvement goes deeper than the level of mere instruction, and this is not without cost to himself. He must pay, for example, "with words," i.e., "if the transmutation that they undergo from the analytic operation raises them to the level of interpretation" (1977, p. 227/587). He must pay, too, "with his person" to the extent that he lends his whole person "as a support for the singular phenomen[on] that analysis has discovered in the transference" (1977, p. 227/587). Finally, he must pay with his very being, for if his analytic action "goes to the heart of being" in his patient, how can he expect "to remain alone outside the field of play" (1977, pp. 227–228/587)? Such talk about being sounds terribly metaphysical, of course, but it is only on the level of being that we can make sense out of such claims as that the "analyst cures not so much by what he says and does as by what he is" (1977, p. 228/587). What about the being of the analyst, then?

At this point, Lacan wastes no time with metaphysics but addresses the question of the analyst's being in terms of how the analyst conceives his function to be his "own oracle," "master" of his own ship, i.e., "free in the timing, frequency and choice of [his] interventions, to the point that it seems that the [analytic] rule has been arranged entirely so as not to impede in any way [his] own freedom of movement" (1977, p. 228/588). Freedom of movement, however, to do precisely what? The answer to this question depends on how each analyst understands the role of *transference* in the analytic venture.

The fact is that every analyst, no matter how questionable his manner of procedure may be, "experiences the transference in wonder at the least expected effect of a relationship between two people that seems like any other" (1977, p. 229/588). The whole issue of how the analyst fulfills his function ("who" it is, then, that "analyses today") turns on how he deals with the phenomenon of transference.

One way to deal with transference is for the analyst to experience it as the alienation of his own freedom "by the duplication to which [his] person is subject in it" (1977, p. 228/588). He experiences this duplication as an intrusion upon himself insofar as his freedom is perceived as residing in the other of the transference. This third dimension, however, does not prevent people from believing that psychoanalysis is a situation involving two persons, one of whom sees his task to be the "training of the 'weak' ego, by an ego that [he] is pleased to believe is capable, on account of its 'strength,' of carrying out such a project" (1977, p. 229/588). The assumption is, of course, that the ego's weakness or strength is measured by its ability to serve as the agency by which the subject adapts to reality, and that reality, i.e., his own relation to reality, is clearly discernible by the analyst. This "relation to reality [in the analyst] goes without saying" (1977, p. 230/590). It is transmitted to him by the educational process of his training analysis and imposed by him in turn on the analysand with all the authoritarianism of an educator, despite the experience of his own analysis which should have made him know better. In this context, one can appreciate the appeal of the notion of the "autonomous ego," developed particularly by American psychology as a "standard of the measure of the real" (1977, pp. 230–231/590). Be this as it may, Lacan dismisses this "American" tradition of ego psychology with bemused disdain: "[this] does not solve the problem of the analyst's being. A team of *egos* no doubt less equal than autonomous . . . is offered to the Americans to guide them towards *happiness*, without upsetting the autonomies, egoistical or otherwise, that pave with their non-conflictual spheres the *American way* of getting there" (1977, p. 231/591).

But this is only one way for the analyst to deal with the transference. There are others. One of these would be simply to deal with transference as resistance. In this case, the analysis of resistance would have to be done very cautiously — the analyst "would look twice before hazarding an interpretation" (1977, p. 231/591). Another way would be to examine and interpret the transference as such, but then how would such an interpretation be received by the analysand? "[T]his interpretation. . .will be received as coming from the person that the transference imputes him to be." Of course, this second level of transference, too, could be interpreted, but "the analyst's words will still be heard as coming from the Other of the transference, [and] the emergence of the subject from the transference is thus postponed *ad infinitum*" (1977, p. 231/591).

None of these solutions to the problem of transference is satisfactory for Lacan, however, and it is to bring out the unsatisfactoriness of them that he poses at the end of this section the questions that in effect summarize the whole: "Who is the analyst? He who interprets, profiting from the transference? He who analyses it as resistance? Or he who imposes his idea of reality?" (1977, p. 232/592). We are left expecting the answer: "None of the above."

What we have seen so far in this section is largely negative. Is there nothing positive, no indication of how the analyst *should* proceed in the analytic situation, transference and all? As a matter of fact, Lacan does propose one way of conceiving the process which is no more than suggested here and will be elaborated elsewhere. The matter arises in his discussion of the role of countertransference in the process. He speaks rather disparagingly of those who throw their feelings, "which they class under the heading of their counter-transference, [on] one side of the scales, thus balancing the transference itself with their own weight" (1977, p. 229/589). This, Lacan claims, indicates "a failure to conceive the true nature of the transference" (1977, p. 229/589).

Lacan then changes the metaphor and continues: "One cannot regard the phantasies that the analysand imposes on the person of the analyst in the same way as a perfect card player might guess his opponent's intentions" (1977, p. 229/589). Rather, by his deliberate reserve (e.g., "impassive face," "sealed lips," etc.), the analyst brings "to his aid what in bridge is called the dummy *(le mort)*, but he is doing so in order to introduce the fourth player who is to be the partner of the analysand here, and whose hand the analyst, by his tactics, will try to expose" (1977, p. 229/589). Here the dummy, i.e., the analyst's manner of austere reserve, enters the game as the analyst's ally—its task being to help the analyst uncover the hand of the fourth player, i.e., the analysand's partner—presumably his unconscious.

Lacan now pursues this metaphor in a way that makes sense if we view the game as in progress, where each player has an opportunity to take the lead and play to the dummy. We could deduce the way the analyst is playing "according to whether he places himself 'on the right' or 'on the left' of the patient, that is to say, in a position to play after or before the fourth player, that is to say, to play...before or after the player with the dummy" (1977, pp. 229–230/589). The dummy enables the transference to take place, to have a place in this four-sided structure, and the patient's unconscious (the fourth player) will at times take the lead and play to the dummy. Where the analyst places himself makes a difference in terms of who takes the lead and whose hand he will force. The essential seems to be that the dummy in analysis plays an important function as an ally of the therapist in helping the unconscious of the patient to reveal its hand. At any rate, this much is certain: the feelings of the analyst have a part in this game only as part of the dummy that he plays (1977, p. 230/589).

II
What is the place of interpretation?

Given the importance of transference in analytic treatment (and we shall return to the matter below), what place does interpretation have in the process? Any answer to such a question depends, of course, on how one understands the term, and the wariness of contemporary psychoanalytic writers in using the term suggests their uneasiness in dealing with it (1977, p. 232/ 592).

The fact is that interpretation seems to involve a "transmutation" in the subject that is somehow uncovered by the interpretation (1977, p. 233/593). This is understandable, however, only if we recognize the radical importance of the signifier in localizing "analytic truth" for the subject.

For interpretation does not consist in just any wild attribution of signification to phenomena, as if it were "a sort of phlogiston: manifest in everything that is understood rightly or wrongly" (1977, p. 233/593) — "signification no more emanates from life than [the] phlogiston in combustion escapes from bodies" (1977, p. 234/594). Rather, in interpretation the signification of a series (i.e., "diachrony") of "unconscious repetitions" is deciphered inasmuch as a given constellation (i.e., "synchrony") of signifiers permits the "missing element" in that series to appear, thus making translation possible. This happens through the function of the Other in the process, "it being in relation to that Other that the missing element appears" (1977, p. 233/593). This Other, of course, we take to be the unconscious, inasmuch as it "is structured in the most radical way like a language" (1977, p. 234/594) — a structure synonymous with the symbolic order that "pre-exists the infantile subject" and to which this subject is introduced in the experience described by Freud in terms of *Fort! Da!* In any case, it is in this fashion that "the signifier effects the advent of the signified, which is the only conceivable way that interpretation can produce anything new" (1977, p. 233/594).

As to rules of interpretation, they can indeed be formulated, though this is not the place to formulate them. Let it suffice to say that the index of a correct interpretation is not acknowledgment by the patient (for, as Freud pointed out, denial, too, is a "form of avowal") but rather "the material that will emerge as a result of the interpretation" (1977, p. 234/594).

More important here, perhaps, is Freud's example in using it, since his manner of proceeding is far different from that of

contemporary analysts. The latter are caught in an initial timid-
ity that goes along with their conception of their role as engaged
in a dual relationship with the patient's ego. For them, then, the
development of transference offers a sense of "security" that permits them to use interpretation in order to reduce the transference (by a kind of "working through") as a way of helping the
patient deal with his relation to the "real" (1977, p. 235/596).
Freud, however, following an "inverse order," "begins by introducing the patient to an initial mapping of his position in the
real" (1977, p. 236/596). He then proceeds to the development
of the transference — in which he recognized the "principle of his
power" (1977, p. 236/597) — and finally to interpretation (1977,
p. 237/598).

Freud's conception of interpretation is a bold one. When
we see, for example, how his notion of "drive" *(Trieb)* as distinct
from "instinct" implies "the advent of a signifier" (1977, p. 236/
597), it is clear that in his conception of interpretation Freud
recognizes, however implicitly, the function of the symbolic order. Hence, far more is involved for him than a "dual relation"
between the analyst's ego and the patient's ego — operative, too,
is the whole dimension of the Other, the role of the "absolute
Father" (1977, p. 237/598).

Lacan concludes this section by offering a clinical vignette
that suggests how his understanding of interpretation differs from
that of the so-called "id" psychologists (e.g., Melitta Schmideberg) on the one hand, and the so-called "ego" psychologists
(e.g., Ernst Kris) on the other. The case is that of an inhibited
intellectual unable to bring his research to a finish because of a
compulsion to plagiarize (1977, p. 238/599). Schmideberg
(1934) allegedly sees the unconscious conflict in straightforward
fashion as the perdurance of an "infantile delinquency" (he had
stolen sweets and books); hence she focuses on the role of the
"id." Kris (1951), taking over the case, resorts to the tools of
"ego" psychology and approaches the problem in terms of defense mechanisms. In other words, the patient has a drive that
is manifest in an attraction to others' ideas but defends himself

against the drive by thinking of himself as a plagiarist lest in fact he become one. The insufficiency of such an interpretation, according to Lacan, appears in the patient's acting out a rejection of it by associating to his own search for his "favourite dish, [fresh] brains" (1977, p. 239/599).

For Lacan, "it is not his defence against the idea of stealing that makes him believe that he steals. It's having an idea of his own that never occurs to him" (1977, p. 239/600). Hence, the idea of being a plagiarist is not a defense mechanism against a drive but rather a metonymy for his desire that is diverted through an entire metonymic chain. The food fantasy (search for fresh brains), then, suggests that the appropriate diagnosis here is not "obsessional neurosis" but rather a kind of "anorexia mentale" (1977, p. 240/601).

III
Where have we got with the transference?

But the issue of transference is far from exhausted, and Lacan returns to it again, taking as his starting point the work of Daniel Lagache, who has made a serious effort to study systematically this notion in Freud. Precisely by his effort at systematization, Lagache's work has highlighted the incompleteness of most current discussions of the notion, particularly the extent to which the very loose signification of the term in popular usage, i.e., as "the positive or negative feelings that the patient has for his analyst" (1977, p. 241/602), has permeated serious psychoanalytic discussion. All of this leaves many subtle issues unresolved, probably because "at each of the stages at which an attempt has been made to revise the problems of the transference, the technical divergences that made such a revision a matter of urgency have left no place for a true critique of the notion itself" (1977, p. 241/603). It is perhaps worthwhile to examine some of these theories precisely to see not only their incompleteness but their noncomplementarity, and thus to be able to understand better that "they suffer from a central defect" (1977, p. 242/603).

The first of these incomplete, "partial" theories to be considered Lacan calls "geneticism." We take him to mean that conception of transference that is based on the tendency "to ground analytic phenomena in the [psychosexual] developmental stages that concern them" (1977, p. 242/603). Such a theory is based on the assumption of a correlation between physiological development and the emergence of psychological drives. Moreover, given Freud's hypothesis of an unconscious dimension of the ego, this theory postulates that in the ego's unconscious, defenses may be erected against the exigencies of these drives. Hence these defense mechanisms may "reveal a comparable law of appearance" (1977, p. 242/603)—an "order of formal emergences" (1977, p. 243/605)—proper to the drives themselves. Such, at least, was Anna Freud's hypothesis in *The Ego and the Mechanisms of Defense* (1936), stimulated by, and finding some confirmation in, her work with children.

This perspective might have become fruitful if it had been focused on "the relations between development and the obviously more complex structures that Freud introduced into psychology" (1977, p. 242/604). Unfortunately, in practice it settled for a facile psychobiological concordism and a technique that contented itself with seeking to differentiate an earlier ("non-contemporaneous") pattern as measured by its departure from a contemporary pattern that "finds in its conformism the guarantees of its conformity" (1977, p. 243/604).

The second of these incomplete, "partial" theories of transference to be considered is that which proceeds from the theory of object relations that has its origin in the work of Karl Abraham (1908), who added to Freud's stages of early libidinal development (oral, anal, phallic, genital) more precise subdivisions, based not only on the sexual aims (i.e., actions) of a drive but on its sexual objects. For Abraham, the subject's relation to his sexual objects is marked by corresponding stages of "love" ranging from "auto-erotism" in the earlier oral stage to full "object-love" in the final genital stage. In the genital phase, the subject ideally overcomes all traces of earlier stages, resolves the

Oedipus and castration complexes, and transfers the feelings of affection or hostility which he entertains toward his patients onto the environment; he thus is ready for subsequent adaptation to society. It is in the elaboration of these different stages in terms of their relevance for character development that Abraham orchestrates differences between "genital" and "pregenital" characters.

Lacan challenges all this, finding much that "begs the question" (1977, p. 243/605). To begin with, the development of libido toward object love "can be explained as a finality that allows itself to be instinctual, in the sense that it is based on the image of the maturation of an ineffable object, the Object with a capital O that governs the phase of objectality (to be distinguished, significantly, from objectivity by virtue of its affective substance)" (1977, p. 243/605). For Lacan, this assumption of a kind of biological final cause is without warrant.

Moreover, the resultant emphasis on the distinction between the "pregenital" character as an "amalgam of all the defects of the object relation" and the "genital" character as the paragon of integration where the " 'style of the relations between subject and object is one of the most highly evolved [sic]' " (1977, p. 244/ 605–606) is wholly unsatisfactory. "And what has this absurd hymn to the harmony of the genital got to do with the real" (1977, p. 245/606)? The point seems to be that such a conception too easily overlooks the "barriers and snubs *(Erniedrigungen)* that are so common in even the most fulfilled love relation" and glamorizes the genital aspect of object relations to the point of confusing "the sublime" with the "perfect orgasm" (1977, p. 245/607), thus placing impossible burdens on the shoulders of "innocents" who cannot achieve it.

There is a third theory about the nature of transference that is likewise inadequate: "the notion of intersubjective introjection...in a dual relation" with the analyst (1977, p. 246/ 607). The principal focus of Lacan's critique here seems to be Sandor Ferenczi (1909)—though he also mentions Strachey and Balint—for whom transference, though fundamentally a "displacement," involves identification and even an introjection, or incorporation, of the other.

The "phantasy of phallic devouring, to which the image of the analyst is subjected" (1977, p. 246/608), would be a case in point. Now Lacan himself, who takes the phallus to be the signifier par excellence of desire (Chapter 8), would be inclined to take this fantasy as an illustration of "the privileged function of the [signifier-]phallus in the mode of the subject's presence to desire" (1977, p. 246/608). But such an interpretation presupposes the "true relations of the analytic situation," i.e., the whole domain of language (the symbolic order) within which analysis takes place, as well as the function of desire in that situation.

When all this is left out of account by limiting the analytic situation to a strictly dual relation, the situation itself is "crushed" (1977, p. 246/608) and the possibility of a truly "symbolic" perspective eliminated. Since analysis as such does not effect any change in the "real," the only remaining register in which a strictly dual relation may be conceived is that of the "imaginary." But "if one confines oneself to an imaginary relation between objects there remains only the dimension of distance to order it" (1977, p. 246/608). If this distance is ideally reduced to zero (1977, p. 247/609), the result is obviously a kind of "mystical consummation" (1977, p. 246/608). That is why the "phantasy of phallic devouring" finds such a congenial place in analysis of this kind, for "it tallies so well with a conception of the direction of the treatment that is based entirely upon the arrangement of the distance between patient and analyst as the object of the dual relation" (1977, p. 246/608).

But if "distance" is the only criterion by which to judge the relation between analyst and patient, then "too much" and "too little" can be measured by different interpreters in completely contradictory fashion, with corresponding variation in recommendations for technique. Carried to the extreme by a kind of "wild" analysis that would transpose the situation from the "imaginary order" into the "real," the result could be quite ludicrous. For since "the olfactory is the only dimension [except for taste] that enables one to reduce distance to zero" (1977, p. 248/610), it would follow, as one work suggests, that to "be able to smell one's analyst" would be an "index of the happy outcome of the transference" (1977, p. 247/609).

At this point Lacan dialogues with an absent partner over a clinical case of "transitory perversion," about which the otherwise uninformed reader is forced to guess the details. He then returns to his theme: the problem of transference. For his "only purpose is to warn analysts of the decline that threatens their technique if they fail to recognize the true place in which its effects are produced" (1977, p. 249/612). If he criticizes the genetic conception of transference or the theory of object relations as inadequate (i.e., "partial"), this is not to say that they have no relevance to "properly analytic realities" (1977, p. 250/612) but only to deny that they define the "true place" in which the effects of technique are produced. The result is a failure on the part of analysts to grasp "their action in its authenticity" so that they end up forcing that action "in the direction of the exercise of power" (1977, p. 250/612). But this power, such as it is, is merely a substitute for "the relation to...being where this action takes place, producing a decline of its resources, especially those of speech" (1977, p. 250/612). We take this to mean that the "true place" where the effects of technique are produced, hence (presumably) where transference finds the source of its power, is in relation to being, which never has been taken sufficiently into account by analysts. *This*, then, would be the "central defect" from which these theories "suffer."

IV
How to act with one's being

Lacan concluded the previous section by referring to the level of "being where [analytic] action takes place" (1977, p. 250/612). We infer that this alludes to the domain of the Other, i.e., the symbolic order. He now echoes the word "being" but, initially at least, speaks of it as if it were the analyst's being that is at

stake. We assume that the two uses of the word are not disconnected, but the connection is far from clear in the text (the text
itself is particularly obscure). This assumption serves as an underlying working hypothesis in our effort to detect the unifying
thread of this section.

To begin with, it was again Ferenczi (1909) who introduced
the question about the being of the analyst when he "conceived
of the transference as the introjection of the person of the doctor
into the subjective economy," i.e., the "absorption into the economy of the subject of all that the psychoanalyst makes present in
the duo as the here and now of an incarnated problematic"
(1977, p. 250/613). What "the psychoanalyst makes present in
the duo" is what Lacan calls in Ferenczi's name the psychoanalyst's "being"—with this nuance, however, that we "distinguish
from the interhuman relation, with its warmth and its allure-
ments *(leurres)*, that relation to the Other in which being finds its
status" (1977, p. 251/613).

In any case, it "is certainly in the relation to being that the
analyst has to find his operating level" (1977, p. 252/615). This
means, first of all, that his purpose is not to bring "happiness" to
the analysand, still less to share with the analysand some puta-
tive "happiness" of his own. It means, too, that the analyst's task
is not first of all to help the analysand to "understand" himself,
nor even to teach the analysand to "think." Rather, the "analyst
is the man to whom one speaks and to whom one speaks freely.
That is what he is there for" (1977, p. 253/616). Speaking "freely," of course, does not necessarily mean that there is a great
deal of "freedom in what [one] says" (1977, p. 253/616), though
it does "open up on to a free speech [of a kind, i.e.], a full speech
that is painful to [the analysand]" (1977, p. 253/616). Such an
experience might prove quite troublesome to the patient if this
"full speech" articulates "something that might be true" (1977, p.
253/616). But truth is what is at stake in the analysis—not as an
abstract intellectualization but as a concrete dynamic grappling
with the "unsayable."

The analyst's first task in all this is to listen *(écouter)* to what is spoken to him. For Lacan, the importance of the analyst's "presence" in the analytic process consists in the fact "that this presence is first of all simply the implication of his listening, and that this listening is simply the condition of speech" (1977, p. 255/618). Having listened, the analyst also must hear *(entendre)* what is said beyond the spoken discourse. This may not necessarily mean, however, that he can understand *(comprendre)* what he hears, and if he does not, he will have nothing to say. Silence, however, is admittedly frustrating to the speaker, for his speech is, after all, a way of asking the analyst for something — at the very least, for a reply — that the analyst by his silence refuses. Such a request "is deployed on the [broader] field of an implicit demand, that for which he is there: the demand to cure him" (1977, p. 254/617). This introduces the whole issue of the role of the patient's requests (i.e., "demands") in the analysis.

Through the articulation of the patient's demands, "the whole past opens up right down to early infancy" (1977, p. 254/ 617), for it is only by making demands that the infant could have survived. This may be the sense of "analytic regression," for "regression shows nothing other than a return to the present of signifiers used in demands" of a speech of long ago (1977, p. 255/618). That is why the analyst sustains the demand if he can, "not, as has been said, to frustrate the subject, but in order to allow the signifiers in which his frustration is bound up to reappear" (1977, p. 255/618).

What the analyst seeks, then, is the articulation of the patient's demands. This is made possible by reason of the "primary transference," which we take to mean transference to the therapist in terms of the "primary identification" with the omnipotent mother. In terms of this identification, the exigencies of the infant's biological structure (i.e., his "needs") cannot just be met by the mother in some concrete physical fashion, for the time comes in his development when the infant must separate from the mother and enter into the symbolic order, where the satisfaction of these needs must be filtered through the "defiles of the structure of the signifier" (1977, p. 255/618). Hence:

> Needs become subordinated to the same conventional con-
> ditions as those of the signifier in its double register: the
> synchronic register of opposition between irreducible ele-
> ments [i.e., the binary pairs of distinctive phonemes], and
> the diachronic register of substitution and combination,
> [by] which language, even if it does not fulfil all functions,
> structures everything concerning relations between human
> beings [1977, p. 255/618–619].

Articulated in this fashion, these needs become "demands,"
and it is with "all the articulations of the subject's demand" that
the analyst must deal in turn (1977, p. 256/619). In doing so, he
is indeed identified with the omnipotent mother, whose task
would be to attend to these articulations and discern the demand for love that lies within them all. Such presumably would
be the situation that "explains the primary transference, and the
love that is sometimes declared in it" (1977, p. 255/618).

To be sure, the analyst "must respond to [this demand]
only from the position of the transference," but what that might
mean and how the transference itself is to be understood as an
"identification with signifiers" (1977, p. 256/619) is far from
clear at the moment. What is clear is that by engaging the patient in this fashion, the analyst "acts with his being," that is, as
grounded in the symbolic order, the unconscious Other in
which all signifiers find their matrix of signification.

V

Desire must be taken literally

The transition from the previous section, with its discussion (however sinuous) of the analyst's relation to being, to this,
where the theme is "desire," calls for an explanation—or at least
for some educated guesswork. We have just seen in what sense
the analyst finds his operating level in relation to being by dealing with the articulations of the subject's demand(s). However,

the fundamental driving force of the subject is not his demand(s) but the desire that lies beneath (or within, or behind, or beyond) this demand(s). Hence, there arises now the necessity of addressing explicitly the question of the role of desire in the treatment and its relation to the source of the treatment's power.

When Lacan in his title to this section tells us that desire must be taken "literally" *(à la lettre)*, we understand this in the sense that this same phrase was used in "The Agency of the Letter in the Unconscious" (Chapter 5), i.e., in terms of the linguistic structure of the unconscious. In other words, we may reasonably expect this section to address the question of desire in its distinction from demand and in relation to the whole role of language in psychoanalysis as Lacan conceives it.

As we know, desire plays a central role for Freud in *The Interpretation of Dreams* (1900a), but the import of the word is not self-evident. Freud's (1900b) word is *Wunsch*, which the *Standard Edition* translates as "wish," with the implication that what is at stake is an individual, isolated act. The French equivalent would be *voeu*. In fact, however, the French have always translated *Wunsch* as *désir*, with the implication of a continuous force (Sheridan, 1977, p. viii). We follow the French (Lacan's) usage here, though the reader should bear in mind the possible ambiguity that results.

Lacan begins his discussion by referring to the familiar dream of the butcher's wife discussed by Freud:

> I wanted to give a supper-party, but I had nothing in the house but a little smoked salmon. I thought I would go out and buy something, but remembered then that it was Sunday afternoon and all the shops would be shut. Next I tried to ring up some caterers, but the telephone was out of order. So I had to abandon my wish to give a supper-party [1900a, p. 147].

The reader will recall how this dream, presented to Freud as a challenge to his theory that dreams express the fulfillment of desire, becomes under Freud's analysis the expression of the dreamer's desire for an unfulfilled desire. This becomes clear when the "salmon" in the dream is seen to be a substitute for "caviar," for which the dreamer has a craving that she wishes to remain ungratified by her husband (1900a, p. 148). Let us begin by seeing how desire functions here according to the laws of language *(à la lettre)*, by which signifiers are related to each other either by reason of the substitution of one for the other (i.e., as metaphor) or through the combination of one with the other (i.e., as metonymy) (1977, p. 258/622).

In the present case, the salmon in the dream signifies the friend's desire for salmon, which is seen by Freud as signifying (by substitution) the dreamer's desire for caviar. The former, then, is a metaphor for the latter. With regard to the desire for caviar as signifier of the desire for an unsatisfied desire, the caviar, by reason of its *in*accessibility, serves as a displacement of the unsatisfied desire, hence serves an expression of that desire by metonymy (1977, p. 259/622). We see, then, how this dream is elaborated according to a "linguistic structure" that Freud discovered—even before Saussure—simply in the "signifying flow" of associations, "the mystery of which lies in the fact that the [conscious] subject does not even know where to pretend to be its organizer" (1977, p. 259/623). The "organizer" obviously is Other.

But to whom does the "signifying flow" reveal its meaning, "before the arrival on the scene of the analyst" (1977, p. 260/623)? After all, this meaning preexists in the flow prior to any reading of the flow or deciphering of that meaning. Both reading and deciphering suggest that a dream is made for the "recognition of desire" (yes, but recognition by whom?) that in turn is a "desire for recognition" (yes, but recognition from whom?) (1977, p. 260/623). Such questions are left unanswered, for the moment at least, and instead Lacan takes us through a review of Freud's analysis of the dream. He concludes by returning to the role of desire in the dream, symbolized in this case by the salmon. He finds in the salmon itself a convenient reminder of the phallus, which, as we know, he takes to be the signifier par excellence of desire, independent of the sex of the subject (1977, p. 263/627).

But before we discuss the signifier of desire we must first understand better "that which structures desire" (1977, p. 263/627). Given some understanding of what "need" means and of how "demand" differs from it in articulating this need according to the exigencies of the symbolic order, there remains a gap, an "interval," between the two, insofar as there is a want-to-be that transcends all satisfaction of physical need, transcends, too, any particular articulation of need, i.e., any specific demand, so as to remain unsatisfied even after any/every demand has been met. Any demand is always addressed to some Other, i.e., to some*one*, about some*thing*, through speech made possible by a sharing of language with that Other. Whatever might be the thing demanded, however, what is really sought in the demand is the Other's "love." But this Other suffers from want, too, and cannot satisfy the subject's want-to-be, even by his "love." For the subject's deepest want is not for the "love" (which we take Lacan to mean here as mere "oblativity") but for recognition. That is why the demand for "love," even if acceded to, cannot satisfy desire. Under such circumstances, the subject may well retreat to sleep, "where he haunts the limbo regions of being, by letting it [*Ça*] speak in him" through his dreams (1977, p. 263/627).

Desire, then, is a want-to-be in the subject that is unsatisfiable either through gratification of his needs or acquiescence to his demands. Taking this as a "premise," Lacan now draws the conclusion that "man's desire is the desire of the Other" (1977, p. 264/628), though the step here is a big one. Mediating between premise and conclusion are the suppositions that desire, as well as demand, must submit to the exigencies of the symbolic order, and that this symbolic order is the Other, i.e., the "other scene" where the speech of analytic discourse is "deployed." If we accept these suppositions and try to understand the sense of desire as "desire of the Other," it should be noted first of all that the Other that is spoken of here, in the sense of the unconscious structured like a language, is to be distinguished clearly from the Other in the above sense of the generalized some*one* of whom a demand is made.

With that in mind, we are left to our own resources here to understand how the subject's desire is "desire of the Other." A full discussion of the matter would probably take account of such considerations as the following: Desire, since it must be channeled through the "defiles of the signifier," is "at the mercy of" *(en proie de)* language. It may thus be thought of as possessed by language and in that sense is desire of language, i.e., "of the Other" (subjective genitive). Furthermore (a variation of the preceding), desire may be "of the Other" (subjective genitive) insofar as the Other is thought of as the being of the subject that is "other" than his conscious ego, i.e., the subject's being insofar as this is in want-of-being, hence the dynamic, propelling dimension of his decentered self. We find some confirmation of such interpretations in the dream under discussion, for the "desire of the dream is not assumed by the subject who says 'I' in [her] speech. Articulated, nevertheless, in the locus of the Other, it is discourse—a discourse whose grammar Freud [began] to declare [as] such" (1977, p. 264/629).

From another point of view, however, desire may be "of the Other" (objective genitive) insofar as the being of which the subject is in want is the being of the Other that will fill out his own ineluctable finitude, restoring the illusion of plenitude that was shattered by entrance into the symbolic order. Again, desire may be "of the Other" (objective genitive) insofar as, given his finitude, the subject thinks he can achieve the self-awareness appropriate to him only in recognition by the Other that simulates, and in a measure restores, the radical affirmation of a primordial unity. It is this last sense that easily masquerades as the demand for "love" from the individual Other, as if the Other possessed a fullness that could complete the subject. Hence, we gain some sense of how delicate is the task of discerning the difference between desire and demand. We find some confirmation of this interpretation when we are told that "the subject has to find the constituting structure of his desire in the same gap opened up by the effect of the signifiers in those who come to represent the Other for him, in so far as his demand is subjected to them" (1977, p. 264/628).

But the distinction between demand and desire (and, by implication, need) remains difficult to grasp, desire being both "beyond" *(au delà)* and "on this side of" *(en deçà)* the demand that "evokes" it. We take this to be another attempt by Lacan to express the transcending quality of desire, the "absolute condition" of the subject's ineluctable want, expressed here provocatively as his "nothing." It is precisely this want that erupts when the infant is "born into language," so that henceforth the subject is in bondage to the laws of language in pursuing whatever will satisfy this want. It is in this sense, we presume, that desire "is, as it were, the mark of the iron of the signifier on the shoulder of the speaking subject" (1977, p. 265/629). Here we are taking desire *à la lettre* indeed.

However that may be, the signifier par excellence of desire is the phallus, in a sense that will be given full orchestration in Chapter 8. It is to the theme of the phallus that Lacan now turns in order to elaborate further the role of desire in terms of this unique signifier, and we must do the best we can with it in tentative, make-do fashion. He broaches the issue by presenting a clinical vignette, the essential details of which are these: Lacan's patient is an obsessional male "of mature years," suffering from impotence with his mistress and ready to explain away the problem as a simple matter of "menopause." Persuaded, however, that the possible intervention of a third person into the dyad might salvage the situation, the patient suggests that his mistress sleep with another man "to see." The mistress then has a dream: "She has a phallus, she feels its shape under her clothes, which does not prevent her from having a vagina as well, nor, of course, from wanting this phallus to enter it." When she recounts this to the patient, he "is immediately restored to his virility and demonstrates this quite brilliantly to his partner" (1977, pp. 266–267/631).

Lacan's interpretation of this vignette is more than ordinarily opaque, but the general drift seems to be as follows. The mistress' dream, when reported to the patient, takes the form of a "discourse" that reveals to the patient her own desire both to "have" the phallus and to receive it. Realizing this, the patient is liberated from whatever it was that inhibited him. Fair enough, but how?

We are told that as a child the patient had experienced "the play of destruction exerted by one of his parents [i.e., his mother] on the desire [i.e., the phallus] of the other [i.e., his father]" (1977, p. 265/630). He therefore presumed that it was impossible for anyone "to desire without destroying [i.e., castrating] the Other" (1977, p. 265/630). In the analysis, indeed, the patient comes to see how he is on guard against the destructiveness of his own desire by manipulating the situation "so as to protect the Other" (1977, p. 265/630). Since his mistress represents for him the "castrating mother" (1977, p. 268/633), whose desire presumably will destroy him, i.e., take away his phallus, he is inhibited from responding to her desire out of fear of his own destruction/castration.

What removes this inhibition? The message of the mistress' dream to the effect that she "has a phallus" and therefore "will not have to take it from him" (1977, p. 268/633). In other words, the fear of castration (whether wisely or not, time will tell) is removed. Moreover, "having this phallus [does] not diminish her desire for it [i.e., for his]. And here it is his own want-to-be that [is] touched on" (1977, p. 268/633). For his own deepest want is to be the object of her desire, not simply by having the phallus but by being it for her (1977, p. 268/632) — if that were only possible.

Vignette concluded, Lacan returns to his principal theme: the role of desire in the direction of the treatment. The essential here seems to be to realize that "all the demands that had been articulated in the analysis . . . were merely transferences intended to maintain in place a desire that was unstable or dubious in its problematic" (1977, p. 271/636). Hence, the need to frustrate these demands in order to let the underlying desire show through; hence, too, the importance of analyzing the transference — and Lacan alludes (in highly condensed form) to some of the subtleties involved in such a procedure (1977, p. 270/635).

But the problem of demand has not been exhausted, and after alluding to it in terms of transference, Lacan turns it over again in terms of the formation of symptoms. Symptoms, he recalls from Freud, are "overdetermined," i.e., are attributable to more than one determining factor (1977, p. 271/636). What does that mean in terms of their formation?

We know well enough that for Freud there was an analogy between symptom formation and dreams, insofar as both involve the process of a "wish-fulfillment" (1899, p. 278). Later Freud would speak of the symptom as a formation that establishes a workable compromise between unconscious wish and need for defense (1916–1917, pp. 358–359). According to Lacan's linguistic model, however, we understand that symptoms, like condensation in the dream-work, are structured as metaphors. They thus arise out of a certain "interference" between (i.e., overlapping of) signifiers in the relationship they bear to their respective signifieds. But what of the "wish-fulfillment" character of the symptom? Here we are told that the "wish" in question is essentially a "particular demand." The "interference" that takes place is between the "effects" of this demand within the subject (in the form of signifiers, we presume) and "the effects of a position in relation to the other. . . that he sustains as subject" (1977, p. 272/637), and enacts through an unconscious fantasy. This fantasy, for Lacan, "is defined as an image set to work in the signifying structure" and "is that by which the subject sustains himself at the level of his vanishing desire, vanishing in so far as the very satisfaction of demand hides his object from him" (1977, p. 272/637). The point seems to be that there is an insurmountable tension between the unconscious fantasy promising fulfillment and the articulated demand that intrinsically fragments and displaces desire. Obscure as this is — and we really need the full text of the seminar on which all this is based to understand it — it seems that Lacan here is underlining the role of the other subject in symptom formation. If so, the point is an important one that sorely needs elaboration.

For Lacan, fantasy assumes its role within the possibilities that the languagelike structure of the unconscious permits. Thus, it is not to be "reduced" to mere "imagination," still less to the "irrational," for its function belongs to that strange realm that Freud referred to as "psychical reality" (1900a, p. 620). It is the "existence" of such a realm that Lacan calls Freud's "discovery," characterized by the certainty (to put it in Hegelian terms) that "the real is rational" (we understand: "symbolizable" through the signifying structures of the symbolic order) and "the rational is real" (we understand: enjoying its own level of "existence" as material aspects of language in dreams, symptoms, fantasies, etc.). Thus, "what presents itself as unreasonable in desire is an effect of the passage of the rational in so far as it is real — that is to say, the passage of language — into the real, in so far as the rational [i.e., the symbolic] has already traced its circumvallation there" (1977, p. 272/637).

However this may be, the fantasy (i.e., image) is to be distinguished from the signification conjoined with it that is structured by the signifying processes of the symbolic order. As indicated above, the signification is determined in part by the other to whom the demand is addressed. When this other, once generalized (hence capitalized as the "Other"), continues to expand until it elides with the very limits of being itself, the subject is forced to become aware of his own insatiable want that shines through any and every specific demand in the guise of desire, always dramatized by fantasy (1977, p. 273/638).

At this point Lacan becomes caught up in a polemic against the "present-day analyst," which is soon highlighted by the notion of "identification" as it appears in Freud's *Group Psychology and the Analysis of the Ego* (1921, pp. 105–110). His argument, however, is tortuous to follow, partly because of the sheer opaqueness of style, partly because of the hidden agenda to which only seminar members are privy, partly because any direct relationship to the problem of taking desire *à la lettre* is not immediately apparent. The general drift seems to be that it is dangerous for the analyst to encourage a process whereby he becomes a part of the patient's fantasy by fostering the patient's identification with his own ego, itself an image. This only results in further alienating the patient from his desire. Happily, Lacan comes out of the underbrush in time to bring the essay to a respectable close.

What is to be said, then, of "the direction of the treatment and the principles of its power"? Lacan enumerates the essentials of his position by noting in conclusion (1977, p. 275/640):

1. The "special powers" of the treatment consist in the power of speech itself.

2. The analyst's task is not to "direct" the subject toward "full speech," nor even toward a "coherent discourse," but rather to help him to be free to attempt such things on his own.

3. Such freedom, however, is not tolerated easily by the subject.

4. The subject's *demands* must not be gratified in the analysis — even the demand to be cured — however difficult such a stance may be for the analyst to maintain (1977, p. 276/641).

5. Instead, every effort must be made to help the subject recognize and acknowledge the thrust of his fundamental *desire*.

6. "Resistance" to this acknowledgment is ultimately attributable to "the incompatability between desire and speech" (1977, p. 275/640), i.e., (we presume) to the incapacity of speech, always finite, to articulate adequately a desire that inevitably transcends it. Demands are articulable, but the full thrust of desire is not.

In sum, then, to take desire *à la lettre* is to see it clearly in distinction from both need and demand, and insinuating its way, usually under the guise of an image (fantasy), through the labyrinthine ways of the symbolic order, structured as it is by the "nets of the letter" (1977, p. 276/641), i.e., the laws of language. The consequences of this for the formation of the analyst are clear enough: "Since it is a question of taking desire, and it can only be taken literally [*à la lettre*], since it is the nets of the letter that determine, overdetermine, its place as a bird of paradise, how can we fail to require that the birdcatcher be first of all literate [*littéraire*]" (1977, p. 276/641)? And no one offers us a better example of this than Freud himself.

MAP OF THE TEXT[1]

I. *Who analyses today?*
   A. Analysis is marked by the person of the analyst just as much as by the person of the analysand.
      1. Our concepts about countertransference are inadequate,
         a. especially if we talk of "an emotional re-education of the patient,"
         b. reflecting a loss of principle and an imposture that must be denounced.
      2. The failure to practice authentically results in the exercise of power.
   B. The psychoanalyst assuredly directs the treatment.
      1. But this does not mean directing the patient.
         a. Hence he must carefully avoid anything like the direction of conscience.
      2. Directing the treatment is quite different.
         a. It first entails making the subject use the analytic rule,
            i. which he cannot learn from being in "the analytic situation."
         b. In explaining it the analyst reveals his own understanding of, and prejudices about, analysis.
            i. and this indicates the ambiguity inherent in the issue of direction.
         c. In this early stage of the treatment we make the patient overlook the fact that he is merely speaking,

---

[1] As in Chapter 6, our subdivisions A, B, etc., correspond to Lacan's numbers 1, 2, etc.

        i. but this does not give the analyst an excuse to forget it himself.

C. We will engage our subject from the side of the analyst.
  1. In this common enterprise, not only the patient, but also the analyst pays.
    a. He pays with words transformed to the level of interpretation,
    b. with his person as support for the transference,
    c. with his most intimate judgment as part of an action that goes to the kernel of being.
  2. I am not giving my opponents the right to accuse me of metaphysics,
    a. for they fail to question statements stressing the thesis that the analyst cures by what he is.
    b. But what is "being" doing here?

D. In cross-examining the analyst again, we see that he is less sure of his action the more he is caught up in his being.
  1. In interpreting what is presented to him in words and deeds, the analyst is his own oracle and articulates what he pleases.
    a. Well aware that he cannot measure the whole effect of his words,
      i. the analyst strives to parry their effect
      ii. by being always free in the timing, frequency, and choice of his interpretations.

E. In the transference the analyst's freedom is placed outside of himself by the duplication to which he is subjected.
  1. Here lies the secret of analysis, for we must go beyond seeing it as a relation of two persons.
  2. Such a situation is conceived as one in which a "weak" ego is trained by a "strong" ego,
    a. despite avowals of a "cure from within,"
      i. for the subject's assent is forced.

3. In experiencing the transference every analyst must wonder at the least expected effects,
   a. although he is not responsible for them, as Freud stressed their spontaneity.
4. But today's analysts think Freud fled from the commitment implied by the situation,
   a. and they throw countertransference feelings about to balance the transference.
5. The analyst's silence is not the strategy of a poker player,
   a. for by it he introduces the dummy *(le mort),*
      i. and thereby the game becomes a four-handed game of bridge.
   b. The fourth player is the analysand's unconscious, whose hand the analyst will try to force.
   c. But it matters where the analyst places himself, for his feelings have only one place — that of the dummy.

F. The analyst should take his bearings, not from his being, but from his want-to-be *(manque à être),*
   1. or else he will fail to understand his action on the patient in its four-sidedness.
   2. Today's analysts presume a relation to reality,
      a. and measure the patient's deviations from it in the authoritarian way educators have always done.
      b. They maintain this relation by relying on didactic analysis at a price,
         i. without realizing that their own responses to the problems of humanity addressed to them are sometimes parochial,
         ii. while making light of their own experience by claiming that analysis provides a simple means for "measuring up to reality."
   3. This precarious notion is propped up by the American concept of "the autonomous ego":

a. as a standard to measure the real;

b. as an organization of disparate functions that buttress a sentiment of interiority;

c. as autonomous because sheltered from conflict.

d. But it solves the problem of the analyst's being

    i. by offering a team of unequal egos to guide the Americans on their way to happiness.

G. If the analyst dealt only with resistances, he would be cautious with interpretation.

1. For his interpretation will be heard as spoken by a transference-figure.

a. This can be useful if the analyst interprets this effect;

    i. otherwise it amounts to mere suggestion.

    ii. But the words of the analyst will still be perceived as issuing from the place of the transference.

    iii. And this postpones forever the subject's emerging from the transference.

2. But after interpretation, what remains of the analyst? Who is he?

a. The "having" implied in *having* an answer (namely, that he is a man) puts "being" in question.

b. The analyst reassures himself by relying on his ego and his own sense of reality,

    i. and thus enters an aggressive relationship between an "I" and a "me" with his patient.

3. To those who thus recast analysis, I ask: "Who is the analyst?"

a. "He who interprets, profiting from the transference?"

b. "He who analyses it as resistance?"

c. "Or he who imposes his idea of reality?"

d. This troublesome question leads to another: "Who is speaking?"

    i. Bluntly answered: the ego *(moi)*.

II. *What is the place of interpretation?*
  A. I have not replied to all the novice's questions, but have
      assembled the current problems involving the direction
      of the treatment.
      1. In speaking of the lesser place held by interpretation
          in contemporary psychoanalysis, we always ap-
          proach its meaning with embarrassment,
          a. witnessed by authors' efforts to detach it from
              every other mode of verbal intervention.
  B. Some kind of transformation in the subject is being
      evaded here,
      1. which escapes thought as soon as it becomes fact.
          a. No criterion suffices to show where interpreta-
              tion acts, unless one radically admits a notion of
              the function of the signifier,
              i. which allows us to see how words affect the
                  subject.
      2. Interpretation makes it possible to translate the sig-
          nifiers of unconscious repetitions.
          a. This in turn is made possible by the function of
              the Other, in relation to which the missing ele-
              ment appears.
      3. The signifier's importance in situating analytic truth
          appears highlighted by its absence in Glover,
          a. who finds interpretation everywhere, even in a
              medical prescription,
          b. and who, perhaps unknowingly, says the forma-
              tion of the symptom is an inexact interpretation
              on the subject's part.
  C. Interpretation produces something new through the
      different ways the signifier brings about the emergence
      of the signified.
      1. Interpretation is not based on any assumption of di-
          vine archetypes,
          a. but on the fact that the unconscious has the radi-
              cal structure of a language,

        i. in which the sign connotes and establishes presence in absence and absence in presence.

D. Although the rules of interpretation can be formulated, their formulas presume notions that cannot be condensed here.

  1. Everyone recognizes that an interpretation is confirmed by the material that emerges, not by the conviction with which it is received.

    a. Yet we operate in terms of the subject's assent, despite what Freud said about denial as a type of avowal.

      i. This is a type of resistance bred by our practice,

      ii. and shows itself to be the analyst's, not the patient's, resistance.

E. But today's authors reverse the sequence by indicating that interpretation is an uncertain stammer compared with a broader relation in which true understanding reigns.

  1. This view sees interpretation as both an exigency of the weakness to which we must give help as well as something unpalatable to the patient.

    a. But here we see only the influence of the analyst's feelings.

    b. This has nothing to do with an individual's countertransference,

    c. but reflects his position in a dual relation,

      i. which he cannot overcome if he sees it as his ideal place.

    d. This undoubtedly shows the desire to avoid a break with the patient.

      i. But this confuses honest civility with technique,

      ii. and confuses the patient's presence with the analytic relation.

F. In this perspective, the transference serves as the analyst's security.
   1. Delaying interpretation until the transference is formed, he now interprets to reduce the transference,
      a. and the field of combat becomes an assumed relation to reality.
      b. Thus interpreting the transference is reabsorbed into a "working through,"
         i. and becomes a mode of revenge for the analyst's earlier timidity.
         ii. The analyst now pressures the patient with insistence in the name of strengthening his ego.
G. Freud follows an inverse order,
   1. by first determining the patient's position in reality.
   2. Hegel's procedure shows the reversal of positions between the *belle âme* and the reality it accuses.
      a. The question is not one of adapting to reality,
      b. but of showing that the ego is implicated in constructing reality.
      c. The path ends here, for the transference shows that something other is at stake than the relations between the ego and the world.
   3. Freud immediately realized that the principle of his power lay in the transference.
      a. In this respect it did not differ greatly from suggestion.
      b. Yet this power offered a solution to the problem only if he did not exercise it,
         i. for only then could it develop fully as transference.
      c. From that moment he no longer addresses the one he holds in his proximity.
   4. Popularization has robbed of its boldness Freud's conception of interpretation.

    a. In his exposure of a drive (different from instinct), we fail to see that the drive implies the advent of a signifier.

H. Pardon me if I must cite well-known examples rather than my own cases in order to preserve anonymity.

    1. The Rat Man is not cited as a case cured by Freud,

        a. for his analysis is not unconnected with his tragic death.

    2. Freud made his fundamental discoveries about obsessional neurosis in the context of a direction of the treatment,

        a. which has the following order:

            i. an initial righting of the subject's relations with the real,

            ii. the development of the transference,

            iii. interpretation.

        b. In reversing this order, have we lost Freud's horizon?

I. The ritualization of Freud's discoveries reveals a basic confusion.

    1. A case from Schmideberg and Kris will serve as an example.

        a. Here the concern about plagiarizing was checked against evidence and interpreted in terms of the patient's wanting to plagiarize as a defense against being a plagiarist.

            i. This interpretation is erroneous because it assumes that defense and drive are from the same world.

            ii. The patient's response (his post-session scanning of menus for fresh brains) proves that the interpretation is erroneous.

        b. Instead, what is important is that the patient steals *nothing:*

            i. for having an idea of his own never occurs to him;

        ii. here "fresh brains" functions as metonymy, suggesting a diagnosis of "anorexia mentalc,"

       iii. since the patient refuses the intellectual rivalry common to his father and grandfather.

  2. There is thus nothing in common between Kris's progress down from the surface and the subject's progress.

    a. There is no topographic priority in Freud's method.

    b. Freud sets out to right the subject by using the subject's words.

      i. Therefore, it is erroneous to appeal to "objective" evidence about plagiarizing (which, in any case, is always a relative matter).

    c. The idea that what is on the surface is superficial is dangerous.

      i. For another topology is needed to avoid being misled as to the place of desire.

III. *Where have we got with the transference?*

  A. We turn to Lagache's account of the work on transference.

    1. He introduces structural distinctions essential for the critique of its function,

      a. such as his distinction "between the need for repetition and the repetition of need."

      b. Such work indicates to what extent only partial aspects are discussed.

      c. It shows, too, to what extent the ordinary use of "transference" is tied to vulgarity,

        i. as when it means the enumeration of the patient's positive or negative feelings for the analyst.

    2. On the question of where we are with the transference, neither agreement nor illumination exists in our scientific community,

      a. regarding the effect of the relation to the analyst on early infatuation and on the transference neurosis.

      b. These ambiguities persist because the technical diversions urging revisions of the transference leave no room for a true critique.

B. The notion of transference is so central to the analytic action that it serves as a measure for the partiality of three established views:

    1. that is, we judge these theories by how they handle the transference.

    2. As a group these theories fail to complement one another, confirming the impression that they suffer from a central defect.

C. The first, geneticism, generally grounds analytic phenomena in developmental stages.

    1. It is linked to a technique focused on the analysis of defenses.

        a. This link is based only on a historical point of view.

    2. Its beginnings lie in Freud's notion of an unconscious ego,

        a. with the mechanisms of defense grouped under its function.

        b. Anna Freud tried to insert them into the stages of sensorimotor and intellectual development.

           i. But nothing emerged from this that shed light on technique.

D. More prominent is the second theory, that of object relations.

    1. It has its origin in Abraham's concept of the part-object,

        a. which is linked to the partial aspect that he detached from the transference,

           i. and which he transformed into terms of the ability to love.

    2. There are two equations here.

        a. Sexual transference is at the foundation of object love.

      b. Transference capability is the index of the patient's relation to the real.

         i. But "this merely begs the question."

   3. In this view the image of a maturing object operates as an instinctual final cause.

   4. Such a view leads to a dichotomy between pregenital and genital character structure,

      a. which makes the pregenital character the sum of all kinds of object-relations defects,

      b. while a simplistic notion governs the movement from pregenital to genital character.

      c. But this does not keep the ego from remaining independent of its objects.

E. If the collector's activity demonstrates the object relation, perhaps the rule is found not in this dichotomy but in some impasse constitutive of desire.

   1. The form of the fragmented object is not necessarily a pathological factor.

   2. What does the "absurd hymn" to the genital have to do with the real?

      a. How can we forget that Freud forged the oedipal drama to explain the barriers common to love?

      b. The sublime in sublimation should not be confused with the perfect orgasm.

      c. Souls tender by nature are now burdened with coping with the delirious "normality" of the genital relation.

      d. The uninformed reader might think our art was employed to treat sexual retardation.

         i. Yet we have made no contribution to the physiology of sex, nor was there much to learn.

F. The third theory is that of introjection established in a dual relation.

   1. This kind of relation is also called identification with the analyst's superego or terminal narcissistic trance.

      a. The fantasy of phallic devouring tallies with a conception of treatment as a dual relation.

      b. This illustrates the special place of the phallus in signifying desire,

         i. but in an experience that is blind and without direction.

  2. Given a misunderstanding of symbolic incorporation, nothing but the imaginary is recognized in analysis,

      a. for any sort of real consummation is excluded.

      b. In limiting oneself to an imaginary relation between two objects, one leaves only the dimension of distance to structure it.

         i. This leads to insurmountable contradictions about how much is too far or too close,

            (a) resulting in an obsession about *rapprochement*.

        ii. Distance then regulates all technical parameters.

G. Misconceptions have eroded analytic practice.

  1. We have heard of such wild analyses that an index of transference resolution was found in the ability to smell one's analyst.

      a. The latter is a consequence of carrying over the development of the analytic situation into the real.

         i. For smell is the only dimension in which one can reduce the distance between two objects to zero,

        ii. although odors can be useful, as an example suggests.

  2. In the example, the fantasy of the phallic mother took the form of a phobia and then was transposed into a perversion.

      a. In harassing the patient toward the real situation, the analyst was situated in the permanence of a castrating intervention.

    b. This raises the question of a boundary between analysis and reeducation when the process is guided predominantly by an eliciting of real effects.

H. My intention is not to deprecate this work,

    1. but to warn analysts that their technique will decline if they do not recognize the true location of its effects.

        a. They do not flag in trying to define that place, and their experience is not always fruitless.

            i. Genetic research, direct observation, and object relations are relevant.

            ii. Specifically, the notion of the transitional object has an explanatory role in the genesis of fetishism.

    2. As analysts fail to grasp their action in its authenticity, they end up making it an exercise of power.

IV. *How to act with one's being.*

A. The question of the analyst's being arose early in the history of analysis.

    1. It was introduced by Ferenczi in 1909.

        a. He saw transference as introjection of the analyst,

            i. no longer as support for a repetition compulsion, maladaptive behavior, or fantasy,

            ii. but as a taking in of all that the analyst makes present in the here-and-now dyad,

            iii. arriving at the extreme conclusion that the completion of the analysis is reached only when the doctor tells the patient of his own feeling of abandonment.

B. Is this the price one must pay for seeing the subject's want-to-be as the key to the analytic experience?

    1. With the exception of the Hungarians, only the British have described the patient's gaping abyss.

    2. Ella Sharpe reveals the neurotic's true concerns.

        a. Her reading list abounds in works that give a central place to the veiled phallus as signifier.

C. Again, the British have most rigorously defined the completion of analysis by the subject's identifying with the analyst.

    1. Whether this be with his ego or superego is unclear.

        a. It helps to master Freud's structure of the subject by distinguishing the symbolic, the imaginary, and the real.

    2. Melanie Klein's dialectic of fantasy objects is in a theory based on identification with these objects.

D. To help the troubled patient it seems the analyst should be free of pathology.

    1. Thus one imagines that the psychoanalyst should be a happy man, since it is happiness that one asks from him.

        a. We do not refuse to promise happiness in a time when its extent has become complicated by politics.

            i. But the progress of humanism hasn't solved the puzzles of happiness either.

    2. The analyst has to grasp his operating level in the relationship to being.

        a. What his training analysis offers to this end is not to be calculated as just a function of the problem his analyst has resolved.

            i. There is a kind of unhappiness that goes along with being that should not be eliminated by schools and false shame.

        b. An ethic remains to be formulated to integrate the Freudian conquests over desire,

            i. so that the question of the analyst's desire would be highlighted.

E. Decadence marks analytic speculation.

    1. Because they understand a pile of things, analysts imagine understanding as an end in itself and "a happy end."

a. But the physical sciences show that the greatest
   successes don't imply that "one knows where one
   is going."
b. It is frequently better not to understand in order
   to think.
   i. And one can travel a great distance in under-
      standing without the least thought resulting.
   ii. Thus the behaviorists renounced under-
       standing but used what we understand with-
       out understanding it.
2. The notion of oblativity gives a sample of our
   thought in the area of morality.
   a. But this is the uncomprehended fantasy of an
      obsessional,
      i. where all is offered for the other, my coun-
         terpart,
      ii. without recognizing there the anxiety the
          Other inspires by not being my counterpart.
F. We do not pretend to teach psychoanalysts to think.
   1. They learned this from psychologists,
      a. and repeat that thought as an attempt at action.
      b. Freud partakes of this too, although he is a bold
         thinker
         i. whose action completes itself in thought.
G. What does it mean to say the analyst is the person to
   whom one speaks freely?
   1. All that one can say regarding the association of
      ideas is psychologistic dressing.
      a. In what he says in analysis the subject does not
         show much liberty,
         i. because his associations open on to a full
            word that is painful for him.
   2. There is nothing more fearful than saying what
      might be true,
      a. for if true it would become so absolutely.
         i. And God knows what occurs when doubt is
            no longer possible.

    b. Is progress toward truth the procedure in analysis?

        i. Although accused of intellectualization, I try to preserve the unspeakable in analysis.

3. That the unspeakable is beyond the discourse that our hearing accommodates is clear to me,

    a. provided I take the path of listening and not of sounding,

        i. certainly not of tapping the resistance, tension, and discharge in which is re-formed a stronger ego.

    b. Listening does not force me to understand.

        i. What I listen to is always a discourse, even when it is an interjection.

    c. What I listen to without doubt I find no fault with.

        i. If I understand none of it, or if I understand something, I am sure to deceive myself.

        ii. Because I keep silent I frustrate both speakers.

4. If I frustrate the analysand, it is because he is asking something of me — to respond.

    a. But he knows this would just be words, and he can get these from anyone.

    b. He's not even sure he'd be thankful for good words, still less bad ones.

    c. To be sure, his asking appears on the field of an implicit demand:

        i. that he be healed, that he be revealed to himself, that he become an analyst.

H. The patient's demand is a radical one.

  1. Macalpine rightly seeks in the analytic rule alone the motive force for transference.

  2. Asking serves as an intermediary to open the past all the way to early infancy,

    a. for the subject could not have survived without asking.

3. By this path analytic regression occurs —
  a. not that the subject makes himself a child, for this is not the usual regression.
  b. Regression is the return to the present of signifiers used in prescribed demands.

I. This is how we understand the love declared in primary transference.
  1. For the lover gives what he does not have,
    a. and the analyst does not even bestow this nothing.
  2. The primary transference is often a shadow,
    a. but this shadow dreams and reproduces its request,
      i. even when there is nothing left to request.
  3. Some say the analyst gives his presence,
    a. but this is implied by his hearing
      i. which "is simply the condition of speech."
    b. His presence will be noted later,
      i. most acutely when the subject can only stay silent in the face of the shadow of asking.
    c. Thus the analyst is the one who carries the asking
      i. not to frustrate the subject
      ii. but so that the signifiers which retain his frustration may reappear.

J. Therefore it is proper to recall that the primary identification is produced in the oldest asking,
  1. elicited by the omnipotent role of the mother
    a. in such a way that need satisfaction now hangs on the signifying chain,
      i. which fragments and filters it through the signifying network.
  2. In this way needs become subject to the same conditions as language:
    a. the synchronic register, as opposition between irreducible elements;
    b. the diachronic register of substitution and combination.

      c. By these means language structures interhuman relations entirely.

   3. Thus we see Freud vacillate about the relations between the superego and reality.

      a. The superego does not ground reality,

         i. but it traces its paths.

  K. We need look no further for the source of identification with the analyst.

   1. It is always an identification with signifiers.

   2. Analysts interested in frustration only maintain a stance of suggestion,

      a. which "reduces" the subject to restate his request.

      b. This surely is how emotional reeducation is to be understood.

   3. People conceive analysis in a way that reduces the basis of symptoms to fear and of treatment to suggestion.

V. *Desire must be taken literally.*

  A. In the dream Freud recognized desire, not drives,

   1. even in the dream presented to disprove that the dream is an expression of a desire.

      a. In that dream the desire for caviar signifies the desire to have an unsatisfied desire,

      b. and the desire for smoked salmon is substituted for the desire for caviar.

  B. The dream reveals a structure common to so-called unconscious mechanisms,

   1. in which desire is unconsciously marked by language.

      a. We are dealing with the opposition between signifier and signified, where the powers of language begin,

         i. whose laws are those of substitution (metaphor) and combination (metonymy).

      b. In this dream, substitution of salmon for caviar is a metaphor of desire.

      c. The desire for caviar is a metonymy, concealing the desire for an unsatisfied desire.

C. Freud's work on dreams is not a psychology.

  1. His interest lies only in the elaboration, the linguistic structure of the dream,

    a. which he discovers in a signifying flow that is not organized by the subject,

      i. since as desirer he is subject to it.

D. The dream is created for the recognition of desire through interpretation.

  1. The desire for recognition stimulates the dream's elaboration.

    a. But such recognition does not come during sleep,

    b. and when the dream is equivalent to conscious demand, I awake.

E. Those who dismiss the dream have found more direct ways to lead the patient to "normal desires";

  1. the patient with thwarted needs responds negatively,

  2. or else symptoms reappear — repetition compulsion, we say.

F. One even reads that the ego produces the dream,

  1. thus showing how important it is to go back to Freud.

    a. The desire of his hysteric for caviar is the desire for gratuitous, unsatisfied needs;

      i. she has everything, but satisfaction of real needs is not enough for her.

G. Freud provides a key with his passing remark about hysterical identification,

  1. by means of which the dreamer identifies with her friend.

    a. Her friend had requested to dine with the dreamer and her husband.

  2. But the dreamer also desires to thwart her friend's desire as well as her husband's interest in her friend.

    a. Thus her desire is to have (by identification) an unsatisfied desire.

H. The woman now identifies herself with the man as the object of his desire,
  1. and the salmon stands for this desire of the Other.
      a. But since the salmon is inadequate, the dreamer must give up the search for her desire.
      b. Psychoanalysts also give up on desire, reducing it to a demand.
      c. But the salmon remains as a metaphor for the phallus.
          i. The phallus as signifier provides the ultimate identification with the desire of the Other.
          ii. This is as far as Freud got, i.e., to the castration complex and penis envy.
I. Desire appears in the interval that demand carves on this side of itself,
  1. insofar as the articulating subject makes the want-to-be appear in his appeal to the Other,
      a. who is asked to give what he himself lacks, namely, what is called love — or he can respond with hate or ignorance.
          i. These feelings are evoked by any demand insofar as it goes beyond need.
          ii. But the subject is deprived of love insofar as the need articulated in his demand is satisfied.
  2. The satisfaction of need crushes the demand for love,
      a. forcing it to be expressed in dreams where being speaks in the subject.
J. The child is disturbed when the Other (mother) confuses its needs with her ministrations.
  1. Thus the child fed most with love is the one who refuses food.
      a. His rejection of her demand indicates that she requires a desire outside him.
K. Thus we state a principle:
  1. Desire is an effect of discourse that passes needs through the defiles of the signifier,

    2. and the Other is the locus (as the other scene) of the deployment of speech:

       a. therefore "man's desire is the desire of the Other."

    3. Signifiers structure those representing the Other, too, as having a gap.

       a. The conscious speaker is other than the discourse of the Other which structures the dream and masks desire.

L. Desire appears both beyond and on this side of demand.

    1. As needs are articulated they are pruned from the subject's life.

       a. Demand highlights the subject's lack of being,

          i. under the forms of love, hate, and ignorance.

    2. Desire is less than the negation contained in discourse;

       a. it is a furrow, a mark created by language,

          i. originating in symbolic castration.

M. The function of the signifier of the phallus is the key to completing analysis.

    1. The case of an impotent obsessional illustrates this.

       a. Its key lies in his partner's dream,

          i. which shows her having a phallus but wanting it too,

          ii. thus allowing him to feel safe from castration and to be the phallus for her.

N. We should orient the place of desire in directing the treatment by reference to the effects of demand.

    1. People today see just these effects as the power of the treatment.

       a. We do not give in to the patient's demand for intercourse,

          i. since the genital act has its place in the unconscious articulation of desire.

          ii. Why then do we treat other demands differently?

2. The subject's demand originates in the Other as the locus of speech and is first of all a message to himself.
   a. Spontaneous speech has a double meaning, concealing the subject's desire
   b. and showing how the subject is split by language.
3. Regression in analysis concerns only the signifiers of demand.
   a. By reducing these signifiers to drives or needs we only appear to reduce desire.
   b. Identification with the other (the patient with the analyst) is also a form of regression.
4. In one's training analysis it must be seen that all demands were merely transferences maintaining a desire.
   a. This is necessary for assuming the direction of an analysis.
   b. To maintain this framework of the transference, frustration is required.
   c. The subject's resistance to suggestion is his desire keeping the analysis on the right track.
O. Symptoms, like dreams and parapraxes, are overdetermined.
   1. This is possible only in a linguistic framework.
   2. Unconscious fantasy "is defined as an image set to work in the signifying structure."
      a. Fantasy supports the subject on the plane of his vanishing desire.
      b. This allowed Freud to confirm Hegel's "the rational is real and the real is rational."
P. The neurotic's position on desire marks his response to demand.
   1. In his fantasy his demand becomes absolute.
      a. The relation between unconscious fantasy and action awaits illumination by analysis.

    2. For the analyst of today the transference is defined by the distance between the fantasy and the adaptive response.

        a. But the norm for adaptation is the analyst's demands.

Q. Thus the patient of the contemporary analyst ends up with a purely imaginary identification.

    1. The appeal for love is to be distinguished from Freud's third mode of identification,

        a. in which the object is indifferent.

        b. But as object of incorporation the analyst can hardly be indifferent.

    2. The patient is further alienated by identifying with the analyst's strong ego.

R. The cunning principle of power is "the power to do good."

    1. But here it is only a question of truth, not power.

    2. The direction of the treatment relies on the means of speech, the subject's freedom, and the incompatability between desire and speech.

    3. The analyst is tempted to respond to demand,

        a. especially the demand to cure,

        b. but instead must utilize silence and the allusive power of interpretation.

S. Since desire must be taken literally, the analyst must first of all be literate.

    1. Freud's own literary style must be studied,

        a. for it reveals his desire

            i. as he fearlessly faced life's one meaning, "that in which desire is borne by death."

            ii. He unveiled the signifier of desire: the phallus, whose symbolic castration splits the subject.

Notes to the Text

230*e*/590   The four-sidedness or fourfold division (*écartelé*, "quartered") appears to continue the bridge game metaphor and suggests that the analyst's action on the patient must always be viewed in the context of the ego/subject distinction proper to each of them (we recall Lacan's earlier statement about the "game for four players" [1977, p. 139*d–e*/429]).

231*b*/590 Wilhelm Wundt (1832–1920) founded the first psychological laboratory in Leipzig (1879) and made scientific introspection into a methodology.

231*g*/591 The subject imputes being to the analyst, thus making him more than he is, and enabling his interpretive words to return to the place of the Other of the transference, from where it affects subsequent responses of the ego/subject pair engaged in analysis.

The word "place" recurs now in a series of statements beginning with whether the analyst places himself *(se place)* on the right or the left of the patient (1977, p. 230*a*/589). The analyst is forced to count on the intelligences that must be in the place *(la place)* dubbed on occasion the healthy part of the ego (p. 232*a*/591). Section II begins with the question, "What is the place [*la place*] of interpretation?" (p. 232/592) and goes on to speak of the less important place *(la moindre place)* held by interpretation in current psychoanalysis (p. 232*h*/592). In his note 9 to the text (of p. 234*b*) Lacan speaks of the essential function of place *(de la place)* in the structure of the signifier (p. 280*e*/594). He speaks of the necessity for another kind of topology if we are not to be misled regarding the place *(la place)* of desire (p. 240*h*/601). All appear to do with his notion of the topological structure of the subject, ego, and signification, which awaits further elaboration.

231*h*/591 The analyst, in response to the query regarding what he is, has something to say, namely, that he is a man. This having of an answer and of his manhood raises the issue of having versus being (the phallus), i.e.,

the issue of castration in which his being is in question. Lacan later explicitly discusses having versus
being the phallus (p. 268*b*/632) and want-to-be in
relation to castration (p. 268*e*/633).

231*i*/591   The aggressivity of the "I and me" relationship recalls the permanent war of "you or me" of the dual
relation of ego to ego (1977, p. 138*d*/428).

232*b*/591   The "Q.E.D." translates "C.Q.N.R.P.D." (*ce qui nous
ramène au problème du départ,* or "that which brings us
back to our original problem").

232*e*/592   The impersonal, pseudo-universal answer given by
the impatient ("an animal of our species") to the
question, "Who is speaking?" is less honest (if less an-
noying) than the answer: the ego (tautological in that
ego speaks to ego in this kind of analytic relation).

232*i*/592   Devereux (the author in question, cited in Lacan's
footnote) uses gestalt concepts in speaking of the patient's experience as comparable to jigsaw puzzle fragments that begin to suggest a pattern that gradually
seeks closure; interpretation provides this closure.

233*c*/593   Unconscious repetitions are diachronic insofar as
they are uniquely structured in the history of the individual; the signifiers that compose their interpretation are drawn from the preexisting synchronic structure of language. It is in the presence of the Other, in
the recesses of the structure of language (made present in the unconscious dimension opened by the analyst's silence), that there emerges the missing element
rendering possible a translation of the symptom.

233*e*/593   Phlogiston was the hypothetical physicochemical
principle of combustion, regarded in the eighteenth
century as a material substance present in combusti-
ble objects. The theory was refuted by Lavoisier.

233*f*/593   Jakob Boehme (1575–1624) was a German mystic
(influenced by Paracelsus), one of whose major works
is *De Signatura Rerum* (*Signature of All Things* [1651]).

235*d*/595   The translation should read: "Interpretation becomes here an exigency of the weakness to which we must offer help" ("L'interprétation devient ici une exigence de la faiblesse à laquelle il nous faut venir en aide").

236*c*/596   The *belle âme* projects internal conflict onto the world and then proceeds to denounce it. Lacan earlier wrote: "The *moi*, the ego, of modern man, as I have indicated elsewhere, has taken on its form in the dialectical impasse of the *belle âme* who does not recognize his very own *raison d'être* in the disorder that he denounces in the world" (1977, p. 70*d*/281).

236*h*/597   The translation should read, "it is the face of Tiresias with which we question ourselves before the ambiguity in which his verdict operates" ("c'est la figure de Tirésias dont nous nous interrogeons devant l'ambiguité où opère son verdict"). The reference to Tiresias, the blind seer in *Oedipus Rex*, suggests the inevitable revelation of the oedipal structure (and thus the symbolic order) in which we are all participants. Tiresias was blinded by Athena after he saw her bathing, but he was then given the gift of prophecy.

237*e*/598   Lacan earlier commented on how Freud's epitaph elevated the case to the beauty of tragedy (1977, p. 89*d*/303).

237*f*/598   Instead of the English "that Freud made the fundamental discoveries," the French text reads "that is situated the horizon where the fundamental discoveries gave themselves up to Freud" ("que se situe l'horizon où à Freud se sont livrées les découvertes fondamentales").

239*b*/599   To translate *cervelles fraîches* by "cold brains" rather than "fresh brains" is to lose some of the metonymy's vigor: the patient wanted fresh—i.e., new—brains to compensate for his *anorexia mentale*.

239*c*/600   Rather than "in the very relation that it makes of it," which is obscure, we translate "in the very report that he makes of it" *(dans le rapport même qu'il en fait).*

239*j*/600   The Jakobson reference (1956) was discussed earlier (see note 148*b*). Lacan puns on *cervelle fraîche* and *rafraîchir.*

240*a*/600   The suggestive wording appears to be in the title of Lacan's bibliographic reference (1977, p. 279, fn. 25/ 645), "Intellectual Inhibition and Eating Disorder."

240*c–d*/   The familiar anorexic patients appear to be the refer-
601   ents of "the thin virgins" with "[t]heir symbolically motivated refusal."

241*c*/602   The triad of frustration, aggression, and regression appeared earlier in the "Discourse at Rome" (1977, p. 41ff./249).

243*a*/604   The Kris paper (discussed just now by Lacan, pp. 238ff./599ff.) has a footnote near the end of the presentation of the case of the plagiarist in which Bibring's approach is described as singling out "a patient's present patterns of behavior and arriving, by way of a large number of intermediate patterns, at the original infantile pattern" (1951, p. 24). On the following page Kris titles a new section of his paper, "Planning and Intuition." Criteria for success, beyond mention of the patient's publishing and finding satisfaction in his home life and career, are not discussed. Those listed by Lacan are typical of his American critique.

243*d*/605   The relation between "object" and "reality" is assumed.

243*e*/605   Geneticism is based on an order of formal changes emerging in the subject, while the object relations position is based on formal changes in the object.

244*g*/606   We may try to understand this phrase in the following way: to put oneself in the limelight, to expose one's private parts by bragging and spelling out this "parade" of genital satisfaction.

245*b*/606   In the paper cited by Lacan, Abraham (1908) writes:

> The excessive value [the collector] places on the object he collects corresponds completely to the lover's overestimation of his sexual object. A passion for collecting is frequently a direct surrogate for a sexual desire; and in that case a delicate symbolism is often concealed behind the choice of objects collected. A bachelor's keenness for collecting often diminishes after he has married; and it is well known that interest in collecting varies in different periods of life [p. 67].

Such variation is incompatible with the fixity of the pregenital-genital antinomy.

245*g*/607   The translation might better read "delirious normality" *(normalisme délirant)* rather than "delusional normality."

246*e*/608   Again, the translation should read "the wrong route effectively practiced" *(la fausse-route effectivement pratiquée).*

246*f*/608   We read the French *du signifiant phallus* as two nouns of apposition, "of the signifier-phallus" rather than "of the signifying phallus." Speech is crushed in the dual relation because, as an essentially imaginary relation, it excludes the Other (the symbolic order and the signifying network).

246*h*/608   Lacan appears to be saying that in the dual-relation model of analysis the objects are related to one another only in the imaginary order, as image to image, and this kind of relating is essentially a spatial one. He describes this somewhat in a later seminar:

> Vision is ordered according to a mode that may generally be called the function of images. This function is defined by a point-by-point correspondence of two unities in space. Whatever optical intermediaries may be used to establish

their relation, whether their image is virtual, or real, the point-by-point correspondence is essential. That which is of the mode of the image in the field of vision is therefore reducible to the simple schema that enables us to establish anamorphosis, that is to say, to the relation of an image, in so far as it is linked to a surface, with a certain point that we shall call the 'geometral' point. Anything that is determined by this method, in which the straight line plays its role of being the path of light, can be called an image [1964, p. 86].

247*d*/609 Rather than "double-Dutch," an easier translation for *chinois* is "involuted."

248*a*/609 Alfred Jarry (1873–1907) was a French author of farces, surrealistic verses, and scatological stories.

248*c*/610 The exhibitionism underlying the patient's anxiety at being teased for his height is incorrectly seen as inverted in the voyeurism, and this has implications for (not "to") the diagnosis *(impliquée . . . au diagnostic)*.

248*f*/610 Alas, we who have not been Lacan's pupils can only guess at his meaning here: the phobic object appears in order to take the place of, or make up for *(suppléer)*, the lack in the Other insofar as this lack means the Other cannot fill the lack in oneself. By avoiding the phobic object this lack is never faced; but the phobic object's general presence (to be avoided) continually signifies the substitution (metaphorically) of the phobic object for the lack. The fetish is an object (metonymically) perceived in the place of castration instead of the absent phallus.

248*g*/611 André Breton (1896–1966) was the founder of the surrealist movement and the first in France to publicize the work of Freud. Lacan was one of his numerous well-known friends, and he apparently had a significant influence on Lacan's thought and style. See Anna Balakian (1971).

In his "Introduction au discours sur le peu de réalité" (1924), Breton imagines donning a suit of armor in order to discover a little of the consciousness of a fourteenth-century man. He then writes:

> O eternal theatre, you require, not only in order to play the role of another, but even to suggest this role, that we disguise ourselves with its likeness, that the mirror before which we pose return us to a foreign image of ourselves. The imagination has every power, except that of identifying ourselves despite our appearance to a character other than ourselves [pp. 8–9; our translation].

In the section "Colloquy of Armours" the question is put: "Can a being be present to a being?" (p. 10). Later Breton reflects:

> The duly established prior existence of this bouquet which I am going to inhale or this catalogue which I am perusing ought to be sufficient for me: alas, it is not. It is necessary that I reassure myself about its reality, as we say, that I make contact with it [p. 11; our translation].

Reflecting later on language, he writes:

> Words are subject to grouping themselves according to particular affinities, which generally have the effect of re-creating at each instant the world according to its ancient model. Everything happens in that case as if a concrete reality existed outside the individual, as if this reality were unchangeable. . . . The mediocrity of our universe, doesn't it depend essentially on our power of enunciation? [pp. 21–22; our translation].

249*h*/611   In the *Georgics* (I, 146) Vergil wrote: *Labor omnia vin-cit improbus* ("Indomitable labor conquers all"). *Impro-bus* has the sense of restless persistance. Vergil also used *improbus* to refer to "bold Aeneas."

249*i*/612   The true place is the symbolic order.

250*d*/612   It is not "the relation to the being" but "the relation to being" *(la relation à l'être)* that is at stake. Also, the dis-course, rather than informing, "rules there" *(qui y règne)*.

250*e*/613   In his article Ferenczi (1909) writes:

> The practical significance and the exceptional position of the kind of introjections that have as their object the person of the physician, and which are discovered in analysis, make it desir-able that the term "transferences" given to them by Freud be retained. The designation "intro-jection" would be applicable for all other cases of the same psychical mechanism [p. 53, fn. 14].

Ferenczi does, however, support a linguistic reading of the unconscious:

> The fact that a transference on the ground of such petty analogies strikes us as ridiculous re-minds me that Freud in a category of wit showed the "presentation by means of a detail" to be the agent that sets free the pleasure, i.e., reinforces it from the unconscious; in all dreams also we find similar allusions to things, persons, and events by the help of minimal details. The poet-ical figure "pars pro toto" is thus quite current in the language of the unconscious [pp. 42–43].

This of course describes the process of displacement or metonymy (more specifically, synecdoche).

252*d*/614   Louis de Saint-Just (1767–1794) was a politcal leader of the French Revolution and ideologue of the perfect state based on Spartan rigor. He was executed by guillotine.

252*m*/615 In the Schreber paper Lacan contrasts *physis* as object of science "in its ever purer mathematization" with *antiphysis*, "the living apparatus that one hopes is capable of measuring the said physis" (1977, p. 179/531).

253*a*/615 In the paper on aggressivity Lacan noted the use behaviorists make "of categories introduced into psychology by psychoanalysis" (1977, p. 9/102).

253*c*/616 The word "doughty" is used to translate *rude*; "fierce" or "rugged" would do as well.

253*g*/616 Full speech is *pénible* ("laborious") for the subject; see the earlier discussion of empty versus full speech (1977, pp. 45–46/254).

253*i*/616 The "unsayable aspect" of analysis admits of several interpretations. One is the radical disparity between the articulation of demands made to another and the underlying desire that can never be adequately expressed in words: that is, the gap that splits the subject because he speaks, making the simple satisfaction of needs no longer possible because the satisfaction becomes mediated by the Other in demands.

253*j*/616 The distinctions (made more precisely in the French) are between listening *(notre écoute)* of which auscultation is a form (as the act of perceiving sounds which arise within organs of the body), and hearing *(entendement)*, which ordinarily implies understanding (although it does not necessarily follow hearing). The word "opisthotonos" refers to a spasm in which the trunk is arched with the head and posterior bent back. Lacan appears to be criticizing the approach of Wilhelm Reich, especially as presented in his *Character Analysis* (1933).

254*d*/617 Only the subject is transitive perhaps in the sense that the subject intends certain goals and demands certain objects. The French words *demander* and *la demande* have been translated into English as "demand," and we have followed this translation for the sake of consistency. It should be noted, however, that the words usually carry the less imperative meaning "request" or "ask for."

255*a*/618 The word "prescription" can be read in several ways, as referring to the regulation or ritualization of demands (or of needs articulated in requests), or as referring to requests which have been already inscribed in the unconscious (in the sense of prescripted).

255*b*/618 The primary transference may refer to the early stage of infatuation in the transference mentioned earlier (1977, p. 241*c*/602). Michael Balint (to whom Lacan refers frequently in the *Écrits*) describes primary transference in terms of "pregenital" or "primary object-love" leading to both love and hate (1951, p. 154).

257*a*/620 For "damp squib" the French text has "wet firecracker" (*pétard mouillé*).

257*f*/621 Lacan here begins to structure the dream analysis in terms of "the laws" of substitution (metaphor) and of combination (metonymy), which he will soon get to (on the following page). Here he distinguishes two registers: one in which "a desire [is] signified by a desire," as, for example, "the desire to have an unsatisfied desire is signified by [the] desire for caviar" — this is the register of metonymy or displacement; in the other register, "one desire [is] substituted for another," as, for example, the desire for smoked salmon substitutes for the desire for caviar — this is metaphor.

258*b*/621 The "mark of language" anticipates the later phrase, "the mark of the iron of the signifier on the shoulder of the speaking subject" (1977, p. 265/629).

The focus here appears to be on the resistance

of "the bar" separating signifier and signified (1977, pp. 149, 152/497, 500), which Lacan takes up in the very next paragraph. The "bar" as language's "mark" specifies the Freudian unconscious by instituting the primary repression that follows upon symbolic castration, that is, the impossibility of being the phallus if one is to enter the symbolic order and be subject to the law of the Father. The phallus as signifier of desire becomes a kind of ultimate signified that slides under all discourse expressive of desire. The following essay, "The Significance of the Phallus" (Chapter 8), develops the links between the phallus as signifier, the mark of the signifier, and the bar.

258*f*/622　This difficult sentence may have an obvious sense: metaphor, as the substitution of one signifier for another (which then becomes the signified of the first), indicates the movement of the subject (not "from the subject" [*du*]) to a new meaning of desire, a new direction *(sens)* taken by the signifier.

259*b–c*/
622　The desire for caviar becomes the metonymy of the desire for an unsatisfied desire by association with the dreamer's words to her husband, begging him not to give her a caviar sandwich every morning, allegedly so that she could continue teasing him about it. The "want-to-be" in which the metonymy is situated is the absence created by her words, but more radically (Lacan goes on to say) the absent phallus. Desire itself (and, specifically, in this case the desire of the hysteric to have an unsatisfied desire) is the metonymy of the "want-to-be" by association with the absent phallus and with the symbolic castration of wanting-to-be the phallus, the signifier of the desire of the Other. Desire as such proceeds out of this radical finitude or lack and seeks to cover it by generating an endless metonymic chain of substitute signifiers, an endless displacement of the original desire to be the phallus.

259*e*/623   The *Traumdeutung* is "mantic" insofar as it foreshad-
                owed Saussure's discoveries in linguistics.

259*h*/623   The word *dérivation* contains the word *rive* ("bank" or
                "shore") and connotes diversion, shunting, or branch-
                ing of water from its proper course. The "channel of
                desire" thus shunted is later described as "the furrow
                inscribed in the course" (1977, p. 265/629). To be-
                come aware of his own movement in the signifying
                chain, the subject must be able to get some orienting
                feedback by switching out of it.

260*c*/623   Lacan spoke earlier of how the desire for recognition
                dominates the desire that is to be recognized (1977,
                p. 141/431).

260*d*/623   Here the English text can seriously mislead the read-
                er. The French text reads: "the elaboration of the
                dream is nourished by desire; why does our voice fail
                to finish, for recognition." Instead, the English has
                "out of recognition," for *de reconnaissance.* Recognition
                "reabsorbs" the other (and the other word, desire)
                insofar as it always has to do with the desire of the
                other; desire seeks to be recognized as the desire (de-
                sired object) of the other.

260*e*/624   We read this paragraph as saying that if my dream
                (as a desire for recognition) comes to rejoin *(vient à re-
                joindre)* or is on the same level of discourse as my
                (consciously articulated) demand to be recognized
                by the other as the object of his request, then there is
                no necessity for the dream to articulate further.

260*f*/624   Instead of "A negative therapeutic reaction, I would
                say," the French has "we will say" *(dirons-nous)*, in ob-
                vious sarcasm.

261*c*/625   The English is misleading about the painter; the text
                should read, "a painter who makes a fuss about him
                . . . over his interesting face" ("un peintre qui lui fait
                du plat. . . sur sa bobine intéressante"). Freud
                (1900a, p. 147) makes it clear that the painter was
                chatting with the husband, not the wife.

261*e*/625 The English is grossly misleading: to be certain that the needs are gratuitous they must *not* be satisfied *(ne pas les satisfaire)*.

261*g*/625 Jean Gabriel de Tarde (1841–1904) was a French sociologist whose social theory distinguished between innovative and imitative persons.

Instead of "in each particular case," "in this particular case" is preferred as the translation of *dans le particulier*.

262*b*/626 The husband's desire — thwarted in the dream — is his interest in his wife's friend.

262*c*/626 "The appeal of the patient" can more simply be stated as "The call *(L'appel)* of the patient" on the telephone.

262*d*/626 The point seems to be that the dreamer wonders if her husband is no longer satisfied with her (for she may have become just a slice of backside for him) and instead is turning to her friend, with whom, as object of his desire, she now identifies. In analyzing the dreamer's unsatisfied desire, Freud wrote: "The process might be expressed verbally thus: my patient put herself in her friend's place in the dream because her friend was taking my patient's place with her husband and because she (my patient) wanted to take her friend's place in her husband's high opinion" (1900a, pp. 150–151).

263*d*–*i*/
627–628 Once again desire is associated with a cavity (channel, furrow) — this time an "interval" which demand digs on this side of itself *(en deçà d'elle-même)*. This "interval" or gap appears insofar as the subject manifests his want-to-be, his deficiency with his appeal to the Other (who shares the deficiency). The paragraphs here are as dense as any in the *Écrits*, but the point, simply put, seems to be that any articulation of a need is addressed to another for a response and above all expresses a desire to be recognized by the other (who, in turn, also desires recognition). The

satisfaction of the need serves to highlight what by contrast remains as surplus in the demand, namely, the desire for recognition. The frustrated expression of desire reemerges in dreams.

264*b*–*c*/ 628

Translation error has "confuses his needs" instead of "confuses its ministrations" *(confond ses soins)*. The mother's ignorance in confusing overfeeding with recognition is unforgiven *(n'est pas pardonnée)*, not "unforgivable." The English continues to be more difficult than the French, which does not present the child as "demanding" from the mother, but rather asks *n'exige-t'il pas que la mère. . . .* ("doesn't he require that the mother. . . ."). Lastly, "the way lacking to him toward desire" *(la voie qui lui manque vers le désir)* is less ambiguous than "the way towards the desire that he lacks."

264*d*/628

This most Lacanian of laconic phrases ("man's desire is the desire of the Other") has a number of related significations: (1) man's desire à la Kojève (1939), is for another desire as its most humanizing object; (2) man's desire is to be the object of the other's desire, i.e., to be the phallus as the signifier of the other's desire; (3) the Other as unconscious is the true locus of man's desire; (4) the Other as symbolic order mediates man's desire, transposing what is sought on the level of (physiological) need to the specifically human level of discourse.

264*e*/628

The gap *(béance)* appears to be the same as "the split . . . which the subject undergoes by virtue of being a subject only insofar as he speaks" (1977, p. 269*i*/634).

264*f*/629

The dream presents itself as a *fait accompli*, a finished story; the verb denoting action in the dream is in the indicative, not optative, mood.

264*h*/629

Desire can be said to ex-sist in the dream insofar as it is displaced into the metonymic chain of signifiers, and this manner of ex-sistence or standing outside of itself is its form of distortion *(Entstellung).*

265*a–c/*
629–630

The text again becomes dense as Lacan grapples with the relationship between need, demand, and desire and the role of language. He seems to say that desire has two ways of emerging in demand: (1) as surplus ("in the beyond of demand") insofar as the articulation and determination of biological needs highlight by contrast what desire is after (i.e., recognition); (2) as the unexpressed element in the unconditional demand for the other's presence and absence which falls "on this side of" the demand *(dans son en-decà)*, rather than "within the demand." The three Buddhist figures of love, hate, and ignorance (mentioned earlier in the "Discourse at Rome" [1977, p. 94/309]) typify responses to demands and call attention to the basis of desire in fundamental lack. The demand for love is motivated by this lack insofar as desire as negativity (undetermined being which becomes determined by negating other beings) seeks the recognition of another desire. Hate seeks to negate the other in the struggle to the death for recognition. And the unsaid (and unsayable) goes unrecognized (or ignored) in the demand either because speech is always inadequate to desire or because the other's response fails to recognize what is expressed.

Desire as the action of the signifier stops when "the living being" (the body) becomes a sign, apparently in the tomb, thus stopping the action of the signifier in speech. The moment of cut *(coupure)* appears related to death, on which desire "is borne" (1977, p. 277/642). This is prefigured by the symbolic castration of the phallus which, when repressed, becomes the signifier of signifiers making possible the entrance into the symbolic order.

Osiris was killed and cut to pieces by his brother; his sister-wife Isis succeeded in piecing together his body, finding all the fragments except his penis. Osiris then became god of the dead and of agriculture.

265*d*/630 Lacan here offers the signifier of the phallus as solution to Freud's final difficulties (see 1977, p. 263*a*/627).

265*e*/630 We can read the Other in terms of the parents — first as father, then as mother. It is with the desire of the mother to destroy the father that the patient identified, hence "his powerlessness to desire without destroying the Other."

265*f*/630 This obscure paragraph appears to be describing the obsessional's ability to so distinguish the symbolic order verbally that he practically gets rid of it and is left with the narcissistic juggling of ego and fantasy objects of attachment.

266*c*/631 In three-card monte three cards are placed face down on a table and the dealer deftly shifts their positions, showing one face (e.g., the Queen of Spades) to bettors and returning it face down to continue switching the cards' positions. The object is to guess which of the three is the previously exposed card.

266*g*/631 The point seems to be that the analysis touches or affects her (not "effects her") in her unconscious position as the patient's mother, as supported by Lacan's later use of *commère* ("godmother" or familiar term of endearment for "partner") (p. 267*b*/631).

267*e*/631 The fable seems to be the notion that repressed homosexuality exists in everyone.

268*a*/632 The impossibility seems to be that the patient desires his mother to *have* a phallus (and thereby not be castrated and not be castrating toward him), but he also desires to *be* the phallus for his mother. From this impossibility flows the metonymic chain of his symptoms: sexual impotence, blaming the menopause, urging his mistress to take a different sexual partner, his notion of repressed homosexuality, and his virile response to her dream. All of these are displacements of the original desire concerning the phallus and his own fear of castration.

268*f*/633 Desire (and therefore one's being as lack) is constituted by the difficulty of being in continual displacement.

269*b*/633 Earlier Lacan discussed how psychoanalysts reduce desires to demands and then convert them to be in conformity with their own demands (p. 262*g*/626)— in other words, for them the power of the treatment lies in the power of suggestion.

269*c*/634 The Latin prescription reads, "normal coitus, with repeated dose."

269*f*/634 The text should read, "to his wife or to his master." The French *tu es* ("you are" in familiar or intimate form) equivocates *tuer* ("to kill").

269*g*–*h*/
634 The murderous desire shows through the above articulation addressed to wife or master but also, as unsaid, thereby transcends it. It is "on this side of" another articulation as follow-up to the first, a counterdependent retort which posits a static relationship fixing the speaker in his given role with his true unconscious desire remaining repressed. Only a speech that would lift the mark of repression (structured by the homophony of the subject's own words) would enable the subject to be absolved of his repressed desire. The text should read "would give him back to his desire" *(qui le rendrait à son désir)*. The word "prohibition" does not appear in the French text, which instead has *marque*, suggestive of the bar separating signifier from signified and the condition of possibility for repression. This repression or mark of the signifier splits the subject as speaker from himself (as signified), from his unconscious desire (which can never be adequately articulated), and from others (who are also split by being subjected to the law of the signifi-

er). We recall Lacan's question in "The Agency of the Letter in the Unconscious": "Is the place that I occupy as the subject of a signifier concentric or excentric, in relation to the place I occupy as subject of the signified?" That is, it is a matter "of knowing whether I am the same as that of which I speak" (1977, p. 165e–f/516–517).

270b/635 Lacan wrote earlier: "For regression shows nothing other than a return to the present of signifiers used in demands for which there is prescription" (1977, p. 255a/618).

270d/635 The phrase "desire is a source of subjection" translates *le désir est assujettissant,* repeating the earlier phrase, "Desire merely subjects what analysis makes subjective" ("Le désir ne fait qu'assujettir ce que l'analyse subjective") (p. 260a/623). Desire can compel the subject only through signifiers (and man is a subject only by being subject to the laws of language).

270g/635 The "all-powerful signifier of demand" seems to be "the genital act" mentioned earlier (1977, p. 269c/633).

Freud (1921) wrote that "*identification has appeared instead of object-choice, and . . . object-choice has regressed to identification.* . . . the ego assumes the characteristics of the object" (pp. 106–107).

270h/635 The French text reads "that is to say, [opens] the way in which are designated the identifications which in stopping this regression punctuate it" ("soit la voie où pourront être dénoncées les identifications qui en stoppant cette régression, la scandent").

270i/635 Scybalum is a hardened fecal mass. The belief about it being noxious may refer to a medieval conception.

271i/637 Overdetermination is possible because the relation between signifier and signified is arbitrary, not rigidly fixed in a one-to-one correspondence.

272a/637 The point may be that a kind of static results from the discrepancy of a determinate demand for a specific object with the indeterminate relationship to the other (which sustains an unconditional demand for love).

272*c*/637   Fantasy is discussed in more detail in Chapter 9.

272*g*/637   The real is rational insofar as it can be symbolized, and the rational, symbolic order is real as the materiality of language.

272*h*/637   The "paradox of desire" may have to do with the subject's inability to recognize himself in his discourse because he is implicated in it not as subject but as signifier (the spoken about "I" recedes from the "I" that enters the spoken discourse — recall the theme of excentric circles [1977, p. 165/516]). Precisely because desire is articulated in discourse, it remains fundamentally inarticulable. This will be the major theme of the final essay.

273*b*/638   The position of the neurotic marks with its (not "his") presence the subject's response to demand, to, that is, the signification of his need.

273*c*/638   The fantasy, existing at a level distinct from that of the conscious articulation of demand, seeks to absolutize the demand and calls attention in the subject to the gap of his desire.

273*d*/638   This is an appeal for a kind of psychohistory which understands the relation between the unconscious fantasy and action. The last sentence is confusing: "all that," referring to the preceding phrases, "gives him [not "it"] a quasi-experimental access" — that is, "all that, together with whatever experience the analyst calls acting-out, gives him a quasi-experimental access" ("tout cela auquel l'expérience de ce que l'analyste appelle l'*acting out*, lui donne un accès quasi expérimental").

273*f*/639   The analyst interposes *himself (s'interpose)* into the patient's fantasy (by telling the patient his behavior relates to him in the transference?).

273*g*/639 The Other in this instance is the analyst.

273*h*/639 To introduce himself into the fantasy is a necessary consequence of taking the path that betrays him.

274*a*/639 Circe was an island magician who changed Odysseus' sailors into pigs. The sense seems to be that the analyst, by imposing himself on the patient's fantasy, becomes a victim of the imaginary order, diverts the authentic manifestation of desire, and causes the treatment to become sidetracked and fragmented.

274*e*/639 Freud (1921) wrote: "There is a third particularly frequent and important case of symptom formation, in which the identification leaves entirely out of account any object-relation to the person who is being copied. . . . The mechanism is that of identification based upon the possibility or desire of putting oneself in the same situation" (p. 107).

274*f*/639 We take "indifferent" here as ironic: The analyst can hardly be an indifferent object in a treatment resolution based on incorporation.

274*g*/640 The ego is the metonymy of desire perhaps as its displaced point of reference (displaced from the subject) and as its substitute narcissistic object.

275*g*/641 The French text reads: "That speech has all the powers, the special powers of the treatment" ("Que la parole y a tous les pouvoirs, les pouvoirs spéciaux de la cure"). Instead of "shepherded," the French has *canalisé*, ("it is toward this that the subject is directed and even canalized"), thus complementing previous images of desire as channel, furrow, etc.

276*a*/641 The only surprise is the unusual clarity of these propositions.

276*d*/641 Hercules killed the centaur Nessus for trying to rape his second wife, Deianira. Before dying Nessus told her that his blood would serve to restore Hercules' love. Later she sent him a tunic smeared with the blood of Nessus. When Hercules put it on, it stuck to him, burning him to the point that it led to his building his own funeral pyre.

276e/641   The horizon of being which has become "disinhabited" by modern analysts would seem to be the unconscious. The raised finger apparently refers to Leonardo's painting of St. John the Baptist in the Louvre — a naked, sensuous, smiling St. John, with affinities pointing to other paintings of St. John cast in the accoutrements of Bacchus. The point may be that the analyst must be silent to the patient's demands in order to hear the expressions of unconscious desire.

276i/642   The artificial river in Mauriac is apparently a reference to his novel *Le Fleuve de feu* (1923).

277b/642   The sense of *il se mire*, translated by "he saw himself reflected," is better expressed as "the ways in which he looked at himself in feeling, domination, and knowledge." To say desire "belongs to being" may be misleading, and a better translation of *c'est de l'être* might be "it is a matter of being," i.e., a matter of being the phallus.

Chapter 8

The Signification of the Phallus

This essay dates from the same year as the preceding one (1958) and therefore represents a corresponding level of development in Lacan's thought. In fact it complements the former insofar as, for Lacan, the essential function of the phallus is to be the signifier of desire, whose importance in the treatment process we have just seen. Both themes received full discussion in the seminar of 1957–1958 on "The Formations of the Unconscious," and the essays crystallize the results of that effort. As in the previous essay, so here, the available text cries for glosses that only the seminar can give. But such is Lacan's manner, and we simply have to live with that fact, settling for what provisional sense we can make out of what he actually says.

The present essay is mercifully brief (is this because the original lecture was delivered in German?). It begins with a reference to the importance of the castration complex for traditional psychoanalytic theory, both in terms of eventual symptom formation and in terms of the unconscious dimension of sexual identification. For how are we to understand the strange anomaly by which a human being assumes "the attributes of [his/her] sex only through a threat—the threat, indeed, of their privation" (1977, p. 281/685)? Are we to admit with Freud "a disturbance of human sexuality, not of a contingent, but of an essential kind" (1977, p. 281/685)? This much is certain: the problem is "insoluble by any reduction to biological givens" (1977, p. 282/686). It must be approached in terms of the "clinical facts," and these "reveal a relation of the subject to the phallus that is established without regard to the anatomical difference of the sexes" (1977, p. 282/686).

The interpretation of this relation presents difficulties, of course, especially in the case of women, whether in terms of the little girl's feeling that she has been deprived of a phallus, or in the fantasy of the mother as possessing a phallus, or in terms of the mother's presumably having been deprived of the phallus— for that matter, the whole *raison d'être* of the "phallic stage" in the sexual development of women.

Having thus indicated his own intention to address the issue of the relation of the subject to the phallus "without regard to the anatomical difference of the sexes," Lacan indulges in a polemic section where he pays his contentious respects to other writers who have dealt formally with the phallic stage of development. In particular, "the most eminent" (Helene Deutsch, Karen Horney, and Ernest Jones) receive honorable mention, with Melanie Klein slipping in through the back door. Jones is singled out for special attention—praised for his introduction of the notion of *aphanisis* (the disappearance of sexual desire) into the psychoanalytic debate, since with this he suggests "the relation between castration and desire" (1977, p. 283/687), but criticized for resorting to the notion of part-object (a Kleinian term that "has never been subjected to criticism since Karl Abraham introduced it" [1977, p. 283/687]). The latter notion leaves Jones victimized by a Kleinian perspective. Lacan's whole critique of object relations theory as developed by Melanie Klein is implicit here and must be left for fuller discussion elsewhere. For the moment, we may expect the brunt of that critique to fall on the failure of this school, with its heavy emphasis on the role of fantasy, to take sufficient account of the function of the symbolic order.

It was Freud's grasp of the functioning of the symbolic order (despite the absence of adequate concepts of linguistics) that Lacan, as we know, sees to be the most significant aspect of Freud's "discovery." This implies not only the distinction between signifier and signified but the conception "that the signifier has an active function in determining certain effects" in what is to be signified (i.e., the "signifiable"). The signifier is determinative to the extent that the signified is accessible only through the signifier, i.e., "appears as submitting to its mark" (1977, p. 284/688) in such fashion that we are forced "to accept the notion of an incessant sliding of the signified under the signifier" (1977, p. 154/502). Moreover, when "the signifier" is concatenated into a chain of signifiers, this chain is governed by the laws of language. Thus we must acknowledge "a new dimension of the human condition in that it is not only man who speaks, but . . . in man and through man *it* speaks *(ça parle)*." The "it" here is to be understood as the "structure of language," that is so woven through man's whole nature as to make it possible for speech "to resound" in him (1977, p. 284/688–689).

What is at stake here, we know, is not "language as a social phenomenon" but language in the sense of "the laws that govern that other scene" (for Freud, the "unconscious"), operating as they do in the "double play of combination and substitution" on which metonymy and metaphor (those "two aspects that generate the signified") are based (1977, p. 285/689). As such, these laws play a "determining" role in the "institution of the subject" — but we shall return to this later. Let it suffice here to observe that when Lacan says that "*It* speaks in the Other," we take him to mean that the laws of language function in such fashion that it is these that are evoked when two subjects engage in speech, these that permit the signifying process, "by means of a logic anterior to any awakening of the signified" (1977, p. 285/689), to emerge in the first place. To recognize the dimension of the unconscious in the subject's speech is to gain some appreciation of the fundamental division in the subject that is ingredient to his very constitution.

This now brings us at last to the role of the phallus in this constitution, and now the waters muddy. For the phallus, according to Lacan, is neither a fantasy, nor an object, nor an organ (whether penis or clitoris), but a signifier — indeed the signifier of all signifiers, "intended to designate as a whole the effects of the signified [we understand: of the whole process of signification], in that the signifier conditions them by its presence [i.e., its function] as a signifier" (1977, p. 285/690). But what precisely is the import of this?

Let us begin by asking: What are the effects of the signifying system? First of all, that the needs of a human being must be channeled through the order of signifiers (i.e., the symbolic order) by the very "fact that he speaks" (1977, p. 286/690). When these needs become articulated through speech and thus take the form of demands, they undergo a certain alienation from the subject, if only because turning them into "signifying form" already submits them to exigencies that belong to "the locus of the Other" (1977, p. 286/690).

Now this "alienation" "constitutes" a form of "repression" in the subject. How? We know that the dynamic thrust that initially took the form of need now must be channeled through the order of signifiers. To the extent that signifiers are able to articulate this thrust, the result is a series of demands. To the extent that they cannot, the dynamic movement remains operative but is now subject to a continual displacement whose pattern is unconsciously structured, and it is in this form that it goes by the name of "desire." Its shunted movement is, of course, governed by the laws of combination and selection, i.e., "the play of displacement and condensation to which [the subject] is doomed in the exercise of his functions" (1977, p. 287/692). If it escapes formulation in demand, it may nonetheless emerge in "the paradoxical, deviant, erratic, eccentric, even scandalous character by which [desire] is distinguished from need" (1977, p. 286/690).

It is the extent to which desire is forced underground and filtered through the symbolic system that we understand it to be "repressed." And it is the extent to which the process is fundamental to the developmental cycle, constituting initiation into the symbolic order, that this repression legitimately may be called "primal" *(Urverdrängung)* (1977, p. 286/690). It should be noted that repression in this sense also constitutes a "splitting" of the subject between the unconscious signification of desire (i.e., the dynamism submissive to the laws of language) and the aboveground chains of signifiers that operate on the level of conscious signification.

Fair enough, but what has this to do with the phallus? The phallus is the signifier par excellence of desire precisely inasmuch as desire undergoes repression and is henceforth marked with unconscious signification: "The phallus is the privileged signifier of that mark in which the role of the logos [i.e., the order of signifiers — the symbolic order] is joined with the advent of desire" (1977, p. 287/692). But why choose the phallus for this delicate task? Lacan replies that it is "because it is the most tangible element in the real of sexual copulation, and also the most symbolic in the literal (typographical) sense of the term, since it is equivalent there to the (logical) copula" (1977, p. 287/692). The verbal correlation between "copula" and "copulation" is obvious enough, but why sexual copulation is of such central importance in this regard is less obvious. We are left to guess at some vague sense of consummation in it, or perhaps resort to the myriad reasons that attempt to explain the importance of the phallus as a symbol throughout the history of human culture. In any case, the final reason given by Lacan for choosing the phallus as signifier of all signifiers is less problematic: "By virtue of its turgidity, [the phallus] is the image of the vital flow . . . transmitted in generation" (1977, p. 287/692). That much, at least, is clear.

Now the paradox of the phallus as a signifier is that it plays its role as veiled, i.e., insofar as it dis-appears when desire, which it signifies, is repressed. Thus, "the living part of [the] being [of the subject] in the *urverdrängt* (primally repressed) finds its signifier by receiving the mark of the *Verdrängung* (repression) of the phallus" (1977, p. 288/693). With this the subject is initiated into the symbolic order, and this brings with it the bar between signifier and signified, so that "the subject designates his being only by barring everything he signifies" (1977, p. 288/693).

Now if the phallus is signifier of desire, and if, as we have seen already (Chapter 7), desire is desire of the Other, then "it is [the] desire of the Other as such that the subject must recognize, that is to say, the other in so far as he is himself a subject divided by the signifying *Spaltung*" (1977, p. 288/693)—victim as well of the primal repression out of which desire emerges, signified by the repressed phallus.

Here the dialectic of desire between subject and Other, in this case the mother, is engaged. Recalling that in Hegelian terms the subject's quest for recognition becomes the desire to be the desired of the other, we are told again that "if the desire[d] of the mother *is* the phallus [i.e., signifier of the Other's desire], the child wishes to be the phallus in order to satisfy that desire" (1977, p. 289/693). But sooner or later the child must be "content to present to the Other what in reality he may *have* that corresponds to this phallus" (1977, p. 289/693)—or not have—and learn to live with the consequences.

Up to this point, "phallus" has been used clearly to designate *not* an organ (whether penis or clitoris) but a signifier. Now Lacan speaks of a "real phallus" rather than a signifier and the sense is the physical organ of the male or the imaginary organ in the female (e.g., the "test of the desire of the Other is decisive not in the sense that the subject learns by it whether or not he has a real phallus, but in the sense that he learns that the mother does not have it" [1977, p. 289/693]). From here, Lacan proceeds to discuss "the structures that will govern the relations between the sexes" "by reference to the function of the phallus" (1977, p. 289/694), but the term "phallus" now assumes a new ambiguity, oscillating as it does between its role as signifier and its role as real or imagined organ.

The issue of relations between the sexes, we are told, turns around either "being" the phallus (signifier of desire) or "having" it. But "having" the phallus is ambiguous: simply "having" it may be opposed to "being" the phallus and thus refer to the struggle with basic human finitude independent of sexual differentiation; or it may refer to having the "real" phallus (the male organ) and thus be distinguished from *not* having it (as a female). This having/not-having polarity, however, soon is replaced by an attitude of seeming-to-have *(paraître)* the organ "in order to protect it on the one side, and to mask its lack on the other" (1977, p. 289/694). It is in terms of this "seeming" that the "typical manifestations of the behaviour of each sex" become apparent and the drama of sexual differentiation is played out.

If all this makes sense, it is conceivable that a subject may "have" the phallus-as-signifier (as opposed to "being" the phallus for the Other) yet "not have" the phallus-as-organ (because female). This suggests a way to avoid dizziness through the following skid:

> Paradoxical as this formulation may seem, I am saying that it is in order to be the phallus, that is to say, the signifier of the desire of the Other, that a woman will reject an essential part of femininity, namely all her attributes in the masquerade. It is for that which she is not that she wishes to be desired as well as loved. But she finds the signifier of her own desire in the body of him to whom she addresses her demand for love [1977, pp. 289–290/694].

Note in this passage the slippage between the two senses of "phallus"; note, too, the overlay of the demand-for-love/desire polarity. If we add allusions to certain familiar Freudian themes (e.g., repression), the result is a palimpsest which, on the evidence given in the text, is all but inscrutable. After touching briefly on certain characteristics of male sexuality, then of homosexuality in both male and female, Lacan goes on to say that "these remarks should really be examined in greater detail," and one is all too ready to agree with him. But greater detail is not forthcoming here, and we must await further elucidation by the publication of the seminar materials.

The essay concludes with a remark that is enormously rich and relatively intelligible. Given all that has been said about the role of the phallus as signifier of desire, "one can glimpse the reason for a characteristic that had never before been elucidated, and which shows once again the depth of Freud's intuition: namely, why he advances the view that there is only one *libido* [grammatically of *feminine* gender in both Latin and German], his text showing that he conceives it as masculine in nature" (1977, p. 291/695). In other words, it is altogether appropriate that the phallus ("masculine in nature") may be taken to signify desire of whatever gender. Lacan adds: "The function of the phallic signifier touches here on its most profound relation," which we take to mean that desire signified by the phallus lies deep within the human subject, deeper than any sexual differentiation between male and female, as deep as that dimension "in which the Ancients embodied the [*Nous*] and the [*Logos*]" (1977, p. 291/695).

This calls for some explanation. We take "embodied" (*incarnaient*: "give flesh to") literally to suggest that desire corresponds to the deepest strivings of the human being where *Nous* and *Logos* permeate human flesh. As to these two Greek terms themselves, both have a rich and complex history among the "Ancients." Long before either was located in a concrete individual to designate specific human functions (e.g., *nous*: "mind"; *logos*: "thought," "speech"), both *Nous* and *Logos* referred to something more like cosmic forces: *Nous* (e.g., Anaxagoras) as an organizing principle of the essentially material universe; *Logos* (e.g., Heraclitus) as a gathering principle that brings beings together, giving them cohesion within themselves and relatedness to one another. Thus, either may be thought of as Other than a human being, yet permeating him. Indeed, it is on the deepest level of penetration that these principles permeate human "flesh" and become one with the striving of desire. But this adds up to saying again that desire is "desire of the Other."

Map of the Text

I. Clinical introduction.
   A. The castration complex functions as a knot:
      1. by structuring symptoms;
      2. by regulating unconscious sexual identity.
   B. One's sex, therefore, is assumed in the face of threatened deprivation.
      1. This shows the radical disturbance in human sexuality.
      2. and repudiates any notion of sex as a biological given.
   C. Clinical findings reveal a relation of the subject to the phallus that transcends sexual difference:
      1. the little girl considers herself deprived of the phallus, first by her mother, then by her father;
      2. both sexes see the mother as provided with a phallus;
      3. castration becomes significant for symptom formation only after its discovery as castration of the mother;
      4. the phallic stage in both sexes is dominated by the imaginary phallus and masturbation, with no marking of the vagina for genital penetration.
   D. Some authors therefore conclude that the phallic stage is the effect of a repression,
      1. in which the phallic object functions as a symptom.
         a. This symptom is variously called a fetish or a phobia, or viewed as a part-object.
   E. The abandoned debate on the phallic stage by Deutsch, Horney, and Jones makes for refreshing reading.
      1. Jones's notion of *aphanisis* correctly poses the relation of castration to desire,
         a. but this only highlights his failure in falling back on biological distinctions,
         b. and on a notion of part-object that is Kleinian.

II. Freud's discovery deals with the relationship between the signifier and the signified.
  A. Because of the signifier, man is structured by language.
    1. The theoretical and practical import of this is not yet glimpsed.
      a. It has nothing to do with cultural, social, or even psycho-ideological positions stressing the role of affect.
  B. Freud shows that what is at stake are the laws governing the unconscious.
    1. These are the laws governing the combination and selection of phonemes to generate metonymy and metaphor,
      a. whereby the subject is instituted,
      b. and the symptom is structured.
  C. Thus we can say "*It* speaks in the Other,"
    1. for it is there that the subject finds his signifying place
    2. and is characterized by a splitting *(Spaltung)*.
  D. In this context "the phallus is a signifier" (not a fantasy, object, or organ),
    1. designating the effects of the signified in their entirety,
    2. and conditioning them by its presence as signifier.
III. The effects of the presence of the phallus as signifier stem from a deviation.
  A. Insofar as man speaks, he must subject his needs to the articulation of a demand,
    1. whereby they become alienated,
    2. since his message must be emitted from the locus of the Other.
  B. What is in this way alienated in needs constitutes a primary repression *(Urverdrängung)*
    1. and, by hypothesis, cannot be articulated in demand,
    2. but appears in an offshoot, namely, desire,

        3. which cannot be reduced to need.

C. A demand always calls for something other than need satisfaction.

    1. The demand is for a presence or an absence,

        a. primordially with reference to the mother who also is subject to the Other,

        b. and who is thus constituted as having the "privilege" of satisfying needs through love.

    2. Demand goes beyond the particularity of every object,

        a. insofar as the object becomes proof of love.

    3. The satisfaction demand obtains for needs crushes the demand for love.

D. But particularity reappears beyond demand in desire.

    1. The unconditionality of the demand for love becomes the "absolute" condition of desire,

        a. so that desire cannot be reduced to an appetite for satisfaction,

        b. nor is it equivalent to a demand for love,

        c. but it is the result of their splitting, the subtraction of the appetite for satisfaction from demand.

IV. Sexual relationships function within this field of desire.

A. The sexual relation arouses and signifies an enigma for both partners.

    1. Each demands a proof of love from the other,

        a. which goes beyond the satisfaction of a need.

    2. But each desires to be recognized by the other.

    3. This gap basic to desire is only camouflaged by referring to genitality.

    4. Marked by his relation as a subject to the signifier, the human being can never be whole.

B. The phallus signifies this mark where language is joined to desire.

    1. This signifier is chosen for several reasons:

        a. it is the most salient element in sexual copulation;

b. it literally functions as a copula;

c. in its tumescence it is the image of the vital flux that passes in generation.

2. As a veiled and disappearing signifier, the phallus is a sign of the latency of the signifiable,

a. and functions as the bar creating the signified,

b. as well as producing a complementary split in the subject.

   i. The signifying subject is barred from himself as signified,

   (a) thus making unrealizable his demand to be loved for himself.

   ii. The primary repression of the phallus as signifier necessitates substitute signifiers,

   (a) thereby structuring the unconscious as language.

3. The phallus as signifier modulates desire,

a. but the subject has access to it in the Other (the unconscious).

b. The phallus is a veiled signifier of the Other's desire,

   i. which must be recognized,

   ii. but the other subject is also divided by the signifying splitting.

C. The function of the phallus is confirmed by psychological development.

1. This enables us to formulate more correctly the Kleinian thesis that the child perceives the mother as "containing" the phallus.

2. The child's development is subject to the dialectical relationship between the demand for love and the experience of desire.

a. If the mother desires the phallus, the child wishes to *be* the phallus for the mother,

   i. whether or not the child *has* the phallus.

b. Yet the child demands to be loved for himself and as the phallus.

3. Upon learning that the mother does not have a real phallus, the castration complex has its effect,
   a. in symptom or structure in the child.
4. The law of the father introduces the outcome of this development.

D. The function of the phallus structures the relations between the sexes.

1. These relations pivot around a *to be* and a *to have*,
   a. where the attempt *to be* the phallus gives the subject a signifying reality,
   b. while *having* or *not having* it is masked by idealized sex-role posturing,
      i. wherein the demand for love reduces desire to demand.
2. As the woman desires to be the phallus, she must reject aspects of her femininity,
   a. for she wishes to be desired and loved for what she is not.
   b. Yet she finds the signifier of her desire in the man,
      i. and so has less difficulty tolerating the lack of satisfaction of her sexual need,
      ii. and her desire is less repressed.
3. To meet the man's desire for the phallus, no woman is adequate,
   a. since the phallus as signifier constitutes her as giving what she does not have.
      i. He therefore tolerates impotence less well,
      ii. but the repression of his desire is more important in his case than the woman's.
   b. However, neither is the man adequate to the phallus which substitutes for him in his relations with the woman.
4. Male homosexuality proceeds from repressed desire (to be or to receive the phallus).
   a. Disappointment is central to female homosexuality by reinforcing the demand for love.

5. Femininity is protected by a mask stemming from phallic repression.
   a. Therefore (by analogy) the unmasking in virile display appears feminine.
6. For Freud there is only one libido, and it is masculine for both sexes.
   a. At a radical level it precedes the distinction between thought and word.

Notes to the Text

281/685   The precise nuance implied in the word "signification" in the title, transliterating the French, is not self-evident. Both English and French translate the German *Bedeutung* of the original text as orally delivered. Lacan may be alluding here to the use of this term by Frege in his famous distinction between *Sinn* ("sense") and *Bedeutung*, which normally would be translated by "meaning." However, since "meaning" in the ordinary English often answers to Frege's *Sinn*, his English translators translate *Bedeutung* as "reference" (1960, pp. ix, 56–78). The point may seem pedantic, since Frege's distinction was not maintained by Freud, Lacan's author of predilection, but Lacan's own shifting use of the word "signification" in his later writings makes us wary of taking this use of the word here for granted.

281*d*/685   The meaning of *ratio* broadly includes the notions of reason, measure, plan, order, principle, and ground. The sense would be that the castration complex regulates development in such a way (by the installation of an unconscious position) that it accounts for or grounds the first role mentioned, namely, the structuring of symptoms.

281*e*/685   In the previous essay Lacan has already alluded to Freud's difficulty with the endless analysis of the se-

quelae of the castration complex and penis envy. Referring to the phallus, Lacan writes:

> Are we going to have to spell out the role of the
> signifier only to find that we have the castration
> complex and penis envy — which, God knows,
> we could be well rid of — on our hands? When
> Freud reached that particular juncture, he
> found himself at a loss as to how to extricate
> himself, seeing ahead of him merely the desert
> of analysis [1977, p. 263/627].

Lacan goes on to offer the signifying phallus as the
key to the solution: "The function of this signifier as
such in the quest of desire is, as Freud mapped it
out, the key to what we need to know in order to terminate his analyses: and no artifice can take its place
if we are to achieve that end" (1977, p. 265/630).

282a/686 The presence of the myth of Oedipus itself indicates
that we are dealing with the symbolic order, not with
biological givens.

282b/686 The French has *artifice* for "trickery," suggesting that
the resort to genetic memory is a contrived or expe-
dient argument. What remains unsolved by it is the
institution of the symbolic order, as enacted in Freud's
myth of the primal horde in *Totem and Taboo* (1913)
and the Oedipus myth.

282c/686 Because of its awkwardness, "from this 'why' " for *de
ce pourquoi* can be better rendered as "in terms of the
reason why."

283a/687 The text of Longus (2nd–3rd c. A.D.) describes the
woman, Lycaenon, as "young and pretty and by coun-
try standards rather elegant" (p. 79). She seduces
Daphnis under the premise of teaching him about
making love, the procedures of which the two pastor-
al teenagers have been shyly struggling to discover —
they were uncertain about what should follow kiss-

ing, embracing, and being naked with one another.

The English translation of the French *vieille* ("old") might better read "older," i.e., more experienced.

283e/687 In his 1964 seminar, *The Four Fundamental Concepts of Psychoanalysis,* Lacan writes:

> What must be stressed at the outset is that a signifier is that which represents a subject for another signifier.
>
> The signifier, producing itself in the field of the Other, makes manifest the subject of its signification. But it functions as a signifier only to reduce the subject in question to being no more than a signifier, to petrify the subject in the same movement in which it calls the subject to function, to speak, as subject. . . .
>
> One analyst felt this at another level and tried to signify it in a term that was new, and which has never been exploited since in the field of analysis—*aphanisis*, disappearance. Ernest Jones, who invented it, mistook it for something rather absurd, the fear of seeing desire disappear. Now, *aphanisis* is to be situated in a more radical way at the level at which the subject manifests himself in this movement of disappearance that I have described as lethal. In a quite different way, I have called this movement the *fading* of the subject [pp. 207–208].

This fading of the subject will be echoed later in the notion of the subject "barring" himself in designating himself (1977, p. 288d–e/686) and in the next essay.

283f/688 The position is contrary to him *(lui),* that is, to Freud, not "contrary to it." Lacan is apparently referring to a text in which Jones states:

> Turning now to the corresponding problem in

girls, we may begin by noting that the distinction mentioned earlier between the proto- and
the deutero-phallic phase is if anything more
prominent with girls than with boys. So much
so that when I made the suggestion that the
phallic phase in girls represents a secondary
solution of conflict I was under the impression
that by the phallic phase was meant what I now
see to be only the second half of it, a misapprehension Professor Freud corrected in recent
correspondence; incidentally, his condemna-
tion of my suggestion was partly based on the
same misunderstanding, since on his part he
naturally thought I was referring to the whole
phase [1933, p. 467].

Jones argues that the proto-phallic phase is marked
by an awareness that the vagina is for penetration by
the penis; the fear of castration (and awareness of
sex difference) leads to the deutero-phallic phase, a
period of neurotic compromise in boys, who must renounce the incest wish, and of a secondary defensive
reaction in girls, who react to the absent penis with
disappointment, resentment, or denial.

283*g*/688   Jones (1933) ends his essay with the words: "Lastly I
think we should do well to remind ourselves of a piece
of wisdom whose source is more ancient than Plato:
'In the beginning. . . male and female created He
them' " (p. 484).

284*c*/688   For a discussion of Saussure's notion of the signifier
and the signified, see the Introduction and Chapter
5. The "signifiable" in this context would seem to be
"reality" insofar as it can be talked about. The "mark"
appears again later (1977, p. 287/692) and suggests
the bar dividing the signifier from the signified. The
word "passion" here and in the next paragraph connotes the submission of the real as signifiable to the

laws of language which structure the unconscious expression of desire.

284e/689 Rather than "if only," the French *même* allows for "even in the form of effects of retreat," that is, even in deviations of technique.

285b/689 As before, "the two aspects" *(les deux versants)* are rendered as "slopes" down which a previous signifier slips to become the signified. A misprint omits "that *it* is impossible" (italics added).

285c/689 The sense is that speech presupposes the symbolic order, largely unconscious (Other), as the foundation of the signifying subject. This reading would then achieve consistency by translating "it articulates," for *il articule*, as "he articulates" (that is, the subject) and "he [not "it"] has thus been constituted" for *il s'est ainsi constitué,* that is, the subject as split.

285d/690 The phallus has a long history spanning diverse cultures. Laplanche and Pontalis (1967) write that in Freud's presentation of the castration complex the phallus has a symbolic function "in so far as its absence or presence transforms an anatomical distinction into a major yardstick for the categorisation of human beings, and in so far as, for each individual subject, this absence or presence is not taken for granted and remains irreducible to a mere *datum*" (p. 313). They go on to discuss the many Greco-Roman figurations of the phallus in sculpture and painting.

Hermes stands out as the most significant Western phallic figure, and Róheim (1952), drawing on classical research, writes:

> What is the origin of this god? . . . '*The oldest form in which the god was presented was the phallos.*' In Kyllene, Pausanias says there is a temple dedicated to Asklepios, one to Aphrodite. Hermes is also one of their gods. They represent him as an erect phallos. The stone piles or pillars called

hermai in Greek are a second form in which the god appears. Finally, we have wooden or stone pillars with a phallos added to them—the ithyphallic Hermes. Eros appears as a herm 'very near akin to the rude Pelasgian Hermes himself, own brother to the Priapos of the Hellespont and Asia Minor' [p. 151].

As the "messenger of the gods," Hermes is intimately linked with language. One inscription even refers to him as "the giver of discourse" *(Sermonis dator)*, as Kerényi (1944) explains:

It is not without good reason that Hermes was supposed to be the inventor of language. It belongs to the Hermetic wisdom of the Greek language itself, to one of its most ingenious chance hits, that the word for the simplest mute stone monument, *herma*, from which the name of the God stems, corresponds phonetically to the Latin *sermo*, 'speech' or any verbal 'exposition.' The word *herma*, which in the Greek does not have this meaning, does however form the basic verbal root for *hermēneia*, 'explanation.' Hermes is *hermēneus* ('interpreter'), a linguistic mediator, and this not merely on verbal grounds. By nature he is the begetter and bringer of something light-like, a clarifier, God of ex-position and inter-pretation (of the kind also that we are engaged in) which seeks and in his spirit—the spirit of the shameless ex-position of his parents' love affair—is led forward to the deepest mystery.

For the great mystery, which remains a mystery even after all our discussing and explaining, is this: the appearance of a speaking figure, the very embodiment as it were in a human-divine form of clear, articulated, play-related and therefore enchanting, language — its appearance in that deep primordial darkness where one expects only animal muteness, wordless silence, or cries of pleasure and pain. Hermes the 'Whisperer' *(psithyristēs)* inspirits the warmest animal darkness [p. 88].

Jung (whose concern for language [see Kugler, 1978, 1981] seems overlooked by Lacan) attempts to establish numerous etymological links among the roots of phallus, tree, speech, and light in Indo-European languages (1912, p. 163, 219, 220).

An additional correlation exists between the phallus and one of the oldest cross-cultural figures, that of the Trickster, a figure especially prominent among American Indians (Radin, 1956).

285e/690 We can understand "the effects of the signified" as a whole in terms of all the consequences of the institution of the bar (the condition for the signifier-signified relationship), which consequences the phallus conditions by its presence below the bar as the primally repressed signifier.

286a/690 Instead of "its message," we read "his message" *(son message)*, referring to man. Lacan here echoes what he said in the previous essay about needs being subordinated to the structure of language (1977, p. 255/ 618).

286b/690 In German *begehren* can mean "want, desire, demand, long for, hanker after, crave (for), covet" (Betteridge, 1958, p. 61).

286c/690 That is, it is wrong to define demand simply in terms of that which must be frustrated in analysis.

286d/691 Rather than "situated *within* the needs," *en deçà* is better translated as "on this side of," or "short of." The sense seems to be that the primordial relation to the mother comports the Other (language, the unconscious) in such a way that simple need satisfaction is not possible. Yet in demanding the mother's love the child approaches her (the Other) as if she *could* meet his demand for need satisfaction through her love; she herself suffers from a basic want *(manque)* from which her love proceeds. In the previous essay the same point is made (1977, p. 263/627).

287*b*/691   The sense of this dense paragraph seems to be that the sexual relation produces an enigmatic reciprocal relation: each partner seeks both love and sexual satisfaction from the other, but furthermore the very demand puts the other in a position to desire recognition as the one who can meet the demand.

287*c*/692   Rather than "to disguise the gap it creates," the French says *et camoufler sa béance* ("to camouflage its gaping abyss"), the abyss of desire basic to the (un)happiness of the subject. The notion of oblativity appeared in the previous essay (1977, p. 253/615) and suggests self-donation, yielding to the other.

288*a–f*/ 692–693   For the sake of a provisional clarity (but at the risk of misunderstanding through oversimplification) we can attempt to paraphrase this section. The real phallus, now a repressed (veiled or disappearing) signifier, is a sign of how the real as signifiable becomes latent in words (latent insofar as a bar separates signifier from signified). This bar, in turn, splits the speaking subject from himself as spoken-about, and this split is evinced in the split between conscious (speech) and unconscious (desire, structured by the laws of metaphor and metonymy). Lacan seems to be saying that primary repression occurs when the child must "cut off" his desire to be the mother's phallus (the signifier of her desire). This cutting off constitutes symbolic castration and primary repression, establishing the unconscious as the other scene wherein the phallus, as unconscious signifier, continues to structure desire through metaphoric and metonymic chains of associated secondary signifiers. The phallus as unconscious signifier provides the anchor-point for the chain and makes possible all the richness of associations by which language serves to cover the original gap and at the same time signify substitute objects. It would be wrong to conclude that the unconscious is the condition for language. Lacan states the opposite: "Now, what I say is that language is the condition for the unconscious" (1970, p. xiii).

289*a*/693   It is in terms of the symbolic order that the Kleinian formula can be corrected.

289*c*/693   The child's demand is to be loved for himself *and* as the phallus.

289*g–h*
694   The line of argument goes from the subject's *being* the phallus, and thereby given a new signifying reality, to the subject's *seeming* (replacing the *having* or *not having*), whereby the sexual relationship is derealized, that is, is subject to the imaginary captations of sex-role posturing.

290*a*/694   The woman sees the signifier of her desire before her and receives it into her body; therefore, Lacan seems to argue, her desire is less repressed and she can tolerate unsatisfied sexual needs.

290*c*/695   The sense here seems to be that the man must avoid impotence if he is to remain busy being the phallus for women, but he must repress his own desire that the woman be the phallus for him in his never-ending quest for the impossible woman-as-phallus.

290*d*/695   The "redoubling" seems to refer to the issue of being versus having the phallus in each sex. We prefer to translate "the Other of love . . . in so far as it [not "he"] is deprived of what it [not "he"] gives, is poorly perceived [*s'aperçoit mal*] in the retreat in which it [not "he"] is substituted." One reading is that the man cannot measure up to the idealized phallus precisely in the moment of detumescence in the woman's body.

291*c*/695 Grammatically speaking *libido* is always feminine for Freud *(die libido)*. His ascription to it of a masculine character occurs in *Three Essays on the Theory of Sexuality* (1905c, p. 219).

Chapter 9

The Subversion of the Subject and the Dialectic of Desire in the Freudian Unconscious

OVERVIEW

In this essay Lacan formally addresses a colloquium not of psychoanalysts but of philosophers, gathered at Royaumont (September 1960), under the leadership of Jean Wahl, to discuss the theme "Dialectic." It is altogether appropriate, then, that Lacan take for his own theme the issue of "dialectic" in Freud and, indeed, the aspect most specific to the Freudian discovery, namely, the nature of the unconscious. For philosophers, dialectic implies movement through a series of negations, each of which is followed by a sublation *(Aufhebung)*, which assumes the negated moment into a higher synthesis. Since the basic dynamism of the subject for Lacan arises from desire, it is not surprising that he focuses attention on the "dialectic of desire," nor should it be surprising that negation and negativity come to play a crucial role in the discussion.

As the essay develops one gets the impression that Lacan

has moved to a new level of reflection — not because the essay is probably the most enigmatic of this particular collection, but rather because over the years his thought has led him into deeper and deeper waters. We know that his doctoral dissertation (1932) left Lacan with a dual interest: in the role of image and the role of milieu in personality formation. The former interest is explored in the first two essays of this collection, "The Mirror Stage" (Chapter 1) and "Aggressivity in Psychoanalysis" (Chapter 2). The latter interest is developed in the essays that begin to elaborate Lacan's conception of the unconscious as "the Other" that is "structured like a language," namely, "The Function and Field of Speech and Language" (Chapter 3), "The Freudian Thing" (Chapter 4) and "The Agency of the Letter in the Unconscious" (Chapter 5). The discussion of the Schreber case in "On a Question Preliminary to Any Possible Treatment of Psychosis" (Chapter 6) raises in a general way the question about the relation between the subject and the unconscious insofar as this is conceived as the Law of the Father and what happens if the subject is somehow "foreclosed" from this Law. Here for the first time in these essays the importance of the phallus in the oedipal resolution becomes explicated. The next two essays in the collection, "The Direction of the Treatment" (Chapter 7) and "The Signification of the Phallus" (Chapter 8), both address with increasing subtlety the problems involved in the castration complex. In the present essay this issue receives a still further refinement on a new level of complexity, insofar as the role that the phallus plays in a dialectical assumption by the subject of his own desire now becomes thematized.

Be that as it may, the obscurity of this essay almost defies paraphrase without support from a complementary text, "Position de l'inconscient" (1966, pp. 829–850), delivered one month later at Bonneval, as well as from the text of the seminars (still unpublished) on which both papers are based. Without these supports we must content ourselves with a kind of make-do coherence which is forced to take its bearings from a few relatively clear points of reference that peek through the shifting clouds from time to time, but then must poke along as best it can through the long, foggy night.

But the fog does not descend really until we put out to sea. At the beginning of the essay there is, so to speak, only the babble of greetings and farewells along the dockside. Lacan greets his audience of philosophers with appropriate allusions to the philosophy of science, to the dialectic of Hegel, to the status of Freud as a scientist (at least of ambition). His "farewells" are to the "empiricist" conception of science (1977, p. 293/795), to Hegel's "immanentism" (the march of the conscious subject to complete identity with itself in total self-awareness) as an account of the vagaries of the history of science (1977, p. 296/798), to the alleged radicality of the so-called "Copernican revolution" that still left man conceiving of himself as a conscious subject, i.e., in the sense of the Cartesian *cogito*.

Since these early passages may be taken as introductory, we shall not delay over them. Rather, let us disregard the order of the text and cull a few propositions that seem to us to articulate the essence of what Lacan is trying to say. "The praxis that we call psychoanalysis," he tells us, "is constituted by a structure" (1977, p. 292/793), so his fundamental question is: What is the nature of this structure that makes psychoanalysis possible? He chooses for special focus in this essay the structure of the subject, the traditional conception of which has been "subverted" by psychoanalysis. He will attempt to discuss this "subversion proper" and explain how radical it is.

Fundamentally at issue is the subversion (i.e., the overthrow) of the Cartesian subject (i.e., the presumed identity of subjectivity and conscious thought). Freud's assault on man's conception of himself as subject was more radical than either the "revolution" of Copernicus (1977, p. 296/798) or that of Darwin (1977, p. 295/797). The overthrow took place through Freud's discovery of the unconscious as "a chain of signifiers that somewhere (on another stage, on another scene, he wrote) is repeated, and insists on interfering in the breaks offered it by the effective [i.e., conscious] discourse and the cogitation that it in-

forms" (1977, p. 297/799). Here "the crucial term is the signifier, brought back to life from the ancient art of rhetoric by modern linguistics" but unavailable as such to Freud because of the
dislocations of history. Nonetheless, "the mechanisms described
by Freud as those of 'the primary process', in which the unconscious assumes its role, correspond exactly to the functions that
this school [of linguistics] believes determines the most radical
aspects of the effects of language, namely metaphor and metonymy" (1977, pp. 297–298/799).

The conception implied here of a divided subject received
direct treatment in "The Agency of the Letter in the Unconscious" (see Chapter 5, pp. 167–168), where we saw that "the
place that I occupy as the subject of a signifier [is] . . . excentric,
in relation to the place that I occupy as subject of the signified"
(1977, p. 165/517). Such a conception obviously is incompatible
with that of any simplistic psychology that takes as its criterion
the "unity of the subject" or assumes that "the psychical had to
obtain its credentials as a double of the physical organism"
(1977, p. 294/795).

What is significant for Freud, then, is not any "state" of
mind (1977, p. 294/795) or "some archetypal, or in any sense
ineffable, experience" of the subject (1977, p. 295/796), even
though such phenomena might offer some auxiliary "illumination." What really matters — even in the case of the hysteric — is
not the "phenomena associated with hysteria" but rather the patient's *"discourse"* (1977, p. 294/795; italics added). An emphasis
of this kind on the discourse of the subject in psychoanalysis
leads us to the question that will polarize the remainder of the
essay: "Once the structure of language has been recognized in
the unconscious, what sort of subject can we conceive for it"
(1977, p. 298/800)?

Lacan now makes his first assay at answering that question. Whatever the answer turns out to be, it must take account
of the relationship between the unconscious and the "I" who
speaks. Lacan begins with a certain "methodological rigor" by
recalling what the linguists have said about "I" as a "shifter," i.e.,

a double structure that functions both as a signifier within the spoken discourse (hence, as "subject of the statement," the "spoken I") and as a designation of the subject as "now speaking" (1977, p. 298/800) by reason of what Barthes calls an "existential bond" (1964, p. 22) (hence, as "subject of the enunciation," the "speaking I"). Now it is obvious enough that the speaking subject may not be represented in the spoken discourse by any signifier at all, or may be signified in only the most subtle ways, as, for example, in the nuances of the expletive *ne* (1977, p. 298/800). Fair enough, but the question we are pursuing is: " 'Who is speaking?', when it is the subject of the unconscious that is at issue" (1977, p. 299/800). The unconscious itself cannot answer if the subject of the unconscious "does not know what [it] is saying, or even if [it] is speaking, [which] the entire experience of analysis has taught us" (1977, p. 299/800).

This unconscious is both immanent and transcendent to individual subjects, and marks the frontier beyond which the traditional subject, presumed to be "transparent" to himself, loses the self-transparency and begins to "fade," with all the consequent effects that lead to those characteristic manifestations of unconscious processes, such as slips of the tongue, witticisms, etc. In more technical terms, what happens here is that the "cut" *(coupure)* in the discourse, i.e., the bar between the signifier and signified — a fundamental principle of linguistics and basic ingredient of the law of the language — begins to have its effect. The result is that the irruptions of unconscious processes into conscious discourse become more manifest — and these are the focus of psychoanalysis. Hence, "the paradox of conceiving that the discourse in an analytic session is valuable only in so far as it stumbles or is interrupted" (1977, p. 299/801). Paradox or not, the fact remains: "If linguistics enables us to see the signifier as the determinant of the signified, analysis reveals the truth of this relation by making 'holes' in meaning the determinants of its discourse" (1977, p. 299/801).

In this context Lacan comes again to the familiar words of Freud: *"Wo Es war, soll Ich werden"* (cf. 1977, pp. 128–129/417–

418). He underlines the fact that the tense of Freud's *war* corresponds not to the French past historical tense but to the imperfect, designating an incomplete action/state-of-being in past time. The point is important and worth stressing. Lacan makes it again, and more clearly, in the complementary essay "Position de l'inconscient" (1966, pp. 829–850). There he is discussing the nature of the subject (barred, of course) as definable only in terms of its relation to the signifying chain in which the signifier is understood essentially as that which "represents the subject for another signifier" (1966, p. 840; our translation). Speaking of the subject in this sense, Lacan clarifies: "What [i.e., the subject who] *was* there ready to speak [has] the double sense that the imperfect tense in French gives to [the expression] *there was*." Here Lacan is referring "to the moment preceding (e.g., "he was here but is no longer") and to the moment following (e.g., "a little longer and he was there"). In other words, he adds, "what *was* there disappears insofar as it is no longer anything but a signifier" (1966, p. 840; our translation). What is important here is not so much the conception of the subject that is at stake (we shall return to this below) but Lacan's use of the double sense of the French imperfect to interpret the "was" *(war)* in Freud's formula. In any case, the complementary text permits a better understanding of his remark in the essay we are presently considering: "There where it was just now, there where it was for a while, between an extinction that is still glowing and a birth that is retarded, I [no quotes] can come into being [as the speaking subject] and [yet] disappear from what I say" (1977, p. 300/801).

This disappearance is what we take to be the "fading" of the subject. To illustrate what he has in mind, Lacan recalls a dream related by Freud:

> A man who had once nursed his father through a long and painful mortal illness, told me that in the months following his father's death he had repeatedly dreamt that *his father was alive once more and that he was talking to him in his usual way. But he felt it exceedingly painful that his father had really died, only without knowing it* [1911a, p. 225].

Now for Lacan, what the father did not know was the fact "that he was dead" (1977, p. 300/802). What life the father had, then, was only in the signifying chain of the dreamer's psyche. But does the dreaming/speaking subject fare any better? The dreaming subject, too, withdraws from the signifying chain of his dream/discourse. "[T]hat is how *I* as subject comes on the scene, conjugated with the double aporia of a true survival that is abolished by knowledge of itself, and by a discourse in which it is death [of the speaking subject in his withdrawal] that sustains existence [in the discourse]" (1977, p. 300/802).

How does a subject conceived in this way compare with the subject as conceived by Hegel? In fact the two conceptions are separated by a "gap" that can be seen most clearly if we compare them in terms of the way the subject in each case relates to knowing *(savoir)*. Traditionally and in the most general terms, knowing has always been considered to be some kind of union between one being (the knower) and another being (the known) that involves a "presence" of the known to the knower and reciprocal "awareness" in the knower of the known that is not purely physical, which often has been called (for want of a better term) "intentional." Traditionally, too, knowledge is considered true if the awareness in the knower corresponds to the object known, and in that sense the knower depends on the object known as a standard to which the knowledge must conform in order to guarantee its truth. With Descartes, however, truth came to be conceived not merely as conformity of knower to known but as certitude in the knowing subject (i.e., "knowing" that he knows). Henceforth, in order to be true the knowing depended not only on its objects but on its own assurance of itself. Now when a Hegel talks about knowledge as "absolute," this must be understood in the most radical sense of "absolute" — at least so one astute commentator (Martin Heidegger [1950, p. 124]), namely, suggests — in the Latin sense *(ab-solvere)* of "to loosen." In other words, if truth is conceived as stated here, then knowing is absolved (loosened) from its complete dependence on the object in the process of truth. The more the nature of self-assurance is explored, the more the object, if it remains part of the process at all, becomes a matter of indifference. To the extent that knowing is released from dependence on the presentation of objects and becomes more aware of itself as knowing, the subject becomes "absolute." In any case, what matters for Hegel is Knowing's knowing itself, i.e., as absolute.

The entire thrust of Hegel's *The Phenomenology of Mind* (1807a) consists in the process by which Knowing comes to know itself. Initially, indeed, what the subject knows is an object *(an sich)*, say, of sense perception. In a second moment, however, the subject becomes aware of itself as knowing the object *(für sich)*, and then becomes aware of its own role in constituting the object for itself *(an und für sich)*, thereby "loosening" itself (in whatever small degree) from dependence on this object to assure itself of the truth of its knowledge.

This, then, is the basic movement of the dialectic. The knowing subject passes from an initial moment of "affirmation" of its object to an awareness of the inadequacy of this perception (hence, negation) to a new moment of reconciliation of these two previous moments in a higher (or deeper) view of the process, which then becomes the starting point of a new cycle of the dialectic. This movement of affirmation-negation-synthesis on the part of the subject is called "mediation," i.e., the means by which the initial im-mediate experience (affirmation) is processed through negation into synthesis. The initial, un-mediated moment of knowing is what we understand by knowledge-as-*connaissance*. Through the mediation it is assumed into the ongoing process of *savoir* coming to know itself. To the extent that the mediation is also a process of self-assurance on the part of the subject, it is also a moment of truth, which, of course, yields to synthesis within a higher truth as the dialectic moves on. What propels the dialectic for Hegel, however, is not some hidden thrust within knowing itself but fundamentally *desire*.

Now for Freud, the relation between truth and *savoir*, as we find it in Hegel, is broken. There is indeed in Freud a desire, but it must be understood as desire of the Other. If one wishes to call this a desire of *savoir*, that may be possible, provided that one understands *savoir* in a very special sense, i.e., not as "knowledge" in any traditional sense of intentional union between knower and known but as a "knowing" that takes the form of an inscription in the discourse of the subject, "of which, like the 'messenger-slave' of ancient usage, the subject who carries under his hair the codicil that condemns him to death knows neither the meaning nor the text, nor in what language it is written, nor even that it had been tatooed on his shaven scalp as he slept" (1977, p. 302/803).

Such a conception of the unconscious has nothing to do, of course, with Freud's so-called biologism. This does not gainsay the fact that this biologism, properly understood, plays an important role in Freud's thought. One form of it is the death instinct, and "to ignore the death instinct in his doctrine is to misunderstand that doctrine entirely" (1977, p. 301/803). For example, the "return to the inanimate" that characterizes the death instinct is a metaphor for "that margin beyond life that language gives to the human being by virtue of the fact that he speaks" — another way of talking about the Freudian unconscious *savoir*. Another form of biologism is the role ascribed to the phallus in the dialectic of desire, as we shall see in more detail below.

But to recognize the central role of biologism in Freud is not to correlate the unconscious with physiology, and the translation of *Trieb* as "instinct" is very misleading. A much better choice would be "drive" *(pulsion)*. "Instinct" might imply "knowledge" *(connaissance)* of some sort, the way a bird has "knowledge" of how to build a nest, but in no way can "knowledge" of this type be identified with *savoir* in the sense we have explained (1977, pp. 301–302/803).

At this point Lacan begins his attempt to describe precisely how desire functions with regard to this subject who is "defined in his articulation by the signifier" (1977, p. 303/805) like the messenger-slave just alluded to. He does so by resorting to a series of graphs that aim to map out "the most broadly practical structure of the data of our experience" (1977, p. 303/804–805)

—and thereby takes us out to sea in heavy fog.

Graph I is the "elementary cell" of this series. We take it to be a kind of general statement of the nature of the subject "defined in his articulation by the signifier" (1977, p. 303/805). We recall that for Lacan signifiers do not refer to any specific signified in a one-to-one correspondence but rather to other signifiers so as to constitute a signifying chain. As a result we "are forced. . . to accept the notion of an incessant sliding [*glissement*] of the signified under the signifier" (1977, p. 154/502). But there are certain privileged moments when the signifying chain comes to fix itself to some signified, and these are "anchoring points" *(points de capiton)*, "points like buttons on a mattress or intersections in quilting, where there is a 'pinning down' *(capitonnage)* of meaning, not to an object but rather by 'reference back' to a symbolic function" (Wilden, 1968, p. 273).

Now Graph I diagrams one of these anchoring points "by which the signifier stops the otherwise endless movement *(glissement)* of signification" (1977, p. 303/805). The vector $\overrightarrow{S.S^1}$ indicates the signifying chain posed by the speaking subject. We may think of it in both diachronic and synchronic terms. "The diachronic function of this anchoring point is to be found in the sentence, even if the sentence completes its signification only with its last term, each term being anticipated in the construction of the others, and, inversely, sealing their meaning by its retroactive effect" (1977, p. 303/805). In other words, the meaning, suspended to the end of the sentence, must be read backwards into the preceding words once the sentence is finished. As for the synchronic structure of the anchoring point, it is less obvious. This consists in the symbolic order itself that in its most elemental form may be seen in the primordial division of the phonemes. It is this basic pattern of the symbolic order that permits even a child to transpose the bark of a dog perceived as sign into a phoneme-signifier, utilizing the latter in the process of signification in the form of a nursery rhyme. We are taking the diagram to suggest, then, that in the progressive-regressive movement of the anchoring point in which signification emerges, the vector $\overrightarrow{S.S^1}$ represents the progressive movement of the diachrony, and the vector $\overrightarrow{\Delta.S}$ represents the regressive movement of contextualized meaning that is made possible by the synchrony of the symbolic order.

Graph II introduces several new elements into Graph I, principally a place in which to locate the Other. Given the interpretation we have offered of the synchronic structure of the anchoring point, it is perfectly understandable that the Other as "treasure of the signifier" be located precisely where the two vectors cross at the beginning of the reverse trajectory at point O, and that the effect of the Other on the eventual signified be indicated there where a given assertion, ending on "its own scansion," receives its final punctuation at point $s(O)$.

The circularity of this process is evident. But who (and where) is the subject of it all? If the subject here means the individual, real subject, then he "is constituted only by subtracting himself" (1977, p. 304/806) in the fading of the "I" from the discourse as spoken. But if the Other is considered the subject, it is "simply the pure subject of modern games theory" (1977, p. 304/806). Lacan adds that this Other as "locus of Speech, imposes itself no less as witness to the Truth" (1977, p. 305/807). The reason is that if, according to a tradition at least as old as Aristotle, the locus of truth is in the judgment and presupposes a correspondence between the judgment and what is affirmed in the judgment, then truth thus understood (as also falsehood) supposes the symbolic order. To be sure, there is a kind of "pretence to be found in physical combat and sexual display" that is essentially a matter of "imaginary capture," and we find this in animals, too. An animal "does not pretend to pretend," however, nor does he "make tracks whose deception lies in the fact that they will be taken as false." Pretense of this kind implies a passage to the order of the signifier, and "the signifier requires another locus—the locus of the Other, the Other witness, the witness Other than any of the partners—for the Speech that it supports to be capable of lying, that is to say, of presenting itself as Truth" (1977, p. 305/807).

But if this much can be said about the subject of the discourse, what can be said about the ego? Recall what we know about Lacan's conception of the ego. As he tells us in his description of the "mirror stage," it is the "specular image" the child jubilantly assumes at the *infans* stage, while still sunk in his "motor incapacity and nursling dependence." Here the "I" is "precipitated in a primordial form" that "would have to be called the Ideal-I, if we wished to incorporate it into our usual register, in the sense that it will also be the source of secondary identifications, under which term [Lacan] would place the functions of libidinal normalization" (1977, p. 2/94). How the ego thus conceived is victimized by a "paranoiac alienation" (1977, p. 5/98) that affects all its knowledge, how it defends itself by "the armour of an alienating identity" (1977, p. 4/97), how its aggressivity is "a correlative tension of [this] narcissistic structure" (1977, p. 22/116)—all this we have seen already. What Lacan seems to add here is the reminder that the ego thus conceived in its origins must now be dealt with by the (presumably adult) subject: "At this point the ambiguity of a failure to recognize that is essential to knowing myself *(un méconnaître essentiel au me connaître)* is introduced. For, in this 'rear view' *(rétrovisée)*, all that the subject can be certain of is the anticipated image coming to meet him that he catches of himself in [the] mirror" (1977, p. 306/808). This is the ego that Descartes discovered and that Kant analyzed in terms of a "transcendental ego," though the analysis was inevitably relativized by the fact that there, too, the ego was "implicated. . . in the *méconnaissance* in which the ego's identifications take root" (1977, p. 307/809). When all is said and done, the emphasis since Descartes on consciousness as essential to the subject is for Lacan "the deceptive accentuation of the transparency of the I in action [*en acte*] at the expense of the opacity of the signifier that determines the I" (1977, p. 307/809), i.e., (as we understand it) the opacity of the symbolic order that, beyond the transparency of consciousness to itself, silently permeates all discourse.

At this point Lacan digresses into Hegel (out of deference

to his philosophy audience?). His intention, it appears, is to suggest how the early development of the ego follows the classical dialectical master-slave struggle between the ego and its counterpart that "is rightly called a struggle of pure prestige, and the stake, life itself, is well suited to echo that danger of the generic prematuration of birth" that sets the stage for the mirror phase (1977, p. 308/810). He suggests, too, how the same master-slave struggle offers an appropriate paradigm for understanding the neurotic patterns of the obsessional, who simply waits out the Master's death (1977, p. 309/811). Implicit here, of course, is the supposition that the dynamic of this dialectical struggle is desire, hence the remonstrance that "philosophers should not make the mistake of thinking that they can take little account of the irruption that Freud's views on desire represented" (1977, p. 309/811).

What, then, were Freud's views on desire? They are not to be understood in terms of familiar clichés about "repressed wishes," or discerned in the kind of aberration that, according to Lacan, passes for psychoanalytic practice today. Nor are they to be grasped by overlooking the subtleties that differentiate desire from need and demand. If the meaning of desire for Freud is to be sought under the guise of sexuality, then this should be done in terms of certain "structural elements" that transcend those common vagaries of sexuality that led Freud to admit that it "must bear the mark of some unnatural split" (1977, p. 310/812). These "structural elements" are most clearly seen in the Oedipus complex.

Central to the Oedipus complex, of course, is the role of the Father. Freud himself saw the paradigm for this in the dead Father of his own hypothetical myth, but Lacan has interpreted the role in terms of the Name-of-the-Father. What is at stake clearly is not the real father but the "paternal function," which for Lacan is grounded in "the Other as the locus of the signifier" (1977, p. 310/812–813). The Other here is Law and, as such, ultimate—"there is no Other of the Other" (1977, p. 311/813). But the "fact that the Father may be regarded as the original

representative of [the] authority of the Law requires us to speci-
fy by what privileged mode of presence he is sustained beyond
the subject who is actually led to occupy the place of the Other,
namely, the Mother" (1977, p. 311/813). This opens up new
difficulties.

The fundamental issue that now comes more and more into focus (however circuitously) is the relationship between desire and the Other (i.e., the Law, the Name-of-the-Father). The
difficulty of this issue will be compounded by the fact that the
desiring subject is also related to the one who occupies the place
of the Other in terms of need and demand. These are the parameters within which the play of the dialectic will be contained.

Let us begin with what is already familiar. Just as we have
been told that the unconscious is "the discourse of the Other,"
where "of" is to be understood in the sense of the Latin *de* (i.e.,
discourse "from" the Other), so, too, we have heard before
(1977, p. 264/628) that "man's desire is the desire of the Other,"
i.e., "it is *qua* Other that he desires (which is what provides the
true compass of human passion)" (1977, p. 312/814). The subject's desire, then, is in fact the Other's desire. That is why the
question coming from the Other to the subject in the form of
"What do you want?" leads him more surely "to the path of his
own desire," provided he is able to respond to it—and for this
the help of a psychoanalyst may be necessary—not in terms of
"What do I want?" but rather "What does he [i.e., the analyst]
want of me?" (1977, p. 312/815). It is through collaboration
with the analyst that he comes to recognize the otherness of desire and is able to invert the original question so as to ask of the
Other, "What do you want of me?" (1977, p. 335/908).

If the subject is able to appreciate the sense of such a question, he may become aware of the alienation of which he has
been the victim by reason of his own ego. Thus, quite possibly,
"what he [as subject] desires presents itself to him as what he [as
ego] does not want" (1977, p. 312/815). That leaves us with the
delicate task of understanding the relationship between subject
and ego, and this is where "fantasy" plays an important role in
the process.

Laplanche and Pontalis define fantasy in the following classical terms: "imaginary scene in which the subject is a protagonist, representing the fulfillment of a wish [i.e., desire] (in the last analysis, an unconscious wish [desire]) in a manner that is distorted to a greater or less extent by defensive processes"; but they conclude their discussion more succinctly by saying that "the primary function of fantasy [is] the [imaginary] *mise-en-scène* of desire" (1967, pp. 314–318). Lacan here is more specific. We understand him to be saying something like this: When the subject becomes "barred" ($) at the moment of "primal repression" (i.e., "the splitting that [he] suffers from [his] subordination to the signifier") and subsequently comes to expression only in the "fading" of the speaking I from his spoken discourse, he maintains an essential liaison with some imaginary "object" called "fantasy" (1977, p. 313/816). This imaginary object has as its fundamental paradigm a body image that is homologous with the image of the infant perceived by itself in the mirror stage and designated by Lacan as the ego.

This body image as paradigm of fantasy now serves as the " 'stuff' of that 'I' that is originally repressed" (1977, p. 314/816), i.e., the manner in which the speaking I, subject to desire, becomes manifest as it fades. At any rate, this relationship between the split/repressed/barred subject and fantasy is expressed in the algorithm $\lozenge o$, where the $\lozenge$ apparently expresses the relationship between the barred subject and the Other, presumably as a function of desire and its "cause."

The precise nature of this relationship is extremely difficult to articulate, for "the place that I occupy as subject of the signified," i.e., as subordinate to the Other, is "excentric" to "the place that I occupy as. . .subject of a signifier" (1977, p. 165/517). Hence, it is difficult to designate the "subject of the unconscious" as "subject of a statement, and therefore as the articulator, when [the subject] does not even know that [it] is speaking" (1977, p. 314/816). It is all the more difficult to speak of the subject of the unconscious in terms of desire. Perhaps this accounts for the fact that this subject often has been spoken of in terms of "drive, in which [it] is designated by an organic, oral, anal, etc. mapping," "inhabiting," as it were, these organic functions (1977, p. 314/816–817).

But the drive isolates from the sheer metabolism of these functions certain "erogenous zones" that are marked by what Lacan calls a "cut *(coupure)*, expressed in the anatomical mark *(trait)* of a margin or border—lips. . . the rim of the anus, the tip of the penis, [etc.]" (1977, p. 314/817). The full force of "cut" here is for the moment not clear to us, though we recall that Lacan spoke earlier of the "cut in discourse, the strongest being that which acts as a bar between the signifier and signified" (1977, p. 299/801). Perhaps the term is intended to suggest a sign of negativity (of discontinuity and therefore of lack, as basis for desire) in the human organism, the supreme form of which would be symbolic castration; perhaps, too, it is an anticipation on the level of the organism of the "bar between the signifier and signified" in the register of the symbolic order. Be that as it may, it is apparently organic parts such as these that coalesce to form the body schema serving as paradigm for the fantasies that become "stuff" through which the speaking I manifests itself as it fades. The "partial features" of these objects are rightly emphasized, of course, "not because [they] are part of a total object, the body, but because they represent only partially the function that produces them," i.e., the drive/desire of the subject (1977, p. 315/817).

By now Lacan is well into the exposition of his Completed Graph, which we shall not follow in detail. Let it suffice to say that as in Graph II he plotted the formulation of a meaningful statement in conscious discourse by "looping its signification" (1977, p. 316/818), so now he attempts to plot this "looping" of signification on the level of unconscious enunciation, presumably by the "subject of the unconscious." "If we are to expect [this looping] effect from the unconscious enunciation, it is to be found here in the S(∅), and read as: signifier of a lack in the Other, inherent in its very function as the treasure of the signifier." The shock of this formulation is soon mitigated when we are told that the "lack referred to here is indeed that which I have already formulated: that there is no Other of the Other" (1977, p. 316/818). This says nothing about the existence or nonexistence of some higher being as specified in any particular religion—all it says is that the Other is not grounded in any order of signifiers beyond itself.

Proceeding to explain this enigmatic formula, Lacan focuses directly on the signifier of the Other-as-lacking. Taking it in linguistic terms, he tells us: "My definition of a signifier (there is no other) is as follows: a signifier is that which represents the subject for another signifier" (1977, p. 316/819). In the case of the fading subject, for example, this subject is represented in its spoken discourse by a signifier that, in place of the speaking I, relates to other signifiers in the self-referential signifying chain. Here, however, there is question of the subject of the unconscious as such. Hence, the signifier in question, $S(\emptyset)$ will be "the signifier for which all the other signifiers represent the subject: that is to say, in the absence of this signifier, all the other signifiers represent nothing" (1977, p. 316/819).

The whole battery of signifiers, then, is complete and self-contained. If this particular signifier is to be distinguished among the rest, it will have to be by some mark that will not separate it from the other signifiers, and Lacan chooses the sign -1. If this signifier, with its corresponding signified, together yields the "statement" (énoncé) articulated by the subject of the unconscious, then a simple algebraic operation will yield the result: s (unconscious statement) equals $\sqrt{-1}$ —an irrational number that is otherwise quite "inexpressible," even "unthinkable," if we try to think it on the level of the conscious Cartesian cogito. If we are to conceive it at all, it will have to be in terms of the faded subject that, through its withdrawal, undergoes a kind of death and therefore resides in a place "from which a voice is heard clamouring 'the universe is a defect in the purity of Non-Being' " (1977, p. 317/820).

Apparently this place to which the speaking I withdraws is where it can experience a form of boundlessness that Lacan calls *jouissance.* The term, though it has appeared in previous essays, has not been thematized heretofore, and we have very little data to help us understand its nature. We are told that *jouissance* is usually experienced as "forbidden" (1977, p. 317/820) — not because of "a bad arrangement of society," nor because of some fault of the Other (as if it existed), nor because of a consequence of some "original sin" (1977, p. 317/820). Rather, *jouissance* is limited by an interdiction imposed by the Law. We take this to mean that when the subject enters into the symbolic order, i.e., when the subject submits to the law of the signifier and becomes barred through primal repression, the subject must accept the consequences of his finitude that are never more apparent than in the limits imposed upon *jouissance* (1977, p. 319/821).

In any case, this lets us see that the limitations of *jouissance* are closely connected with the barring of the subject in primal repression. Since these are intimately connected with the castration complex, it would be impossible to exaggerate the importance of this complex as "structural of the subject" (1977, p. 318/820). With regard to it, Lacan suggests a second meaning for the term "subversion" of the subject. "In the castration complex we find the major mainspring of the very subversion that I am trying to articulate here by means of its dialectic" (1977, p. 318/820).

Castration involves a sacrifice of the phallus, "image of the penis." We must distinguish, however, "between the principle of sacrifice, which is symbolic, and the imaginary function that is devoted to that principle of sacrifice, but which, at the same time, masks the fact that it [the imaginary function] gives it [the principle] its instrument [of sacrifice]" (1977, p. 319/822). We take this to mean that Lacan wants to distinguish clearly between the phallus as symbolic (hereafter capital Phi [Φ]) and as image (hereafter small phi [φ]). According to our understanding of the matter, the phallus as imaginary is (on the psychic level) the bond with the Source of All, which, like the umbilical cord, must be severed in order to enter into human existence in the symbolic order (though at the cost of the irreparable loss of *jouissance*). As image, the phallus forms part of the body schema perceived in the specular image that, for Lacan as well as for Freud, "is the channel taken by the transfusion of the body's libido towards the object" and serves as paradigm for fantasy (1977, p. 319/822).

The detachability of the phallus may be understood in a broad sense, for insofar as the phallus is erectile (hence also detumescent and in that way "detachable"), it may be experienced as "lacking" to, or "negatived" in, the body image (1977, pp. 319–320/822). As a result of this negative quality, it bears a certain affinity with the negativity of the signifier (-1) as with the negativity of its signification ($\sqrt{-1}$). Since "the erectile organ comes to symbolize the place of *jouissance*," there is a natural correlation between the phallus imagined as castratable and the limitation of *jouissance*, by reason of which the erectile organ may be said to "bind [*nouer*] the prohibition of *jouissance*" (1977, p. 320/822).

The transformation of the phallus as imaginary and detachable ($-\phi$) (implying a castration equally imaginary) into the phallus as symbolic (Φ) is a step forward in the emergence of the subject and in that sense "positive," even though it may be correlated with the filling up of some lack (1977, p. 320/823) and, as signifier of the Other's desire, signifies the lack in the Other. However that may be, the castration of the phallus brings into play some kind of object on the level of fantasy that Lacan refers to as *objet a*. How this may be understood admits of various interpretations. After scrutinizing relative texts in Lacan, Lemaire suggests two possible ways of understanding the *objet a*: the first sense would be to take *objet a* as "the first image to fill in the crack of separation" from the mother, hence necessarily referring to the phallus "in the symbolic sense of the hyphen, *par excellence*, of the impossible unification" with her that in the separation is severed; a second (broader) sense would take *objet a* as the "representative of the object of lack," i.e., "the metonymic object of desire" (1970, p. 174).

As a case in point, an example of *objet a* would be the "inestimable treasure" that in Plato's *Symposium* Alcibiades fantasizes as contained in hidden fashion within Socrates. Recall how Alcibiades had projected onto Socrates the ideal of the "perfect master" (1977, p. 323/826). Yet because Socrates refuses to respond to any of his advances, Alcibiades fantasies Socrates as deprived of the imaginary phallus (– ϕ) and in that sense as "castrated," hence, "ideal Master" or not, as "completely imaginarized." This does not make Socrates any less "the object of desire," however, for, like "the woman concealed behind her veil, it is the absence of the penis that turns her into the phallus, the object of desire" (1977, p. 322/825). We understand this to mean that the absent penis in the woman makes her desirable to the subject, i.e., the object of the subject's desire, in the sense that, not having the phallus, she can now be the phallus for/to him, i.e., the object of his desire. Phallus in this case, however, is obviously used in the symbolic sense (Φ) as signifier of desire or of lack. Similarly, Socrates remains the "symbolic" phallus for Alcibiades, even though (or rather precisely because) he is castrated of the imaginary phallus (– ϕ). In all this, Lacan claims that Alcibiades (though he may well be a lecher and a lush) "is certainly not a neurotic," for he is "*par excellence* [one] who desires," i.e., is in touch with his own desire. Socrates, "the precursor of psychoanalysis," is shrewd enough to discern the true focus of Alcibiades' desire, "object of the transference," i.e., Agathon (1977, p. 323/825–826), insofar as he matches (as homosexual object) the object in Alcibiades' unconscious fantasy, the object marked by the – ϕ "as castrated" (1977, p. 323/825).

For the neurotic, the same issue is not so straightforward. When the subject is split through primary repression ($\math$), the neurotic's ego remains strong and, essentially imaginary itself, functions in the imaginary order. The phallus on this level, as also the castration of it, is equally imaginary. The neurotic's relation to the Other is such that "he imagines that the Other demands his castration" (1977, p. 323/826). But in his imaginary struggle against an imaginary castration, the neurotic fails to appreciate the genuine role of the symbolic phallus and the need for symbolic castration as the price of any satisfactory relationship of the subject to the Other. We understand this satisfactory relationship to involve the dialectic of desire through reciprocal recognition of subject and Other. In other words, it is as if the neurotic played out the scenario of the classic oedipal stereotype on the imaginary level and failed utterly to appreciate the symbolic significance of castration. In any case, what analytic experience shows us is that, whether in the normal or abnormal, castration is the condition for desire to become human. In that sense it "governs" desire (1977, p. 323/826). Reciprocally, it implies the forfeit of *jouissance* of primordial union, which can then be approached only on "the inverted ladder. . . of the Law of desire," i.e., by overturning the Law governing the articulation of desire (1977, p. 324/827).

But all this, along with the tantalizing allusions to different kinds of neuroses (phobic, obsessional, hysterical) and to perversion, suggests a clinical relevance to Lacan's reflections here that the paucity of clinical facts simply does not permit us to explicate further. In other words, we must be content with what few misty glimmers have been allowed us in the course of this long, foggy night.

MAP OF THE TEXT

I. Analytic practice rests on a structure.
    A. Philosophy claims to deal with what interests everyone without their knowing it.
       1. This relation of the subject to knowledge was mapped by Hegel,
          a. but it is an ambiguous relation, even in science.
       2. The scientist is a subject who ought to know what he is doing,
          a. but he does not know what in the impact of science is of interest to everyone.
       3. Thus we consider Hegel's epistemology regarding the subject,

        a. in order to show what psychoanalysis subverts in the question of the subject.

B. Our psychoanalytic experience qualifies us to proceed in this way,

    1. in the face of gaps in theory and transmission,

        a. which consequently jeopardize practice,

        b. and nullify its scientific status.

    2. Its social basis is not at issue,

        a. not even its deviations in Britain and America.

    3. It is subversion itself that we will try to define.

C. Science cannot be founded on empiricism,

    1. not even the so-called science of psychology,

        a. since the Freudian subject disqualifies what lies at the root of academic psychology.

    2. Psychology's criterion is the presupposed unity of the subject,

        a. as a subject of knowledge or as a double of the physical organism.

    3. We must take stock of the notion "state of knowledge,"

        a. insofar as it can be authenticated by a theory

            i. that relates knowing to connaturality.

        b. Hegel had no use for it, nor does modern science,

            i. except in plotting the coordinates of its objects.

        c. So-called depth psychology gets no direction from it.

        d. Freud himself took his distance from hypnoid states,

            i. preferring the discourse of the hysteric.

D. People fail to see that when we question the unconscious,

    1. its reply is a discourse.

    2. We lead the subject to decipher its logic,

        a. provided our voice enters at the right place.

      3. Our goal is not some archetypal or mute experience.

E. In this approach to the subject we see how Freud took a Copernican step.

      1. With Copernicus, the earth was dislodged from its central place.

        a. But heliocentrism is no less a lure,

        b. and Darwinian man still believes he's the pick of the basket.

      2. A doctrine of double truth still shelters our knowledge,

        a. for science has closed the frontier of its knowledge from the Freudian truth.

        b. If we keep the shifting history of science in view, psychoanalysis can still have an earth-shaking role.

II. From this vantage point we reexamine what help we can expect from Hegel.

A. Hegel's phenomenology ideally resolves the relation between truth and knowledge.

      1. Truth emerges in knowledge by putting ignorance to work,

        a. yielding a new symbolic form by resolving the imaginary.

      2. The dialectic leads to an absolute knowing wherein the real and the symbolic are conjoined,

        a. for the absolute subject is complete and perfect, the fully conscious self

        b. that is the basic hypothesis of the entire movement.

      3. But the history of Western science shows detours that are inconsistent with Hegel's dialectic.

        a. Creative physicists remind us that in scientific knowledge as well as in other areas the hour of truth strikes elsewhere than in consciousness.

        b. The consideration shown psychoanalysis by science indicates a wish for theoretical enlightenment.

i. This has nothing to do with the categories of psychology, whose fate is sealed.
B. By thus referring to Hegel's absolute subject and the abolished subject of science, we shed light on Freud's dramatic entry,
  1. the return of truth into the field of science,
    a. at the same time that it imposes itself on the field of practice.
  2. Hegel's unhappy consciousness is basically just a suspension of knowing;
    a. it is far from Freud's malaise of civilization,
      i. marked by the skewed relation separating the subject from sexuality.
  3. We cannot situate Freud in terms of a predictive psychology,
    a. nor in terms of a phenomenology that would reassure idealism.
    b. In the Freudian field consciousness cannot found the unconscious;
    c. nor can affect ground the subject.
C. The unconscious, since Freud, is a chain of signifiers,
  1. which repeats itself "on another stage,"
    a. and which interferes in discourse and thought.
  2. The notion of "signifier" of modern structural linguists was unavailable to Freud,
    a. but his descriptions of primary-process mechanisms match exactly their description of the two poles of language (metaphor and metonymy).
D. Given the structure of language in the unconscious, what kind of subject can we conceive for the unconscious?
  1. We can begin with the I as signifier, defined in linguistics
    a. in terms of its status as shifter.
  2. The shifter indicates the speaking subject,
    a. but does not signify it.

3. The subject does not always know what he is saying, or even that he is speaking,
   a. for the subject fades from discourse,
   b. a discourse marked by parapraxes.
4. As analysts we must return to the function of the
gap in discourse,
   a. the strongest being the bar that separates the
   signifier and the signified.
5. We thus arrive at the subject as bound to signification and thereby under the sign of the preconscious.
   a. This leads us to the paradox of conceiving the
   analytic discourse as of value only in its lapses
   and parapraxes.
6. The subject is therefore structured as discontinuity
in the real,
   a. with holes in meaning as determinants of analytic discourse.

E. Freud's imperative, *"Wo Es war, soll Ich werden,"* emphasizes a presence as having-been.
1. From this presence I can come to being,
   a. but only to disappear in my discourse.
2. The Hegelian subject of absolute knowledge fails to
see the vanity of its discourse,
   a. and thus risks madness.
3. The Freudian subject, as being of non-being, is
separated from Hegel's by an abyss.

III. The subject's relation to knowledge has its roots in the
dialectic of desire.
A. In both Hegel and Freud desire is linked to knowledge.
1. Hegel's "cunning of reason" implies that the subject
knows what he wants.
2. In Freud desire is tied to the desire of the Other.
   a. In this tie we find the desire to know.
B. The biologism of Freud is far from the psychoanalytic
theory of instinct.
1. The tone of Freud's biology is found only by living
the death instinct.

2. The metaphor of the return to the inanimate shows the "margin beyond life" that language gives to being,

   a. in the fact that there is speech,

   b. and body parts are engaged as signifiers.

3. Freud's *Trieb* is incorrectly translated as "instinct."

   a. Instinct is a mode of awareness without knowledge.

   b. The Freudian discourse is a mode of knowledge without awareness.

   c. The unconscious has little concern for physiology,

      i. while psychoanalysis has contributed nothing to physiology.

C. Psychoanalysis involves the real body and its imaginary schema.

  1. Psychosexual development provides symbolic elements.

   a. The phallus holds a privileged place in the dialectic of the unconscious.

D. Hegel provides a basis for criticizing contemporary psychoanalysis.

  1. Yet it would be wrong to accuse me of being lured by his dialectic of being,

   a. for I find desire to be irreducible to demand or need.

  2. Precisely because desire is articulated it remains inarticulable.

IV. A simplified graph (I) illustrates the topological structure showing how desire is related to a subject defined by its articulation through the signifier.

A. The graph's "elementary cell" shows the anchoring point by which the signifier stops the sliding of signification.

  1. The diachronic sentence which is thus anchored completes its meaning retroactively.

    2. The synchronic structure of metaphor is more hidden.

        a. It is apparent in the child's song that raises sounds which serve as signs to the level of signifiers.

B. The two points of intersection (on Graph II) show the role of the Other.

    1. The intersection point O is the place of the treasure of the signifiers,

        a. the synchronic ensemble of reciprocally opposed phonemes.

    2. The intersection point $s(O)$ can be designated the punctuation whereby the articulated meaning is completed.

    3. Both participate in the gap in the real:

        a. the first as a concealed hollow,

        b. the second as "boring-hole" for escape (in articulation).

C. The submission of the subject to the signifier is shown in the circular movement between these two points.

    1. Assertions are circular insofar as they cannot be grounded outside of themselves in the certitude of an action.

        a. They refer only to their own anticipated meaning.

    2. The subject must subtract himself from this circle and function as a lack

        a. while remaining dependent on it.

D. The Other is the pre-given "site of the pure subject of the signifier."

    1. It holds the master position,

        a. determining all codes.

        b. It is from here that the subject receives the message which he emits and whereby he is constituted.

    2. The Other constitutes the place of speech and is Truth's witness.

   a. Without this dimension, verbal deception could
      not be distinguished from the imaginary pre-
      tense of animals,
         i. who can present the hunter with a false start,
        ii. but cannot pretend to pretend.
   b. Speech is possible only in the signifying realm,
      beyond "pretense."
         i. This requires the locus of the Other as third-
            party witness to the speakers,
        ii. thus making lying possible.
   3. Truth draws its guarantee not from Reality but
      from Speech.
V. The first words spoken are a decree conferring authority
   on the real other.
   A. The emblem of symbolic identification is the "unbroken
      line" joining $ to I(O), the castrated subject to the ego
      ideal.
      1. This line fills out the invisible mark that the subject
         receives from the signifier.
      2. This line separates the subject from himself in his
         ego ideal as first identification,
         a. for it establishes a retroactive effect by which he
            announces himself only in terms of what he will
            have been,
         b. and his self-certainty lies in meeting his antici-
            pated mirror image.
      3. This process installs the ambiguity of a misunder-
         standing that is an essential aspect of understanding
         myself.
   B. The ego as originating in the mirror stage is counter-
      posed to the American notion of the "autonomous ego."
      1. The narcissistic mirror image tinges with hostility
         the objects reflected in the mirror.
      2. The mirror image becomes the idealized ego,
         a. established as a function of mastery, martial
            bearing, and rivalry.

3. In its alienating identifications the ego's consciousness is based outside of itself.
4. The ego achieves itself by being articulated not as the speaking I, but as the displacement of its meaning,
   a. that is, only opaquely as shifter,
   b. despite the deceptive emphasis on the self-consciousness of the acting I.
5. The ego is the source of aggressivity toward one's counterpart in the master-slave relation.
C. The master-slave struggle is one of pure prestige.
   1. Its stake, life itself, echoes the danger of our specific prematurity at birth,
      a. which is the dynamic basis of specular capture.
   2. The pact that defines the relation of master and slave requires that the loser not perish,
      a. thus showing that the pact precedes the violence,
      b. and that "the symbolic dominates the imaginary."
   3. Murder is not the absolute Master,
      a. for we must distinguish between physical death,
      b. and the death brought about in language.
   4. We have repressed the truth of the cunning of reason,
      a. whose lure makes us think the slave's work and renunciation of *jouissance* through fear of death is his way to freedom.
      b. In fact the slave's *jouissance* lies in waiting for the master's death,
      c. for the obsessional installs himself in the place of the Other.
D. Philosophers must take seriously Freud's views on desire.
   1. They should not be misled by current psychoanalytic practice
      a. which wrongly emphasizes demand and frustration

      b. and reduces what Freud discovered to repressed wishes.

  2. Demand introduces incompatibility into needs,

      a. for every demand must "pass through the defiles of the signifier."

  3. Man's dependence is maintained by a universe of language,

      a. whereby needs have passed into the register of desire.

  4. Even the sexual function bears the mark of an unnatural split.

VI. The coordinates of the Oedipus complex come down to the question: "What is a Father?"

  A. For Freud it is the dead Father.

    1. Lacan considers this in terms of "The Name-of-the-Father,"

      a. calling attention to the paternal function,

      b. which is not a cultural-anthropological notion, as some analysts believe.

    2. We embark from the notion of the Other as the place of the signifier.

      a. No authoritative statement can find a guarantee outside of itself,

      b. and we look in vain for another signifier outside of this place, for a "metalanguage,"

      c. for "there is no Other of the Other."

    3. The Law's authority is represented by the Father.

      a. We must specify how he becomes present beyond the Mother, who really occupies the place of the Other.

      b. Rather than focusing on demand as a request for love, we concentrate on desire,

      c. for man's desire finds form as desire of the Other.

VII. By representing need, man's subjective opacity produces the substance of desire.

A. Desire is outlined in the margin where demand separates itself from need.
   1. Demand is characterized by an unconditional appeal to the Other,
      a. thereby introducing anxiety insofar as desire cannot be satisfied,
      b. as well as introducing the phantom of the Other's omnipotence.
   2. This phantasm of the Other's omnipotence must be checked by the mediation of the Law.
   3. This mediation originates in desire's reversal of the unconditional demand for love,
      a. which keeps the subject in subjection to the Other,
      b. and through this reversal desire instead becomes absolute and detached.
   4. Control over anxiety and detachment from the Other is achieved by means of the transitional object.
      a. This object functions as an emblem, a "representation of a representation,"
      b. with a place in the unconscious structure of the phantasm as cause of desire.
B. In relation to desire, it is not so much that man doesn't know what he demands, but where he desires.
   1. The "unconscious is [the] discourse of the Other,"
      a. insofar as it is from the Other.
   2. "Desire is . . . the desire of the Other,"
      a. insofar as it is as Other that man desires.
   3. The best path to the subject's own desire is the question of the Other, "What do you want?",
      a. provided he reformulates it in analysis as "What does the analyst want of me?"
   4. The subject comes to see that what he desires is also what he denies.
      a. This negation reveals the *méconnaissance* whereby the subject transfers the permanence of his desire to an intermittent ego,

b. and in turn protects himself from his desire by attributing this intermittent quality to it.

C. In analysis we link the structure of the fantasy to the condition of an object.

1. In the structure of the unconscious fantasy ($\$\Diamond o$) the subject is eclipsed.

a. This "fading" is linked to the subject's condition as split by his subordination to the signifier.

2. The fantasy structures desire just as the image of the body structures the ego.

3. The fantasy is the "stuff" of the I as primordially repressed,

a. because in the "fading" of discourse the I can only be indicated, not signified.

D. We now turn to the signifying chain in its unconscious status.

1. We have been asking about what supports the subject of the unconscious,

a. since it is difficult to designate him as speaking subject of a statement

i. when he doesn't even know that he speaks.

2. Hence arises the concept of drive as an organic registration all the more removed from speaking the more he speaks.

3. Drive ($\$\Diamond D$) can be situated in relation to the treasure of the signifiers ($S[\emptyset]$) and linked with diachronic articulation in demand.

a. It is what comes to pass from demand when the subject vanishes there.

4. Demand too disappears but the cut *(coupure)* remains,

a. for the cut distinguishes the drive from the physical function it inhabits.

b. This cut is the drive's "grammatical artifice" as seen in the reversions of the drive's articulation to its source as to its objects.

E. The "erogenous zone" is what the drive isolates from the metabolism of the organic function.
  1. The erogenous zone is delimited by a cut that is supported by the anatomical trait of a border — lip, rim, tip, etc.
  2. This trait of a cut is also evident in the part-objects described in analytic theory,
    a. but they are partial
      i. not in relation to the whole body
      ii. but to the function that produces them (the drive-fantasy that structures desire).
  3. These objects have no alterity,
    a. that is, they can't be seen in the mirror as partial.
    b. This allows them to function as the "stuff" or lining of the subject of consciousness,
      i. who cannot arrive at himself by designating himself in his statement.
  4. It is this "invisible" object that receives a shadow-substance from the reflection in the mirror.
VIII. The drive-fantasy that structures desire is an unconscious enunciation.
  A. This unconscious enunciation loops back on the signifier of a lack in the Other: $S(\emptyset)$.
    1. This lack is intrinsic to its function as "treasure of the signifier."
    2. The Other must answer for the value of this treasure,
      a. by responding from its place in the lower (verbal) chain,
      b. as well as in the unconscious signification constituting the upper chain.
    3. This lack is formulated as: "There is no Other of the Other."
      a. This implies nothing about a transcendent Other of religion.

B. The lack in the Other parallels a lack in the I.
   1. A signifier is what represents the subject for another signifier.
      a. The signifier of the Other-as-lack, $S(\emptyset)$, therefore, stands for the finite other to whom the subject is represented by all other signifiers.
      b. Remove this signifier of the ensemble of the Other's treasure, and all the other signifiers would represent nothing.
      c. Since the ensemble of signifiers forms a complete battery, this signifier cannot be outside the ensemble but is only a line (-1) inherent in the ensemble.
      d. Although this signifier cannot be pronounced, its effects are present whenever a proper noun is spoken.
   2. An algebraic transformation of this signifier's role in discourse yields the algorithm of the subject's lack in signification: $\sqrt{-1}$.
      a. This is the unthinkable aspect of the subject,
      b. present as "defective in the sea of proper nouns,"
      c. and whose origin is problematic.
   3. We cannot question the subject as I for he does not know if he exists,
      a. since the word "I" can designate, with equal rigor, the dreamer or dead man dreamt.
      b. The Other's existence, however, can be demonstrated in love.
   4. The place of I is the place of *jouissance*,
      a. whose constriction enervates Being,
      b. and whose absence makes everything empty.
      c. Its lack makes the Other incomplete.
      d. We tend to believe it is usually forbidden to us because of the defect of the Other or because of original sin.

IX. What Freud teaches regarding the castration complex is no myth.

   A. In this complex lies the basis of the subversion that we are attempting to articulate.

      1. Freud's discovery of the castration complex cannot be ignored by any thinking about the subject.

         a. Contemporary psychoanalysis, however, makes use of it to avoid any thinking about it,

         b. and thereby has become subservient to general psychology.

      2. This bone of contention which structures the subject has been avoided by all thought.

      3. This is why we lead our students over the disconcerting terrain of the disjunction between the imaginary and the symbolic.

   B. The notion of *mana* is not equivalent to the signifier of the lack in the Other, $S(\emptyset)$.

      1. This signifier is not founded in the inadequacy of society,

         a. nor is it equivalent to Lévi-Strauss' notion of zero symbol.

      2. It signifies, rather, what is lacking to this zero symbol,

         a. and can be written as $\sqrt{-1}$,

         b. or as the "*i*" in the theory of complex numbers.

   C. What we must hold to is that *jouissance* is prohibited to the speaker as such.

      1. It can be spoken only between the lines for one who is subject to the Law,

         a. since the Law grounds itself in this very prohibition.

      2. The Law itself does not bar the subject from *jouissance*,

         a. but it does create a barred subject.

      3. Concrete pleasure sets limits to *jouissance*,

         a. until pleasure, in turn, is structured by the laws of primary process.

4. In his notion of the "pleasure principle" Freud was not merely echoing a traditional idea,

    a. otherwise his notion of the castration complex would not have been spurned.

    b. For this anomalous idea indicates the infinity of *jouissance* that comports the mark of its prohibition,

    c. a mark that involves the sacrifice of the phallus.

D. The phallus is chosen as symbol of this sacrifice,

    1. because the image of the penis as detachable denotes negativity in the specular image.

    2. We must distinguish between symbolic castration as principle of sacrifice,

        a. and the imaginary castration that veils it.

E. The imaginary function presides over the narcissistic investment of objects.

    1. The specular image is invested in this way by the transfusion of the body's libido,

        a. but part of it remains focused on the penis,

        b. giving rise to the fantasy of its detachability,

        c. and of part-objects.

F. The erect penis symbolizes the place of *jouissance*,

    1. not as an image or physical organ,

        a. but as what the desired image lacks.

    2. Thus the erectile organ is equivalent to the algorithm $\sqrt{-1}$.

    3. The erectile organ knots the prohibition of *jouissance* not as imaginary form but as symbolic structure,

        a. with the consequence that lust is reduced to the brevity of auto-eroticism.

    4. The lineaments of the body offer a path to wisdom for some,

        a. but Freud does not promote a technique of the body.

        b. Otherwise analytic practice would not induce guilt,

      c. which appears in the contrast between auto-erot-
         icism and desire.
  G. The passage from the imaginary to the symbolic is here
     indicated.
     1. The imaginary absent phallus ($-\phi$) becomes the
        symbolic phallus (Φ),
        a. signifier of the lack in the Other
        b. which cannot be negated.
X. The structure of unconscious fantasy sheds light on perver-
  sion and neurosis.
  A. Perversion emphasizes the function of desire in the
    man.
     1. In the case of perversion in the man, dominance
       comes to occupy the place of *jouissance*,
       a. dominance over the object *o* of the fantasy that
         he substitutes for the lack in the Other: $S(\emptyset)$.
     2. Perversion adds to it the imaginary phallus (ϕ)
       which involves the Other in a particular way,
       a. whereby the subject becomes the tool of the Oth-
         er's *jouissance*.
  B. In the neurotic there is an identification of Φ and D, of
    the Other's lack and his demand.
     1. Therefore the demand of the Other takes on the
       function of object in his fantasy,
       a. so that his fantasy is reduced to the drive ($\$ \Diamond D$).
     2. This emphasis given by the neurotic to demand
       hides his anxiety about the desire of the Other.
       a. We see anxiety clearly when it is covered by the
         phobic object.
     3. If we understand the fantasy as desire of the Other
       we can also understand the anxiety of the hysteric
       and the obsessional.
       a. The obsessional denies the desire of the Other by
         structuring his fantasy so that he emphasizes the
         impossibility of vanishing as subject.
         i. The obsessional has a basic need to stand in
           the place of the Other.

b. In the case of the hysteric, desire is maintained by the dissatisfaction introduced when he conceals himself as object,

    i. as evidenced in the denial present in hysterical intrigue.

C. The neurotic's fantasy includes the idealized Father as image.

  1. He stands beyond the Mother, the real Other of demand,

    a. for the subject wishes she would abate her desire,

    b. and wants a Father who can ignore desire.

  2. This fantasy calls attention to the Father's true function,

    a. which is not to oppose but to unite a desire with the Law.

  3. The Father sought by the neurotic is therefore the dead Father,

    a. who would perfectly master his desire,

    b. for this is what the subject seeks.

  4. The analyst must show a calculated variability in his neutrality,

    a. and preserve the imaginary dimension of his necessary imperfection through his ignorance of the case,

    b. or else the transference may be interminable.

D. In perversion the subject imagines he is the Other to guarantee his *jouissance*.

  1. But in perversion desire is a defense setting a limit on *jouissance*.

  2. The neurotic imagines himself to be a pervert to make sure of the existence of the Other.

    a. This pretended perversion lies in the neurotic's unconscious as fantasy of the Other.

E. The structure of the fantasy ($ \$ \Diamond o$) contains the imaginary function of castration ($-\phi$).

1. This function is hidden and alternatively makes imaginary one or the other of the terms of the unconscious fantasy.
2. A woman's clothing, veiling the absence of the penis, transforms her into the phallus, the object of desire.
3. Because Socrates does not show his penis to Alcibiades, he becomes castrated in fantasy,
   a. and thereby can be the phallus.
   b. But Socrates sees that Alcibiades perceives his desired object as castrated, and so directs the focus to the handsome Agathon.

F. In the neurotic the $-\phi$ slips under the $\mathcal{S}$ of the unconscious fantasy.
1. This reinforces the imagination proper to it, that of the ego,
   a. for the neurotic's lifelong imaginary castration supports this strong ego.
   b. It is beneath this ego that the neurotic covers the castration that he denies but clings to.
2. The neurotic refuses to sacrifice his castration to the *jouissance* of the Other who, he thinks, would be served by it.
   a. He wants to preserve his difference as a want-to-be,
   b. while imagining that the Other demands his castration.

G. Castration in all cases regulates desire — normal or abnormal.
1. By oscillating between the $\mathcal{S}$ and o of the fantasy, castration turns it into a supple unconscious chain,
   a. whose fantasized object guarantees the *jouissance* of the Other,
   b. which transmits this chain to me in the Law.
2. To confront the Other is to experience not only his demand but his will.

    a. In response one can become an object or a mummy,

    b. or one can fulfill the will to castration inscribed in the Other.

       i. The extreme form of this is the hero's narcissistic death for a lost cause.

  3. Castration means that *jouissance* must be denied.

NOTES TO THE TEXT

293*c*/794   The phrase, "a subject of science" *(un sujet de la science)* refers to the scientist.

293*e*/794   Instead of "while presenting no danger to the praxis itself," we translate "while not being without danger for the practice itself" *(pour n'être sans danger pour la praxis elle-même).*

293*i*/795   "At a second stage" *(De second temps)* suggests that general psychology is an offshoot of the broader field of general science just discussed.

294*c*/795   Rather than "We must take as our standard here the idea" for *Il faut ici prendre étalon de l'idée*, we translate: "We must here take stock of the idea." Lacan goes on to show that the notion of "state of knowledge" is *not* a standard for thought.

294*e*/795   Hegel's *Aufhebung* was briefly defined earlier (see note 46*f*). For an extended discussion, the reader is referred to Lauer's treatment of negation (1976, pp. 29, 35ff.) and to Hyppolite (1946, pp. 13–15).

    The word "noophoric" implies bearing or begetting understanding.

294*h*/795   A simple misprint in the English has "hynoid" instead of "hypnoid" *(hypnoïdes).* The meaning of "fruitful moments" is unclear; it may have to do with the way the ego in paranoiac knowledge projects its own attributes onto things (as discussed earlier [1977, p. 17/111]).

295a/796   The phrase "it says why" *(il dise pourquoi)* suggests the familiar discourse of the child.

295e/796   Freud's reference to Copernicus was discussed earlier (see note 165d/516).

295f/796   After Copernicus the privilege is not "consigned to it," referring back to "our subject" of the preceding paragraph, but is, on the contrary, "excluded" from it *(relégué)*, namely, the privilege of having the earth in the central place.

295g/797   The ecliptic is the circle cut out by the plane containing the orbit of the earth around the sun, which is inclined to the plane of the equator by an angle of approximately 23°.

295i/797   The title of Copernicus' famous work is *De revolutionibus orbium coelestium* ("On the Revolutions of Heavenly Spheres"). The "ellipse" suggests the shape of the graphs that follow in Lacan's text.

296b/797   The doctrine of double truth was a theological vehicle aimed at preserving the "truth" of a literal reading of the scriptures while acknowledging the "truth" of the findings of the science of astronomy.

296e/798   The Scholastic "antinomy" is unclear; perhaps it has to do with the relationship between *esse* and *essentia*, the principle of "existence" whereby a being exists and that of "essence" whereby it has a determinate structure. Lacan interprets Hegel as viewing such a distinction as spurious.

297e/799   Rather than "the suspension of a corpus of knowledge," we translate *suspension d'un savoir* as "the suspension of knowing," a mere interruption on the dialectical path to absolute knowing. The allusion to Freud's title, with single quotation marks in the English highlighting "discontents of civilization," varies from the French which has simply *malaise de la civilization* ("the discontentment of civilization") without quotation marks.

297*f*/799   The "judicial astrology in which the psychologist dabbles" appears to refer to a predictive psychology that makes judgments of people.

Lacan's reference to Aquinas is puzzling, for Aquinas, as far as we know, does not use the word *inconscius*. He does speak, from time to time, about one who is not conscious *(non conscius)* of something and about beings that lack cognition *(non cognoscentia)*, but such usage simply denotes the negation of conscious knowledge.

The "protopathic" is related to cutaneous sensory reception that is responsive only to gross stimuli.

297*g*/799   The French for "breaks" is *coupures* ("cuts"), a word that will receive repeated emphasis in the essay.

298*a*/799   Geneva and Petrograd refer, respectively, to the work of Saussure and Jakobson. For a succinct and remarkably lucid history of modern linguistics, see Jakobson (1973).

299*a*/800   The example of equivocation involved here was used earlier by Lacan (1977, p. 269/634). The French for "from which I eye them" is *dont je les toise*, continuing the play of words.

299*d*/801   In Heidegger Being's presencing comes to pass through *Dasein*'s openness to the Being of beings.

299*e*/801   Rather than "There the subject that interests us is surprised," we translate "There the subject who is of interest to us catches himself" ("Là se surprend le sujet qui nous intéresse").

The "sign of the pre-conscious" appears to refer to the way latent significations appear in homophonic resonances (as exemplified in the example of *tue*).

Rather than "if the session itself were not instituted" for *si la séance elle-même ne s'instituait*, we take the *ne* not as a negative but as denoting emphasis (in the mode Lacan has just exemplified on p. 298*e*/800)

and therefore translate, "if the session itself were instituted."

Mallarmé's metaphor of the worn coin was alluded to in the "Discourse at Rome" (1977, p. 43g/
251).

299f/801   Instead of "by making 'holes' in the meaning of the
determinants of its discourse," the translation should
read "by making holes in meaning the determinants
of its discourse" ("à faire des trous du sens les
déterminants de son discours").

300c/801   For the double sense of the imperfect tense in French,
see Guillaume (1968). It should be remarked that
Lacan's tortured version of the future sense of the
imperfect (il y était d'avoir pu y être [1966, p. 840]) admits of no convenient counterpart in English. Collo-
quial English would accept a future imperfect such
as "another minute and I was dead," but this is at
best a hasty abbreviation of what in formal English
would be ". . . I would have been dead." This raises
the question as to whether Freud's German war has
any more flexibility than the English "was," and if
not, whether Lacan is interpreting Freud here by
saying (however ingeniously) what Freud did not
say, perhaps could not say. If this turned out to be the
case, the implications for Lacan's entire hermeneutic
of Freud would be far-reaching.

The French does not have quotes around I.

300e–i/   Freud's relevant text in German reads: "das der Va-
802   ter doch schon gestorben war und es nur nicht wusste"
(1911b, p. 238). Lacan's sentence, "He did not know
that he was dead," is therefore a paraphrase of the
text in Freud (1911a), which presents the dream as
follows: "his father was alive once more and he was
talking to him in his usual way. But he felt it exceed-
ingly painful that his father had really died, only
without knowing it" (p. 225). Freud interpolates "that

his father had really died" (as the dreamer wished)
and "without knowing it" (that the dreamer wished
it). Lacan is comparing the status of the father as
dead subject with the status of the dreamer as subject
of the unconscious. The dead father achieves presence in the words of the dreamer while the "I" of the
dreamer necessarily recedes from the dream's discourse and therefore undergoes a kind of death
"there where it was" *(là où c'était)*; between the place of
unconscious desire (for the death of the father) and
the enunciation of the dream, I fade.

301*b*/802 This sentence should read: "And to show that there is
no firmer root [for the distinction between the
Freudian and Hegelian subjects and their relation to
knowing] than the modes in which the dialectic of
desire becomes conspicuous" ("Et qu'il n'en est pas de
plus sûre racine que les modes dont s'y distingue la
dialectique du désir").

301*h*/803 The "margin beyond life" assured by language *(le langage)* would seem to refer to the way the symbolic order dominates and structures human existence, from
the name and kinship relation present before birth to
the gravesite, legends, and judgments that follow
one after death. The theme is a repeated one (1977,
p. 68/279), but here specific attention is drawn to the
way in which body parts can serve as signifiers (that
is, go beyond their function in the living body), with
the phallus as preeminent signifier with which the
body as a whole comes to be identified and which
also functions "as that in which being is at stake"
(comme enjeu de l'être).

301*i*/803 The French word *dérive* means "drift" or "leeway" and
is related to *dérivation*, literally a "de-banking," which
was discussed earlier (in note 259*h*/623).

302*d*/804 To be more precise, the French text reads "the real of
the body and of the imaginary of its mental schema"

("le réel du corps et de l'imaginaire de son schéma mental").

303*b*/805   We do not pretend to have an exact comprehension of these graphs as they grow in complexity. What begins here as a relatively intelligible presentation of the structure of the speaking subject becomes multi-leveled, as Lacan introduces the discoursing ego (p. 306/808), the unconscious fantasy (p. 313/815), and the discourse of drive in neurosis (p. 315/817). The many arrows and shifts in direction suggest how the subject is channeled in criss-cross fashion among these many levels and between the various poles at each level (ego [*e*] and specular image [$i(o)$], diachrony [$s(O)$] and synchrony [O], the unconscious fantasy [$\$ \Diamond o$] and desire [*d*], the Other as lacking [$S(\emptyset)$] and drive [$\$ \Diamond D$]). We shall attempt to say something about each of these terms as they come up in the text, though here, even more than elsewhere, a satisfactory explanation of their import must await the publication of the seminars in which these formulas were developed. The reader's attention is called to the comments of the French editor on these graphs (1977, pp. 334–335/907–908).

With respect to the symbol (Δ), Pontalis (1958) describes it as "that by which the human subject, in its essence as problematic subject, is situated in a certain relationship with the signifier" (p. 253).

303*c*/805   Wilden (1968, p. 275) argues that this "retroactive effect" is what Lacan means by the subject receiving his own message back from the Other in inverted form. Lacan seems to confirm this: "it is from the Other that the subject receives even the message that he emits" (1977, p. 305*b*/807).

304*b*/806   The "four-cornered game" echoes the earlier use of bridge to illustrate the relation of subject to analyst (1977, p. 229–230/589–590) and also echoes the structure of schemas L (p. 193/548) and R (p. 197/553). This raises the question whether we have to include in these graphs a dialogue in process (i.e., between two subjects) "if the subsequent construction must be dependent on it."

304c/806   Since the signifier's treasure appears to lie in its phonemic structure as reciprocally distinctive features, and the code is limited to "the univocal correspondence of a sign with something," it seems inappropriate to speak of "the code's treasure"; the French text allows us to translate instead "the locus of the signifier's treasure, which does not mean [the locus] of the code" ("le lieu du trésor du signifiant, ce qui ne veut pas dire du code").

304e/806   Lacan elsewhere (1959) speaks of the "hole in the real" caused by the death of another (pp. 37–38). We recall, again, that language is "the murder of the thing" (1977, p. 104/319), since the brute facticity of objects is negated by words where objects come to have a presence in absence, a presence that is hidden in the synchronic ensemble of the storehouse of language, but is expressed in articulated diachronic speech in which desire is channeled from lack to substitute objects.

304g–h/   Lacan seems to be saying that the previous topology
806   of the square, in which subject is related to the Other, must be modified ("such a squaring is impossible"), since we must subtract the subject from his discourse and therefore the more appropriate notation is "the barred subject" ($), while the emphasis shifts to the structure of the self-referential discourse (expressed in the various loops of the graphs).

305a/807   Rather than "and to make it function as a lack" for *et n'y faire fonction que de manque*, we translate "and to only function there as a lack," referring to the subject's role in the signifying battery.

305b/807   Hegel uses the phrase "the absolute Master" when discussing the slave's experience of the fear of death: "denn es hat die Furcht des Todes, des absoluten

Herrn, empfunden" (1807b, p. 148; 1807a, p. 237). In coming close to death, the slave experiences the true nature of self-consciousness as absolute negativity. Lacan here puts the symbolic order, as affording a "margin beyond life" (see the earlier note 301*h*/803), in a place prior to death and operative in death. The symbolic order as Other is not reducible to a code and is the foundation for the message which constitutes the subject. The English is misleading: rather than "in the message, since it is from this code that the subject is constituted," we translate "in the message, since it is from it that the subject is constituted" ("dans le message, puisque c'est de lui que le sujet se constitue"). The notation "O" would then represent the Other as synchronic system, while "*s*(O)" would be the articulated, diachronic message, with the arrows in Graph II (1977, p. 306/808) suggesting the circular movement between them, i.e., that articulated sentences borrow words from the storehouse of language and "that it is from the Other that the subject receives even the message that he emits." The dominant position of the symbolic order is emphasized again when Lacan goes on to discuss the master-slave dialectic in more detail (p. 308/810).

305*c*/807 The reference is to Lacan's earlier essay on Schreber (1977, pp. 184–187/537–540).

305*d*/807 Pretending to pretend is illustrated by Freud's joke, mentioned by Lacan (1977, p. 173*b*/525).

306*b*–
307*c*/
808–809 In grappling with this passage, we can try to make tentative sense in the following way. Just as the child's first words in the *Fort! Da!* moment lead to separation from the mother, the "first words spoken" here appear to be the mother's words conferring a symbolic identification upon the infant through naming. The *trait unaire* we take to be a scratch mark or line observed on prehistoric artifacts, which functions as an inchoative signifier opening up all the potentiali-

ties of the symbolic order, making possible primary repression, and differentiating the subject from objects by mediating his relationships to them. (In a later seminar [1964] Lacan refers to notch marks used to count kills [p. 141]). The mother's act of naming achieves inchoative differentiation of mother and child and puts in place the ego ideal as the primary symbolic identification. Since all naming and symbolic identification is a function of the Law of the Father (the law of language), this earliest moment in which the "first words" are spoken involves an eventual barring of the subject, and acknowledgment of a lack in both mother and infant, and a kind of anticipated castration (see the discussion of the "paternal metaphor" in Chapter 6, specifically note 199*i*/557). The *trait unaire*, then, would be a foreshadowing of symbolic castration (*trait* is repeated later in the context of the Other-as-lacking [1977, p. 316*f*–*g*/819]). It is the observable mark that "fills out" *(combler)*, i.e., gives form to, "the invisible mark the subject derives from the signifier," i.e., the mark of primary repression.

Once the mirror stage is entered, the ego ideal (taken here to refer to primary symbolic identification) is overlaid by the ideal ego *(moi idéal)*, that "function of mastery" that develops from the narcissistic identification with the reflected specular image (as discussed earlier in Chapters 1 and 2).

307*d*/809 Lacan now adds to the graph the structure of the discoursing ego. The imaginary identification with the image of the other (*i*[*o*]) leads to the development of the ego *(e)*, and this process of ego development is "doubly articulated"—first in an aborted manner (the "short circuit" from $ to I[O], pertaining to the primary symbolic identification), second as excluded from articulated speech (the relation between diachrony [s(O)] and synchrony [O]). The ego is not present in articulated speech as the I who speaks but rather is associated to the I who speaks by a kind of displacement, hence as the "metonymy of its signification." Earlier the ego was called "the metonymy of desire" (see note 274g/640), which is channeled in signification.

The work of Damourette and Pichon (1911–1940) is an exhaustive study of the expression of negation in French.

308b/810   Rather than "this initial enslavement. . . of the 'roads to freedom,' " we prefer to translate, "[T]his enslavement ushering in the ways of freedom" ("Cette servitude inaugurale des chemins de la liberté"). The irony suggested by the translator's use of single quotes does not appear warranted in our text. The structuring of the imaginary order appears quite necessary before full entrance into the symbolic order is possible.

308d-e/   The scenario for the master-slave dialectic, the
810   reciprocal roles of master and slave, is prescribed in the symbolic order, which has a dominant function over the imaginary struggle. We must therefore distinguish between physical death "which is brought by life" and the symbolic death "which brings life." The signifier is the murder of the thing; hence symbolic death is the symbolic castration requisite for participation in the symbolic order.

308f/   Hegel (1807a) writes:
810–811
> In the master, the bondsman feels self-existence to be something external, an objective fact; [but] in fear [of death] self-existence is present within himself [i.e., in the slave]; in fashioning the thing [in work], self-existence comes to be felt explicitly as his own proper being, and he attains the consciousness that he himself exists in its own right and on its own account [p. 239].

The obsessional, who toils in anticipation of the master's death, does not achieve liberation in this way, for he installs himself in the master's place (in imagination), assumes a kind of immortality through outlasting him, and lives and works not in the present but in that anticipated future moment.

309*e*/811   The French text does not say "repressed desires," but rather "repressed wishes" (*des envies rentrées*).

310*f*/813   Rather than translating "artificially inseminating women who have broken the phallic bounds," we translate "artificially inseminating women in [by or through] rupturing the phallic order" ("d'inséminer artificiellement les femmes en rupture du ban phallique").

310*g*/813   Tragedy assumes a universe in which there is some kind of underlying harmony or order. In "Some Reflections on the Ego" (1951), Lacan wrote:

> It may well be that the oedipus complex, the cornerstone of analysis, which plays so essential a part in normal psycho-social development, represents in our culture the vestigial relics of the relationships by means of which earlier communities were able for centuries to ensure the psychological mutual interdependence essential to the happiness of their members [p. 17].

311*a*/813   The "gap" referred to in the English is that there is no Other of the Other; no one can presume to stand outside the symbolic order and have authority over it.

311*g–h*/814   Once again, a very tentative reformulation: Demand becomes separated from need in the margin of the "defiles of the signifier" (1977, p. 309/811), i.e., as articulated. In this margin desire takes form as channeled and structured by the laws of language operative in the concrete statement of a demand. Demand is an appeal for unconditional love from the

Other. Embedded in this appeal is the articulation of desire, which has no universal object of satisfaction — and this condition of impossible satisfaction is called anxiety. Since the Other is addressed as capable of providing this satisfaction, the Other takes on a fantasized omnipotence vis-à-vis the subject, which sets up the necessity (*la nécessité*, woefully translated in this context as "the need") for its curbing by the Law.

The function of the Law (of language) as mediation between subject and the omnipotent Other originates in desire (for desire presupposes the structure of primary repression, symbolic castration, and the "cut" or differentiating power of symbolic articulation). Desire then enables the subject to transcend "the unconditional nature of the demand for love, in which the subject remains in subjection to the Other" (as omnipotent) by raising this unconditional nature to the power of an "absolute" condition, that is, a detached and differentiated status. In its root meaning "absolute" (*ab-solvere*, "to loosen or to free") implies "detachment." Desire, then, comports a differentiation from the Other, initially achieved in the *Fort! Da!* moment (for the moment "in which desire becomes human is also that in which the child is born into language" [1977, p. 103/319]) but prefigured by the transitional object, an object that is on its way toward becoming a signifier.

312*f*/815 We are told that the *"Che vuoi?"* is taken from *Diable amoureux* (1772), a novel by the French author, Jacques Cazotte (1719–1792).

313c–d/ The English translation is misleading. Lacan com-
815–816 pletes the structure of the fantasy not by linking *it* to the condition of an object, but rather by linking in it the moment of a "fading" to the condition of an object: *y liant. . .à la condition d'un objet. . .le moment d'un fading*. The fading or barred subject is tied to an ob-

ject in fantasy ($◊o), and this appears to serve as substitute object inciting desire *(d)*, but incapable of satisfying it.

Regarding the sign (◊) in the formula, Lacan comments on its meaning elsewhere (1977, p. 280, n. 26/634, n. 1). Clément (1981, pp. 206–207) provides a helpful interpretation of the *poinçon* (Lacan's symbol ◊ that links the barred subject to the object *a* [*o*] and to demand [D]). She makes two points: first, that the *poinçon* ("stamp"), not unlike the mark on French coins that guarantees authenticity, is that feature of the subject's implication in his or her unconscious fantasy that marks it as his or her own, that "authenticates" the fantasy as *mine*. Second, she sees the symbol   as a combination of the mathematical symbols for "less than" (<) and "greater than" (>); such a combination, of course, is contradictory and thus the fantasy is marked as impossible.

313*e*/816   The French has *a* (for *autre*) in the formula. In terms of "the phonematic element," we wonder about a play on the letter *a* as first letter of the alphabet, as element of the *Fort! Da!*, etc.

314*b*/816   The graph indicates parallel levels, both participating in the imaginary register, wherein the specular image structures the ego in *méconnaissance*, $i(o) \rightarrow e$, with a homologous relation wherein desire is regulated and disguised in the fantasy, $d \rightarrow ($◊$o)$. This completes the structure of the imaginary, "there where [not "and where"] the unconscious was *itself*" ("là où *s*'était l'inconscient").

314*c*/816   Rather than "the grammatical 'I,'" the French text has "the grammatical ego" *(le moi grammatical)*. In addition, there are no single quotes around the following I *(de ce Je)* that is primordially repressed *(primordialement refoulé)*.

314*d*/816   Our attention is now drawn to the unconscious signifying chain (structured not by the imaginary but by the symbolic order): this is the uppermost level, $S(\emptyset) \rightarrow (\$ \Diamond D)$, paralleling the level of conscious discourse, $s(O) \rightarrow O$.

314*f*–
316*a*/817–
818

The following is, once more, highly tentative: The formula for drive *(pulsion)* expresses a relationship between the barred subject and demand $(\$ \Diamond D)$. For the neurotic, Lacan tells us later (1977, p. 321/823), demand is identified with the lack in the Other; the signifier of this lack, taken abstractly, is $S(\emptyset)$ while its concrete expression is Φ, the symbolic phallus as signifier of the desire (hence lack) of the Other. The movement expressed in the topmost level of the completed graph would then seem to be, in the neurotic: first, *jouissance* is necessarily lost when the signifier of the lack in the Other is installed in the symbolic order (unconscious to be sure)—that is, the Other is accepted as castrated and the *jouissance* of imaginary symbiosis as impossible—and then this lack is assumed to be a demand in which the subject is implicated in fantasy, $S(\emptyset) \rightarrow (\$ \Diamond D)$. For the neurotic, "the demand of the Other assumes the function of an object in his phantasy"—we recall the formula for fantasy is $(\$ \Diamond o)$—and his fantasy, therefore, is "reduced to the drive $(\$ \Diamond D)$" (p. 321/823).

Since demand is a diachronic articulation, it has a temporal duration and "disappears." In saying, "I want, I must have . . ." the neurotic is saying this in identification with the assumed lack in the Other (he is saying this in the place of the Other), and for him this demand is bound up with a part-object related to a bodily function. When Lacan states that "the cut remains," we take this to mean that the unconscious content of the drive in relation to body-part with which the subject is implicated remains structured linguistically, i.e., in an unconscious signifying manner. This is not to say that the part-object in the drive is a signifier (the signifiers are in the demand which expresses the drive), for it remains related to a bodily function. But the kind of bodily function relevant to drive, Lacan appears to be saying, is of a particular sort: it is marked by a cut, a pattern of opening and closing, a rhythmical discontinuity analogous to the gap that differentiates signifiers. It is this "cut" that "distinguishes the drive from the organic function it inhabits" and opens a place for the advent of a signifier. Conceived in this way (albeit vague to us at the present time), the part-object involves a lack which has "no specular image," i.e., is not governed by the processes of reflection indigenous to the imaginary order. The lack, moreover, is camouflaged by the image returned by the mirror, which serves to buttress the ego in a fictional manner.

The reference to Freud appears to be to his *Three Essays on the Theory of Sexuality* (1905c), and to the variability among source, aim, and object in which "active" and "passive" modes are evident.

316*b*–*c*/
818

Since we have been translating *répondre de* as "answer for," we do not read "the Other is required...to respond to the value of this treasure," but rather "the Other is required...to answer for the value of this treasure" ("l'Autre est requis...de répondre de la valeur de ce trésor"). An alternative reading is that the Other is required to respond *from* the value of "this treasure," i.e., from the place of the signifiers. We have seen that the Other (O), on the level of conscious articulation, is the ensemble of phonematic features (1977, p. 304/806); at the level of unconscious signification, the Other is also barred, correlatively with the lack inherent in symbolic castration that makes symbolic exchange possible, and is designated by the signifier of a lack in the Other: S(Ø). The Other without a lack is the fantasized complete Other present in psychosis or symbiotic *jouissance*. The Other "answers for" the value of its treasure (the storehouse of language) by responding *(de répondre)* from its place not only in the conscious chain, but also in the chain of unconscious signification that structures drive.

In specifying the lack in the Other as "there is no Other of the Other," no claim is made about religious belief, for as analysts "We have to answer for no ultimate truth" ("Nous n'avons à répondre d'aucune vérité dernière").

316*f*–
317*b*/819

It is striking that the transposition into English of Lacan's algorithm for the barred Other, S(Ⱥ), should yield the symbol that in mathematical set theory represents the "empty"/"null" set: S(Ø), i.e., a set which contains no members. Lacan's intention seems to be to designate a signifier for the universal set of signifiers that should itself be included within the set, because it is a signifier, and therefore cannot be taken out of the set to signify it lest the universal set thereby continue to expand. Such a signifier, then, must be somehow *inside* the universal set and conceived of as a lack (-1) within it. In this sense it is the complement of the universal set, i.e., an "empty," or "null," set.

While we cannot explore mathematical group theory here, the algebraic transformation is fairly straightforward. The statement (s) is equal to signifier over signified $\frac{S}{s}$. Let $S = -1$ (the signifier of lack in the ensemble) in the case of a proper noun (the designator of symbolic identification which presupposes symbolic castration). By multiplying both sides of the equation by $\frac{s}{s}$ and cancelling, we get

$s = \sqrt{-1}$ (whose denotation is i, an irrational or imaginary number). But what does this mean? It suggests to us that there is an unspeakable dimension inherent in the use of a proper name (as well as in the use of "I") such that it functions only by pointing or designating, not by reference to a meaning outside of itself: "Its statement equals its signification." Thus the speaking I, when speaking of itself, is never present in discourse as a substantive entity spoken about (in this sense it "fades" from the discourse).

For additional commentary on the phrase "a signifier is that which represents the subject for another signifier," see the section "The Primacy of the Signifier" in the linguistic dictionary by Ducrot and Todorov (1972, pp. 351–356).

317*d–f*/ 819   The English translation's use of single quotes around *I* is absent in the French text, which repeats *Je* [italics added]. The French text's *à se garder*, translated as "by protecting itself," includes the sense of "restricting itself."

317*h*/820   The English "insubstantial" translates the French *inconsistant*, which has the sense of lacking in solidity or compactness. The meaning appears to be that contrary to the Other in psychosis that is unbarred, complete, and implicated in the *jouissance* of symbiosis, the Other in the absence of *jouissance* is not compact, full, whole, but marked by a lack—the barred Other. The question of the Other's existence ("if he existed") would appear then to refer to the fantasized, whole, and omnipotent Other.

318*e*/820   Rather than "would spoil the secret," we translate *ferait tomber le secret* as "would push down the secret," i.e., render it inaccessible.

318*g–h*/ 821   Regarding *mana*, Mehlman (1972a) writes:

> Lévi-Strauss's paradox is that whereas the linguistic totality (of meaning) must have come in-

to existence (as structure) all at once, that which we *know* has been acquired progressively. With the irruption of language, the whole world began to take on meaning all at once, before anyone could *know (connaître)* what the meaning was. "But, from the preceding analysis, it follows that it (the world) meant *(a signifié)*, from the beginning, the totality of what humanity could expect to know of it." This dissymmetry between the synchronic (structural) nature of the *meant* and the diachronic nature of the *known* results in the existence of "an overabundance of signifier *(signifiant)* in relation to the *signifiés* to which it might apply." And it is this "floating signifier," this "semantic function whose role is to allow symbolic thought to operate despite the contradiction inherent in it" which Lévi-Strauss sees, in this elusive essay, as the reality of *mana*. It is "a symbol in the pure state," thus apt to be charged with any symbolic content: "symbolic value zero" [p. 23].

Lacan appears to be saying that S($\emptyset$) signifies the lack inherent in *mana* or the zero symbol ("mais c'est plutôt du signifiant du manque de ce symbole zéro qu'il nous paraît s'agir en notre cas").

319*b–c*/
821   The *jouissance* is "no more than understood" as innuendo *(sous-entendue)*, that is, as heard "between the lines." The symbolic castration that is prerequisite for entrance into the symbolic order makes direct access to *jouissance* impossible. Therefore the Law can be said to be "grounded in this very prohibition" ("la Loi se fonde de cette interdiction même") in the sense that it "founds itself" there where its impact appears.

319*d*/821   "Pleasure" is taken to mean the concrete (and therefore delimited) satisfaction found in bodily (or other) functioning of the living being. Pleasure sets limits on *jouissance* but in turn pleasure is subjected to the regulation of the laws governing primary process, which are the laws of language (as Lacan has told us earlier [1977, p. 298/799]).

319e/821 Thorndike's Law of Effect may be an example of the kind of course being pursued in Freud's time.

319f/822 The heteroclite (deviant or anomalous) nature of the castration complex which checked Freud gives an indication of the un-boundedness of *jouissance* (not "of" but "in" [*dans*] its infinitude) which calls for *(qui comporte)* its own interdiction.

319g/822 The image of the penis is not "negativity" but "negatived" *(négativé)* "in its place in the specular image." We take this to mean that the penis is imagined to be detachable from the image of the body (in imaginary castration). The later reference to "phantasy of decrepitude" *(fantasme de caducité)* suggests the transitory detumescence that lends support to this detachability. The phallus, therefore, comes "to embody *jouissance* in the dialectic of desire" by representing what is missing, and therefore what is capable of completing.

320a/822 One way to read this dense paragraph is to see the erectile organ, the part lacking in the desired image, as functioning like the lack present in signification $(\sqrt{-1})$ correlative with the fading of the subject, and like the lack inherent in the ensemble of signifiers (-1). The erectile organ promises a wholeness that would restore *jouissance* on the level of image as well as on the level of discourse—both impossible.

320b/822 The erectile organ's role is to knot *(nouer)* the interdiction of *jouissance* because as desired object that is lacking it comes to represent symbolic castration. It does this not for "these reasons of form" *(ces raisons de forme)*, i.e., not on the level of the desired image, the imaginary level, but insofar as these forms are super-

seded by symbolic structures. Once symbolic differentiation and exchange are established, *jouissance*
that is lusted after (*jouissance convoitée*, misleadingly
translated as "desired *jouissance*") is reduced to an
auto-erotic moment (presumably as in masturba-
tion, suggested by the reference to the hand). Auto-
eroticism is then, in analysis, seen to be inadequate
to desire (for desire presupposes the symbolic order,
while auto-eroticism is a kind of turning away from
it) and this inadequacy is referred to as guilt.

320*e*/823   The English "negated" translates the French *négativer*,
the same verb used earlier which we translated as
"negatived" (note 319*g*/822). The point seems to be
that the symbolic phallus cannot be "detached" in the
same way the image of the penis can be from the
specular image: symbolic castration and imaginary
castration are different.

320*f*/823   The French text suggests that the pervert sets up
dominance concerning or with regard to the object *a*
of his fantasy (*dominance. . . de l'objet* a *du fantasme*).

321*d*/824   Instead of "conceals its anxiety from the desire of the
Other," we translate "conceals his anxiety concerning
the desire of the Other" (*cache son angoisse du désir de
l'Autre*).

322*d*/825   The imaginary castration ($-\phi$) "imaginarizes" either
the barred subject ($\mathcal{S}$) or the object (o) when either of
them is imagined to be castrated in the fantasy ($\mathcal{S} \Diamond o$).
"A complex number has the form ($a + ib$), where a, b
are real numbers and $i = \sqrt{-1}$. It thus consists of a
real part a and a pure imaginary part ib" (Considine,
1976, p. 632).

322*e*/825   The Greek word ἄγαλμα has the meaning of "glory,
delight, honour," or "pleasing gift" or "image," or
"statue" as "an object of worship" (Liddell and Scott,
1897, p. 5).

In Plato's *Symposium* Alcibiades says: "Agathon,

give me back some of those ribbons, will you? I want to crown Socrates' head as well—and a most extraordinary head it is" (p. 565). Later, he tries to seduce Socrates:

> So I got up, and, without giving him a chance to say a word, I wrapped my own cloak around him—for this was in the winter—and, creeping under his shabby old mantle, I took him in my arms and lay there all night with this godlike and extraordinary man—you can't deny that, either, Socrates. And after *that* he had the insolence, the infernal arrogance, to laugh at my youthful beauty and jeer at the one thing I was really proud of, gentlemen of the jury—I say 'jury' because that's what you're here for, to try the man Socrates on the charge of arrogance— and believe it, gentlemen, or believe it not, when I got up next morning I had no more *slept* with Socrates, within the meaning of the act, than if he'd been my father or an elder brother [p. 570].

323*e*/826   The neurotic may be said to be someone without a name *(un Sans-Nom)* because he attempts to deny symbolic castration (the prerequisite for symbolic identification) by focusing on imaginary castration.

323*i*/826   It would be more consistent to translate *si...il existait, il en jouirait* not "if...it did exist" but rather "if ...he did exist [i.e., the fantasized uncastrated Other of *jouissance*], he [this Other] would enjoy it [one's own castration]."

Afterword

Well, a rebus is a rebus is a rebus. What we have seen in these pages is a selection of texts, chosen by Lacan himself to introduce the English-speaking reader to his thought. Or should we not rather say to his style? For they convey, at least to us, less clearly an impression of *what* Lacan thinks than *how*. Allegedly, he is sharing with us through his *Écrits* his own experience of how the unconscious works, and we are left with the task of interpreting these writings more or less as we would a dream, searching for a signification that *in*sists in the web of signifiers he has spun rather than *con*sists in any particular thing he has said. In other words, these *écrits* offer us, like dreams for Freud, essentially a rebus.

This means that understanding them is not exactly guesswork but, nonetheless, a highly precarious business, and sharing our impressions with the reading public may be utter folly. After all, it exposes us to the embarrassment of being told how wrong we are, especially when the master's many disciples are there to say, "that's not what he meant at all." Yet we take this risk, for we feel that with the publication of this translation the

415

time has come to begin to discern the value of Lacan's efforts so as to be able to profit from them, especially if they can offer some help in clinical practice. And this must be, we feel, a collective effort on the part of his English-speaking readers, for which the present pages pretend to be no more than a first assay. As such it offers, at most, some tools for the task, perhaps to be discarded when more sophisticated instruments are available.

The texts in *Écrits: A Selection* cover a signficant span of years (1948–1960). In that sense they are representative of the general drift of Lacan's concerns during a decisive period of his development. We have already indicated (Chapter 9), how that drift appears to us in this particular group of essays. In broader terms, however, it is worth remarking on one characteristic in particular that seems to mark the whole movement: the ever more radical depersonalization of the subject. We recall that Lacan's earliest professional interest focused on the function of image and the role of milieu in personality formation. By 1960, the term "personality" has no place in the articulation of his own thought. Instead, we hear only of "subject," "ego," and "I," where the "ego" is clearly not the "I" but an object present to the experience of the subject, fulfilling an imaginary function there. What, then, is the "I"? And just what sort of ontology does it presuppose? By the end of the present collection, it would seem that the most we can say is that the "I" has a sheerly linguistic role, the function of shifter, not signifying but simply designating the speaker. But who is the speaker?

Is it the "subject"? Since discourse is multileveled and since words always say more than they pronounce, the speaker does not coincide with the conscious presence speaking, but appears in parapraxes as unaware of what is being said. The speaker, then, includes an "unconscious." In 1953 (Chapter 3), it is the "unconscious" of the subject, the *Kern unseres Wesens*, who appears to utter "full" speech in distinction from the "empty" speech of the ego. This relatively straightforward duality is not so difficult to comprehend, but by 1960 (Chapter 9), we no longer hear of the unconscious of the subject but rather of "the

subject of the unconscious." This subject, like the "I" that fades
from discourse, appears to be not a perduring, substantial entity, but rather a kind of intermittent presence caught between
desire and discourse, subject to the laws of language and their
impersonal processes. The subject becomes more and more
"decentered," then, in these formulations as the consequences
of Lacan's fundamental structuralism become more rigorously
pursued.

Another index of this increasing radicalization is the manner in which Lacan formulates the "laws" of the unconscious. In
1957 (Chapter 5), these laws were formulated after the manner
of structural linguistics, according to which the basic paradigm
of the bipolar correlation of the phonemes is ordered according
to the axes of combination and selection to form signifiers that
relate to one another along these axes, i.e., as metonymy and
metaphor. The unconscious, structured like a language, follows
the same laws, too. In 1960 (Chapter 9), however, Lacan's drift
toward the mathematization of these laws (e.g., set theory, irrational numbers, quasi-topological graphs to diagram discourse),
already hinted at along the way, is very apparent. So significant
is this shift that one highly authorized interpreter, Jacques-
Alain Miller (editor of Lacan's seminars), tells us recently (1978)
that the most precise formulation of these laws is that the unconscious "consists in a ciphering," so that the earlier essay, "The
Agency of the Letter," might properly be retitled now as "The
Agency of the Cipher" (*L'Instance du chiffre*, p. 11). Such a development in the direction of mathematics in general and topology
in particular marks a shift, too, in the philosophical mood of Lacan's thought from the more "ontological" tones of Hegel and
Heidegger (1953) to the more astringent formalizations of the
philosophy of science and mathematics (1960). In any case, this
direction is perhaps the most difficult and problematic aspect of
the recent evolution of Lacan's thought.

Ideally, of course, all this calls for a rigorous critique that
should be preceded by a concise and accurate summary of the
essentials of Lacan's conceptual framework. Indeed, such a dis-

cussion should form part of the conclusion of any careful study. But that is just the point: what we write here is not in conclusion, for a "conclusion" would be a closing word, and what we terminate these pages with is not a closing but rather an opening word, i.e., one that opens up the study of these selected texts for others by sharing with them the results of our own initial efforts at understanding. Summary and critique must wait for another day, when we have greater familiarity with the rest of the *Écrits* and with the seminars (many still unpublished), on which most of them are based.

Similarly, to another day must be left the expansion of, or extrapolation upon, Lacan's doctrine as it has emerged here. We have in mind not only such matters as the clinical application of these concepts but the exploration of certain issues which have not been treated in the texts made available in this collection, and which invite consideration. For example, in the discussion of the symbolic order should not something be said about the relation between the verbal signifiers and behavioral comportment, when the latter is not merely a matter of relatively superficial "body language" but is part of the discourse of a whole cultural context — that phenomenon which sociolinguistics has made its own (e.g., Mohatt and Erickson, 1979)? But such a question leads to other still broader issues, whose number is beyond limit.

When all is said and done, one thing, we feel, is certain: however obscure Lacan's thought, no one, after listening to him, can ever read Freud in the same way again. Working from the German original, Lacan reads Freud with a rigor and care that forces his own readers into a searching reconsideration of all of Freud's most fundamental insights, thus stimulating the transmission of psychoanalysis through a radical return to its source.

Is the result a distortion? Surely Lacan goes beyond what Freud said to experience what he did not say and could not say. At its very best, this may be what Heidegger would call a "retrieve" *(Wiederholung)* of Freud, the re-collection of Freud's "unsaid." At its best! If the result is more Lacan than Freud, then it must stand on its own merits and submit to the scrutiny proper to any "original" thought—i.e., one that descends into the origins of the matter at issue to reemerge with a new life of its own. This much can be said for Lacan, at least: he has indeed returned to the origins of psychoanalysis and in that sense enabled it to be born again. Whether that rebirth by passage through the dark, inscrutable world of the Lacanian rebus is worth the pangs that it costs, the reader must decide.

References

Abraham, K. (1908), The Psycho-Sexual Differences between Hysteria and Dementia Praecox. In: *Selected Papers of Karl Abraham, M.D.*, trans. D. Bryan & A.
Strachey. London: Hogarth Press, 1948, pp. 64–79.

Aulagnier-Spairani, P. (1964), Remarques sur la structure psychotique. *La Psychanalyse*, 8:47–67.

Avant, L. L., & Helson, H. (1973), Theories of Perception. In: *Handbook of General
Psychology*, ed. B. Wolman. Englewood Cliffs, N.J.: Prentice-Hall, pp. 419–
448.

Balakian, A. (1971), *André Breton: Magus of Surrealism*. New York: Oxford University
Press.

Baldwin, J. M. (1902), *Fragments in Philosophy and Science*. New York: Scribner.

———— (1906), *Thoughts and Things: A Study of the Development and Meaning of Thought
or Genetic Logic*, Vol. 1. New York: Macmillan.

Balint, M. (1938), Ego-Strength, Ego-Education, and 'Learning.' In: *Primary Love
and Psycho-Analytic Technique*. New York: Liveright, 1965, pp. 189–200.

———— (1951), On Love and Hate. In: *Primary Love and Psycho-Analytic Technique*.
New York: Liveright, 1965, pp. 145–156.

Bär, E. (1971), The Language of the Unconscious According to Jacques Lacan.
Semiotica, 3:241–268.

———— (1974), Understanding Lacan. *Psychoanalysis and Contemporary Science*, Vol. 3,
ed. L. Goldberger & V. H. Rosen. New York: International Universities
Press, pp. 473–544.

Barthes, R. (1964), *Elements of Semiology*, trans. A. Lavers & C. Smith. New York:
Hill & Wang, 1978.

Bartlett, J. (1882), *Familiar Quotations*, ed. E. M. Beck. Boston: Little, Brown, 1968.

Baudelaire, C.-P. (1857), *Les Fleurs du mal*. Paris: Librairie Larousse, 1934.

Betteridge, H. T., Ed. (1958), *The New Cassell's German Dictionary*. New York: Funk
& Wagnalls.

Boehme, J. (1651), *Signature of All Things and Other Writings*. London: Clarke, 1969.
Bowie, M. (1979), Jacques Lacan. In: *Structuralism and Since,* ed. J. Sturrock. Oxford: Oxford University Press, pp. 116–163.
Breton, A. (1924), Introduction au discours sur le peu de réalité. In: *Point du Jour.* Paris: Gallimard, 1970, pp. 7–30.
Bühler, C. (1927), *Soziologische und psychologische Studien über das erste Lebensjahr.* Jena: Fischer.
Cairns, R. B. (1980), Developmental Theory before Piaget: The Remarkable Contributions of James Mark Baldwin. *Contemp. Psychol.,* 25:438–440.
Carroll, L. (1923), *Through the Looking Glass.* New York: Winston.
Cazotte, J. (1772), *Le Diable amoureux.* Paris: Livre Club du Librairie, 1964.
Chrzanowski, G. (1977), Some Present Day Psychoanalytic Currents on the European Continent. *J. Amer. Acad. Psychoanal.,* 5:175–185.
Clément, C. (1981), *Vies et légendes de Jacques Lacan.* Paris: Grasset.
The Compact Edition of the Oxford English Dictionary, Vol. 1. (1971). Oxford: Oxford University Press.
Considine, D. M., Ed. (1976), *Van Nostrand's Scientific Encyclopedia,* 5th Ed. New York: Van Nostrand Reinhold.
Conze, E. (1951), *Buddhism: Its Essence and Development.* New York: Harper Torchbooks, 1959.
Damourette, J., & Pichon, E. (1911–1940), *Des mots à la pensée,* Vol. I–IX. Paris: D'Artrey.
De George, R. T., & De George, F. M. (1962), *The Structuralists: From Marx to Lévi-Strauss.* Garden City, N.Y.: Anchor Books.
Deleuze, G. (1979), The Schizophrenic and Language: Surface and Depth in Lewis Carroll and Antonin Artaud. In: *Textual Strategies in Post-Structuralist Criticism,* ed. J. V. Harari. Ithaca: Cornell University Press, .pp. 277–295.
De Waelhens, A. (1972), *Schizophrenia: A Philosophical Reflection on Lacan's Structuralist Interpretation,* trans. W. Ver Eecke. Pittsburgh: Duquesne University Press, 1978.
Ducrot, O., & Todorov, T. (1972), *Encyclopedic Dictionary of the Sciences of Language,* trans. C. Porter. Baltimore: Johns Hopkins University Press, 1979.
Eco, U. (1976), *A Theory of Semiotics.* Bloomington: Indiana University Press, 1979.
Ehrmann, J., Ed. (1970), *Structuralism.* Garden City, N.Y.: Anchor Books.
Eliot, T. S. (1922), *The Waste Land and Other Poems.* New York: Harcourt, Brace, & World, 1967.
Erasmus, D. (1509), *In Praise of Folly,* trans. L. F. Dean. New York: Hendricks House, 1969.
Fenichel, O. (1949), The Symbolic Equation: Girl = Phallus. *Psychoanal. Quart.,* 18: 303–324.
Ferenczi, S. (1909), Introjection and Transference. In: *First Contributions to Psycho-Analysis,* trans. E. Jones. London: Hogarth Press, 1952, pp. 35–93.
———— (1912), Transitory Symptom-Constructions during the Analysis. In: *Sex in Psychoanalysis,* trans. E. Jones. New York: Dover, 1956, pp. 164–180.
Forrester, J. (1980), *Language and the Origins of Psychoanalysis.* New York: Columbia University Press.
Frege, G. (1960), *Translations from the Philosophical Writings of Gottlob Frege,* 2nd Ed., ed. P. Geach & M. Black. Oxford: Blackwell.
Freud, A. (1936), *The Ego and the Mechanisms of Defense,* trans. C. Baines. New York: International Universities Press, 1946.

Freud, S. (1887–1902), *The Origins of Psychoanalysis: Letters to Wilhelm Fliess, Drafts and Notes,* ed. M. Bonaparte, A. Freud, & E. Kris, trans. E. Mosbacher & J. Strachey. New York: Basic Books, 1954.

_____ (1899), Extracts from the Fliess Papers. *Standard Edition,* 1:177–280. London: Hogarth Press, 1966.

_____ (1900a), The Interpretation of Dreams. *Standard Edition,* 4 & 5. London: Hogarth Press, 1953.

_____ (1900b), Die Traumdeutung. *Gesammelte Werke,* 2 & 3. London: Imago, 1942.

_____ (1901), The Psychopathology of Everyday Life. *Standard Edition,* 6. London: Hogarth Press, 1960.

_____ (1905a), Fragment of an Analysis of a Case of Hysteria. *Standard Edition,* 7: 7–122. London: Hogarth Press, 1953.

_____ (1905b), Jokes and Their Relation to the Unconscious. *Standard Edition,* 8. London: Hogarth Press, 1960.

_____ (1905c), Three Essays on the Theory of Sexuality. *Standard Edition,* 7:130–245. London: Hogarth Press, 1953.

_____ (1908), Creative Writers and Day-Dreaming. *Standard Edition,* 9:143–153. London: Hogarth Press, 1959.

_____ (1909a), Analysis of a Phobia in a Five-Year-Old Boy. *Standard Edition,* 10: 5–149. London: Hogarth Press, 1955.

_____ (1909b), Notes upon a Case of Obsessional Neurosis. *Standard Edition,* 10: 155–318. London: Hogarth Press, 1955.

_____ (1911a), Formulations on the Two Principles of Mental Functioning. *Standard Edition,* 12:218–226. London: Hogarth Press, 1958.

_____ (1911b), Formulierungen über die zwei Prinzipien des psychischen Geschehens. *Gesammelte Werke,* 8:230–238. London: Imago, 1943.

_____ (1911c), Psycho-Analytic Notes on an Autobiographical Account of a Case of Paranoia (Dementia Paranoides). *Standard Edition,* 12:9–82. London: Hogarth Press, 1958.

_____ (1911d), Psychoanalytische Bemerkungen über einen autobiographisch beschriebenen Fall von Paranoia (Dementia Paranoides). *Gesammelte Werke,* 8: 239–320. London: Imago, 1943.

_____ (1913), Totem and Taboo. *Standard Edition,* 13:1–161. London: Hogarth Press, 1955.

_____ (1914a), On Narcissism: An Introduction. *Standard Edition,* 14:73–102. London: Hogarth Press, 1957.

_____ (1914b), Remembering, Repeating and Working-Through. *Standard Edition,* 12:147–156. London: Hogarth Press, 1958.

_____ (1916–1917), Introductory Lectures on Psycho-Analysis. *Standard Edition,* 16:243–463. London: Hogarth Press, 1963.

_____ (1917), A Difficulty in the Path of Psycho-Analysis. *Standard Edition,* 17:137–144. London: Hogarth Press, 1955.

_____ (1918), From the History of an Infantile Neurosis. *Standard Edition,* 17:7–122. London: Hogarth Press, 1955.

_____ (1919), The 'Uncanny.' *Standard Edition,* 17:219–256. London: Hogarth Press, 1955.

_____ (1920), Beyond the Pleasure Principle. *Standard Edition,* 18:7–64. London: Hogarth Press, 1955.

_____ (1921), Group Psychology and the Analysis of the Ego. *Standard Edition,*

18:69–143. London: Hogarth Press, 1955.
_____ (1923), The Ego and the Id. *Standard Edition*, 19:12–66. London: Hogarth Press, 1961.
_____ (1924a), The Economic Problem of Masochism. *Standard Edition*, 19:159–170. London: Hogarth Press, 1961.
_____ (1924b), The Loss of Reality in Neurosis and Psychosis. *Standard Edition*, 19:183–187. London: Hogarth Press, 1961.
_____ (1925a), An Autobiographical Study. *Standard Edition*, 20:7–74. London: Hogarth Press, 1959.
_____ (1925b), Negation. *Standard Edition*, 19:235–239. London: Hogarth Press, 1961.
_____ (1926a), Inhibitions, Symptoms and Anxiety. *Standard Edition*, 20:87–172. London: Hogarth Press, 1959.
_____ (1926b), The Question of Lay Analysis. *Standard Edition*, 20:183–258. London: Hogarth Press, 1959.
_____ (1927), Fetishism. *Standard Edition*, 21:152–157. London: Hogarth Press, 1961.
_____ (1933), New Introductory Lectures on Psycho-Analysis. *Standard Edition*, 22:5–182. London: Hogarth Press, 1964.
_____ (1937), Analysis Terminable and Interminable. *Standard Edition*, 23:216–253. London: Hogarth Press, 1964.
_____ (1940), An Outline of Psycho-Analysis. *Standard Edition*, 23:144–207. London: Hogarth Press, 1964.
Gadamer, H.-G. (1960), *Truth and Method*, trans. G. Barden & J. Cumming. New York: Seabury Press, 1975.
Gallup, G. G. (1977), Self-Recognition in Primates: A Comparative Approach to the Bidirectional Properties of Consciousness. *Amer. Psychol.*, 32:329–338.
Gardner, H. (1973), *The Quest for Mind: Piaget, Lévi-Strauss, and the Structuralist Movement*. New York: Knopf.
Glover, E. (1932), On the Aetiology of Drug-Addiction. *Internat. J. Psycho-Anal.*, 13:298–328.
Gould, S. J. (1976), Human Babies as Embryos. *Natural History*, 84:22–26.
Guillaume, G. (1968), *Temps et verbe. Théorie des aspects, des modes et des temps.* Suivi de: *L'Architectonique du temple dans les temps classiques.* Avant propos de R. Valin. Paris: Champion.
Harris, W., & Levey, J., Eds. (1975), *The New Columbia Encyclopedia*. New York: Columbia University Press.
Hegel, G. W. F. (1807a), *The Phenomenology of Mind*, Rev. 2nd Ed., trans. J. B. Baillie. London: Allen & Unwin, 1949.
_____ (1807b), *Phänomenologie Des Geistes*. Hamburg: Meiner, 1952.
Heidegger, M. (1927), *Being and Time*, trans. J. Macquarrie & E. Robinson. New York: Harper & Row.
_____ (1943), Heimkunft: An die Verwandten. In: *Erläuterungen zu Hölderlins Dichtung.* Frankfurt: Klostermann, 1944, pp. 9–30.
_____ (1950), *Holzwege*. Frankfurt: Klostermann.
_____ (1951), Logos (Heraklit, Fg. 50). In: *Vorträge und Aufsätze.* Pfullingen: Neske, pp. 207–219. (English translation in: *Early Greek Thinking*, trans. D. F. Krell & F. A. Capuzzi. New York: Harper & Row, 1975, pp. 59–78).
_____ (1952), *What Is Called Thinking*, trans. F. D. Wieck & J. G. Gray. New York: Harper & Row, 1968.

Hudgins, C. V. (1933), Conditioning and the Voluntary Control of the Pupillary Light Reflex. *J. Genet. Psychol.*, 8:3–51.

Hugo, V. (1859), Booz endormi. In: *La Légende des siècles*. Paris: Hachette, 1921, p. 82.

Husserl, E. (1929), *Cartesian Meditations: An Introduction to Phenomenology*, trans. D. Cairns. The Hague: Nijhoff, 1964.

Hyppolite, J. (1946), *Genesis and Structure of Hegel's Phenomenology of Spirit*, trans. S. Cherniak & J. Heckman. Evanston: Northwestern University Press, 1974.

Jaeger, W. (1939), *Paideia: The Ideals of Greek Culture*, Vol. 1, trans. G. Highet. Oxford: Blackwell, 1954.

Jakobson, R. (1956), Two Aspects of Language and Two Types of Aphasic Disturbances. In: *Fundamentals of Language*, by R. Jakobson & M. Halle. The Hague: Mouton, pp. 53–87.

———— (1973), *Main Trends in the Science of Language*. New York: Harper Torchbooks, 1974.

———— & Halle, M. (1956), *Fundamentals of Language*. The Hague: Mouton.

Jones, E. (1916), The Theory of Symbolism. In: *Papers on Psychoanalysis*, 5th Ed. Baltimore: Williams & Wilkins, 1948, pp. 87–144.

———— (1933), The Phallic Phase. In: *Papers on Psychoanalysis*, 5th Ed. Baltimore: Williams & Wilkins, 1948, pp. 452–484.

Jung, C. G. (1912), *Symbols of Transformation: An Analysis of the Prelude of a Case of Schizophrenia*, 2nd Ed. (Bollingen Series XX, Vol. 5), trans. R. F. C. Hull. Princeton, N.J.: Princeton University Press, 1956.

Katan, M. (1950), Schreber's Hallucinations about the 'Little Men.' *Internat. J. Psycho-Anal.*, 31:32–35.

Kerényi, K. (1944), *Hermes, Guide of Souls: The Mythologem of the Masculine Source of Life*, trans. M. Stein. Zurich: Spring Publications, 1976.

Kesey, K. (1962), *One Flew Over the Cuckoo's Nest*. New York: Viking.

Kierkegaard, S. (1843), *Repetition: An Essay in Experimental Psychology*, trans. W. Lowrie. New York: Harper Torchbooks, 1964.

Kirk, G., & Raven, J. (1957), *The Presocratic Philosophers*. London: Cambridge University Press.

Klein, M. (1957), *Envy and Gratitude: A Study of Unconscious Sources*. New York: Basic Books.

Köhler, W. (1925), *The Mentality of Apes*, trans. E. Winter. New York: Liveright, 1976.

Kojève, A. (1939), *Introduction to the Reading of Hegel*, trans. J. Nichols, Jr. New York: Basic Books, 1969.

Kris, E. (1951), Ego Psychology and Interpretation in Psychoanalytic Therapy. *Psychoanal. Quart.*, 20:21–25.

Kugler, P. (1978), Image and Sound: An Archetypal Approach to Language. In: *Spring: An Annual of Archetypal Psychology and Jungian Thought*, pp. 136–151.

———— (1981), *The Alchemy of Discourse*. Lewisburg, Pa.: Bucknell University Press.

Lacan, J. (1932), *De la psychose paranoïaque dans ses rapports avec la personnalité, suivi de premiers écrits sur la paranoïa*. Paris: Éditions du Seuil, 1975.

———— (1938), La Famille. In: *Encyclopédie française*, Vol. 8, Sec. 40 (La Vie mentale), ed. A. de Monzie. Paris: Librairie Larousse, pp. 3–16.

———— (1951), Some Reflections on the Ego. *Internat. J. Psycho-Anal.*, 34:11–17, 1953.

———— (1953–1954), *Le Séminaire: Livre I. Les Écrits techniques de Freud*, ed. J.-A. Miller. Paris: Éditions du Seuil, 1975.

_____ (1954–1955), *Le Séminaire: Livre II. Le Moi dans la théorie de Freud et dans la technique de la psychanalyse*, ed. J.-A. Miller. Paris: Éditions du Seuil, 1978.

_____ , Trans. (1956), "Logos," de M. Heidegger. *La Psychanalyse*, 1:59–79.

_____ (1958a), Les Formations de l'inconscient, ed. J.-B. Pontalis. *Bulletin de Psychologie*, 12:250–256.

_____ (1958b), D'une question préliminaire à tout traitement possible de la psychose. *La Psychanalyse*, 4:1–50.

_____ (1959), Desire and the Interpretation of Desire in *Hamlet*. In: *Literature and Psychoanalysis: The Question of Reading: Otherwise*, ed. S. Felman. *Yale French Studies*, 55/56:11–52, 1977.

_____ (1964), *The Four Fundamental Concepts of Psychoanalysis*, ed. J.-A. Miller, trans. A. Sheridan. New York: Norton, 1978.

_____ (1966), *Écrits*. Paris: Éditions du Seuil.

_____ (1970), Preface. In: *Jacques Lacan*, by A. Lemaire, trans. D. Macey. London: Routledge & Kegan Paul, 1977, pp. vii–xv.

_____ (1977), *Écrits: A Selection*, trans. A. Sheridan. New York: Norton.

Lacoue-Labarthe, P., & Nancy, J.-L. (1973), *Le Titre de la lettre (Une Lecture de Lacan)*. Paris: Éditions Galilée.

Laplanche, J. (1970), *Life and Death in Psychoanalysis*, trans. J. Mehlman. Baltimore: Johns Hopkins University Press, 1976.

_____ & Leclaire, S. (1960), The Unconscious: A Psychoanalytic Study, trans. P. Coleman. *Yale French Studies*, 48:118–175, 1972.

_____ & Pontalis, J.-B. (1967), *The Language of Psychoanalysis*, trans. D. Nicholson-Smith. New York: Norton, 1973.

Lauer, Q. (1976), *A Reading of Hegel's Phenomenology of Spirit*. New York: Fordham University Press.

Leavy, S. A. (1977), The Significance of Jacques Lacan. *Psychoanal. Quart.*, 46:201–219.

Lemaire, A. (1970), *Jacques Lacan*, trans. D. Macey. London: Routledge & Kegan Paul, 1977.

Lévi-Strauss, C. (1949a), The Effectiveness of Symbols. In: *Structural Anthropology*, trans. C. Jacobson & B. Schoepf. New York: Basic Books, 1963, pp. 186–205.

_____ (1949b), *The Elementary Structures of Kinship*. Boston: Beacon Press, 1969.

_____ (1951), Language and the Analysis of Social Laws. In: *Structural Anthropology*, trans. C. Jacobson & B. Schoepf. New York: Basic Books, 1963, pp. 55–66.

_____ (1976), Preface. In: *Six Lectures in Sound and Meaning, 1942–1943*, by R. Jakobson, trans. J. Mepham. Cambridge, Mass.: MIT Press, 1978, pp. xi–xxvi.

Lewin, K. (1931), The Conflict between Aristotelian and Galilean Modes of Thought in Contemporary Psychology. In: *A Dynamic Theory of Personality: Selected Papers*, trans. D. Adams & K. Zener. New York: McGraw-Hill, 1935, pp. 1–42.

Lewis, C. T., & Short, C. (1955), *A Latin Dictionary*. Oxford: Clarendon.

Lewis, M. (1977), The Busy, Purposeful World of a Baby. *Psychology Today*, 10:53–56.

Liddell, H. G., & Scott, R. (1897), *A Greek-English Lexicon*, 8th Ed. New York: American Book Company.

Loewenstein, R. M. (1956), Some Remarks on the Role of Speech in Psychoanalytic Technique. *Internat. J. Psycho-Anal.*, 37:460–467.

Longus (2nd–3rd c. A. D.), *Daphnis and Chloe*, trans. P. Turner. Baltimore: Penguin Books, 1968.

Macalpine, I., & Hunter, R. A., Trans. (1955), *Memoirs of My Nervous Illness*, by

D. P. Schreber. London: Dawson & Sons.

Mannoni, O. (1968), *Freud*, trans. R. Bruce. New York: Pantheon Books, 1971.

───── (1971), A Brief Introduction to Jacques Lacan. *Contemp. Psychoanal.*, 8:97–106.

Mauriac, F. (1923), *Le Fleuve de feu*. Paris: Bernard Grasset.

Mehlman, J. (1972a), The 'Floating Signifier': From Lévi-Strauss to Lacan. In: *French Freud: Structural Studies in Psychoanalysis. Yale French Studies*, 48:10–37.

───── , Trans. (1972b), "The Seminar on the Purloined Letter," by J. Lacan. *Yale French Studies*, 48:39–72.

Meissner, W. W. (1976), Schreber and the Paranoid Process. *The Annual of Psychoanalysis*, 4:3–40. New York: International Universities Press.

Merleau-Ponty, M. (1945), *Phenomenology of Perception*, trans. C. Smith. London: Routledge & Kegan Paul, 1962.

Miel, J., Trans. (1966), "The Insistence of the Letter in the Unconscious," by J. Lacan. In: *Structuralism*, ed. J. Ehrmann. Garden City, N.Y.: Anchor Books, 1970, pp. 101–137.

Miller, J.-A., (1978), Introduction à la transmission de la psychanalyse. In: *Lettres de L'École: 25, Vol. 1. La Transmission (I)*. Bulletin Intérieur de L'École Freudienne de Paris. Paris: Claude Conté, 1979, pp. 9–18.

Mohatt, G. V., & Erickson, F. (1979), Cultural Differences in the Social Interaction of Two Teachers in an Odawa School: A Sociolinguistic Approach. In: *Culture and the Bilingual Classroom: Studies of Classroom Ethnography*, ed. H. Trueb, G. Gutherie-Ping, & K. Au. Rawley, Mass.: Newberry Press, pp. 105–119.

Muller, J. P. (1979), The Analogy of Gap in Lacan's *Écrits: A Selection. Psychohistory Rev.*, 8(3): 38–45.

───── (1980), Psychosis and Mourning in Lacan's *Hamlet. New Literary History*, 11(1), 147–165.

Mussen, P. H., Ed. (1970), *Carmichael's Manual of Child Psychology*, Vol. 1, 3rd Ed. New York: Wiley.

Niederland, W. G. (1951), Three Notes on the Schreber Case. *Psychoanal. Quart.*, 20:579–591.

───── (1974), *The Schreber Case*. New York: Quadrangle.

Nordentoft, K. (1972), *Kierkegaard's Psychology*, trans. B. H. Kirmmse. Pittsburgh: Duquesne University Press, 1978.

Onions, C. T., Ed. (1966), *The Oxford Dictionary of English Etymology*. Oxford: Clarendon Press.

Pascal, B. (1670), *Pensées*, ed. L. Brunschvicg, trans. W. Trotter. New York: Modern Library, 1941.

Petronius, (1st c. A. D.), *The Satyricon*, trans. W. Arrowsmith. Ann Arbor: University of Michigan Press, 1959.

Piaget, J. (1968), *Structuralism*, trans. C. Maschler. New York: Basic Books, 1970.

Plato (385 B.C.?), The Symposium, trans. M. Joyce. In: *The Collected Dialogues Including the Letters*, ed. E. Hamilton & H. Cairns. (Bollingen Series LXXI). Princeton, N.J.: Princeton University Press, 1963, pp. 526–574.

Pontalis, J.-B., Ed. (1958), Les Formations de l'inconscient. *Bulletin de Psychologie*, 12:250–256.

Radin, P. (1956), *The Trickster: A Study in American Indian Mythology*. New York: Schocken Books, 1972.

Rank, O. (1925), *Der Doppelgänger; eine psychoanalytische Studie*. Leipzig: Internationaler Psychoanalytischer.

Reich, W. (1933), *Character Analysis,* trans. T. P. Wolfe. New York: Orgone Institute Press, 1949.

Richardson, W. J. (1963), *Heidegger: Through Phenomenology to Thought.* The Hague: Nijhoff.

────── (1978-1979), The Mirror Inside: The Problem of the Self. *Rev. Existential Psychol. Psychiat.,* 16:95-112.

Róheim, G. (1952), *The Gates of the Dream.* New York: International Universities Press, 1970.

Roussel, J. (1968), Introduction to Jacques Lacan. *New Left Rev.,* 51:63-77.

Ryan, M.-L. (1979), Is There Life for Saussure after Structuralism? *Diacritics,* 9(4): 28-44.

Sartre, J.-P. (1943), *Being and Nothingness: An Essay on Phenomenological Ontology,* trans. H. Barnes. New York: Philosophical Library, 1956.

Saussure, F. de (1916), *Course in General Linguistics,* ed. C. Bally & A. Sechehaye, trans. W. Baskin. New York: McGraw-Hill, 1966.

Schatzman, M. (1974), *Soul Murder: Persecution in the Family.* New York: New American Library.

Schmideberg, M. (1934), Intellektuelle Hemmung und Ess-störung. *Zeitschr. psychoanal. Pädagogik,* 8:109-116.

Schneiderman, S., Ed. & Trans. (1980), *Returning to Freud: Clinical Psychoanalysis in the School of Lacan.* New Haven: Yale University Press.

Schotte, J. (1975), The Basic Perspectives of Jacques Lacan. Lecture to the staff of the Clinic of the William Alanson White Institute, May 20, ed. W. J. Richardson.

Schreber, D. P. (1903a), *Memoirs of My Nervous Illness,* trans. I. Macalpine & R. A. Hunter. London: Dawson & Sons, 1955.

────── (1903b), *Denkwürdigkeiten eines Nervenkranken.* Frankfurt: Ullstein, 1973.

Segal, H. (1967), Melanie Klein's Technique. In: *Psychoanalytic Techniques: A Handbook for the Practicing Psychoanalyst,* ed. B. Wolman. New York: Basic Books, pp. 168-190.

Sheridan, A. (1977), Translator's Note. In: *Écrits: A Selection,* by J. Lacan. New York: Norton, pp. vii-xiv.

Sokolowski, R. (1978), *Presence and Absence: A Philosophical Investigation of Language and Being.* Bloomington: Indiana University Press.

Strauss, L. (1952), *Persecution and the Art of Writing.* Glencoe, Ill.: Free Press.

Swift, J. (1726), *Gulliver's Travels,* ed. G. Cumbertege. Oxford: Oxford University Press, 1949.

Tarde, G. de (1890), *The Laws of Imitation.* New York: Holt, 1903.

Times Literary Supplement [London] (1968), Healing Words: Dr. Lacan's Structuralism. Jan. 25, No. 3439, pp. 73-75.

Turkle, S. R. (1975), Contemporary French Psychoanalysis: I. The History of the French Psychoanalytic Movement. *Human Context,* 7:333-342.

────── (1978), *Psychoanalytic Politics: Freud's French Revolution.* New York: Basic Books.

Vergil, P. (1st c. B.C.), *The Eclogues and Georgics,* trans. C. D. Lewis. Garden City, N.Y.: Anchor Books, 1964.

Wallon, H. (1934), *Les Origines du caractère chez l'enfant: Les Préludes du sentiment de personnalité,* 2nd Ed. Paris: Presses Universitaires de France, 1949.

Webster's New International Dictionary of the English Language (1960). Springfield, Mass.: Merriam.

Webster's New Collegiate Dictionary (1974), Springfield, Mass.: Merriam.

Wilden, A., Trans. & Ed. (1968), *The Language of the Self: The Function of Language in Psychoanalysis,* by J. Lacan. Baltimore: Johns Hopkins University Press, 1975.

Wilson, E. (1975), *Sociobiology: The New Synthesis.* Cambridge, Mass.: Harvard University Press.

Wollheim, R. (1979), The Cabinet of Dr. Lacan. *New York Review of Books,* 21/22: 36–45.

Name Index

Index to Works of Freud

Subject Index